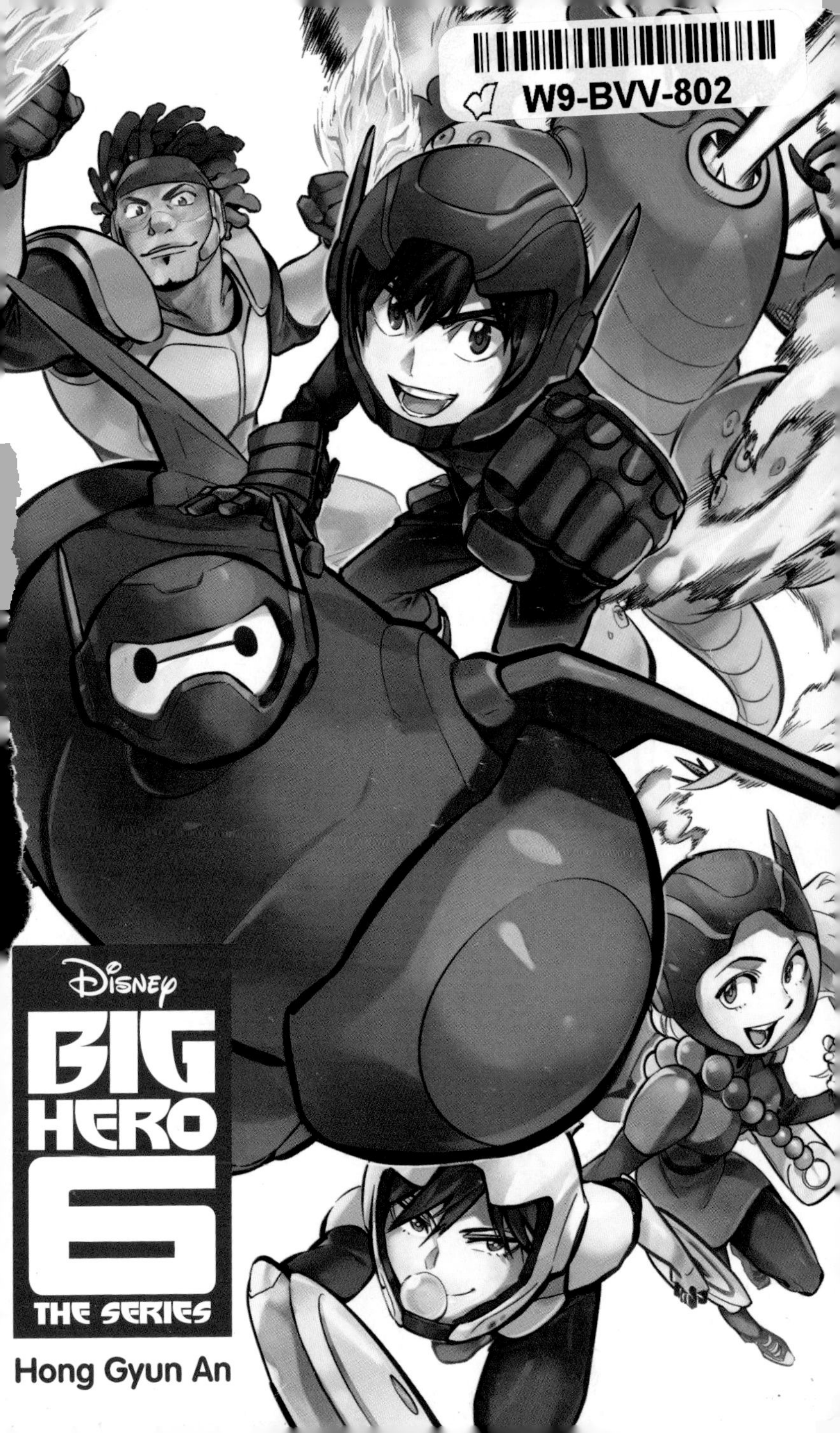

Disney

BIG HERO 6 THE SERIES

Hong Gyun An

CONTENTS

Chapter 1

Issue 188 ········ 3

Chapter 2

Failure Mode ········ 77

Chapter 3

Baymax Returns: Part 1 ········ 139

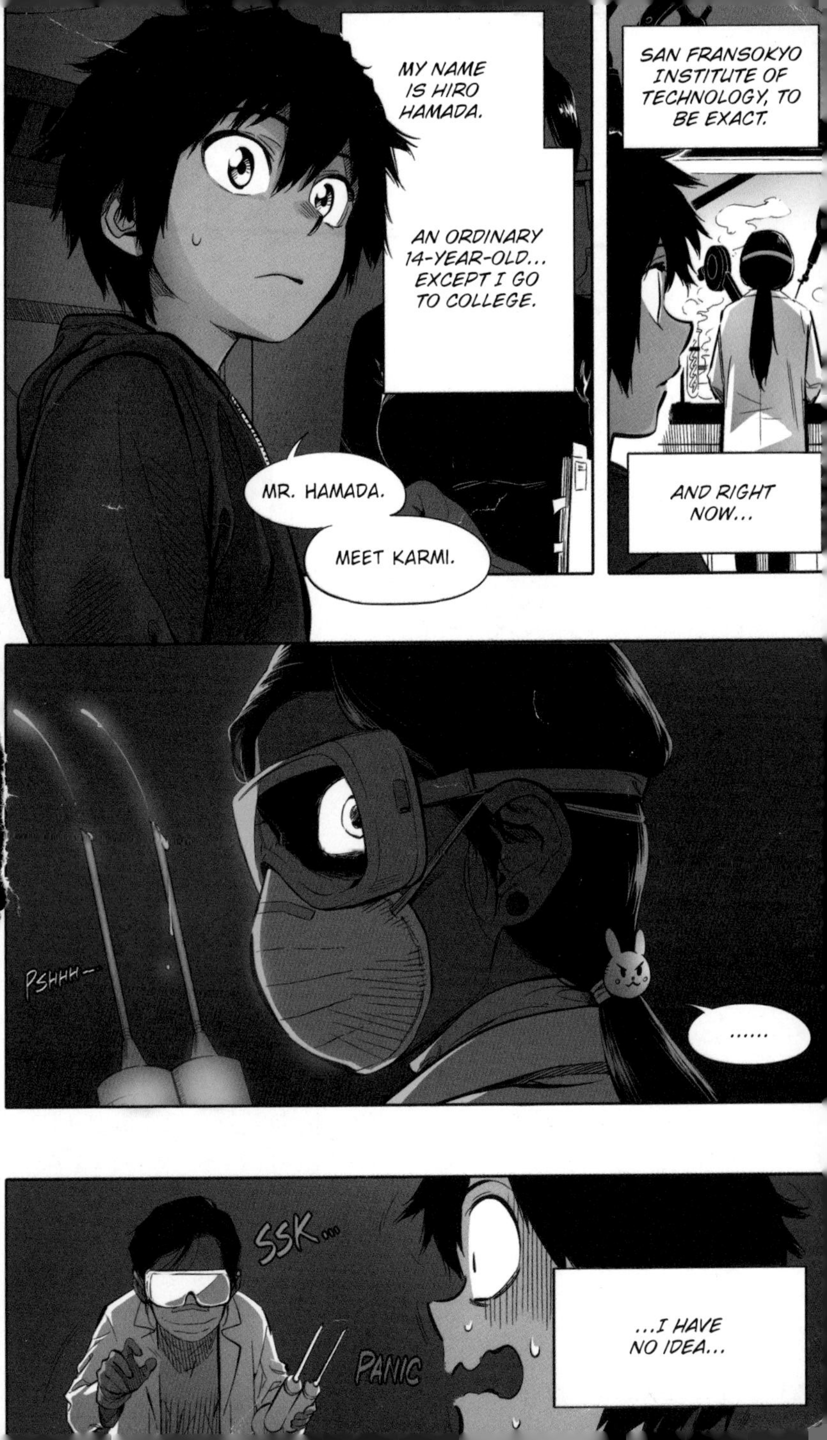
MY NAME IS HIRO HAMADA.
AN ORDINARY 14-YEAR-OLD... EXCEPT I GO TO COLLEGE.
MR. HAMADA.
MEET KARMI.
SAN FRANSOKYO INSTITUTE OF TECHNOLOGY, TO BE EXACT.
AND RIGHT NOW...
PSHHH—
......
SSK...
PANIC
...I HAVE NO IDEA...

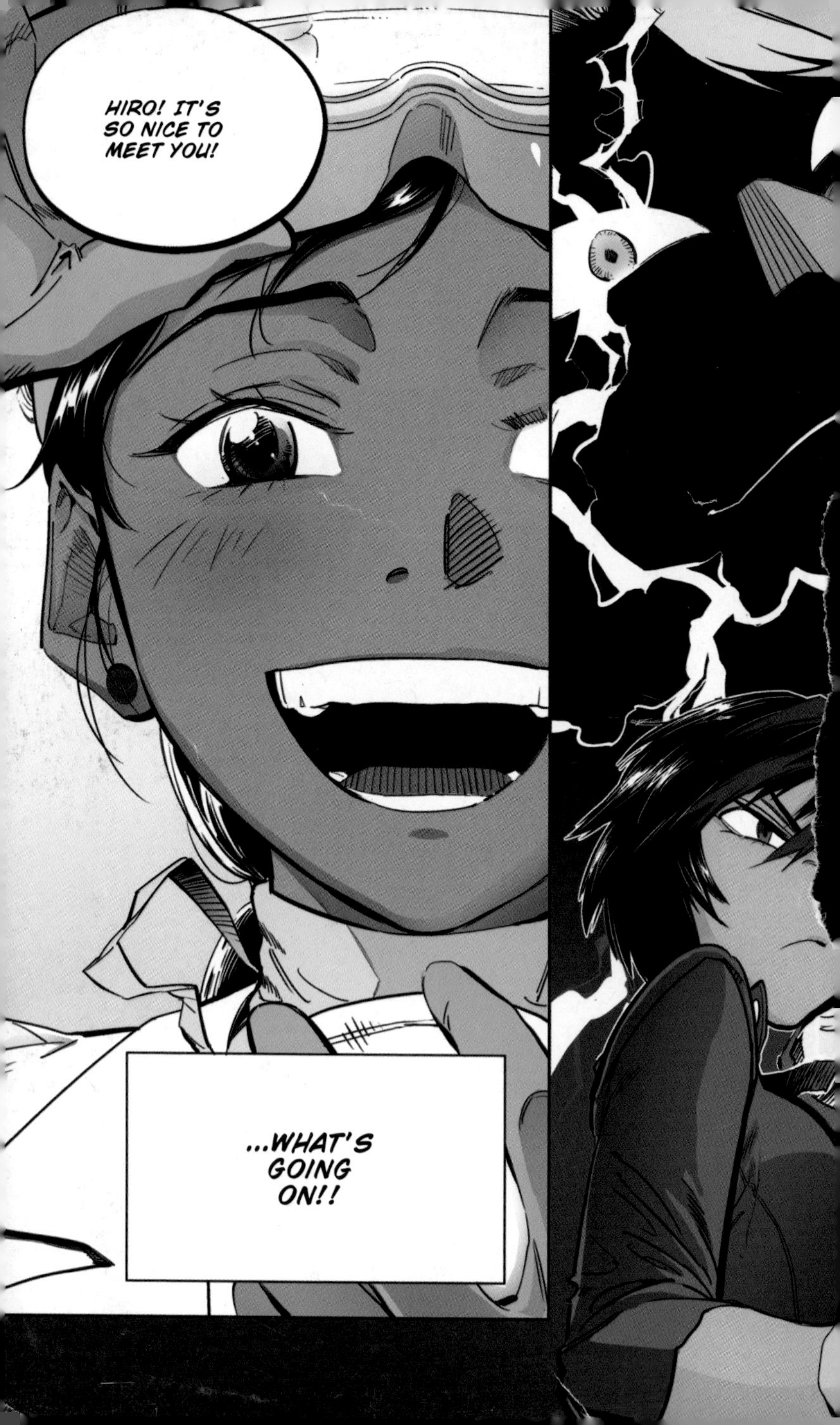
HIRO! IT'S SO NICE TO MEET YOU!
...WHAT'S GOING ON!!

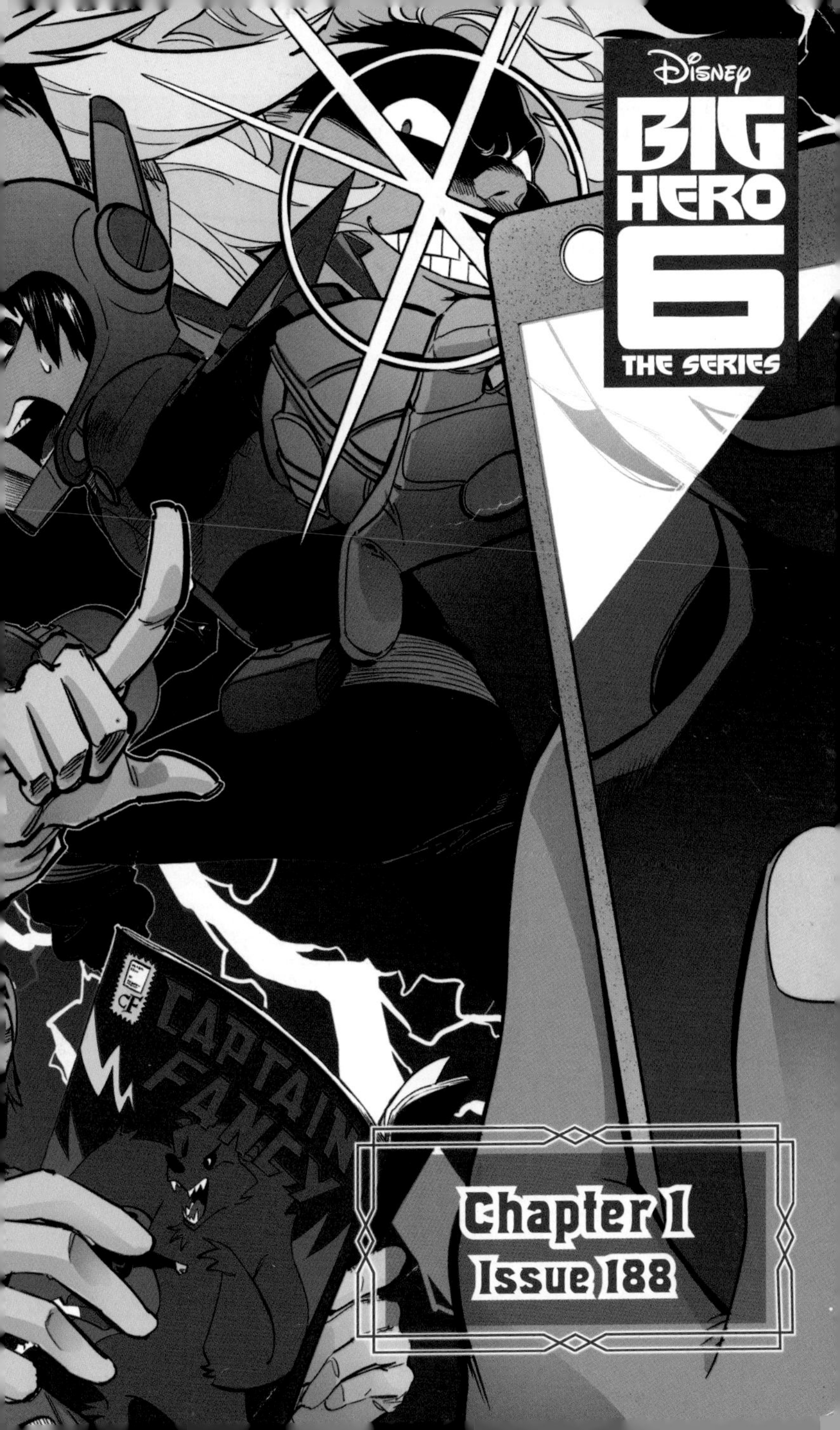
Disney
BIG HERO 6
THE SERIES
CAPTAIN FANCY
Chapter 1
Issue 188

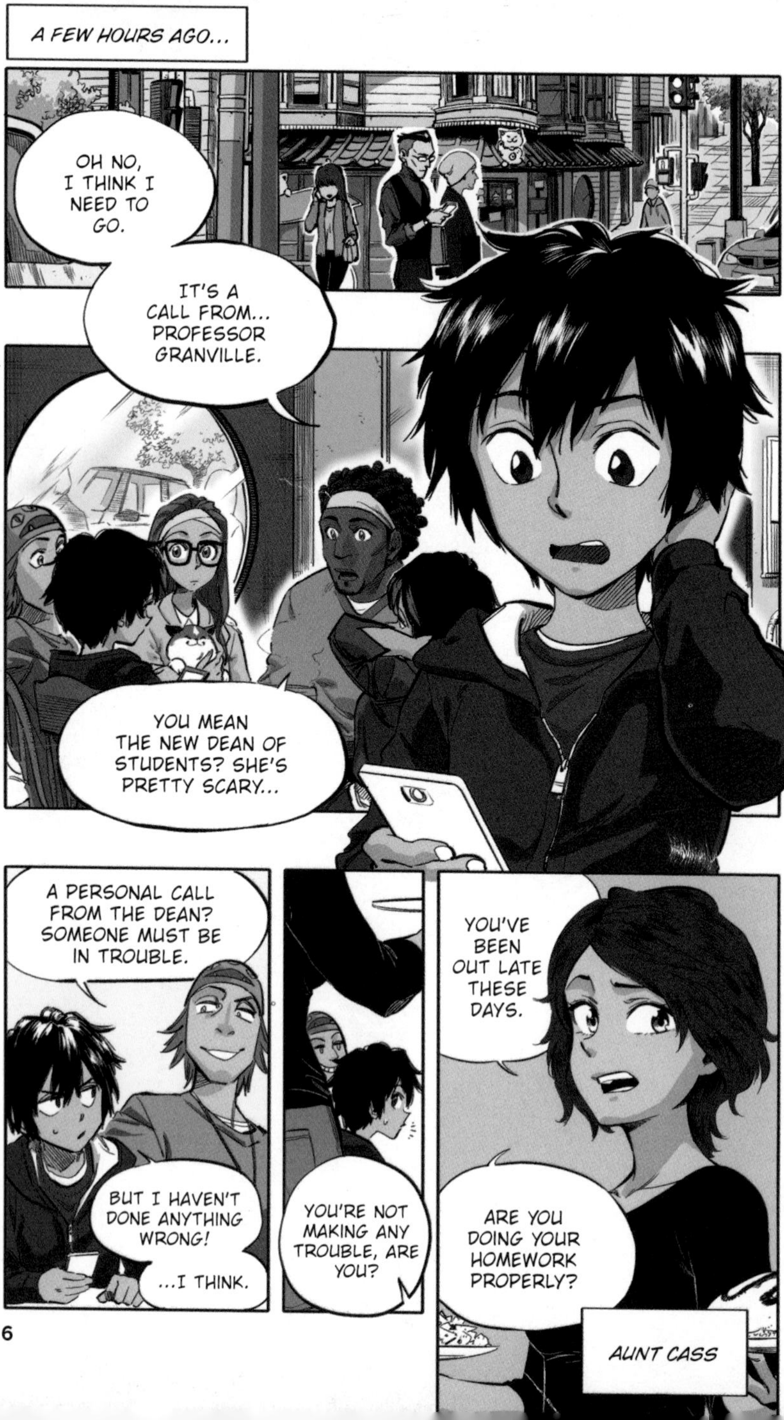
A FEW HOURS AGO...
OH NO, I THINK I NEED TO GO.
IT'S A CALL FROM... PROFESSOR GRANVILLE.
YOU MEAN THE NEW DEAN OF STUDENTS? SHE'S PRETTY SCARY...
A PERSONAL CALL FROM THE DEAN? SOMEONE MUST BE IN TROUBLE.
BUT I HAVEN'T DONE ANYTHING WRONG!
...I THINK.
YOU'RE NOT MAKING ANY TROUBLE, ARE YOU?
YOU'VE BEEN OUT LATE THESE DAYS.
ARE YOU DOING YOUR HOMEWORK PROPERLY?
AUNT CASS

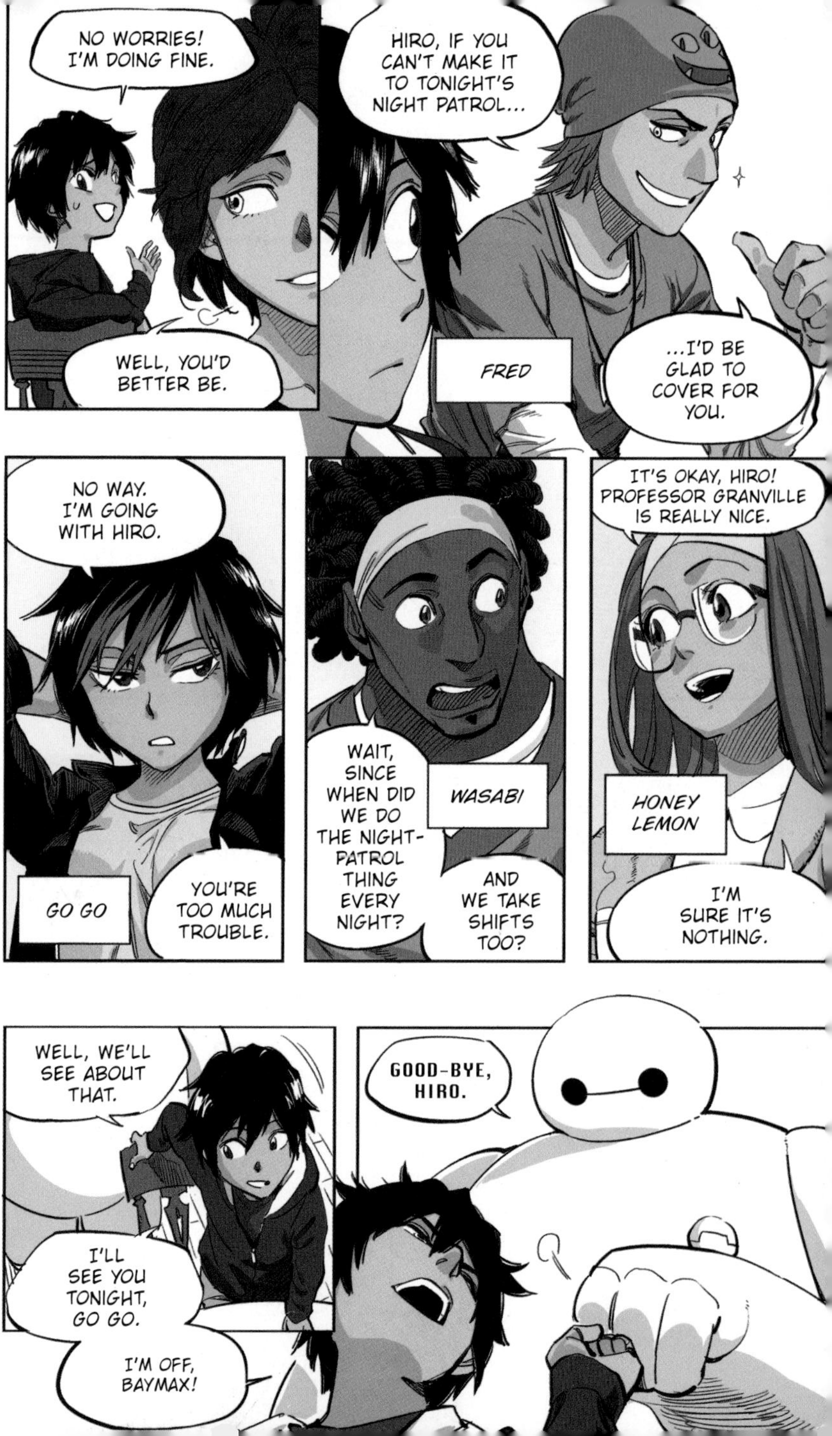
NO WORRIES! I'M DOING FINE.
WELL, YOU'D BETTER BE.
HIRO, IF YOU CAN'T MAKE IT TO TONIGHT'S NIGHT PATROL...
FRED
...I'D BE GLAD TO COVER FOR YOU.
NO WAY. I'M GOING WITH HIRO.
GO GO
YOU'RE TOO MUCH TROUBLE.
WAIT, SINCE WHEN DID WE DO THE NIGHT-PATROL THING EVERY NIGHT?
WASABI
AND WE TAKE SHIFTS TOO?
IT'S OKAY, HIRO! PROFESSOR GRANVILLE IS REALLY NICE.
HONEY LEMON
I'M SURE IT'S NOTHING.
WELL, WE'LL SEE ABOUT THAT.
I'LL SEE YOU TONIGHT, GO GO.
I'M OFF, BAYMAX!
GOOD-BYE, HIRO.

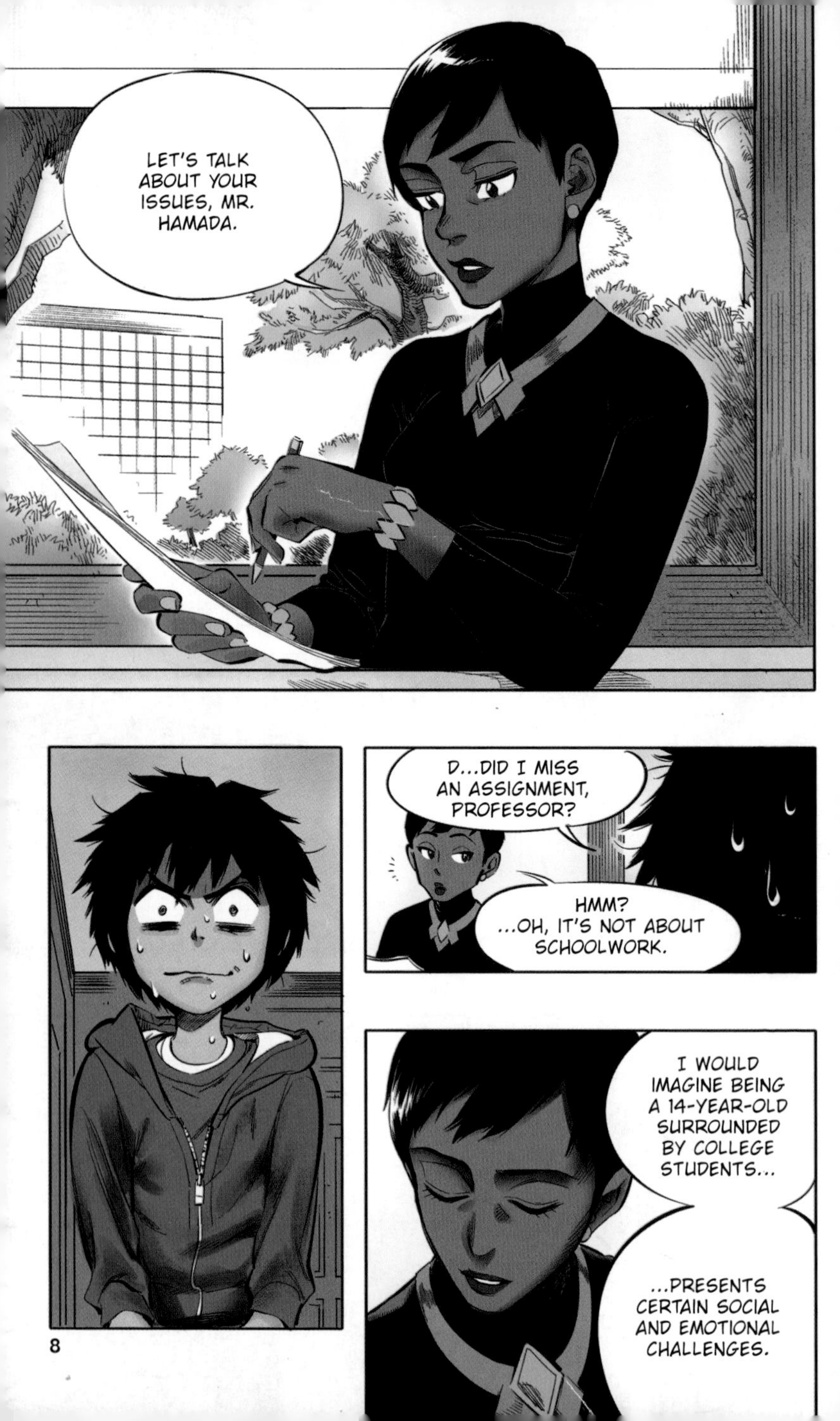

LET'S TALK ABOUT YOUR ISSUES, MR. HAMADA.
D...DID I MISS AN ASSIGNMENT, PROFESSOR?
HMM? ...OH, IT'S NOT ABOUT SCHOOLWORK.
I WOULD IMAGINE BEING A 14-YEAR-OLD SURROUNDED BY COLLEGE STUDENTS...
...PRESENTS CERTAIN SOCIAL AND EMOTIONAL CHALLENGES.

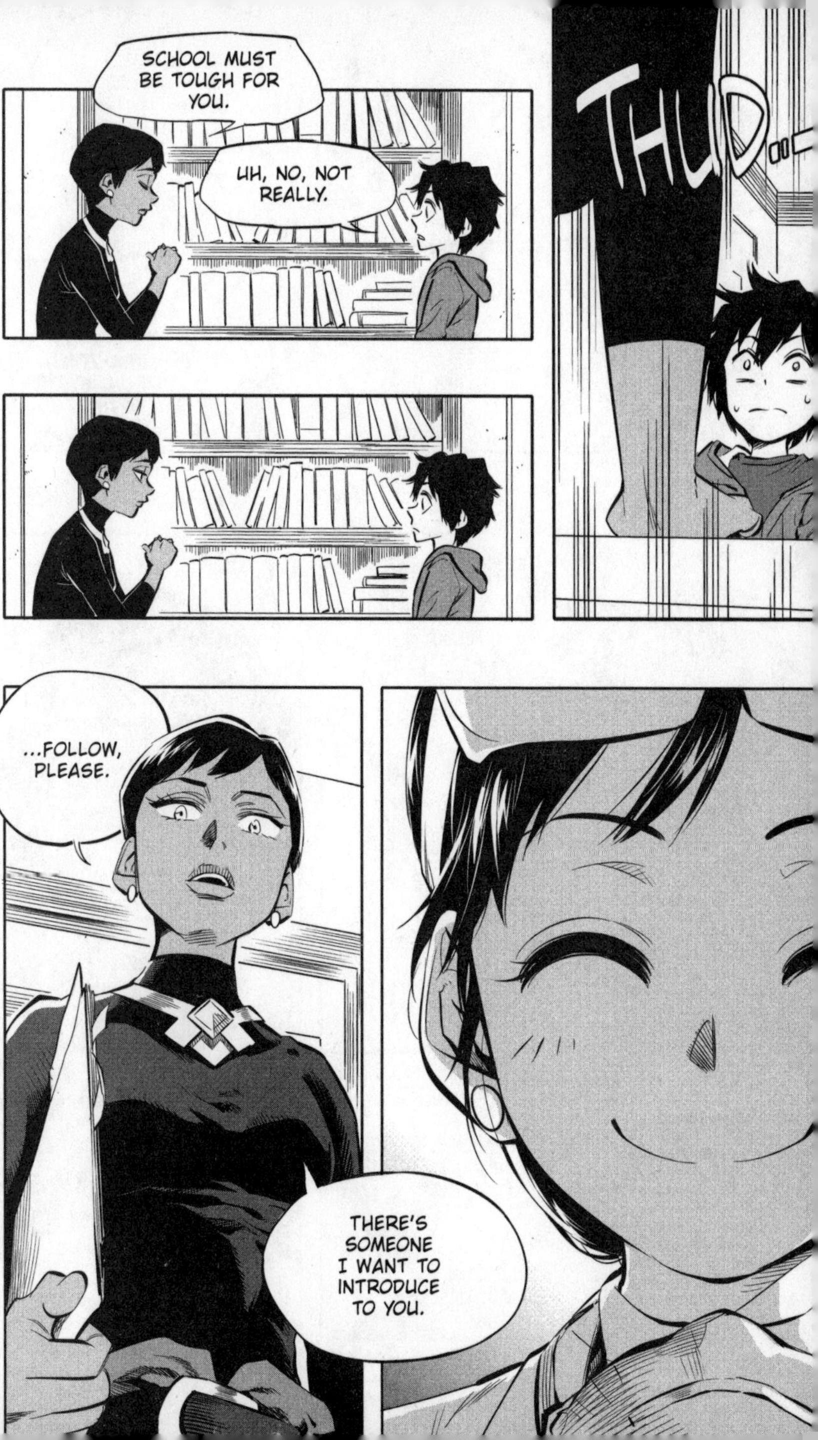
SCHOOL MUST BE TOUGH FOR YOU.
UH, NO, NOT REALLY.
THUD...
...FOLLOW, PLEASE.
THERE'S SOMEONE I WANT TO INTRODUCE TO YOU.

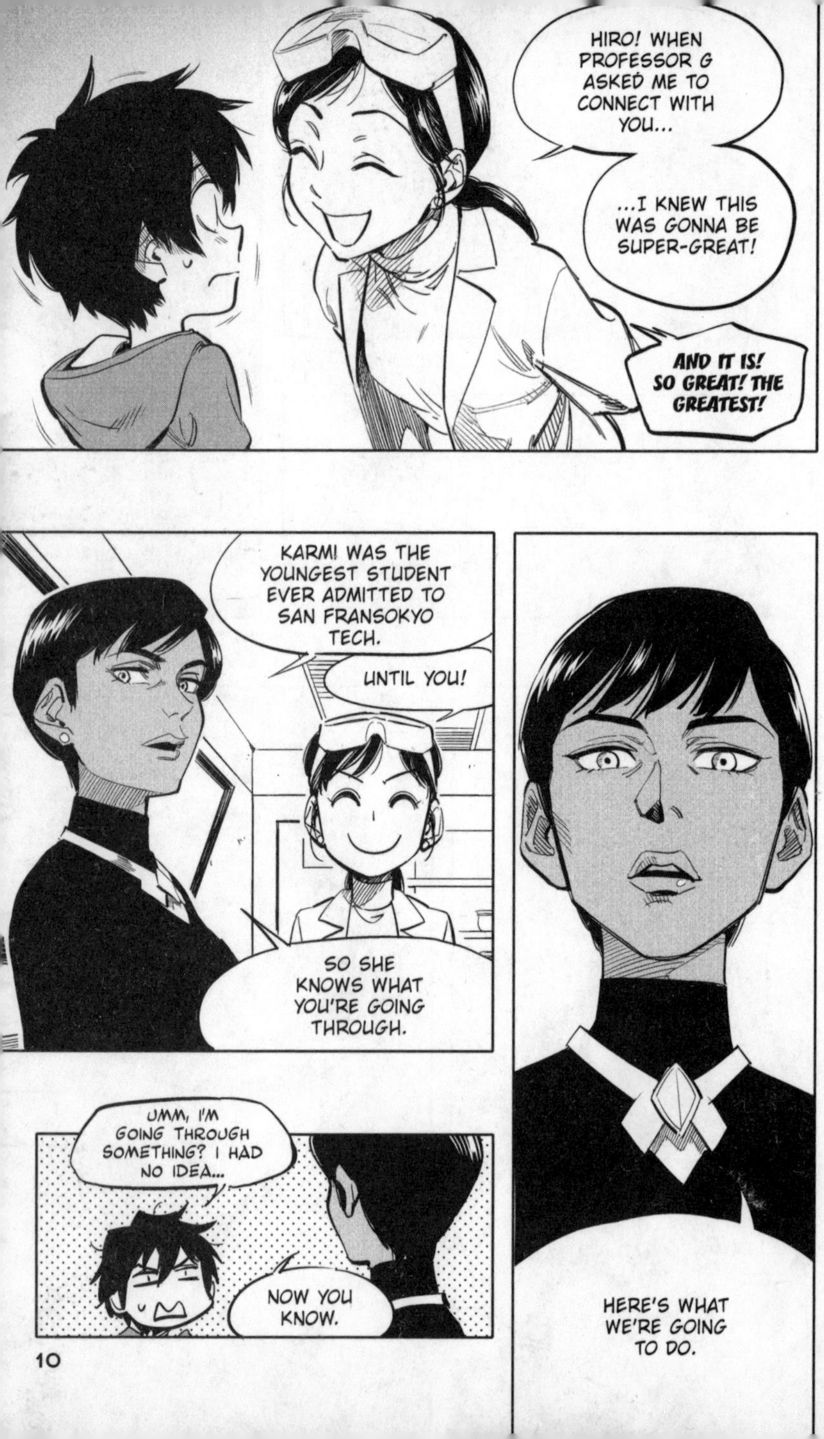
HIRO! WHEN PROFESSOR G ASKED ME TO CONNECT WITH YOU...
...I KNEW THIS WAS GONNA BE SUPER-GREAT!
AND IT IS! SO GREAT! THE GREATEST!
KARMI WAS THE YOUNGEST STUDENT EVER ADMITTED TO SAN FRANSOKYO TECH.
UNTIL YOU!
SO SHE KNOWS WHAT YOU'RE GOING THROUGH.
UMM, I'M GOING THROUGH SOMETHING? I HAD NO IDEA...
NOW YOU KNOW.
HERE'S WHAT WE'RE GOING TO DO.

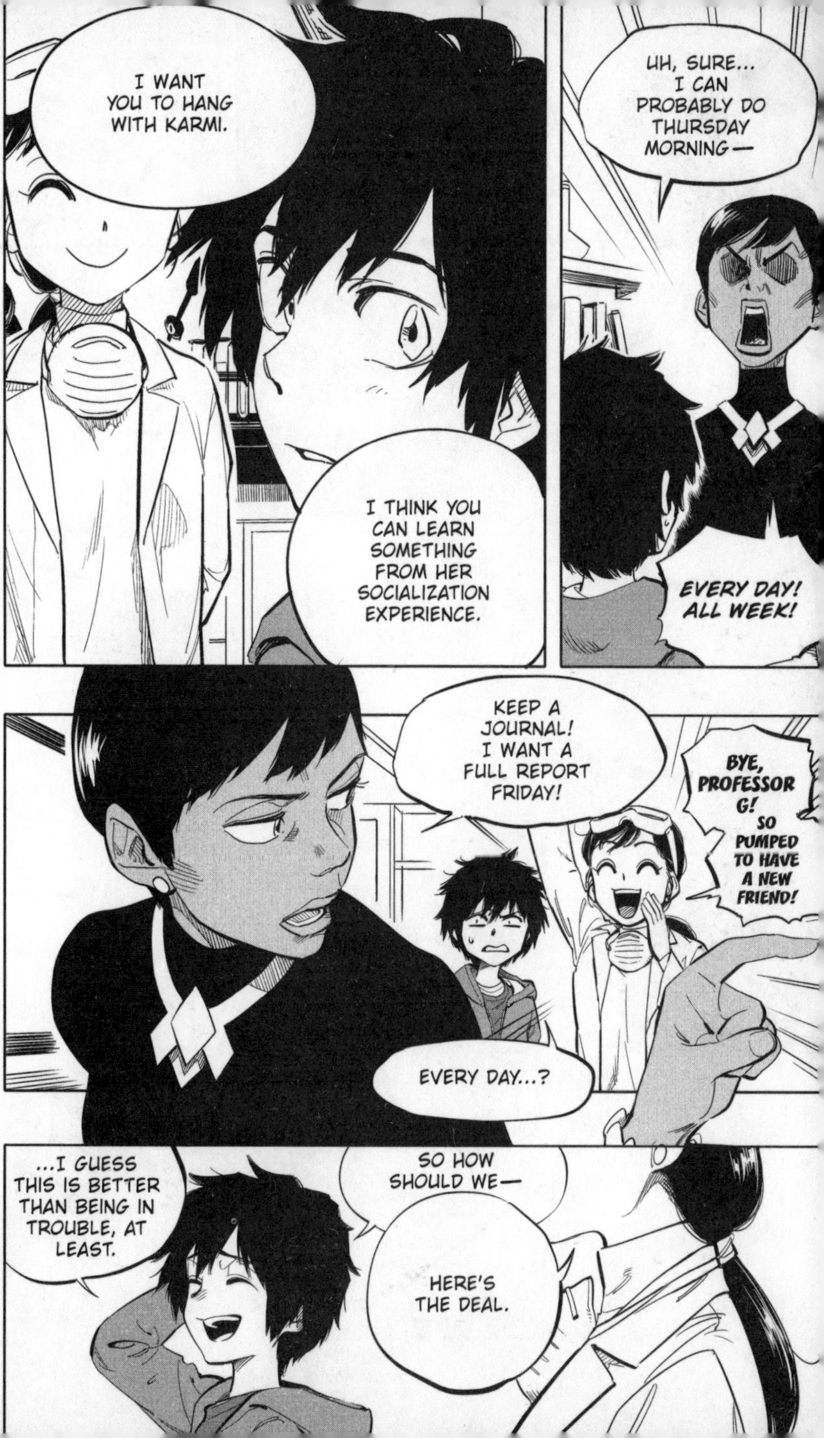
I WANT YOU TO HANG WITH KARMI.
I THINK YOU CAN LEARN SOMETHING FROM HER SOCIALIZATION EXPERIENCE.
UH, SURE... I CAN PROBABLY DO THURSDAY MORNING—
EVERY DAY! ALL WEEK!
KEEP A JOURNAL! I WANT A FULL REPORT FRIDAY!
EVERY DAY...?
BYE, PROFESSOR G!
SO PUMPED TO HAVE A NEW FRIEND!
...I GUESS THIS IS BETTER THAN BEING IN TROUBLE, AT LEAST.
SO HOW SHOULD WE—
HERE'S THE DEAL.

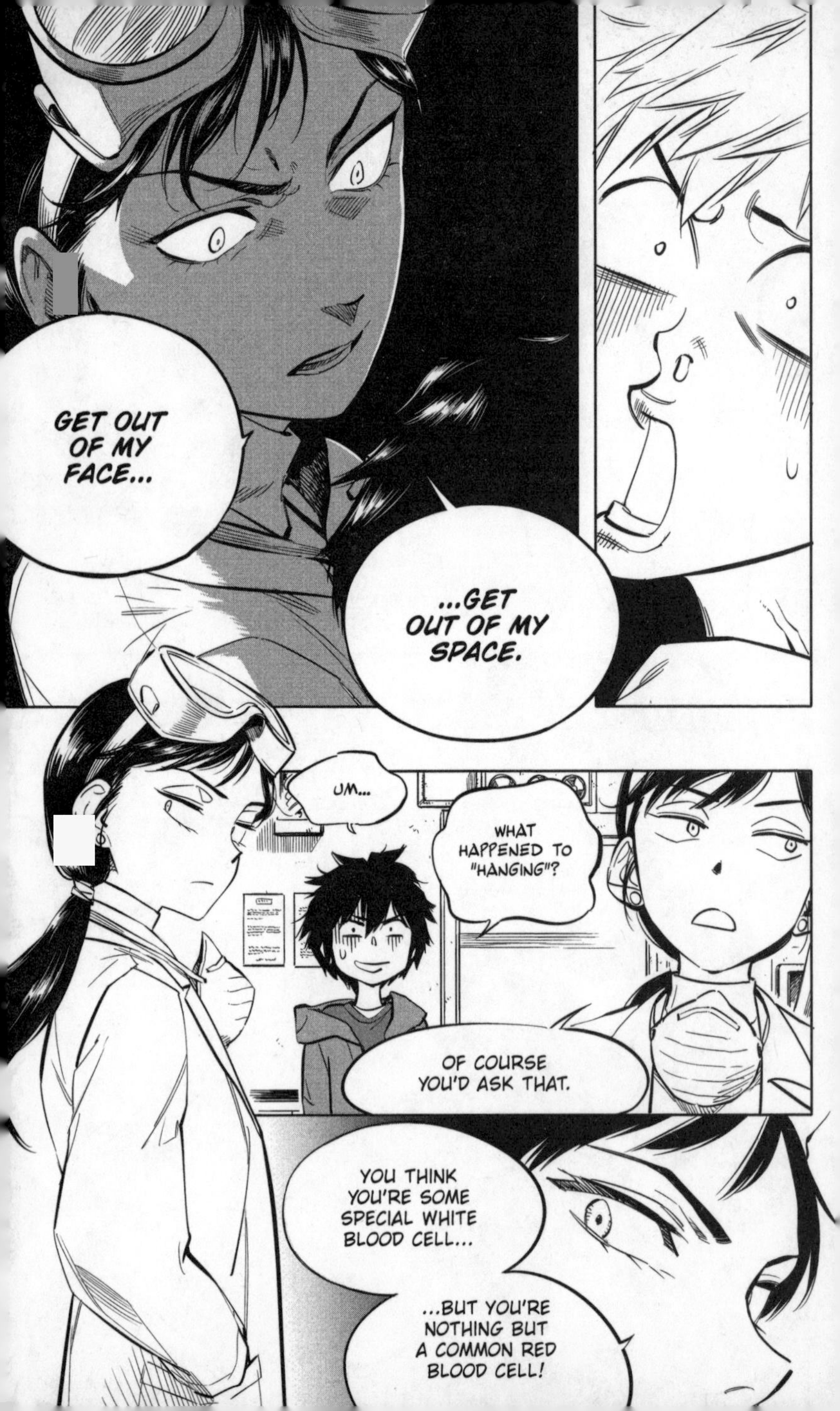
GET OUT OF MY FACE...
...GET OUT OF MY SPACE.
UM...
WHAT HAPPENED TO "HANGING"?
OF COURSE YOU'D ASK THAT.
YOU THINK YOU'RE SOME SPECIAL WHITE BLOOD CELL...
...BUT YOU'RE NOTHING BUT A COMMON RED BLOOD CELL!

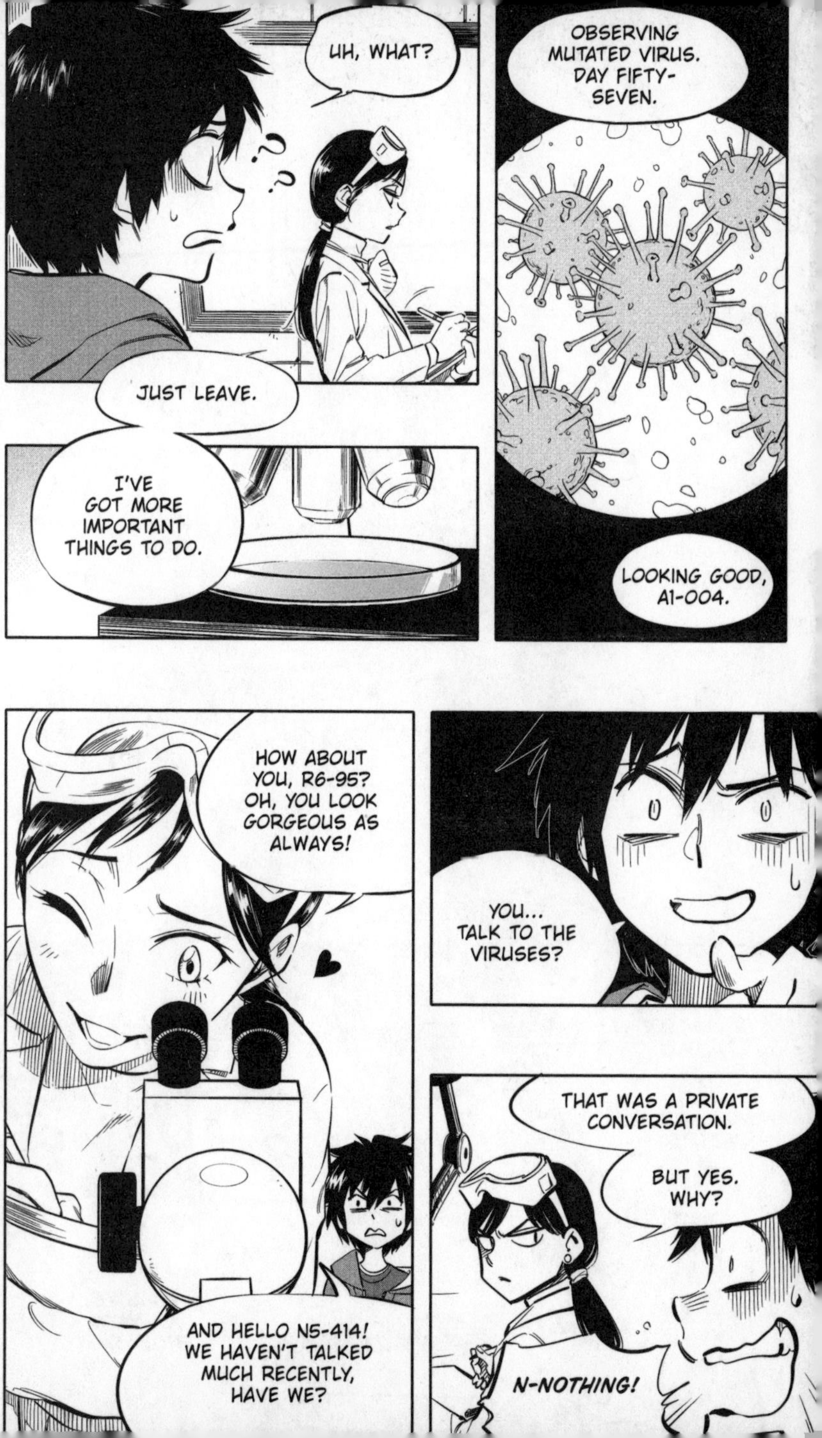
UH, WHAT?
JUST LEAVE.
I'VE GOT MORE IMPORTANT THINGS TO DO.
OBSERVING MUTATED VIRUS. DAY FIFTY-SEVEN.
LOOKING GOOD, A1-004.
HOW ABOUT YOU, R6-95? OH, YOU LOOK GORGEOUS AS ALWAYS!
AND HELLO N5-414! WE HAVEN'T TALKED MUCH RECENTLY, HAVE WE?
YOU... TALK TO THE VIRUSES?
THAT WAS A PRIVATE CONVERSATION.
BUT YES. WHY?
N-NOTHING!

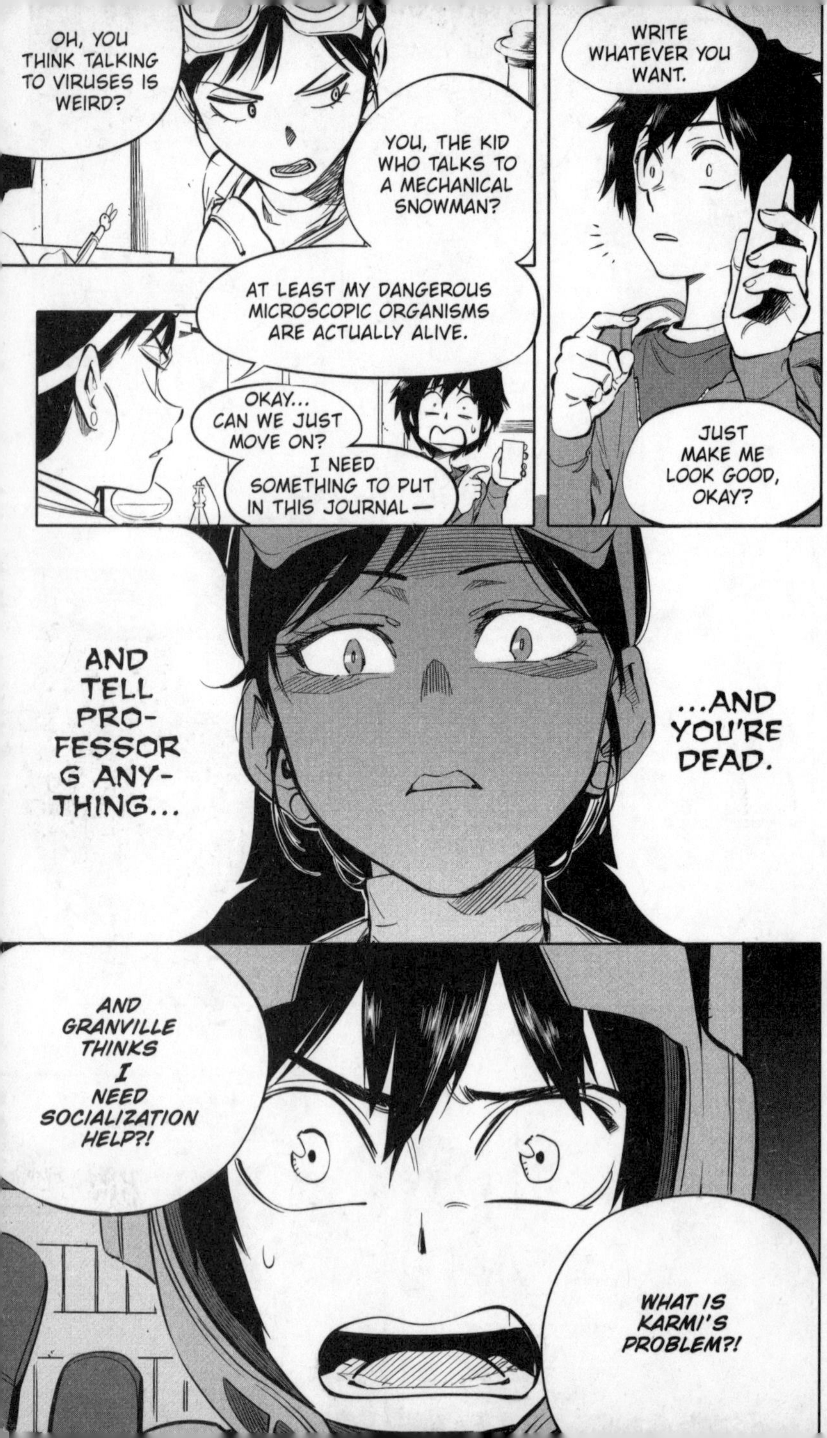
OH, YOU THINK TALKING TO VIRUSES IS WEIRD?
YOU, THE KID WHO TALKS TO A MECHANICAL SNOWMAN?
AT LEAST MY DANGEROUS MICROSCOPIC ORGANISMS ARE ACTUALLY ALIVE.
OKAY... CAN WE JUST MOVE ON?
I NEED SOMETHING TO PUT IN THIS JOURNAL—
WRITE WHATEVER YOU WANT.
JUST MAKE ME LOOK GOOD, OKAY?
AND TELL PRO-FESSOR G ANY-THING...
...AND YOU'RE DEAD.
AND GRANVILLE THINKS *I* NEED SOCIALIZATION HELP?!
WHAT IS KARMI'S PROBLEM?!

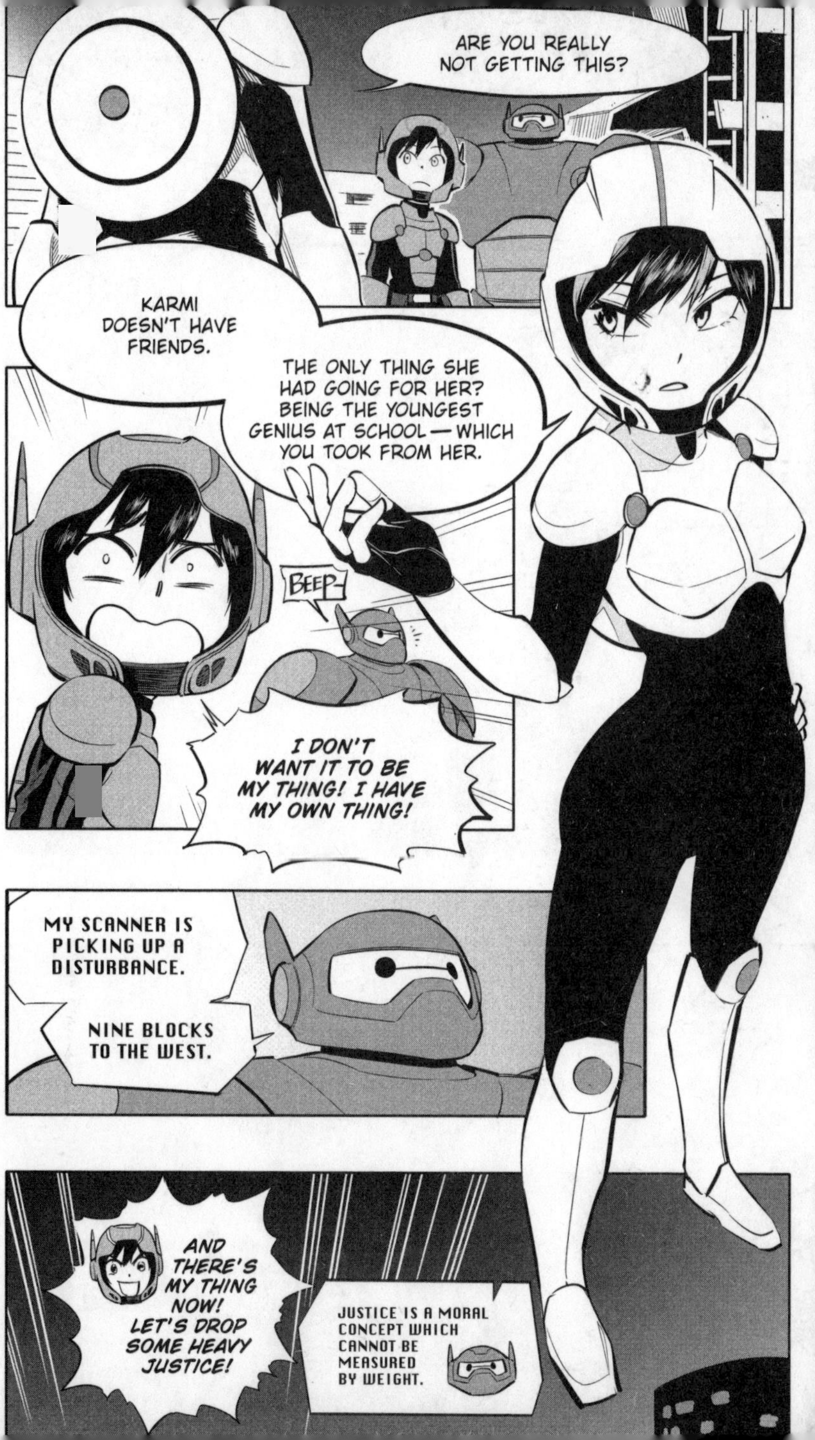
ARE YOU REALLY NOT GETTING THIS?
KARMI DOESN'T HAVE FRIENDS.
THE ONLY THING SHE HAD GOING FOR HER? BEING THE YOUNGEST GENIUS AT SCHOOL—WHICH YOU TOOK FROM HER.
BEEP-
I DON'T WANT IT TO BE MY THING! I HAVE MY OWN THING!
MY SCANNER IS PICKING UP A DISTURBANCE.
NINE BLOCKS TO THE WEST.
AND THERE'S MY THING NOW! LET'S DROP SOME HEAVY JUSTICE!
JUSTICE IS A MORAL CONCEPT WHICH CANNOT BE MEASURED BY WEIGHT.

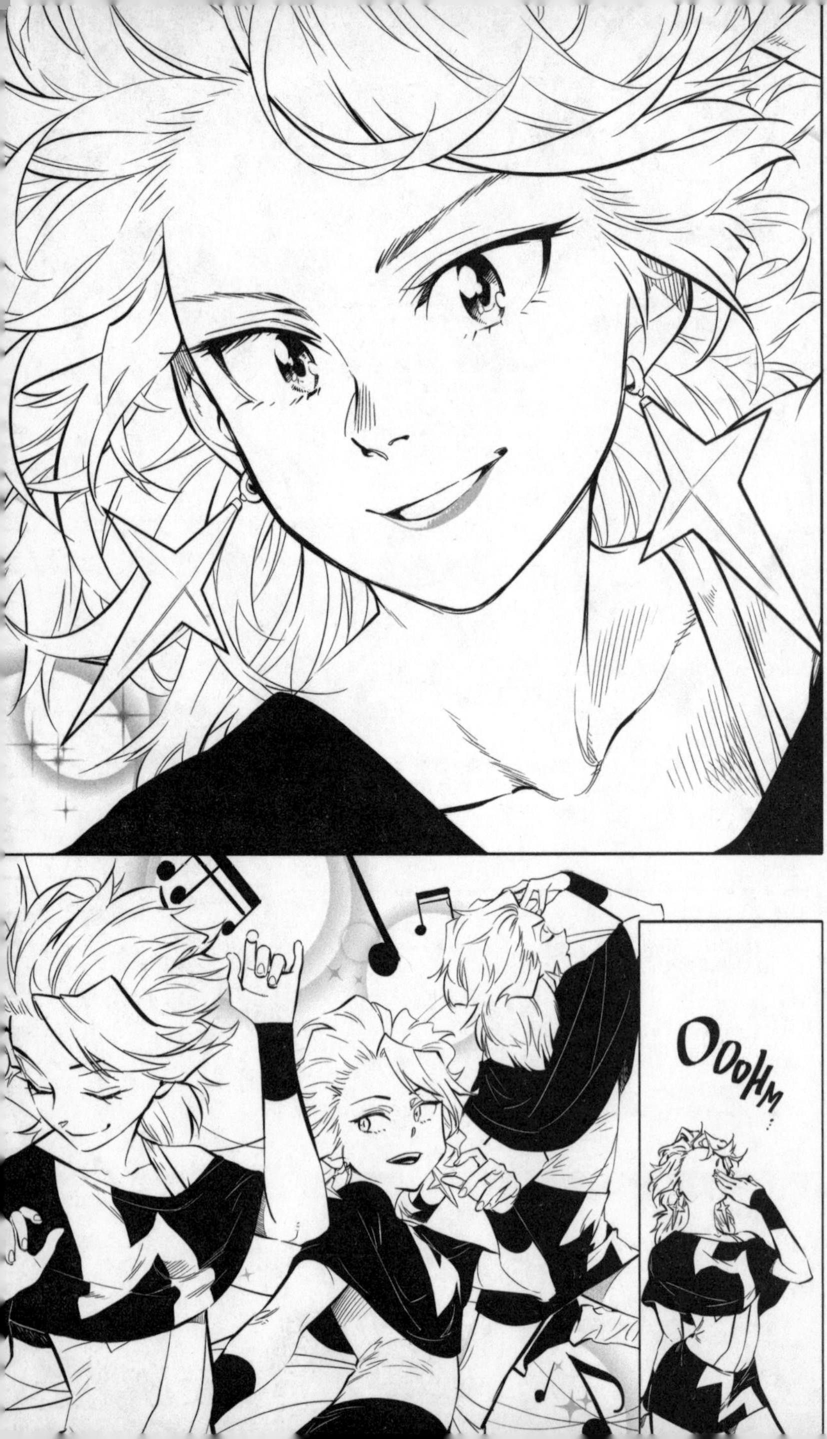
OOOHM

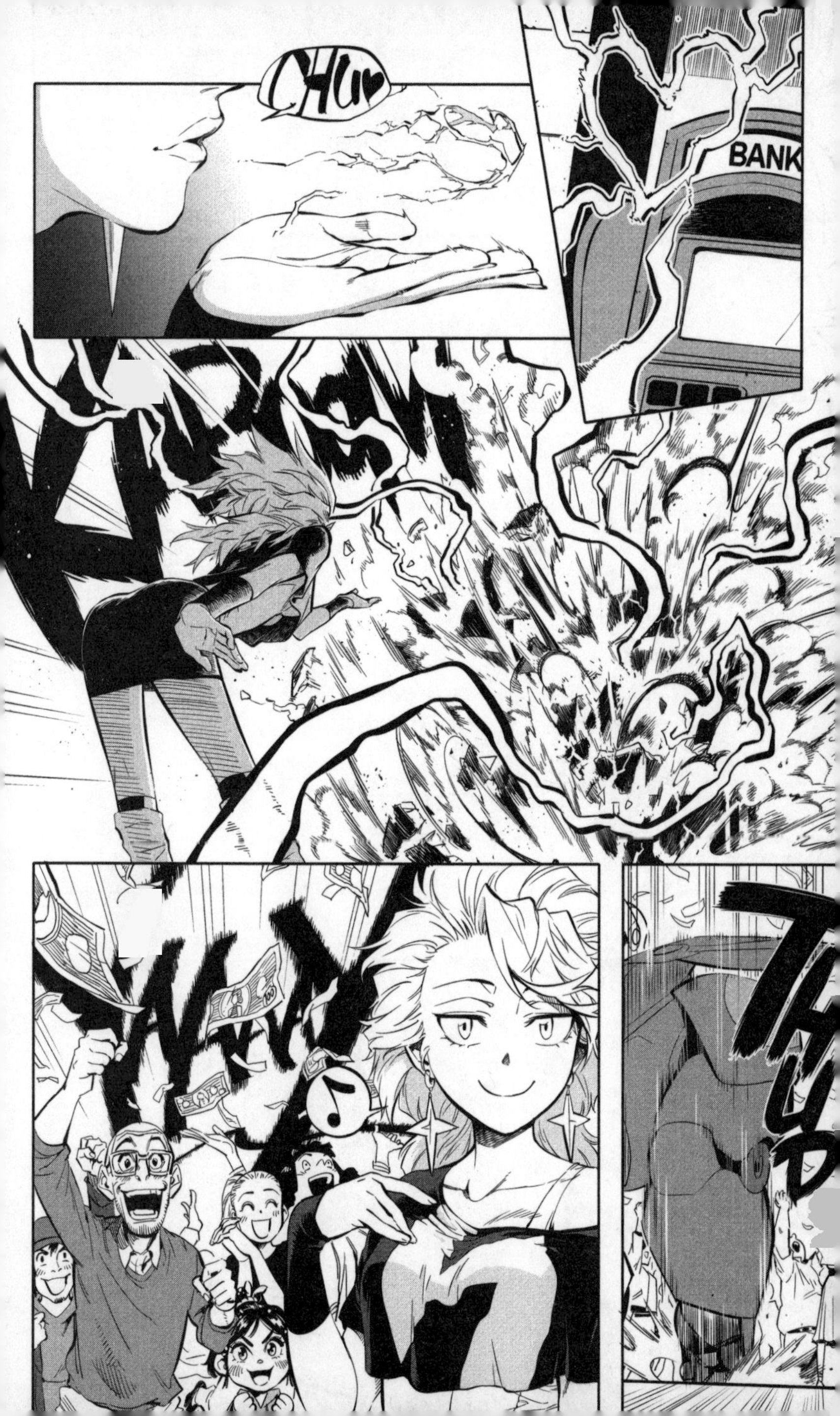
CHU♥
BANK

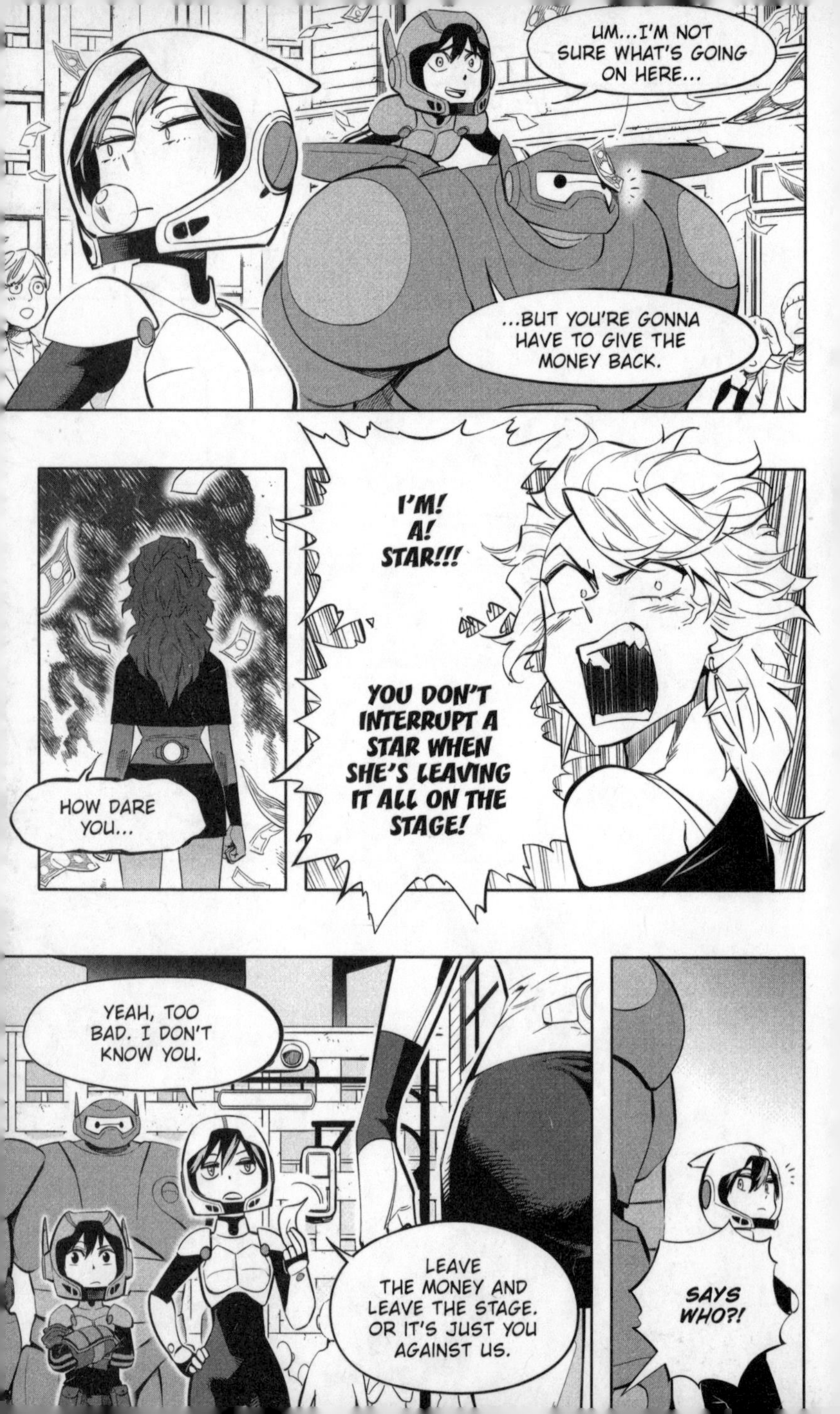
UM...I'M NOT SURE WHAT'S GOING ON HERE...
...BUT YOU'RE GONNA HAVE TO GIVE THE MONEY BACK.
HOW DARE YOU...
I'M! A! STAR!!!
YOU DON'T INTERRUPT A STAR WHEN SHE'S LEAVING IT ALL ON THE STAGE!
YEAH, TOO BAD. I DON'T KNOW YOU.
LEAVE THE MONEY AND LEAVE THE STAGE. OR IT'S JUST YOU AGAINST US.
SAYS WHO?!

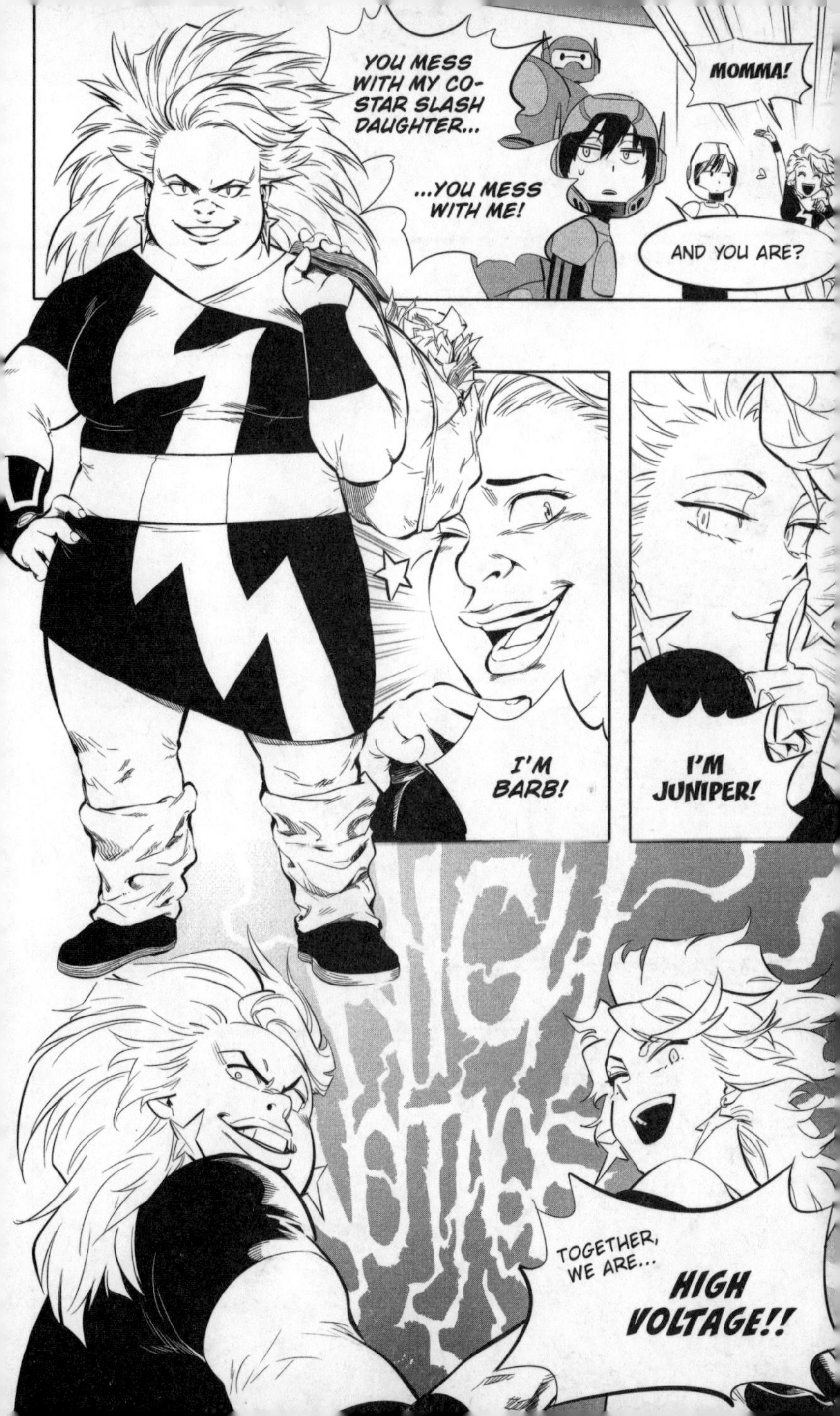
YOU MESS WITH MY CO-STAR SLASH DAUGHTER...
...YOU MESS WITH ME!
MOMMA!
AND YOU ARE?
I'M BARB!
I'M JUNIPER!
HIGH VOLTAGE!
TOGETHER, WE ARE...
HIGH VOLTAGE!!

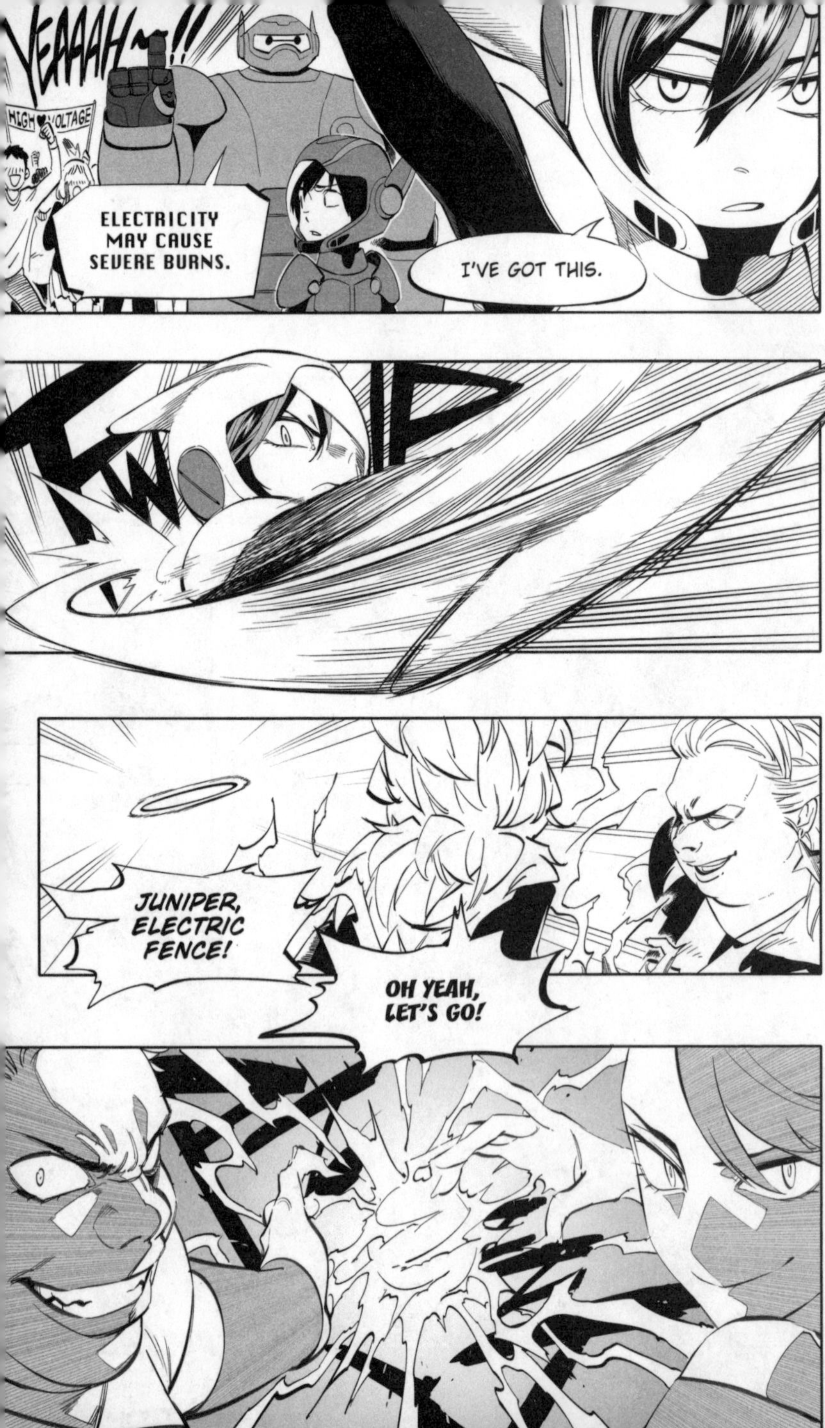
YEAAAH~~!!
HIGH ♥ VOLTAGE
ELECTRICITY MAY CAUSE SEVERE BURNS.
I'VE GOT THIS.
FWIP
JUNIPER, ELECTRIC FENCE!
OH YEAH, LET'S GO!

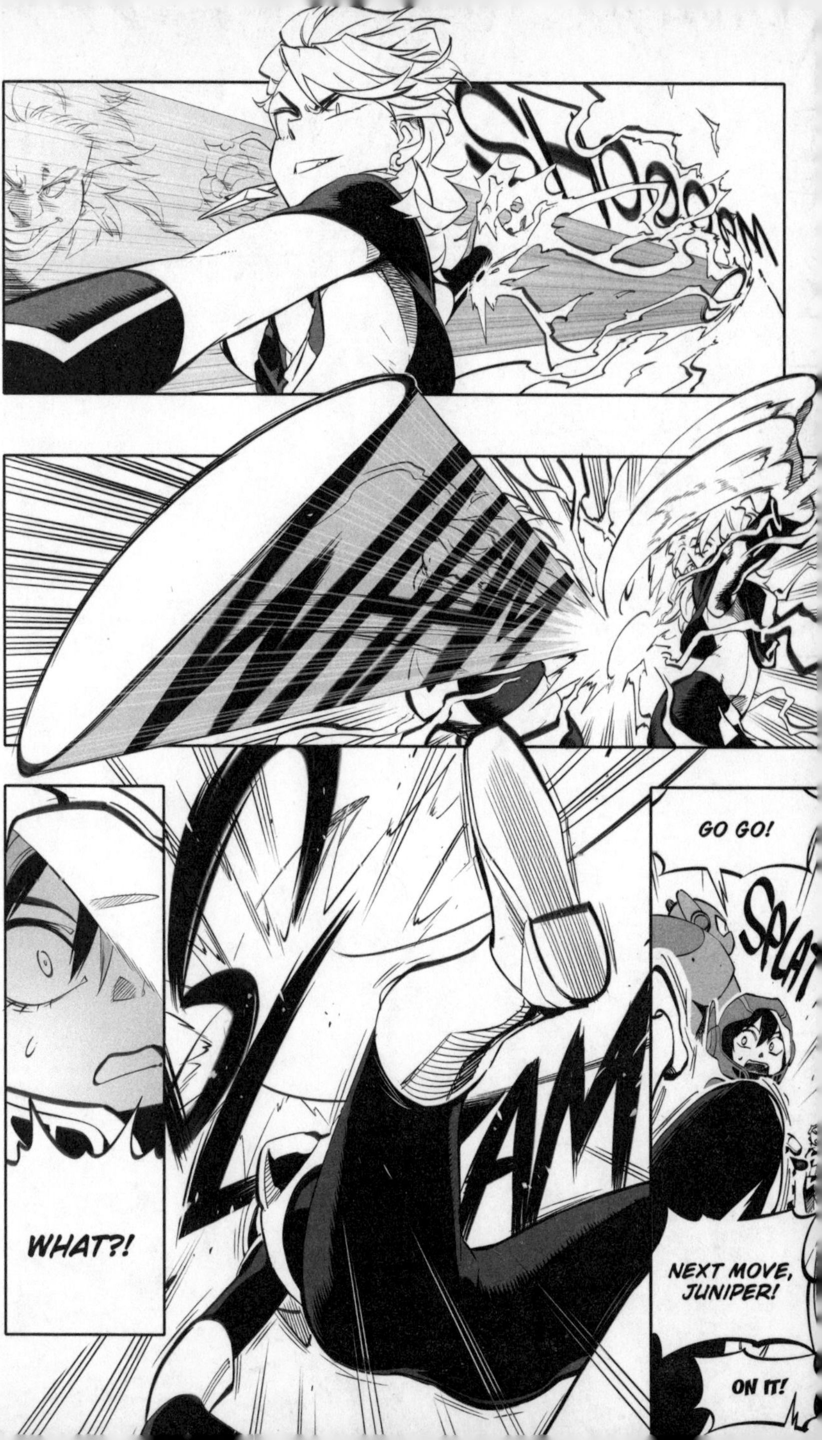

WHAT?!
GO GO!
SPLAT
NEXT MOVE, JUNIPER!
ON IT!

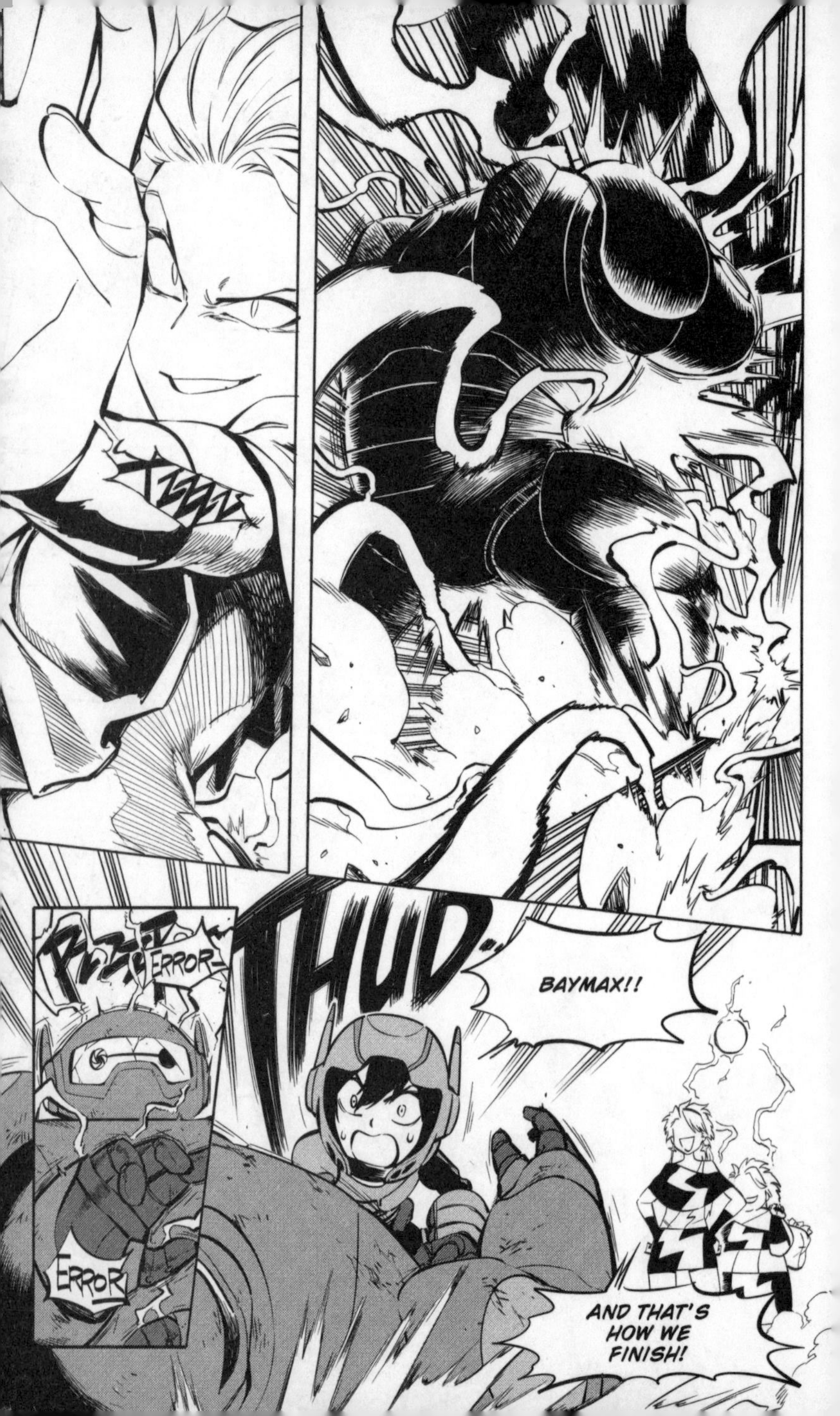
XZZZZ
THUD
BZZT
ERROR
BAYMAX!!
ERROR
AND THAT'S HOW WE FINISH!

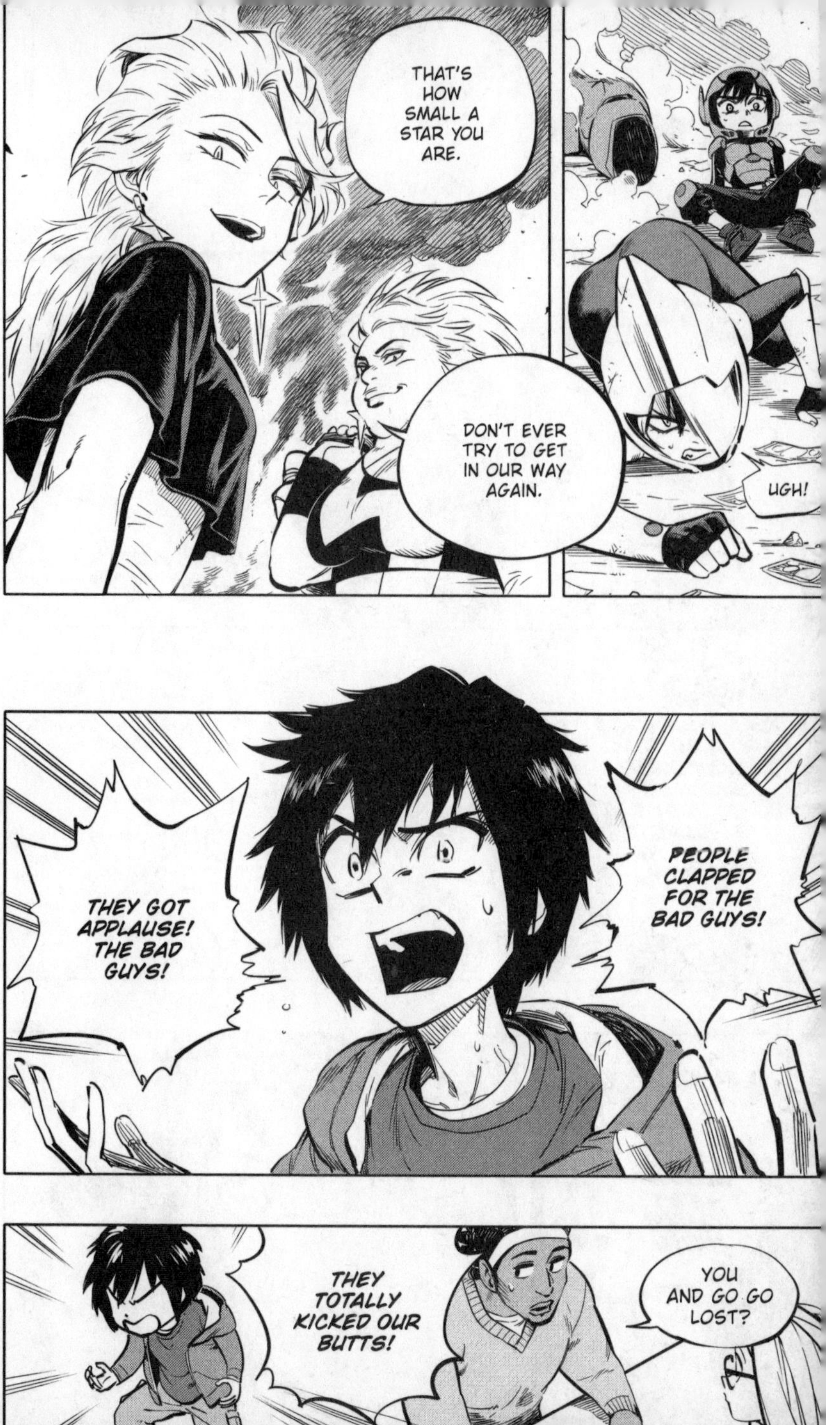
THAT'S HOW SMALL A STAR YOU ARE.
DON'T EVER TRY TO GET IN OUR WAY AGAIN.
UGH!
THEY GOT APPLAUSE! THE BAD GUYS!
PEOPLE CLAPPED FOR THE BAD GUYS!
THEY TOTALLY KICKED OUR BUTTS!
YOU AND GO GO LOST?

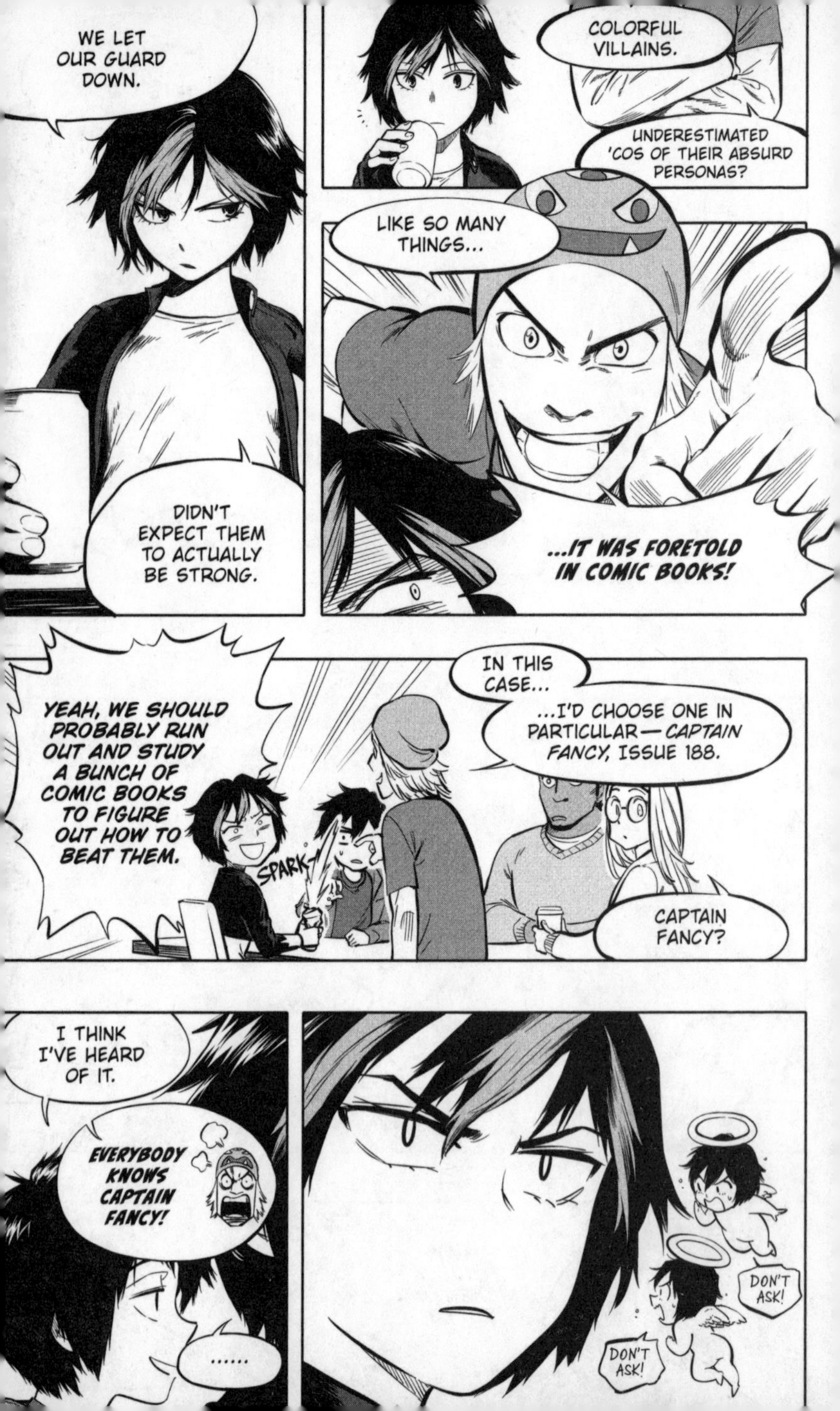
WE LET OUR GUARD DOWN.
DIDN'T EXPECT THEM TO ACTUALLY BE STRONG.
COLORFUL VILLAINS.
UNDERESTIMATED 'COS OF THEIR ABSURD PERSONAS?
LIKE SO MANY THINGS...
...IT WAS FORETOLD IN COMIC BOOKS!
YEAH, WE SHOULD PROBABLY RUN OUT AND STUDY A BUNCH OF COMIC BOOKS TO FIGURE OUT HOW TO BEAT THEM.
SPARK
IN THIS CASE...
...I'D CHOOSE ONE IN PARTICULAR—CAPTAIN FANCY, ISSUE 188.
CAPTAIN FANCY?
I THINK I'VE HEARD OF IT.
EVERYBODY KNOWS CAPTAIN FANCY!
......
DON'T ASK!
DON'T ASK!

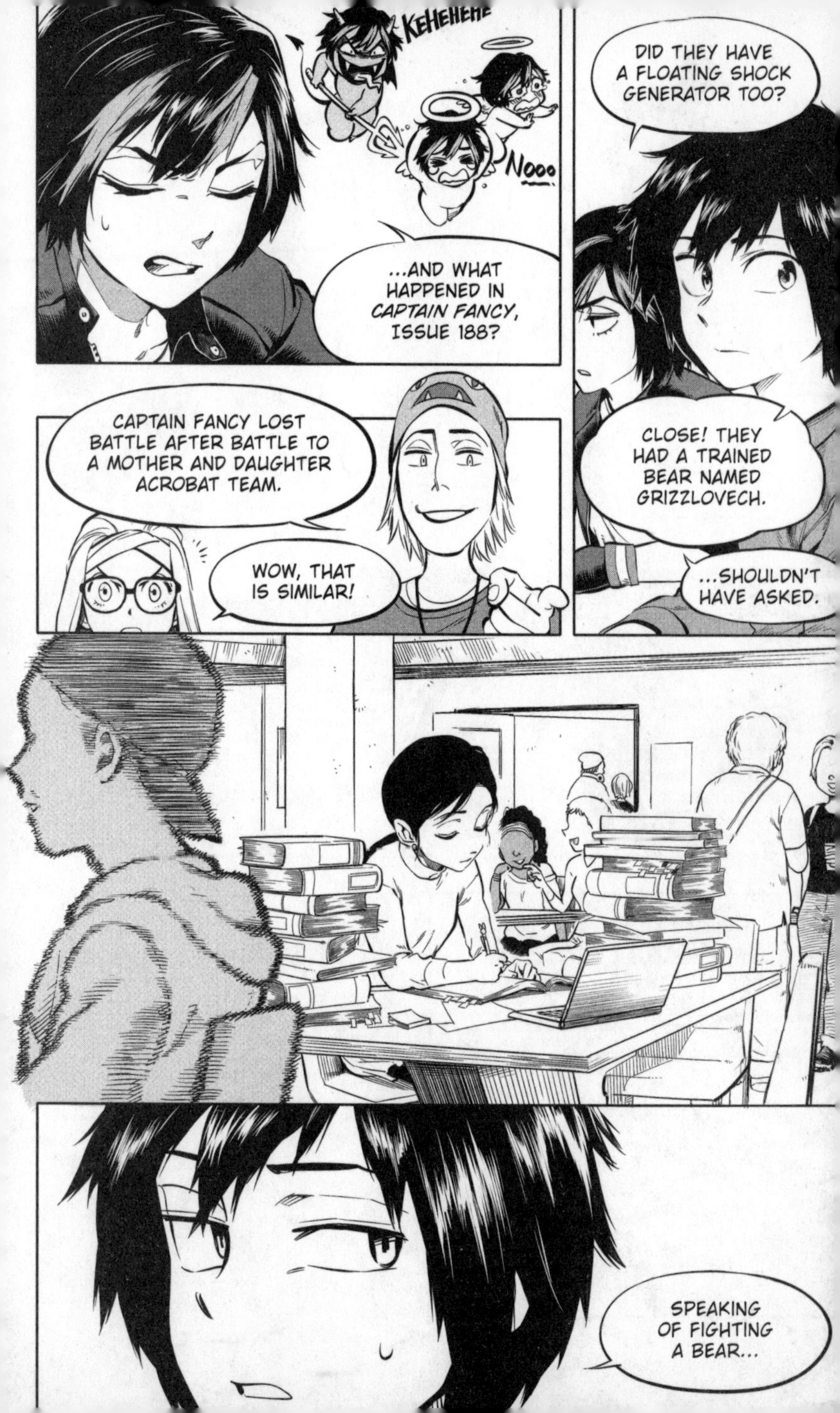
KEHEHEHE
NOOO
...AND WHAT HAPPENED IN *CAPTAIN FANCY*, ISSUE 188?
DID THEY HAVE A FLOATING SHOCK GENERATOR TOO?
CAPTAIN FANCY LOST BATTLE AFTER BATTLE TO A MOTHER AND DAUGHTER ACROBAT TEAM.
WOW, THAT IS SIMILAR!
CLOSE! THEY HAD A TRAINED BEAR NAMED GRIZZLOVECH.
...SHOULDN'T HAVE ASKED.
SPEAKING OF FIGHTING A BEAR...

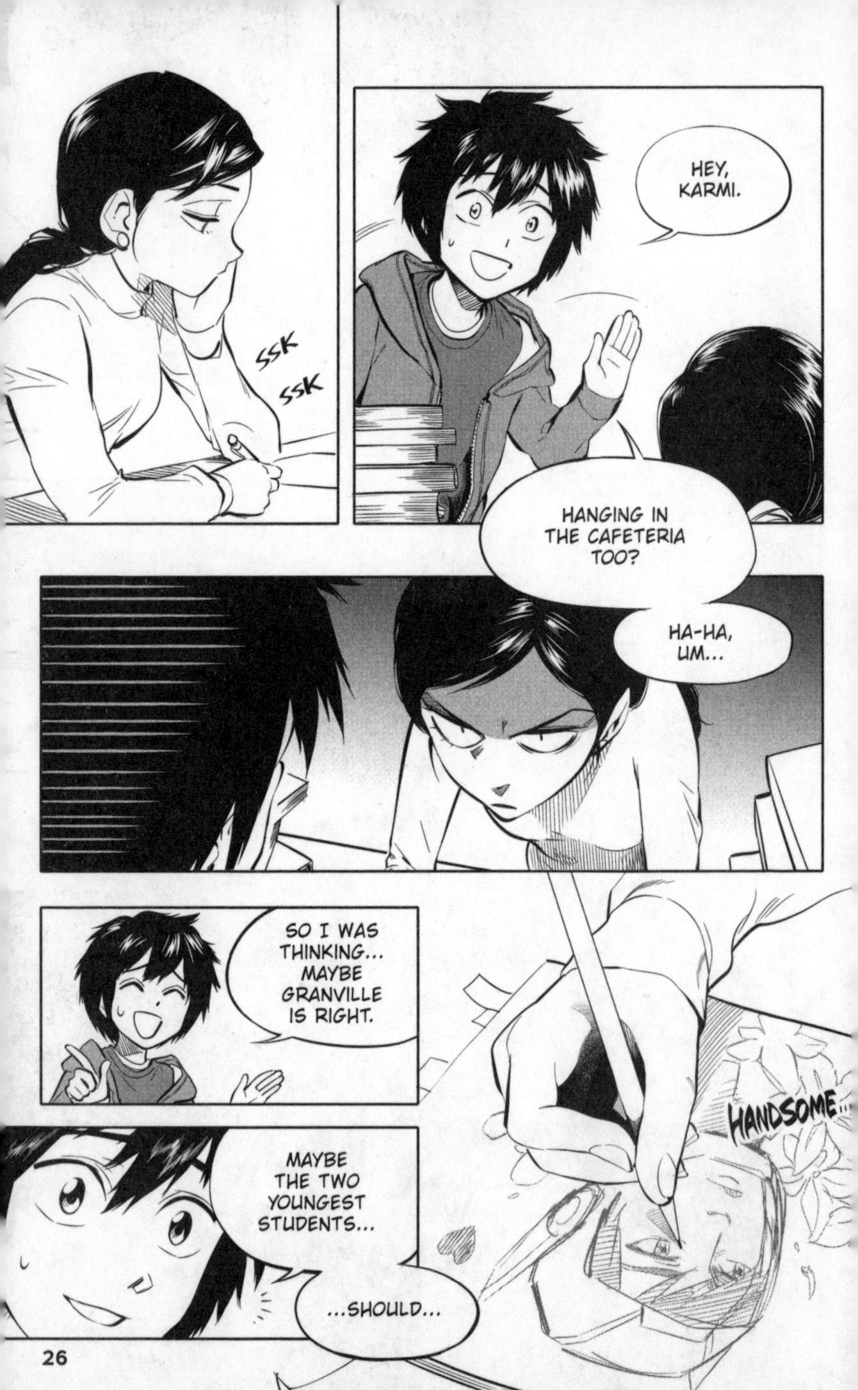
SSK
SSK
HEY, KARMI.
HANGING IN THE CAFETERIA TOO?
HA-HA, UM...
SO I WAS THINKING... MAYBE GRANVILLE IS RIGHT.
HANDSOME...
MAYBE THE TWO YOUNGEST STUDENTS...
...SHOULD...

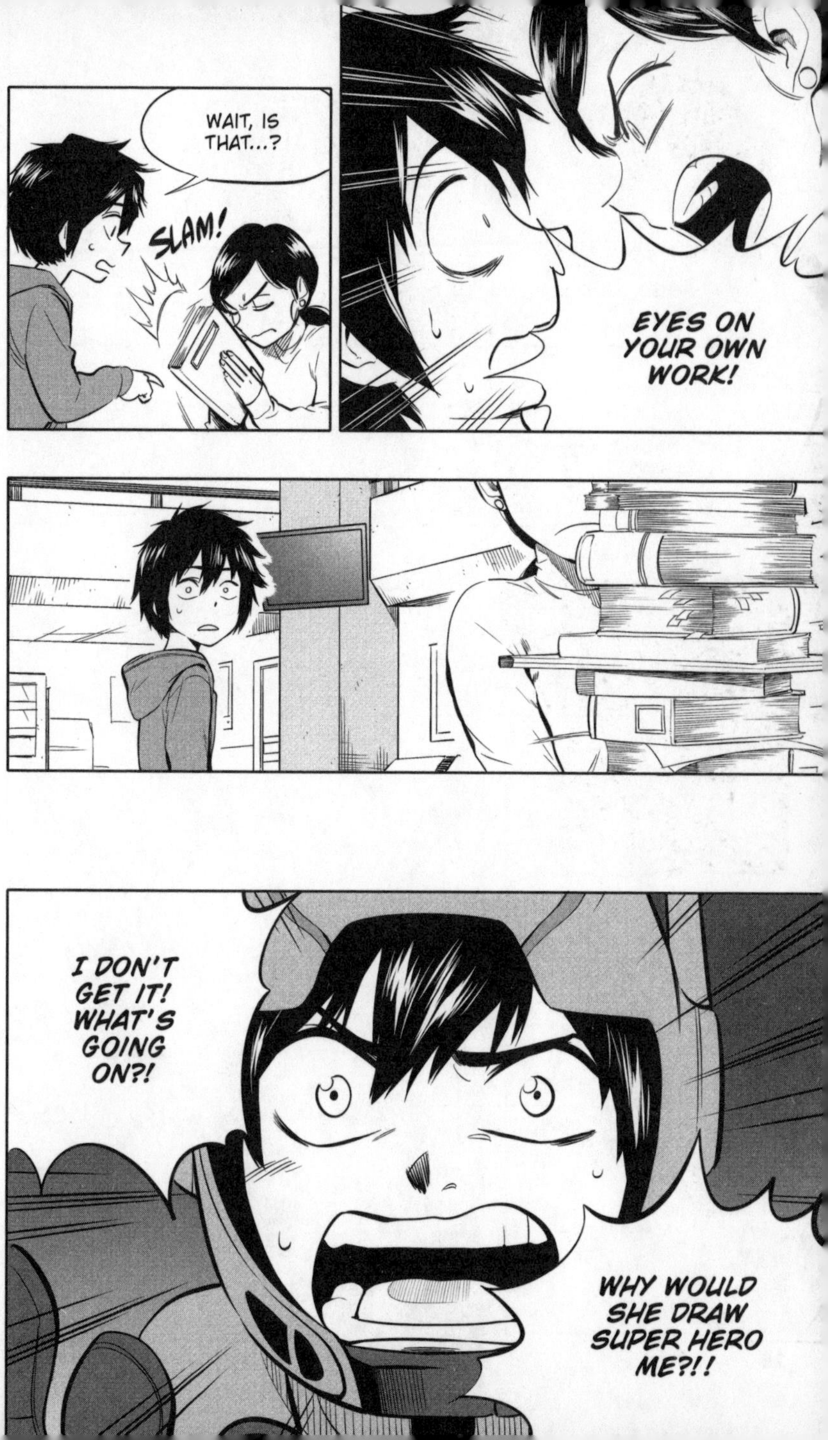
WAIT, IS THAT...?
SLAM!
EYES ON YOUR OWN WORK!
I DON'T GET IT! WHAT'S GOING ON?!
WHY WOULD SHE DRAW SUPER HERO ME?!!

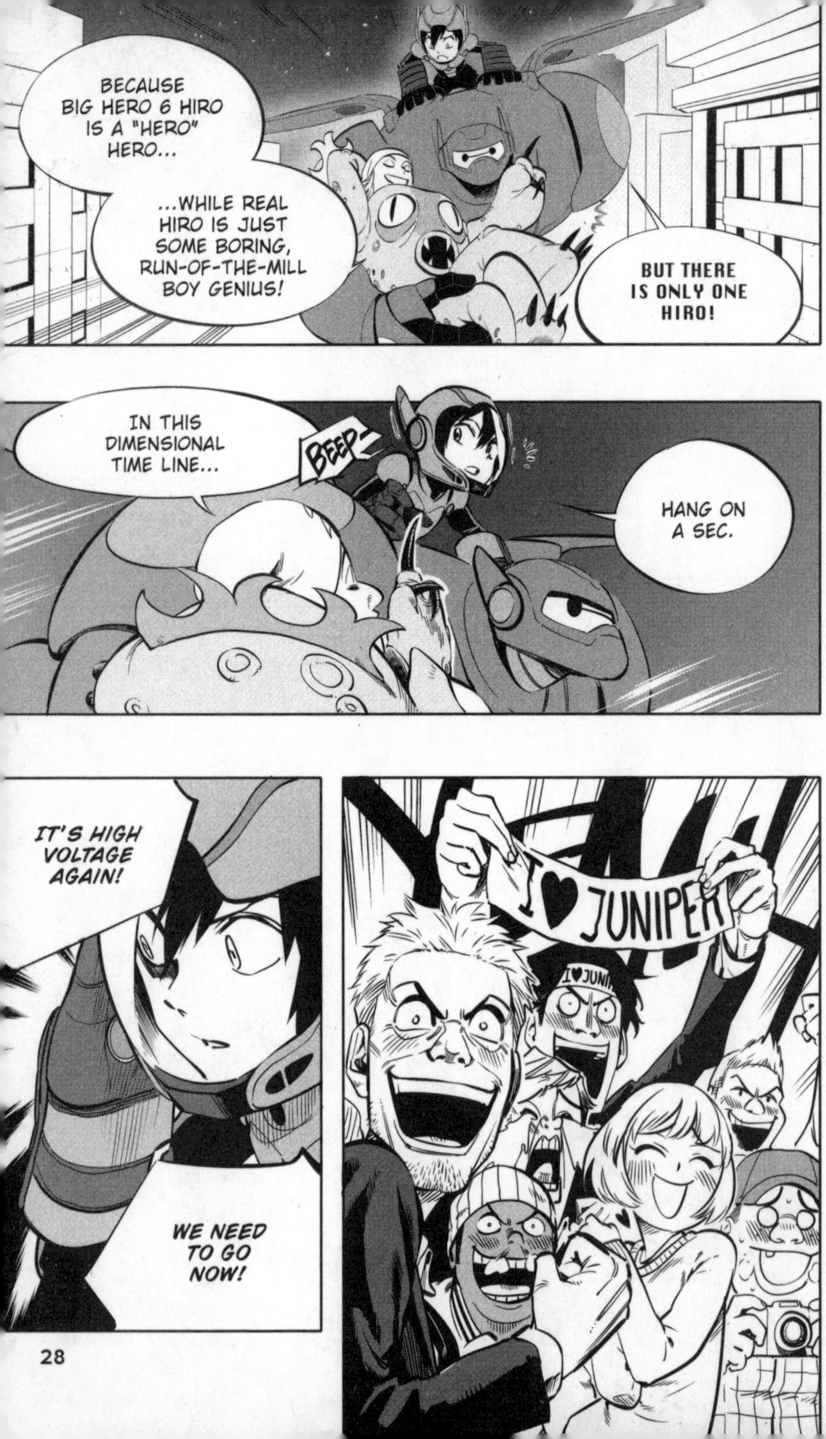

BECAUSE BIG HERO 6 HIRO IS A "HERO" HERO...
...WHILE REAL HIRO IS JUST SOME BORING, RUN-OF-THE-MILL BOY GENIUS!
BUT THERE IS ONLY ONE HIRO!
IN THIS DIMENSIONAL TIME LINE...
BEEP-
HANG ON A SEC.
IT'S HIGH VOLTAGE AGAIN!
WE NEED TO GO NOW!
I ♥ JUNIPER

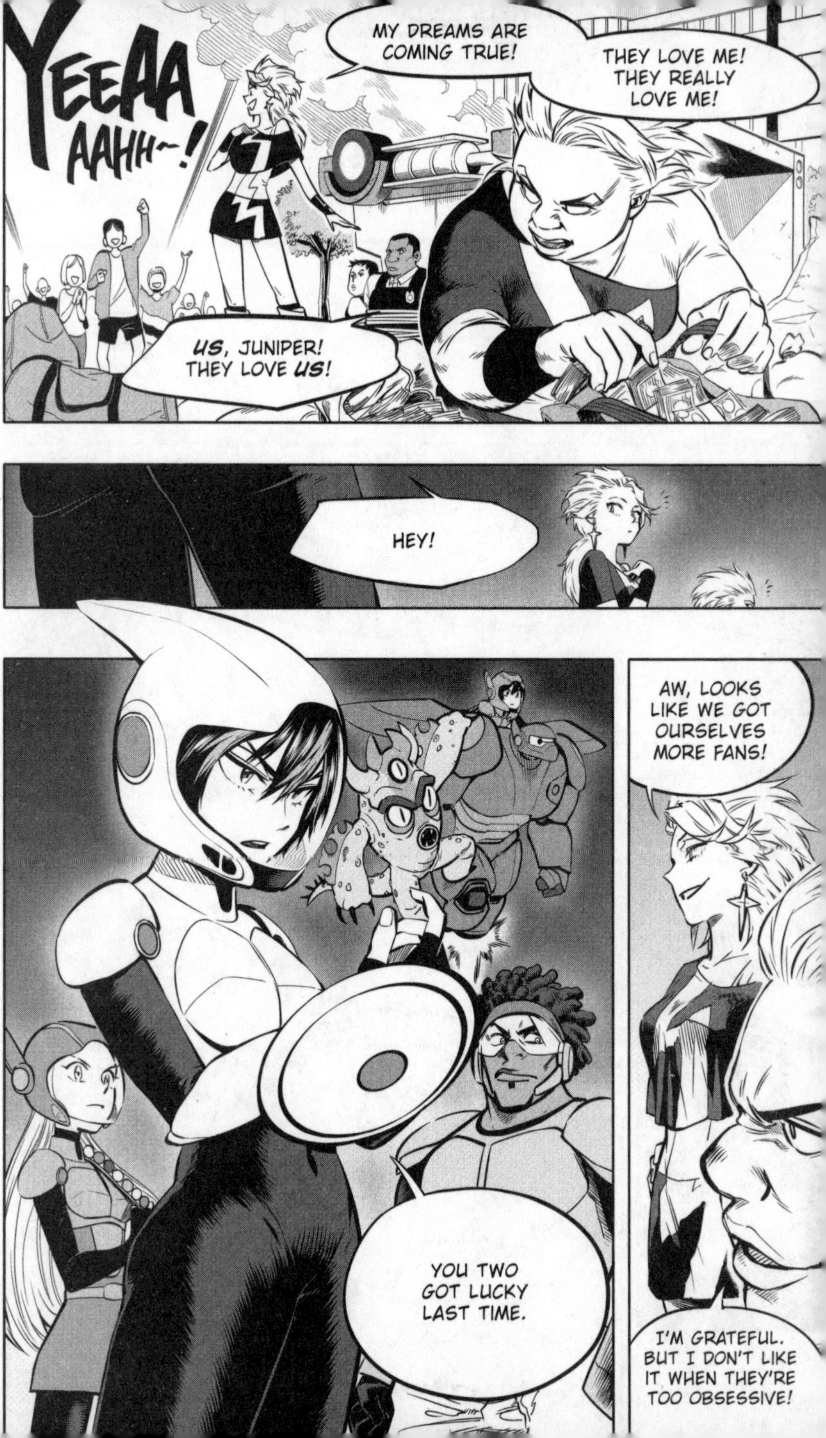
YEEAA AAHH~!
MY DREAMS ARE COMING TRUE!
THEY LOVE ME! THEY REALLY LOVE ME!
US, JUNIPER! THEY LOVE US!
HEY!
YOU TWO GOT LUCKY LAST TIME.
AW, LOOKS LIKE WE GOT OURSELVES MORE FANS!
I'M GRATEFUL. BUT I DON'T LIKE IT WHEN THEY'RE TOO OBSESSIVE!

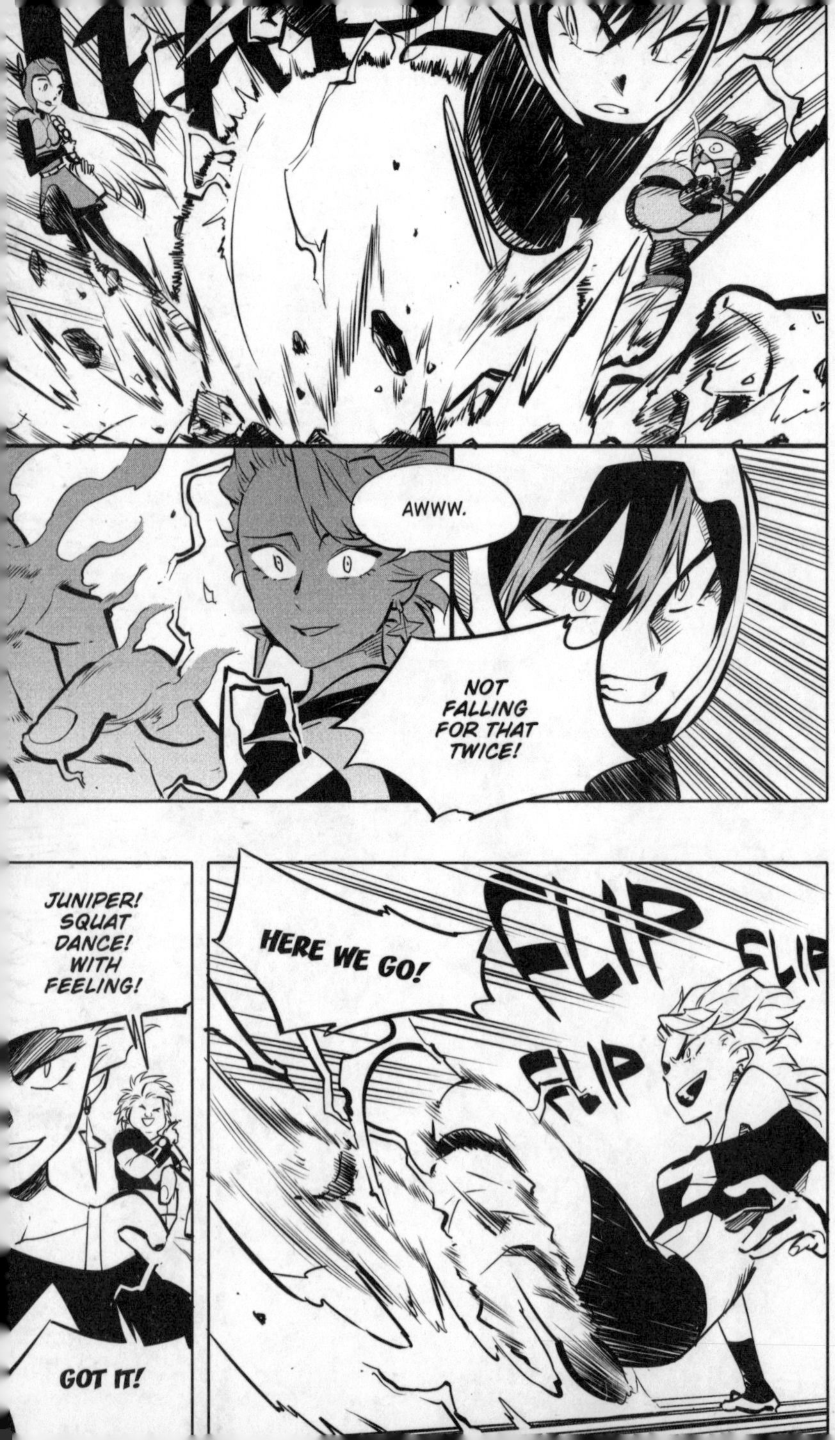
AWWW.
NOT FALLING FOR THAT TWICE!
JUNIPER! SQUAT DANCE! WITH FEELING!
GOT IT!
HERE WE GO!
FLIP
FLIP
FLIP

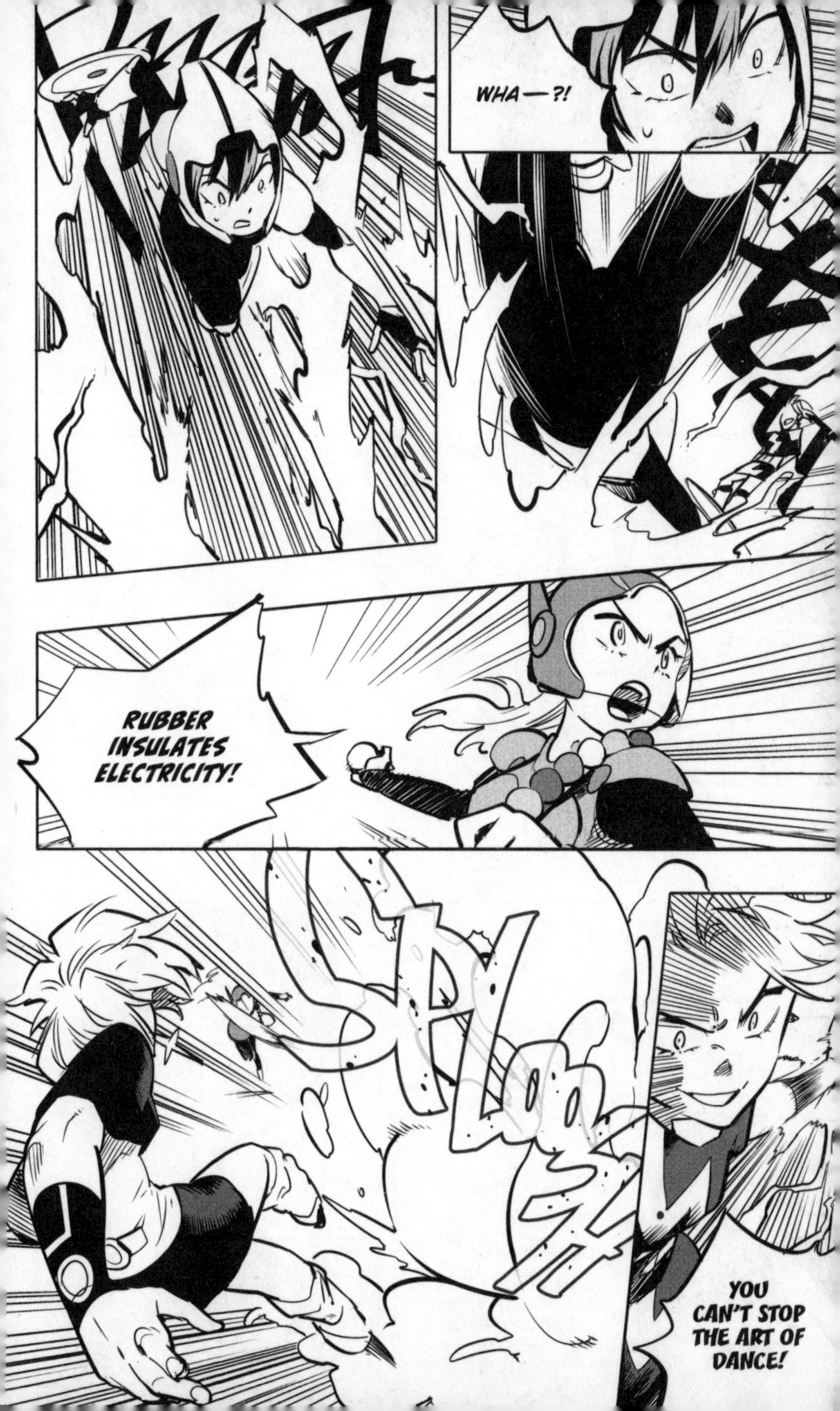
WHA—?!
RUBBER INSULATES ELECTRICITY!
YOU CAN'T STOP THE ART OF DANCE!

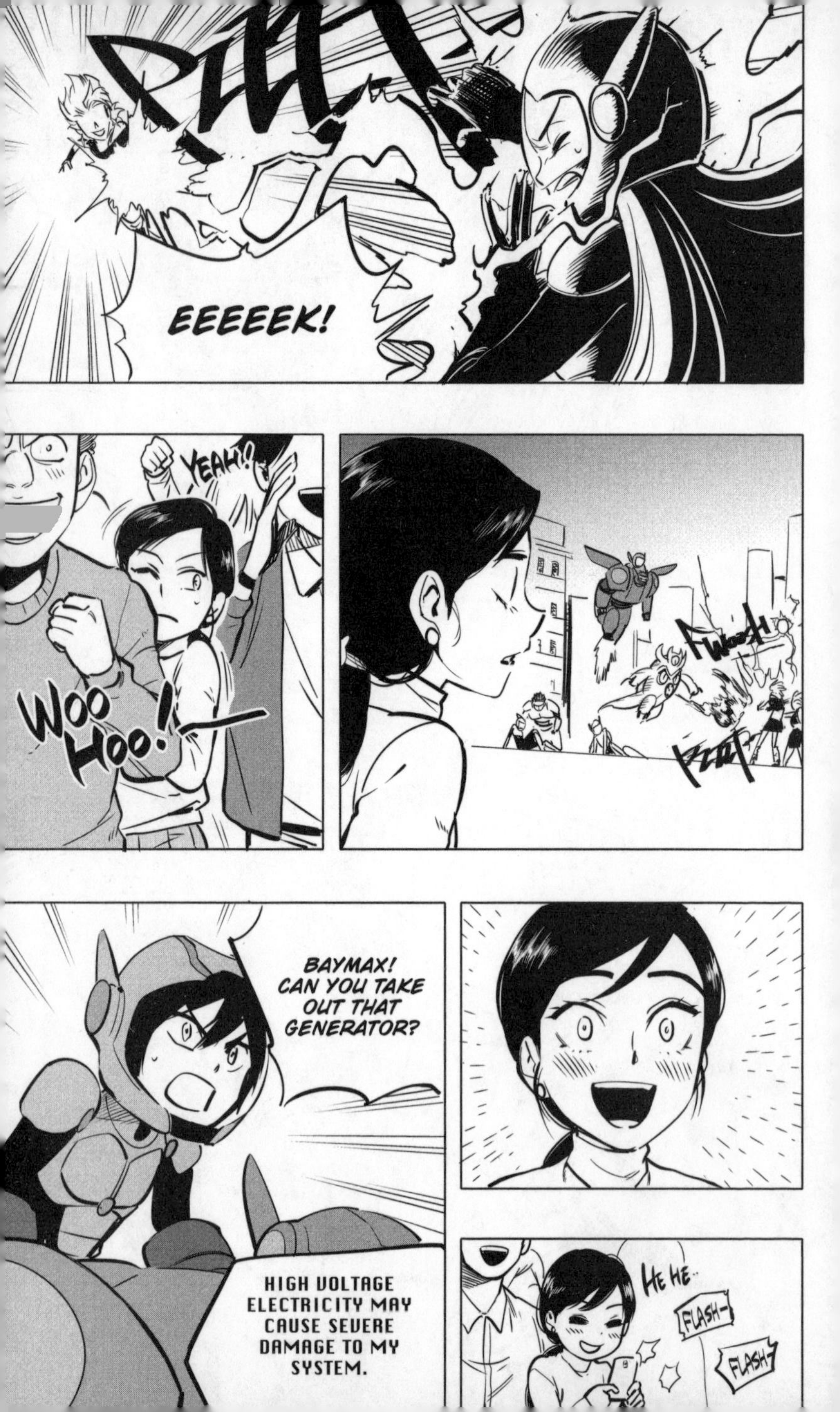
EEEEEK!
YEAH!
WOO HOO!
BAYMAX! CAN YOU TAKE OUT THAT GENERATOR?
HIGH VOLTAGE ELECTRICITY MAY CAUSE SEVERE DAMAGE TO MY SYSTEM.
HE HE..
FLASH-
FLASH-

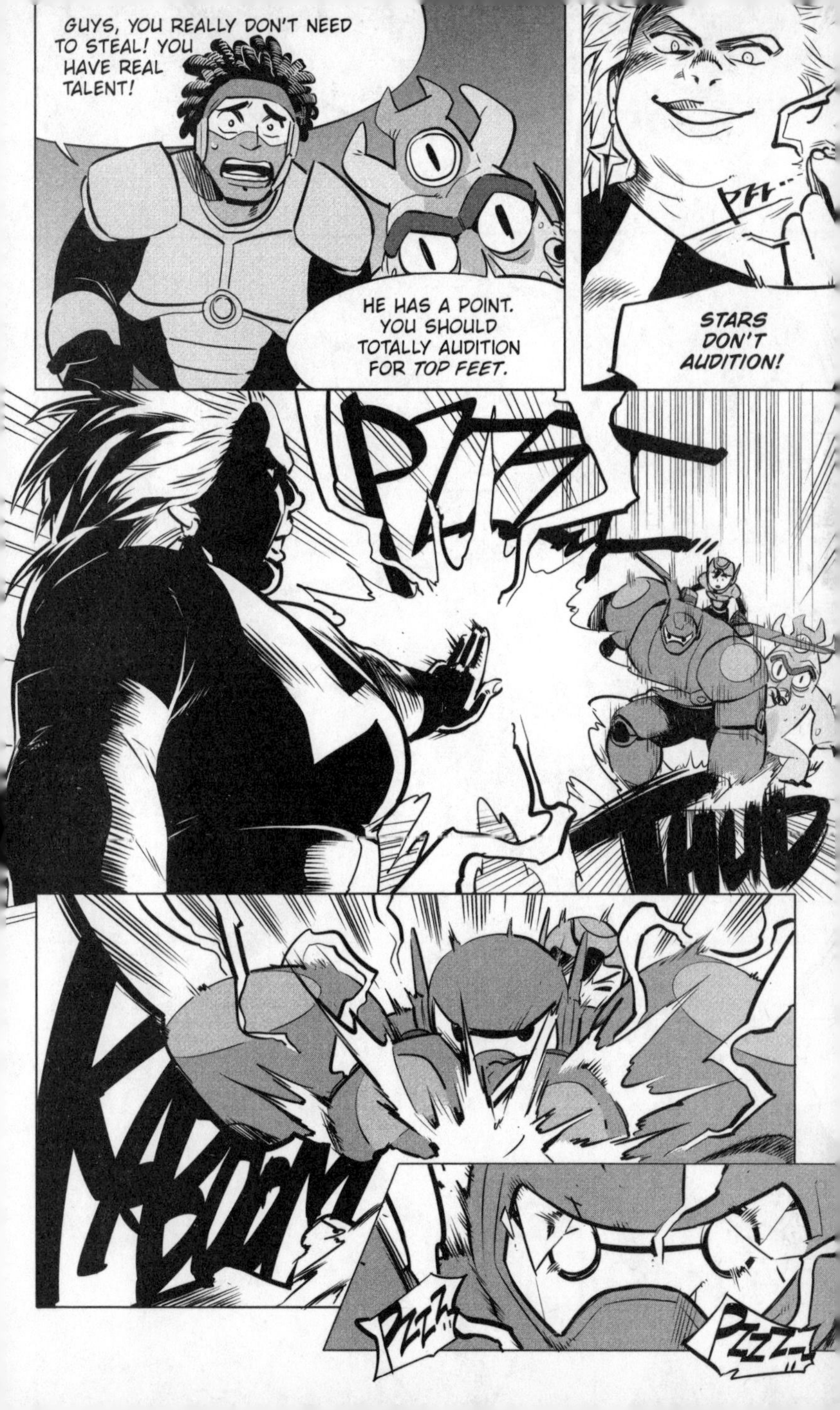

GUYS, YOU REALLY DON'T NEED TO STEAL! YOU HAVE REAL TALENT!
HE HAS A POINT. YOU SHOULD TOTALLY AUDITION FOR *TOP FEET*.
PFF...
STARS DON'T AUDITION!
PZZZT
THUD
PZZZ
PZZZ

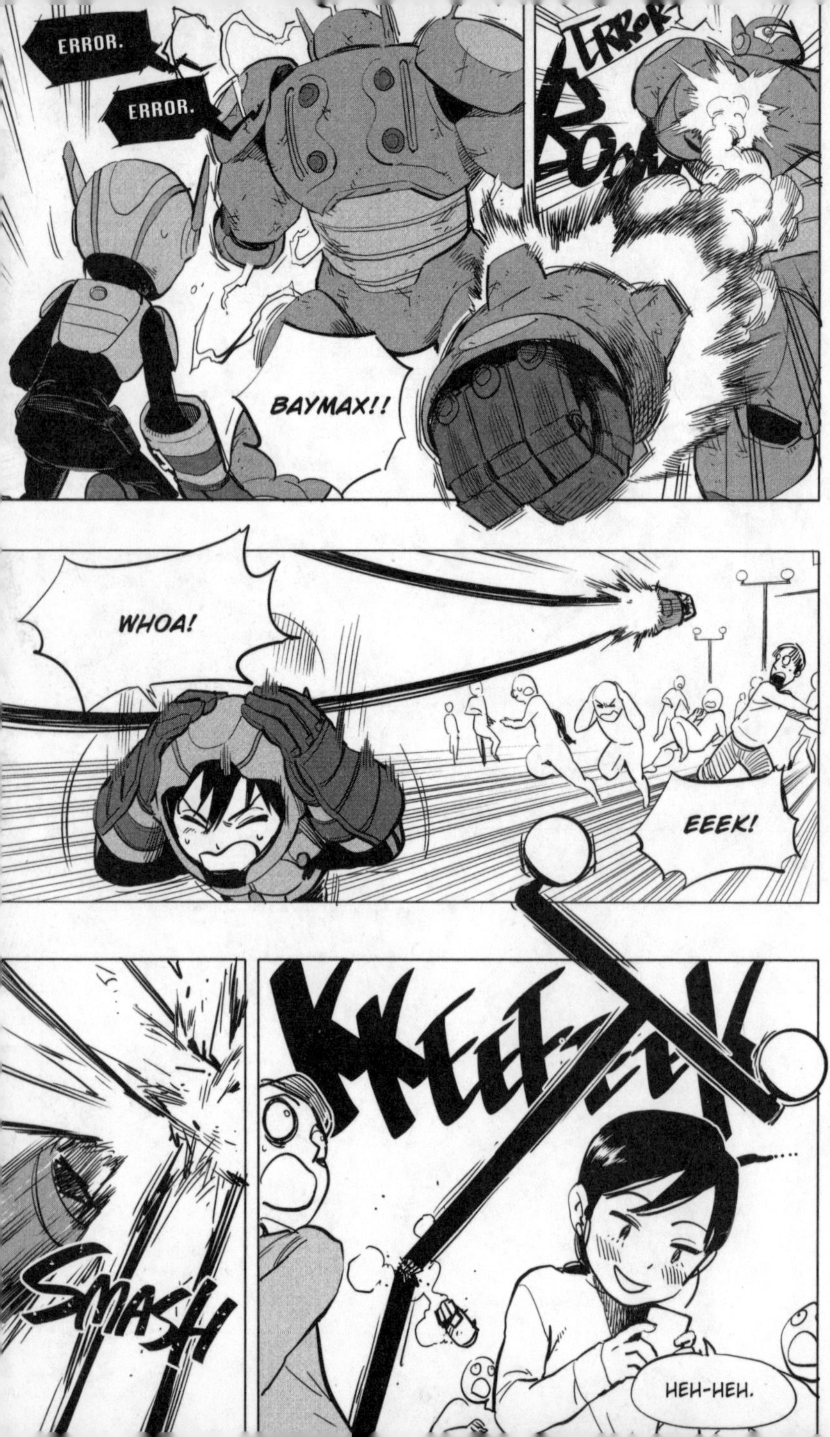
ERROR.
ERROR.
BAYMAX!!
ERROR
WHOA!
EEEK!
SMASH
HEH-HEH.

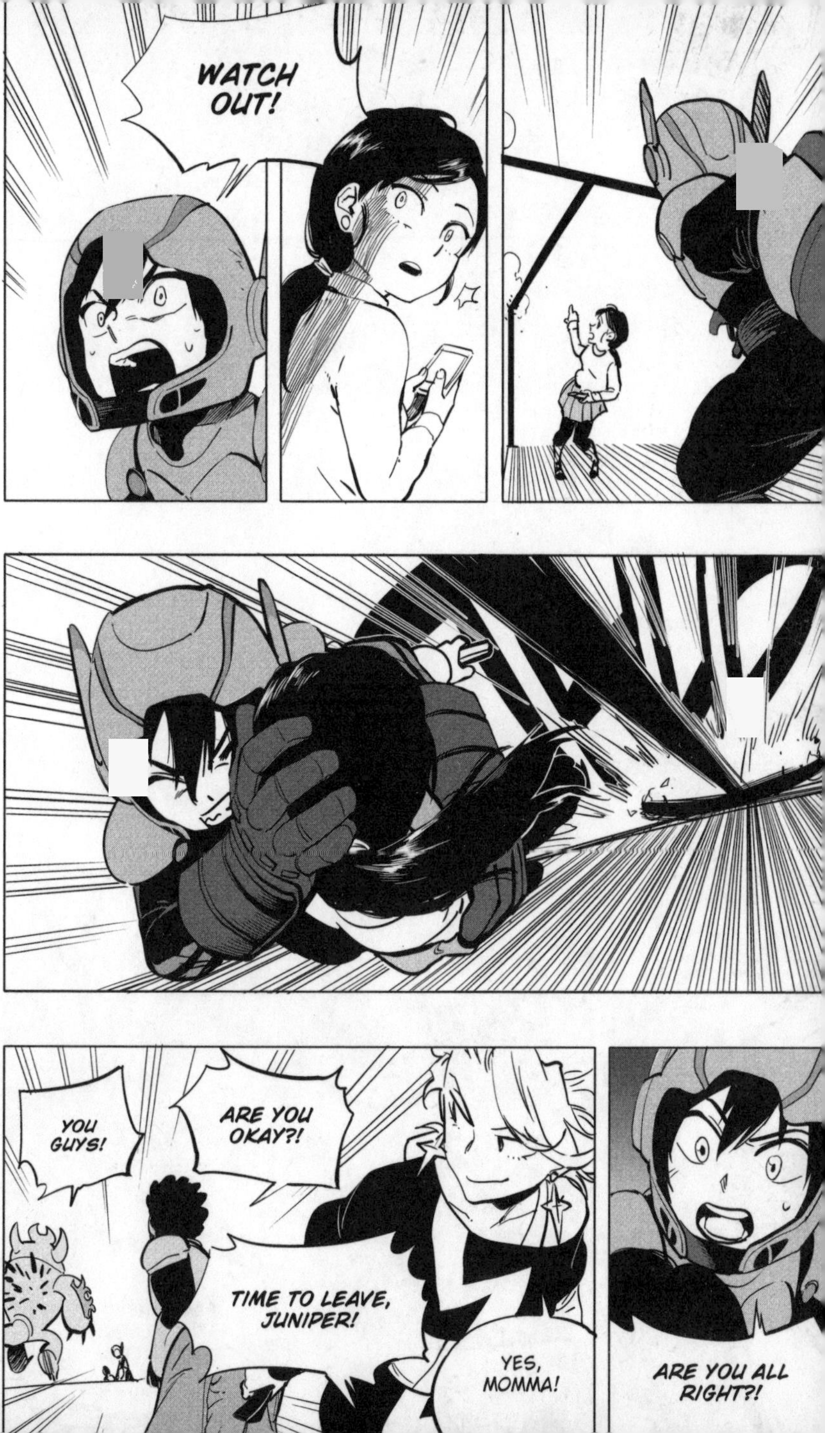
WATCH OUT!
YOU GUYS!
ARE YOU OKAY?!
TIME TO LEAVE, JUNIPER!
YES, MOMMA!
ARE YOU ALL RIGHT?!

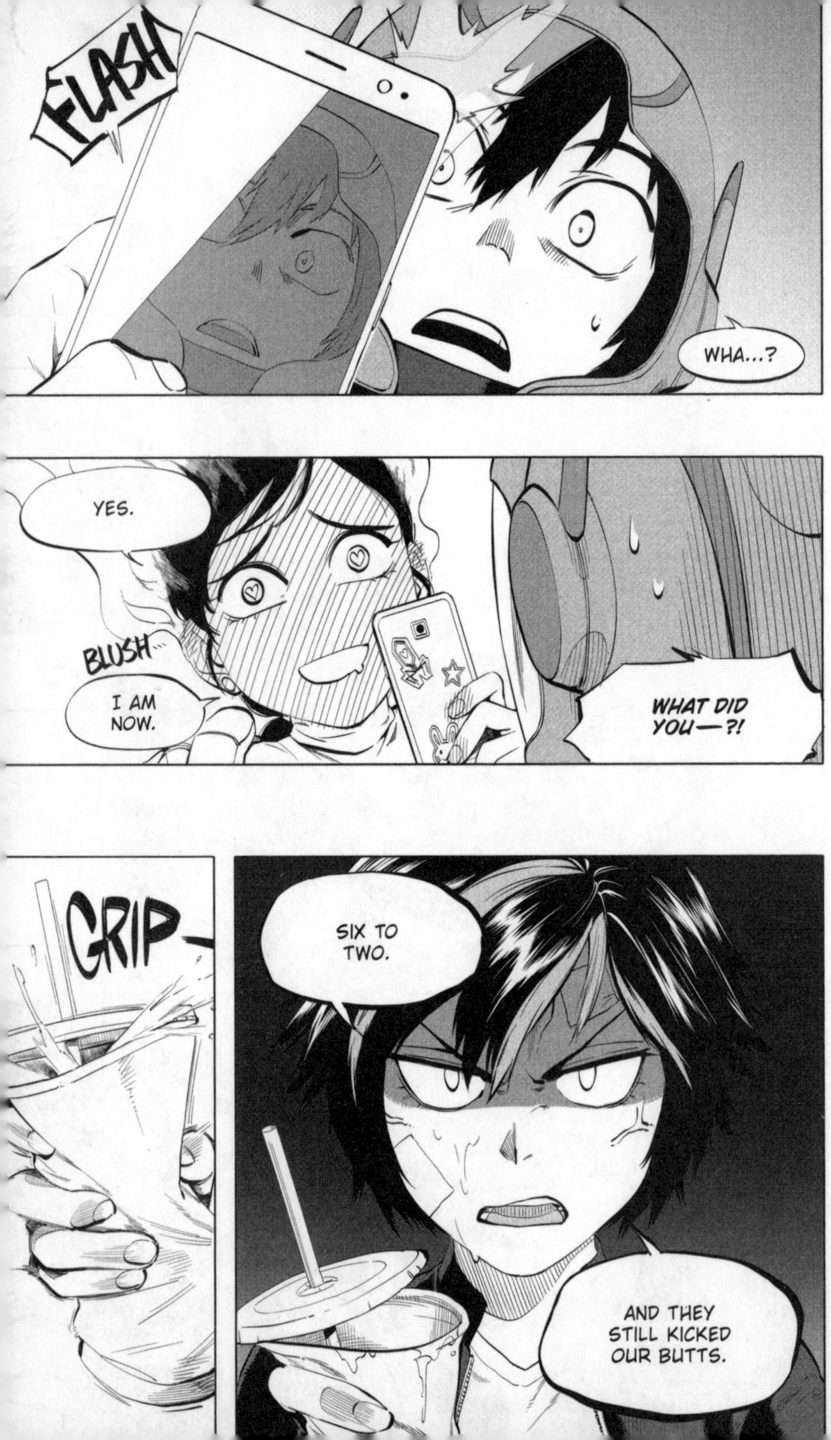
FLASH
WHA...?
YES.
BLUSH...
I AM NOW.
WHAT DID YOU—?!
GRIP—
SIX TO TWO.
AND THEY STILL KICKED OUR BUTTS.

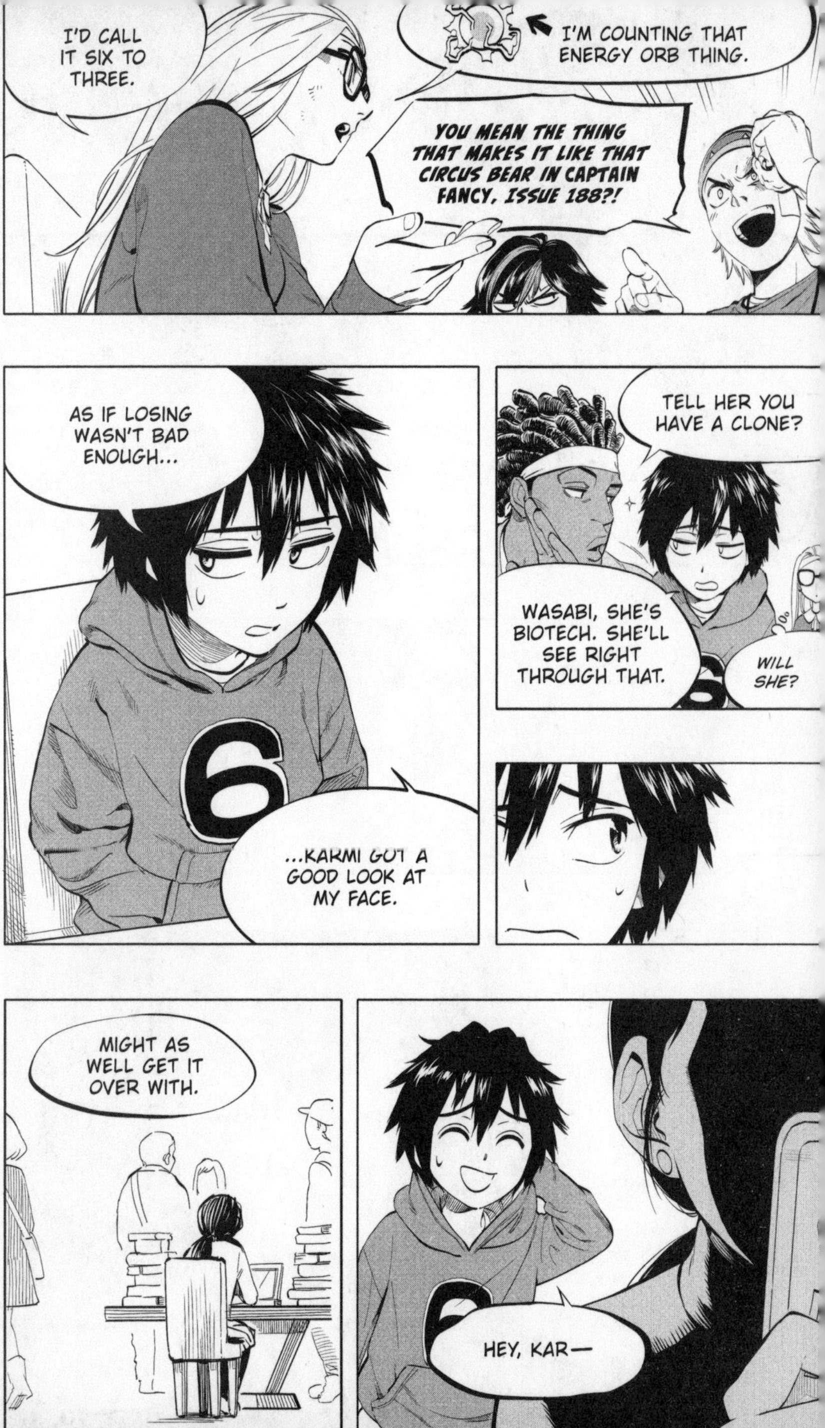
I'D CALL IT SIX TO THREE.
I'M COUNTING THAT ENERGY ORB THING.
YOU MEAN THE THING THAT MAKES IT LIKE THAT CIRCUS BEAR IN CAPTAIN FANCY, ISSUE 188?!
AS IF LOSING WASN'T BAD ENOUGH...
...KARMI GOT A GOOD LOOK AT MY FACE.
TELL HER YOU HAVE A CLONE?
WASABI, SHE'S BIOTECH. SHE'LL SEE RIGHT THROUGH THAT.
WILL SHE?
MIGHT AS WELL GET IT OVER WITH.
HEY, KAR—

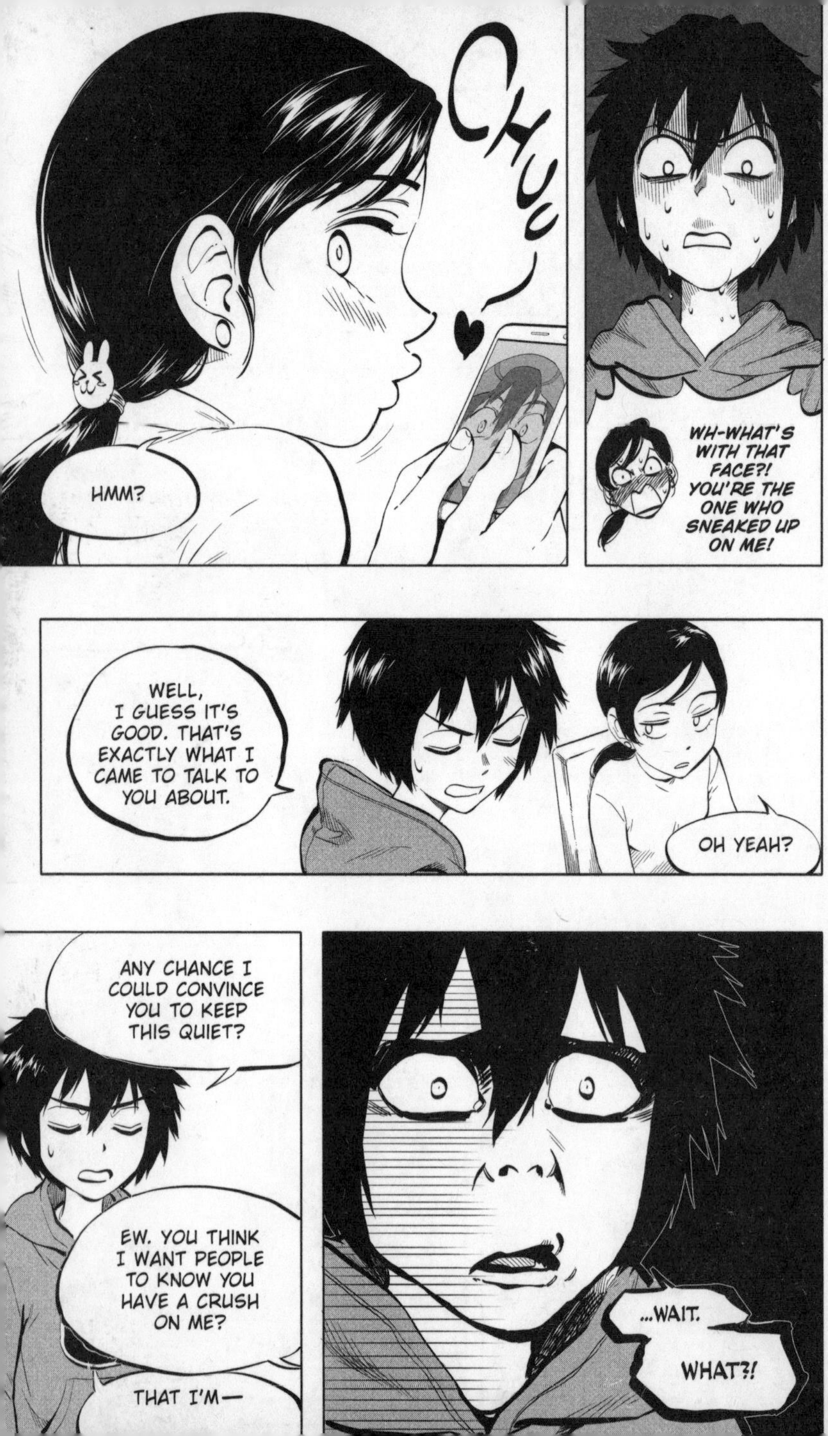
CHUU
HMM?
WH-WHAT'S WITH THAT FACE?! YOU'RE THE ONE WHO SNEAKED UP ON ME!
WELL, I GUESS IT'S GOOD. THAT'S EXACTLY WHAT I CAME TO TALK TO YOU ABOUT.
OH YEAH?
ANY CHANCE I COULD CONVINCE YOU TO KEEP THIS QUIET?
EW. YOU THINK I WANT PEOPLE TO KNOW YOU HAVE A CRUSH ON ME?
THAT I'M—
...WAIT.
WHAT?!

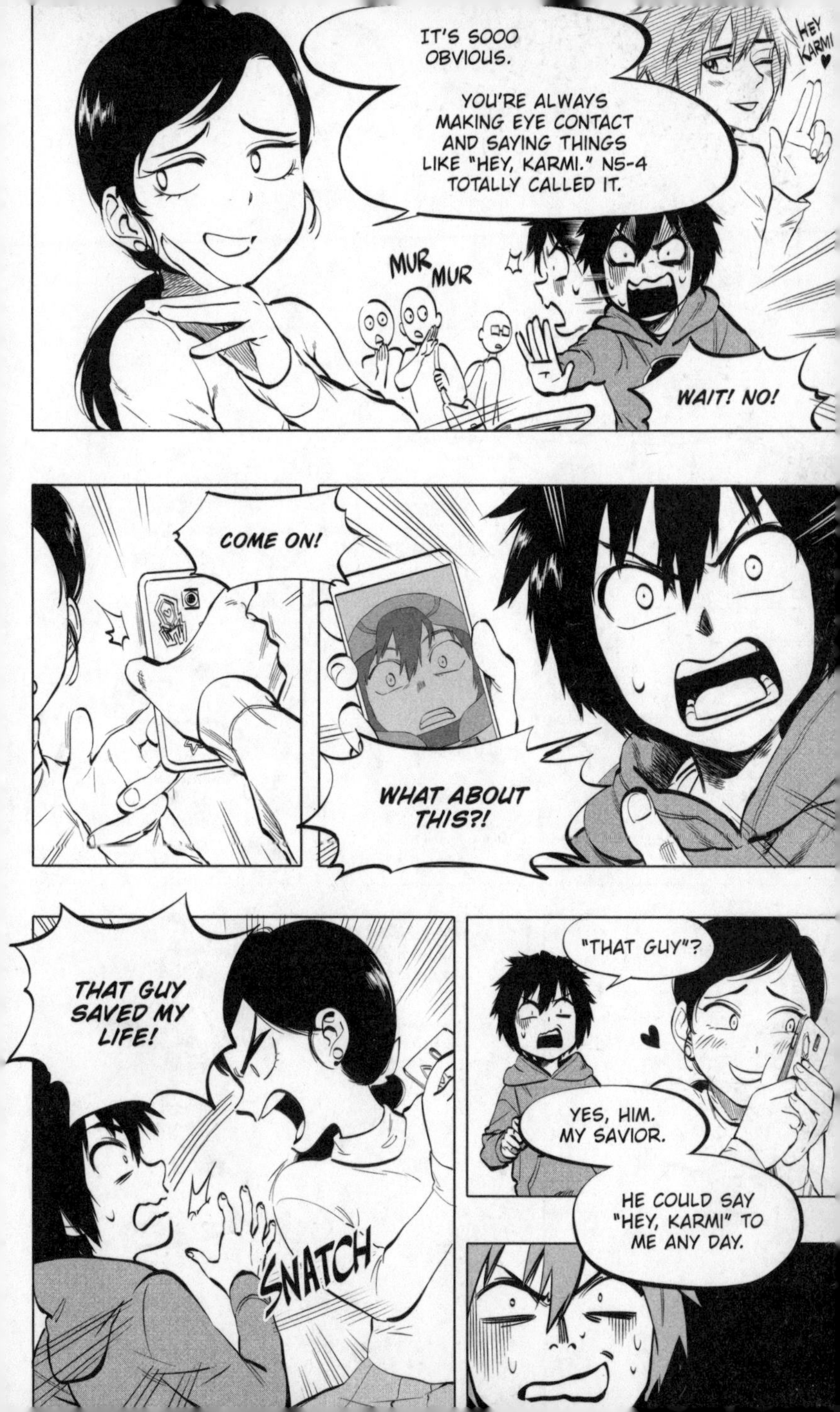
IT'S SOOO OBVIOUS.
YOU'RE ALWAYS MAKING EYE CONTACT AND SAYING THINGS LIKE "HEY, KARMI." N5-4 TOTALLY CALLED IT.
HEY KARMI ♥
MUR MUR
WAIT! NO!
COME ON!
WHAT ABOUT THIS?!
THAT GUY SAVED MY LIFE!
SNATCH
"THAT GUY"?
YES, HIM. MY SAVIOR.
HE COULD SAY "HEY, KARMI" TO ME ANY DAY.

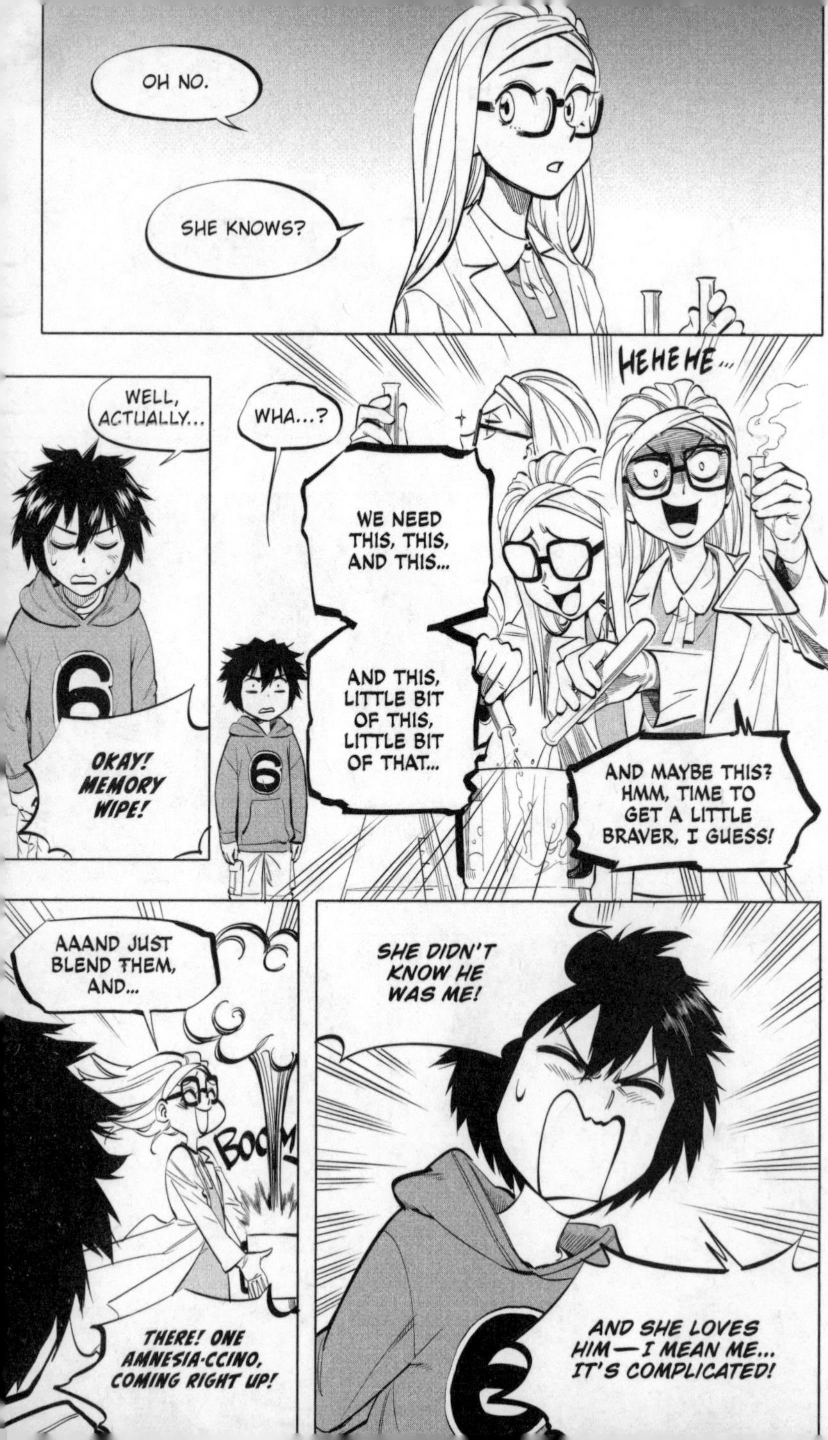
OH NO.
SHE KNOWS?
WELL, ACTUALLY...
OKAY! MEMORY WIPE!
WHA...?
HEHEHE...
WE NEED THIS, THIS, AND THIS...
AND THIS, LITTLE BIT OF THIS, LITTLE BIT OF THAT...
AND MAYBE THIS? HMM, TIME TO GET A LITTLE BRAVER, I GUESS!
AAAND JUST BLEND THEM, AND...
BOOM!
THERE! ONE AMNESIA-CCINO, COMING RIGHT UP!
SHE DIDN'T KNOW HE WAS ME!
AND SHE LOVES HIM—I MEAN ME... IT'S COMPLICATED!

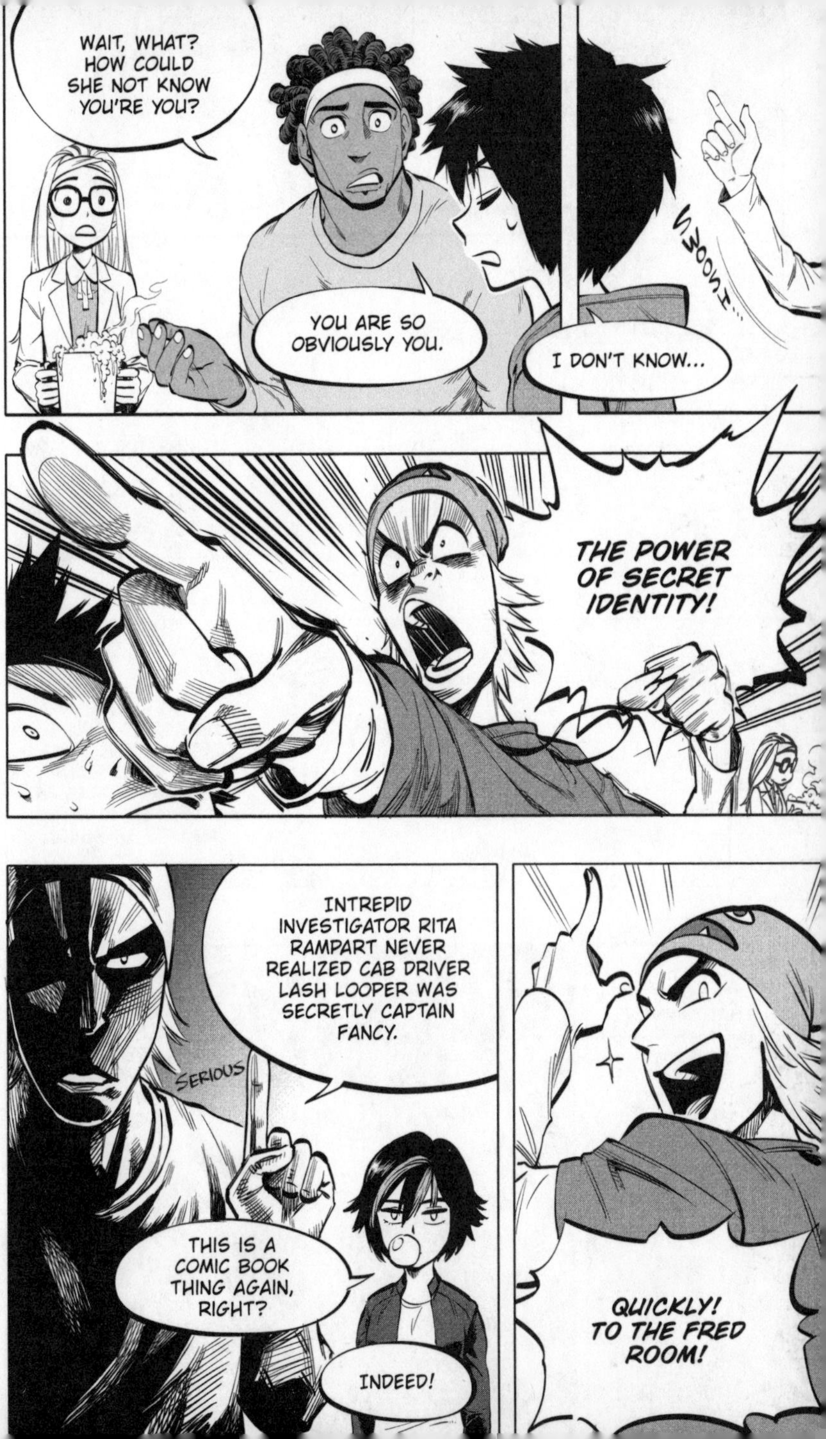
WAIT, WHAT? HOW COULD SHE NOT KNOW YOU'RE YOU?
YOU ARE SO OBVIOUSLY YOU.
SWOOSH...
I DON'T KNOW...
THE POWER OF SECRET IDENTITY!
INTREPID INVESTIGATOR RITA RAMPART NEVER REALIZED CAB DRIVER LASH LOOPER WAS SECRETLY CAPTAIN FANCY.
SERIOUS
THIS IS A COMIC BOOK THING AGAIN, RIGHT?
INDEED!
QUICKLY! TO THE FRED ROOM!

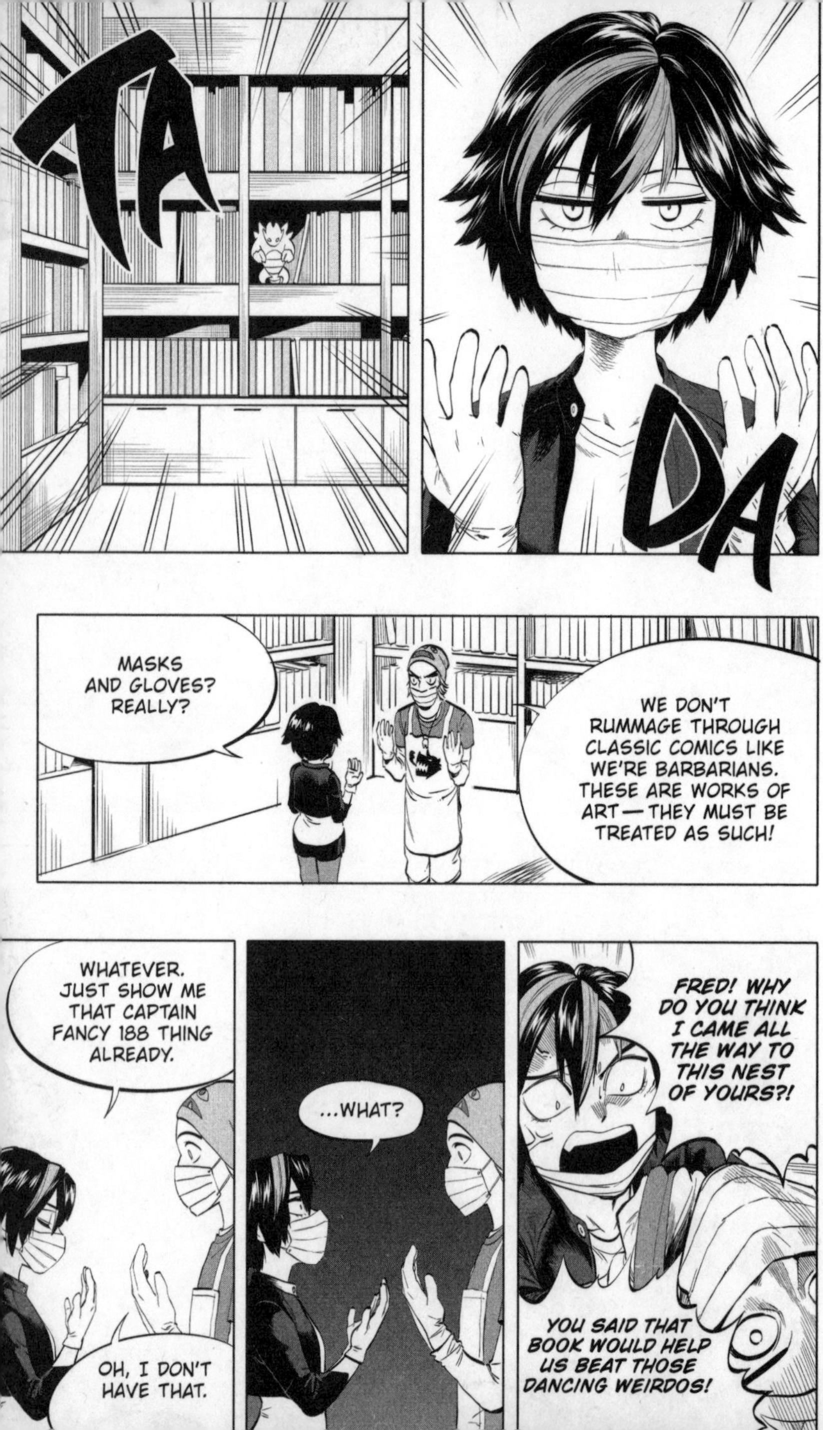
TA
DA
MASKS AND GLOVES? REALLY?
WE DON'T RUMMAGE THROUGH CLASSIC COMICS LIKE WE'RE BARBARIANS. THESE ARE WORKS OF ART—THEY MUST BE TREATED AS SUCH!
WHATEVER. JUST SHOW ME THAT CAPTAIN FANCY 188 THING ALREADY.
OH, I DON'T HAVE THAT.
...WHAT?
FRED! WHY DO YOU THINK I CAME ALL THE WAY TO THIS NEST OF YOURS?!
YOU SAID THAT BOOK WOULD HELP US BEAT THOSE DANCING WEIRDOS!

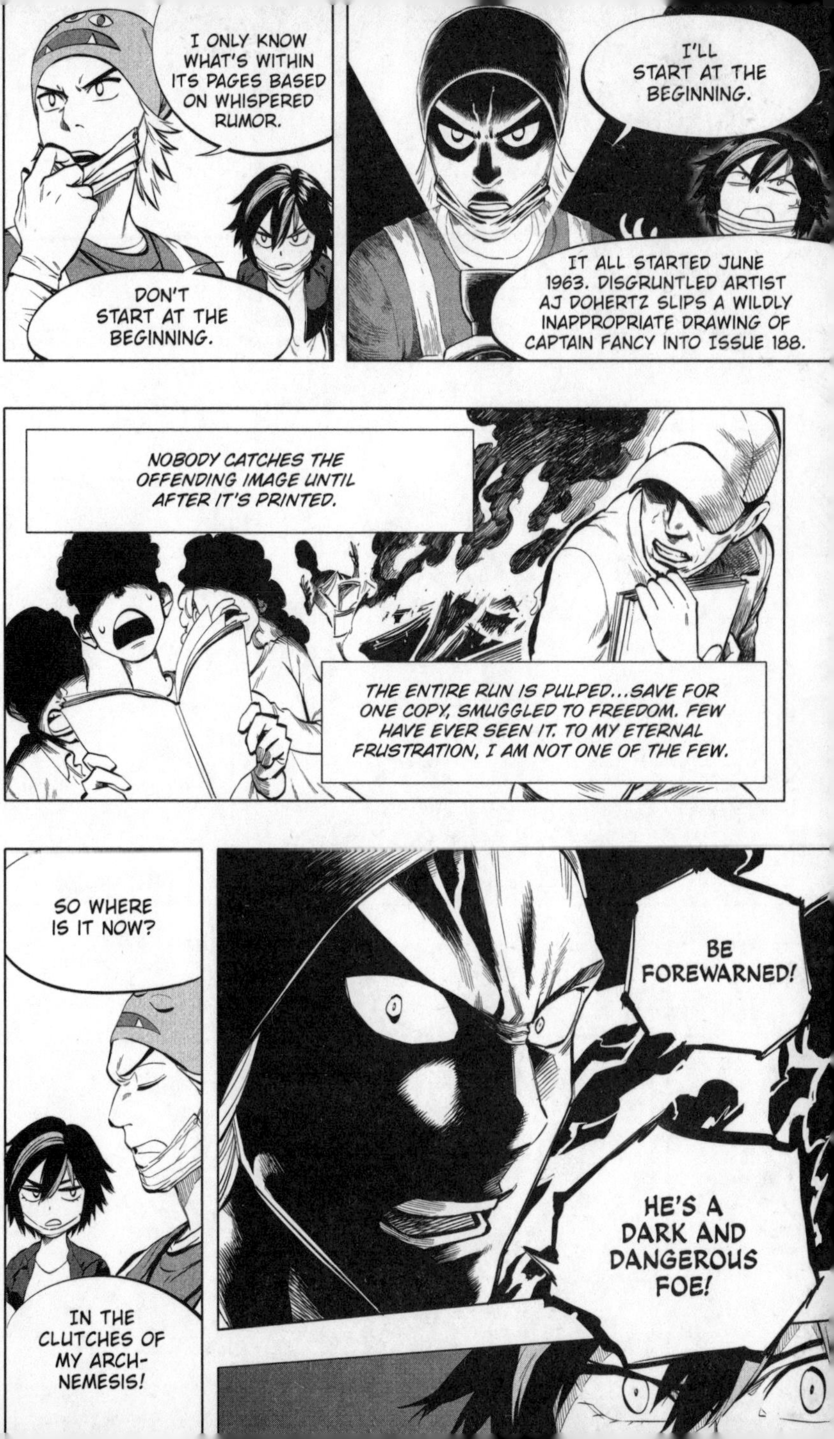
I ONLY KNOW WHAT'S WITHIN ITS PAGES BASED ON WHISPERED RUMOR.
DON'T START AT THE BEGINNING.
I'LL START AT THE BEGINNING.
IT ALL STARTED JUNE 1963. DISGRUNTLED ARTIST AJ DOHERTZ SLIPS A WILDLY INAPPROPRIATE DRAWING OF CAPTAIN FANCY INTO ISSUE 188.
NOBODY CATCHES THE OFFENDING IMAGE UNTIL AFTER IT'S PRINTED.
THE ENTIRE RUN IS PULPED...SAVE FOR ONE COPY, SMUGGLED TO FREEDOM. FEW HAVE EVER SEEN IT. TO MY ETERNAL FRUSTRATION, I AM NOT ONE OF THE FEW.
SO WHERE IS IT NOW?
IN THE CLUTCHES OF MY ARCH-NEMESIS!
BE FOREWARNED!
HE'S A DARK AND DANGEROUS FOE!

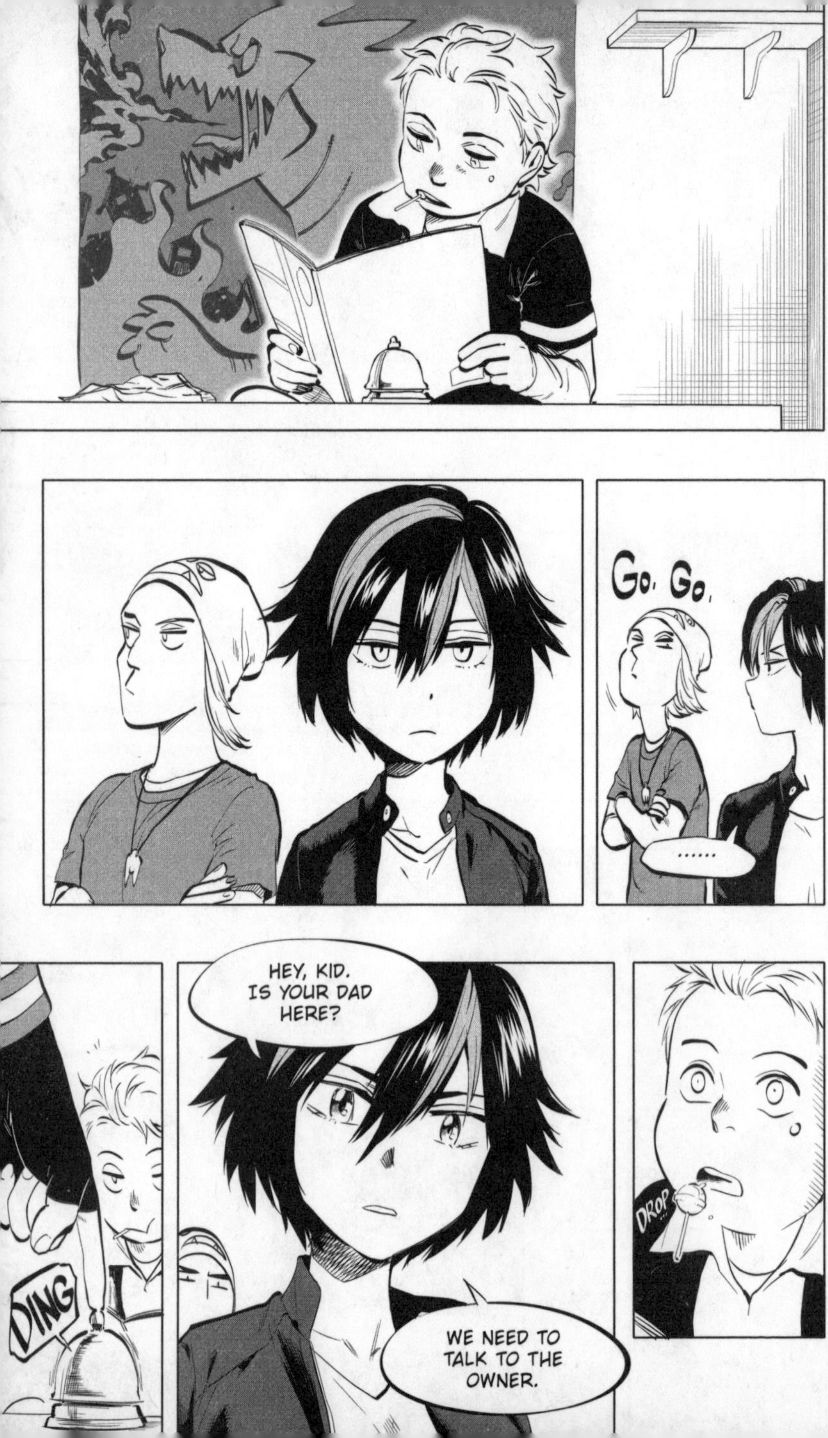
Go. Go.
......
DING
HEY, KID. IS YOUR DAD HERE?
WE NEED TO TALK TO THE OWNER.
DROP

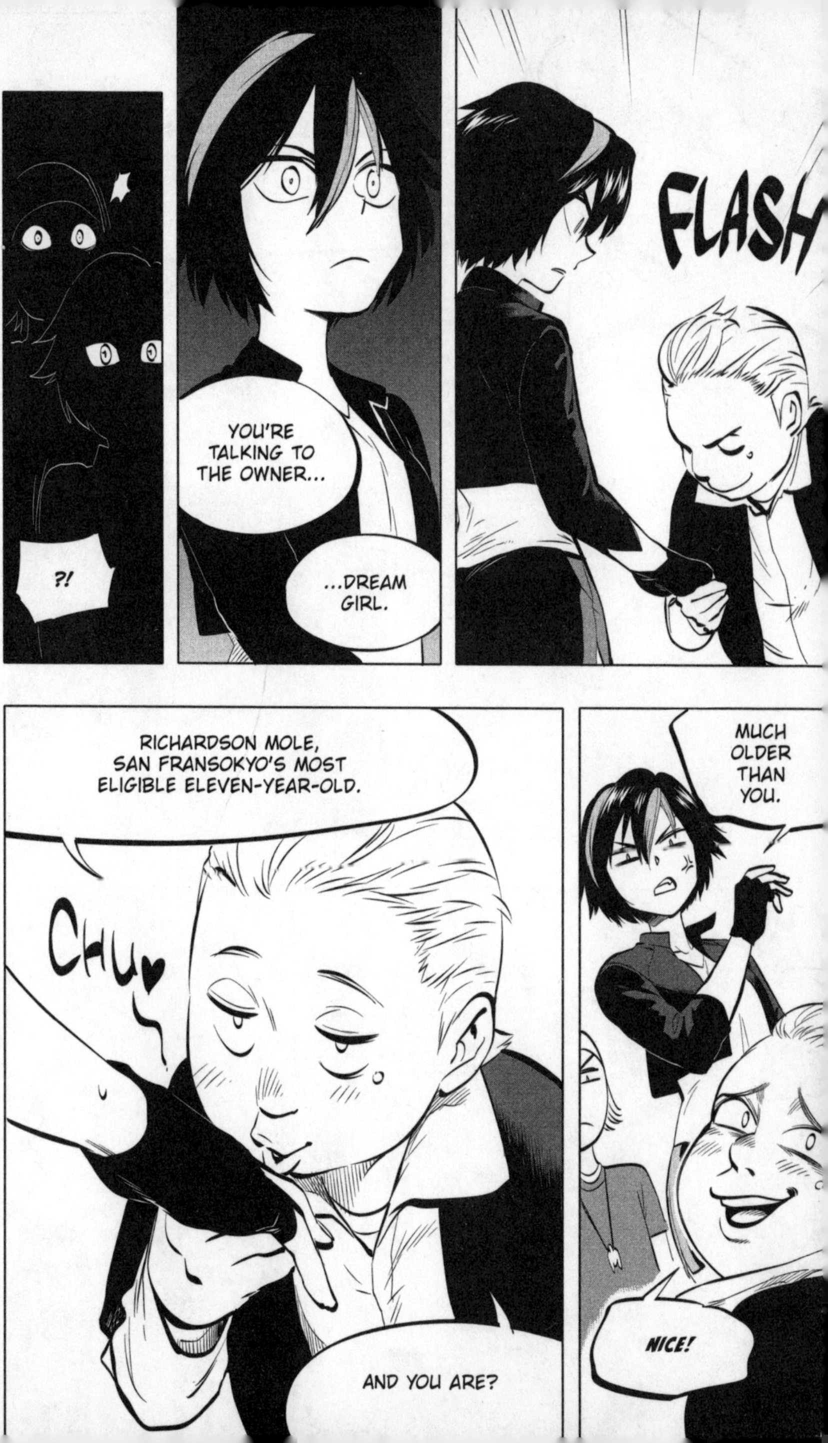
?!
YOU'RE TALKING TO THE OWNER...
...DREAM GIRL.
FLASH
RICHARDSON MOLE, SAN FRANSOKYO'S MOST ELIGIBLE ELEVEN-YEAR-OLD.
CHU♥
AND YOU ARE?
MUCH OLDER THAN YOU.
NICE!

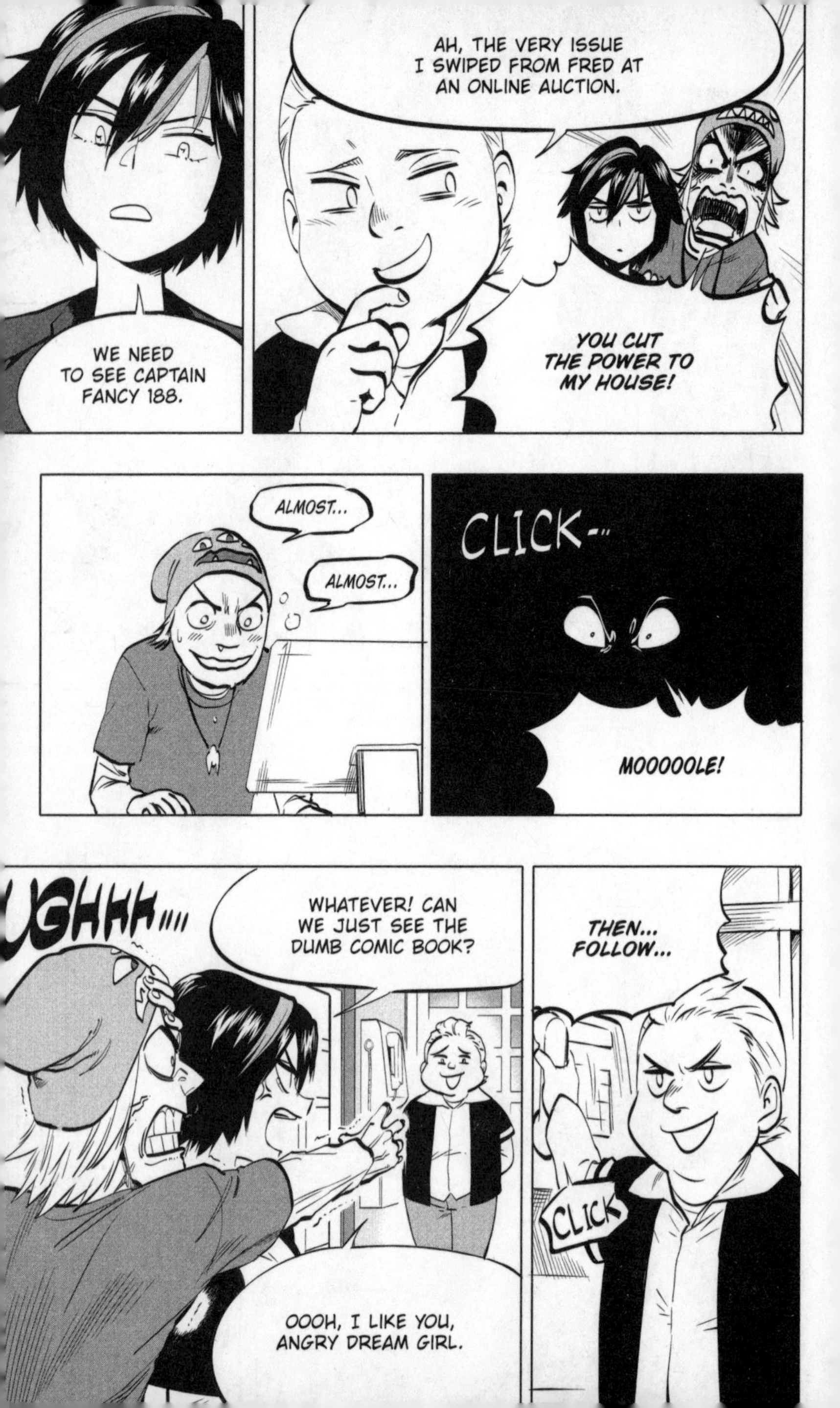
WE NEED TO SEE CAPTAIN FANCY 188.
AH, THE VERY ISSUE I SWIPED FROM FRED AT AN ONLINE AUCTION.
YOU CUT THE POWER TO MY HOUSE!
ALMOST...
ALMOST...
CLICK
MOOOOOLE!
UGHHH
WHATEVER! CAN WE JUST SEE THE DUMB COMIC BOOK?
OOOH, I LIKE YOU, ANGRY DREAM GIRL.
THEN... FOLLOW...
CLICK

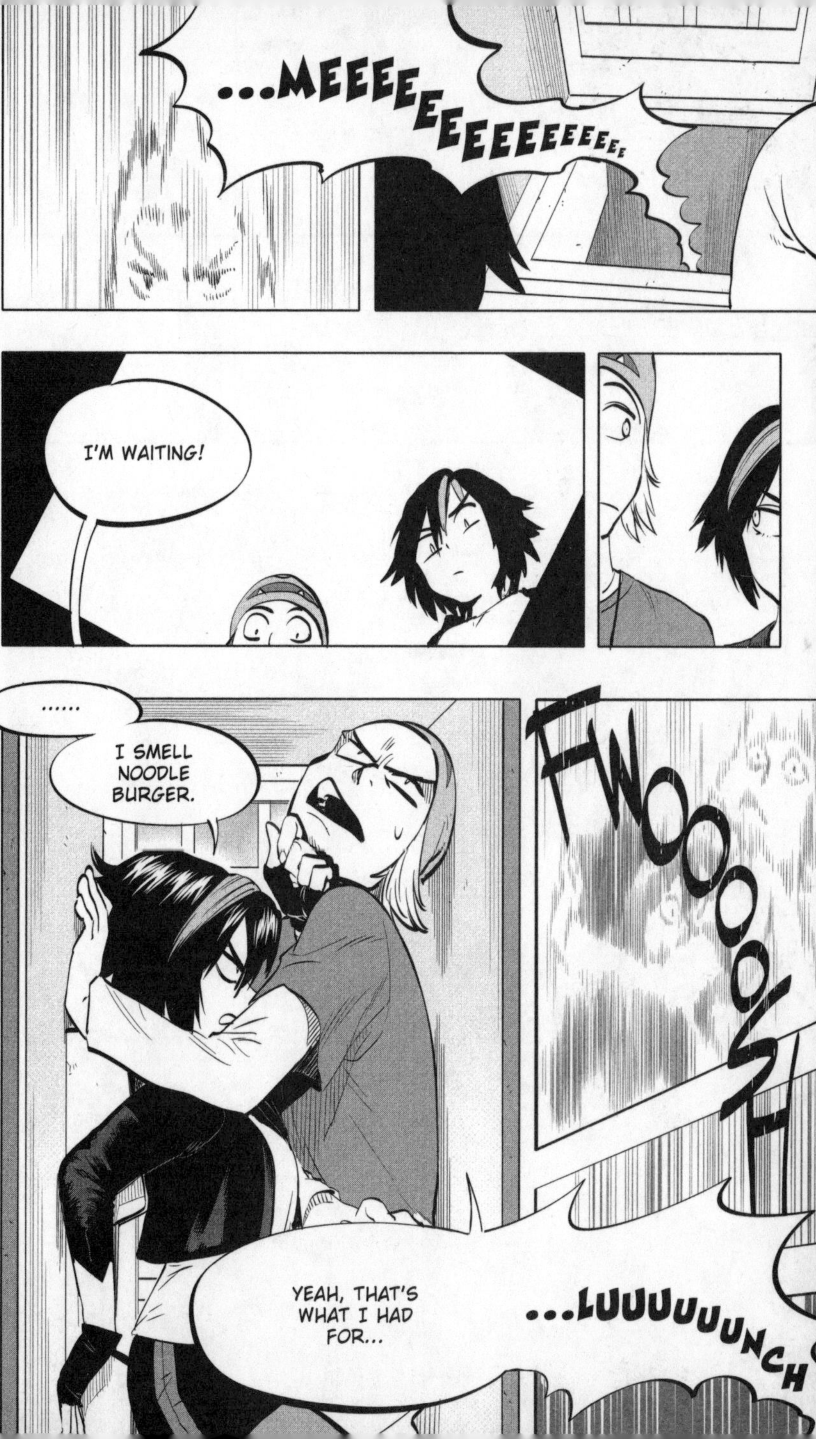
...MEEEEEEEEEEEEEE
I'M WAITING!
......
I SMELL NOODLE BURGER.
FWOOOOOSH
YEAH, THAT'S WHAT I HAD FOR...
...LUUUUUUUNCH

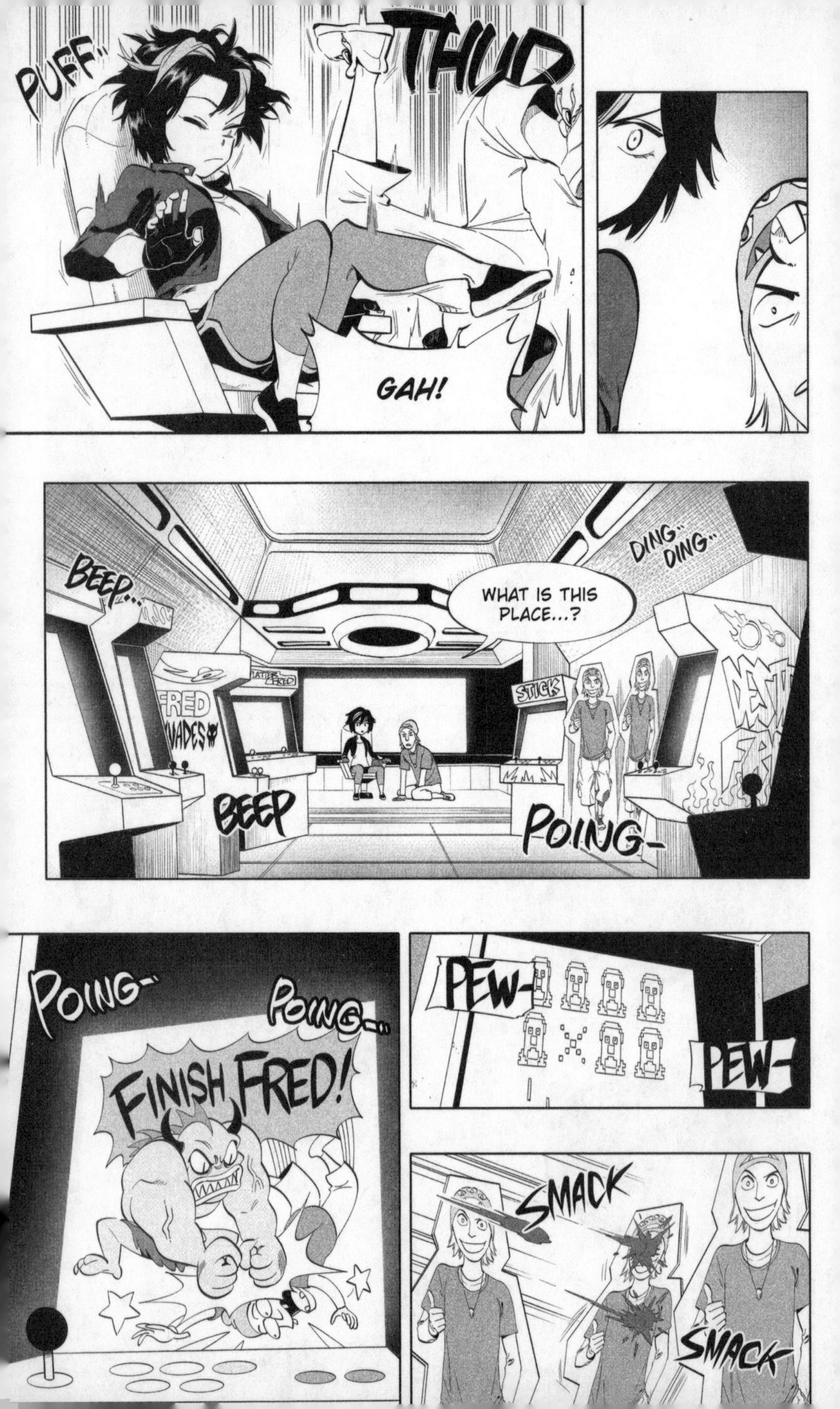
PUFF..
THUD
GAH!
BEEP...
DING.. DING..
WHAT IS THIS PLACE...?
FRED INVADES
STICK
BEEP
POING-
POING-
POING...
FINISH FRED!
PEW-
PEW-
SMACK
SMACK

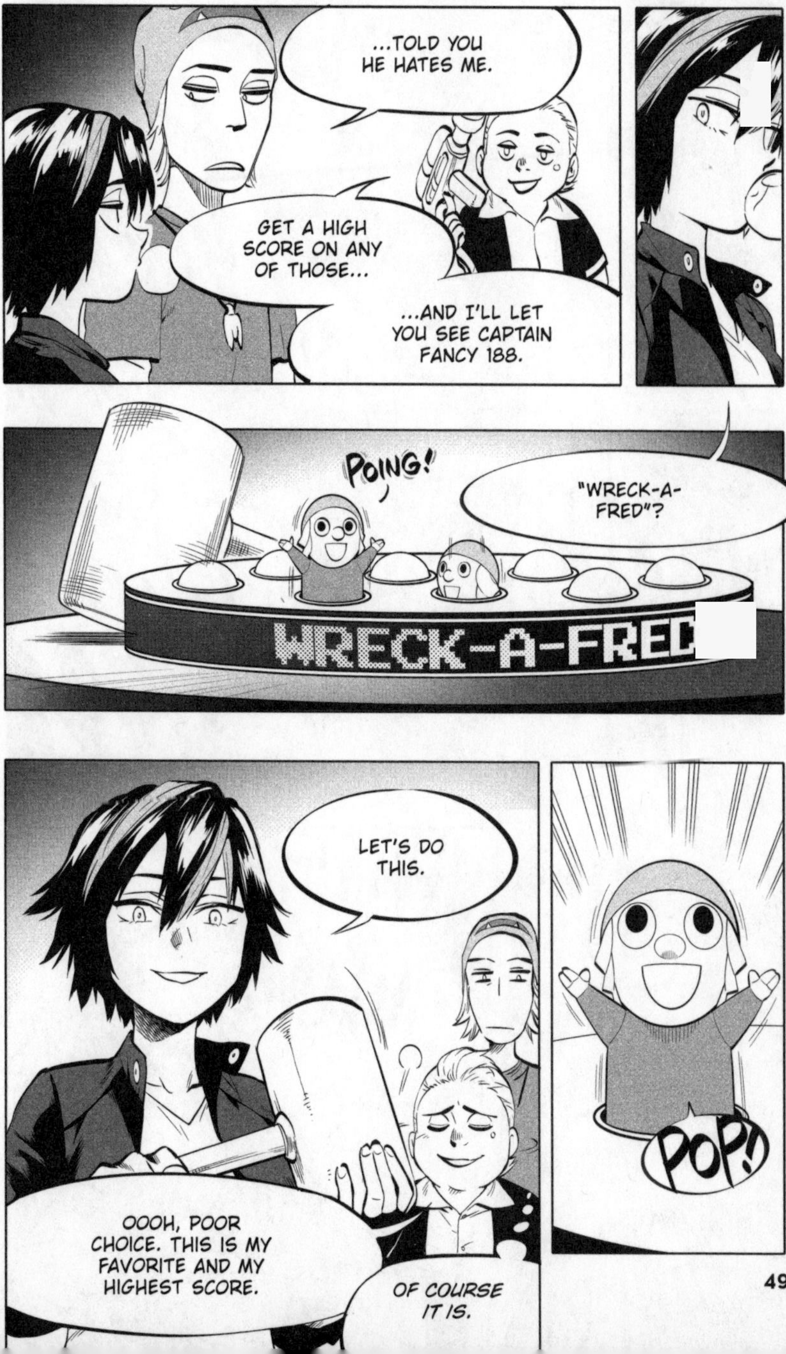

...TOLD YOU HE HATES ME.
GET A HIGH SCORE ON ANY OF THOSE...
...AND I'LL LET YOU SEE CAPTAIN FANCY 188.
POING!
"WRECK-A-FRED"?
WRECK-A-FRED
LET'S DO THIS.
OOOH, POOR CHOICE. THIS IS MY FAVORITE AND MY HIGHEST SCORE.
OF COURSE IT IS.
POP!

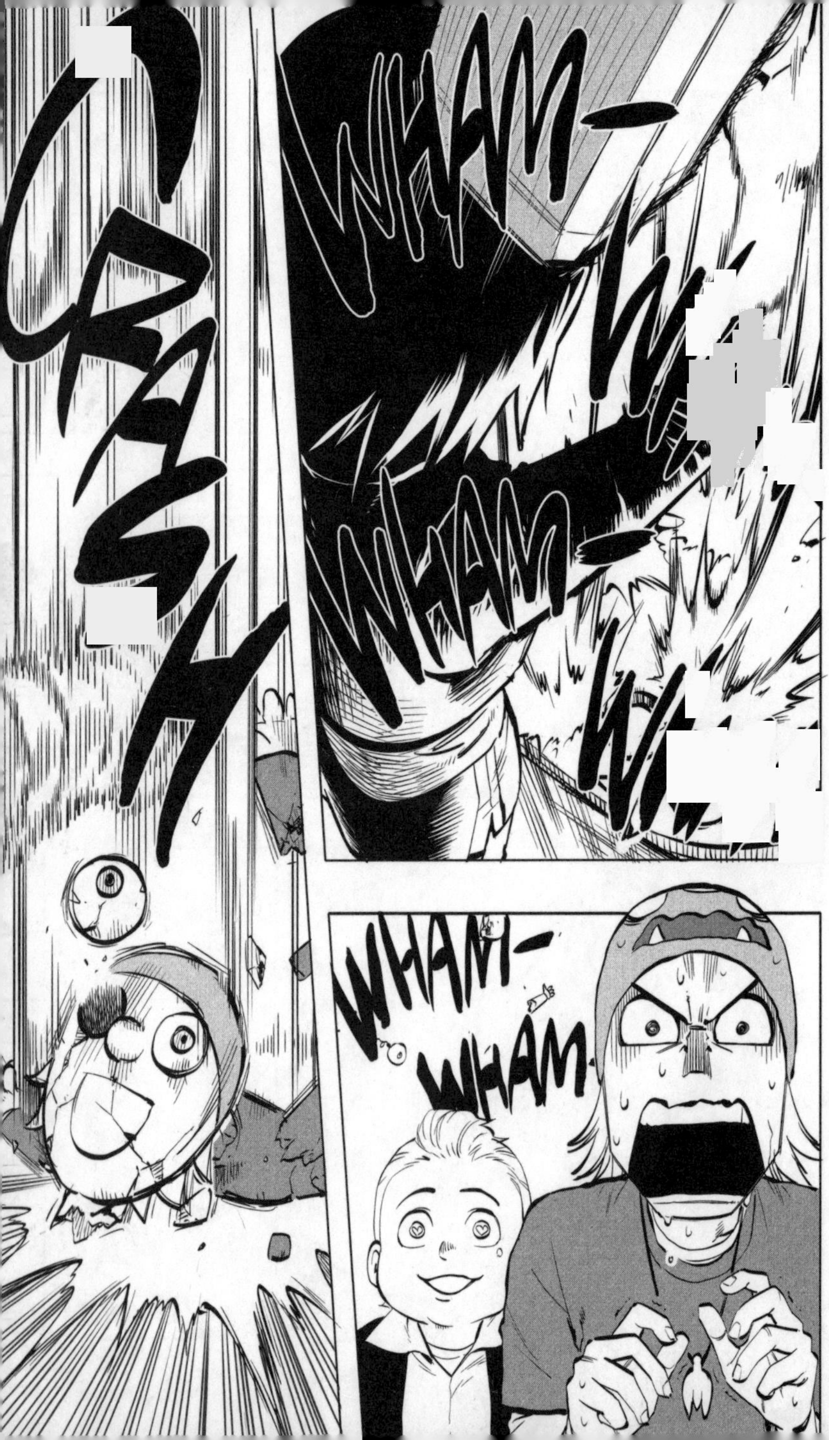
CRASH
WHAM-
WHAM-
WHAM-
WHAM-

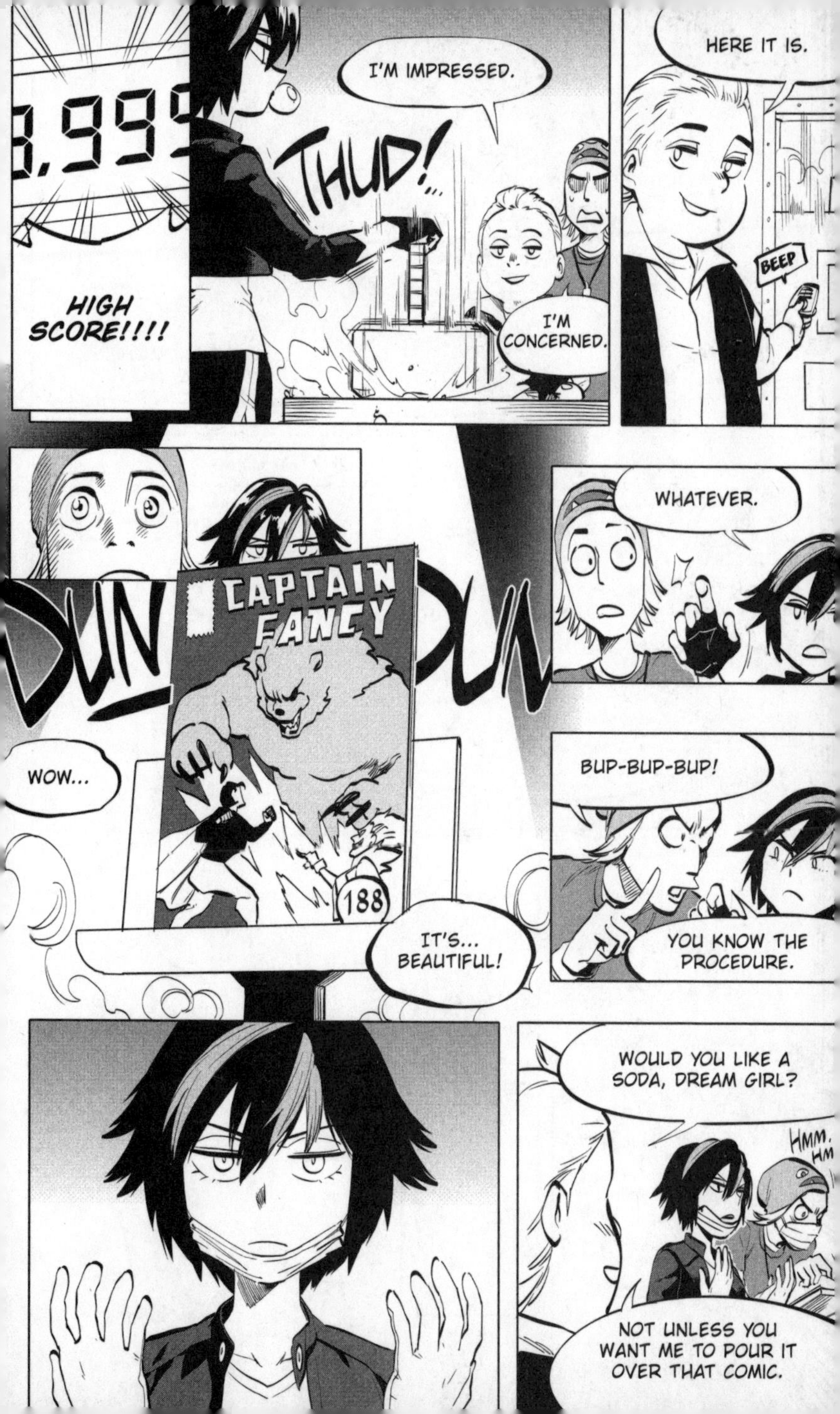
8,999
HIGH SCORE!!!!
I'M IMPRESSED.
THUD!
I'M CONCERNED.
HERE IT IS.
BEEP
DUN
CAPTAIN FANCY
188
DUN
WHATEVER.
WOW...
IT'S... BEAUTIFUL!
BUP-BUP-BUP!
YOU KNOW THE PROCEDURE.
WOULD YOU LIKE A SODA, DREAM GIRL?
HMM. HM
NOT UNLESS YOU WANT ME TO POUR IT OVER THAT COMIC.

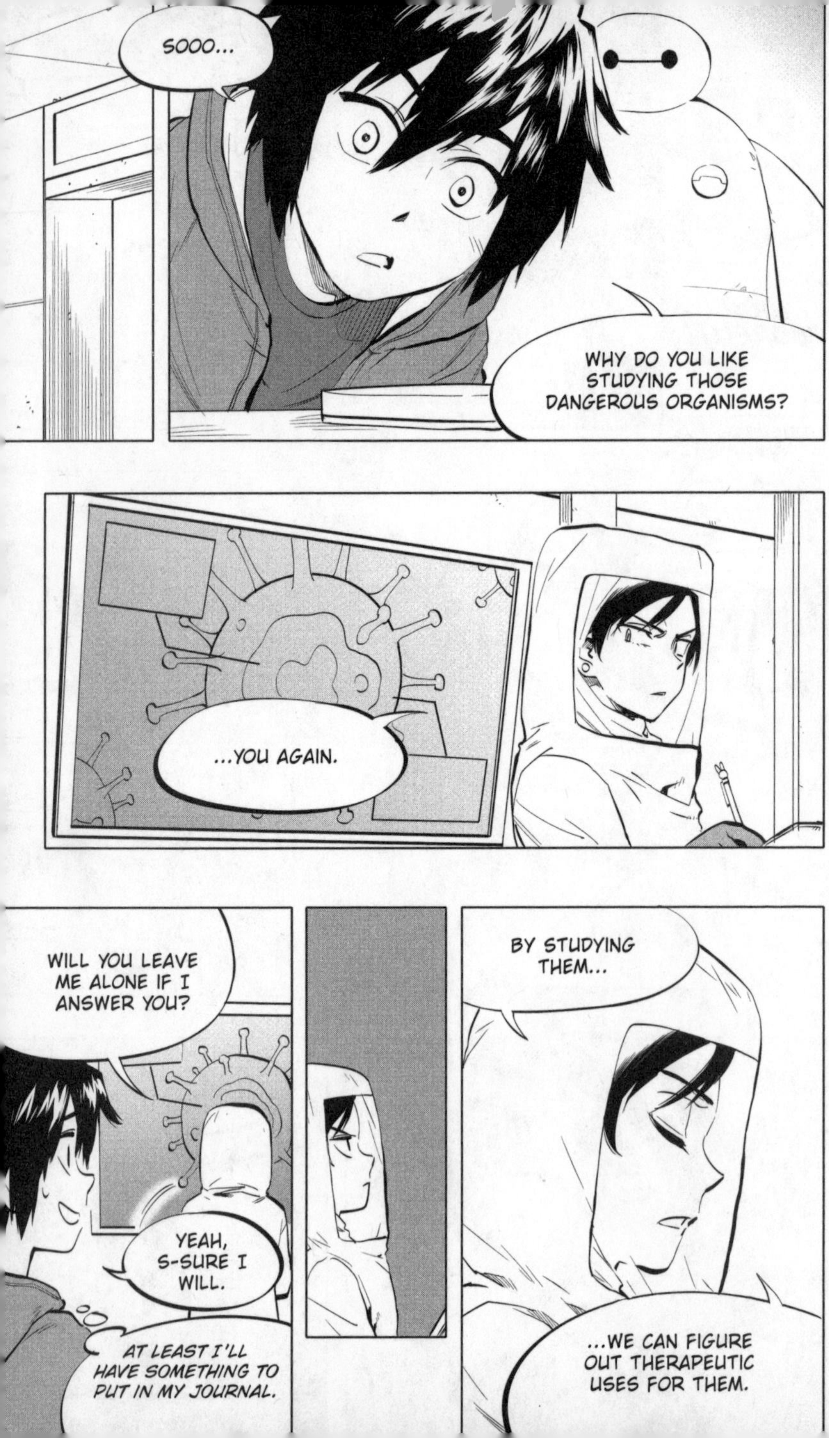
SOOO...
WHY DO YOU LIKE STUDYING THOSE DANGEROUS ORGANISMS?
...YOU AGAIN.
WILL YOU LEAVE ME ALONE IF I ANSWER YOU?
YEAH, S-SURE I WILL.
AT LEAST I'LL HAVE SOMETHING TO PUT IN MY JOURNAL.
BY STUDYING THEM...
...WE CAN FIGURE OUT THERAPEUTIC USES FOR THEM.

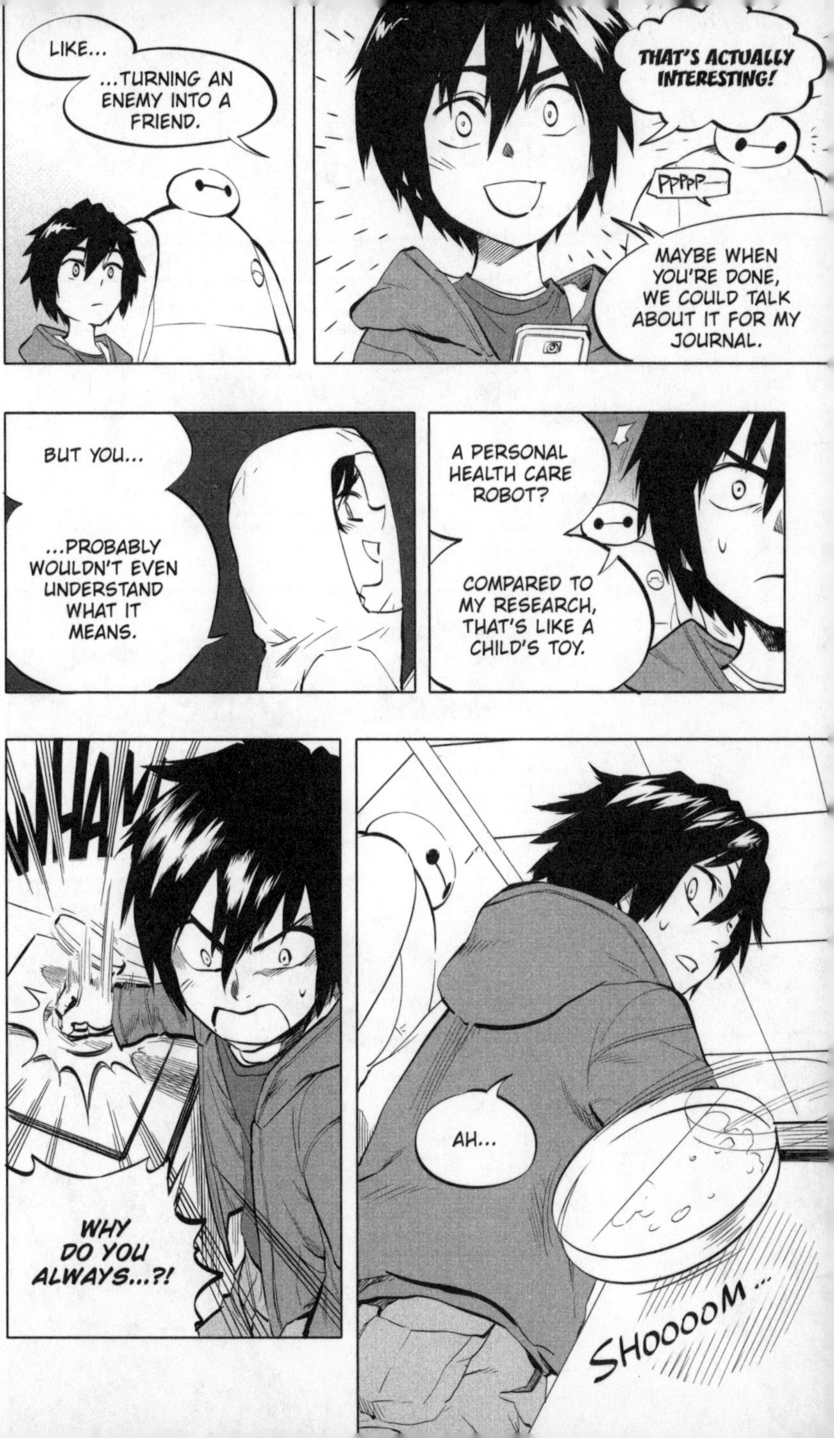
LIKE...
...TURNING AN ENEMY INTO A FRIEND.
THAT'S ACTUALLY INTERESTING!
PPPPP
MAYBE WHEN YOU'RE DONE, WE COULD TALK ABOUT IT FOR MY JOURNAL.
BUT YOU...
...PROBABLY WOULDN'T EVEN UNDERSTAND WHAT IT MEANS.
A PERSONAL HEALTH CARE ROBOT?
COMPARED TO MY RESEARCH, THAT'S LIKE A CHILD'S TOY.
WHAM
WHY DO YOU ALWAYS...?!
AH...
SHOOOOM...

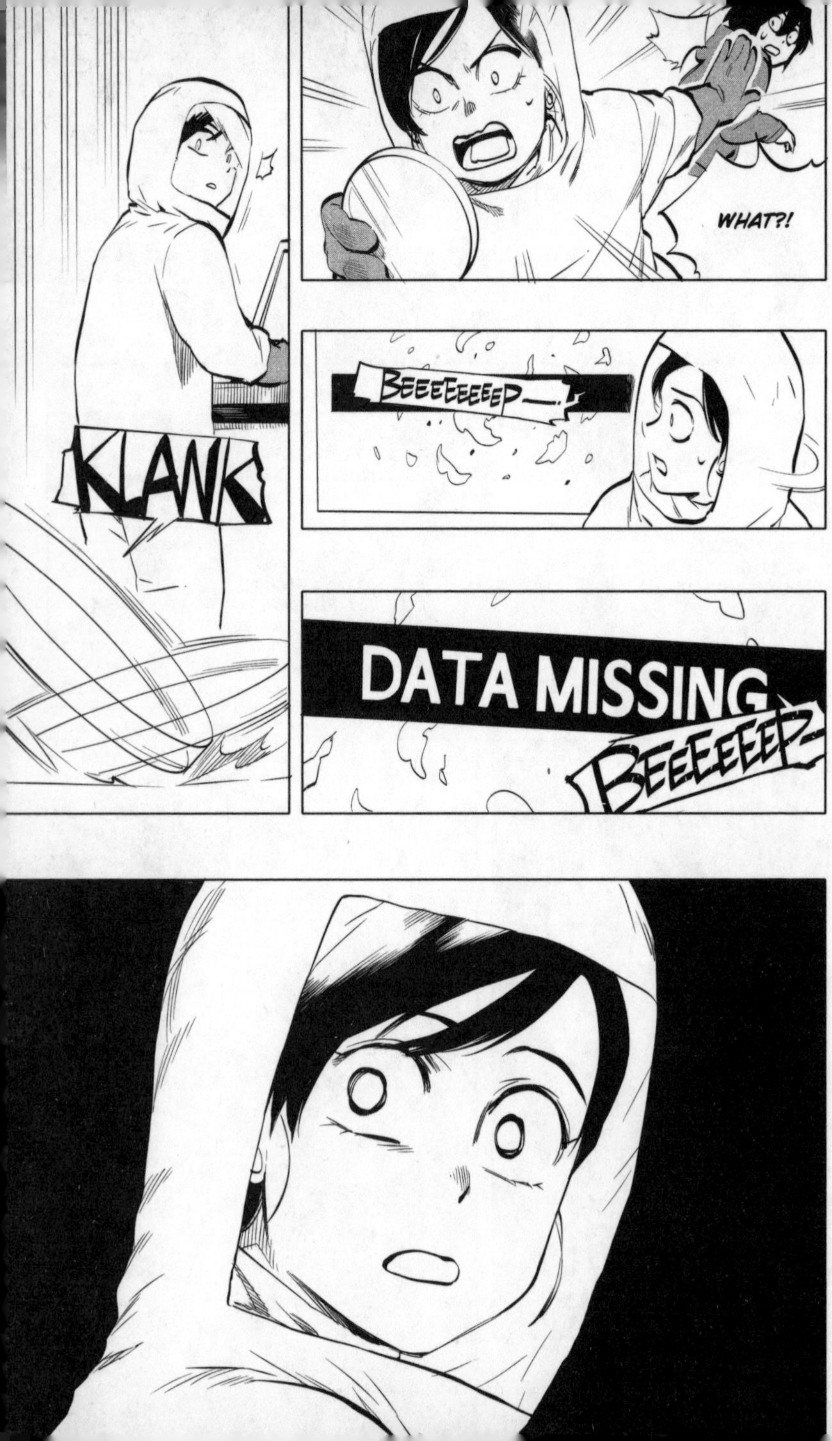
KLANK
WHAT?!
BEEEEEEEEEP—
DATA MISSING
BEEEEEEP

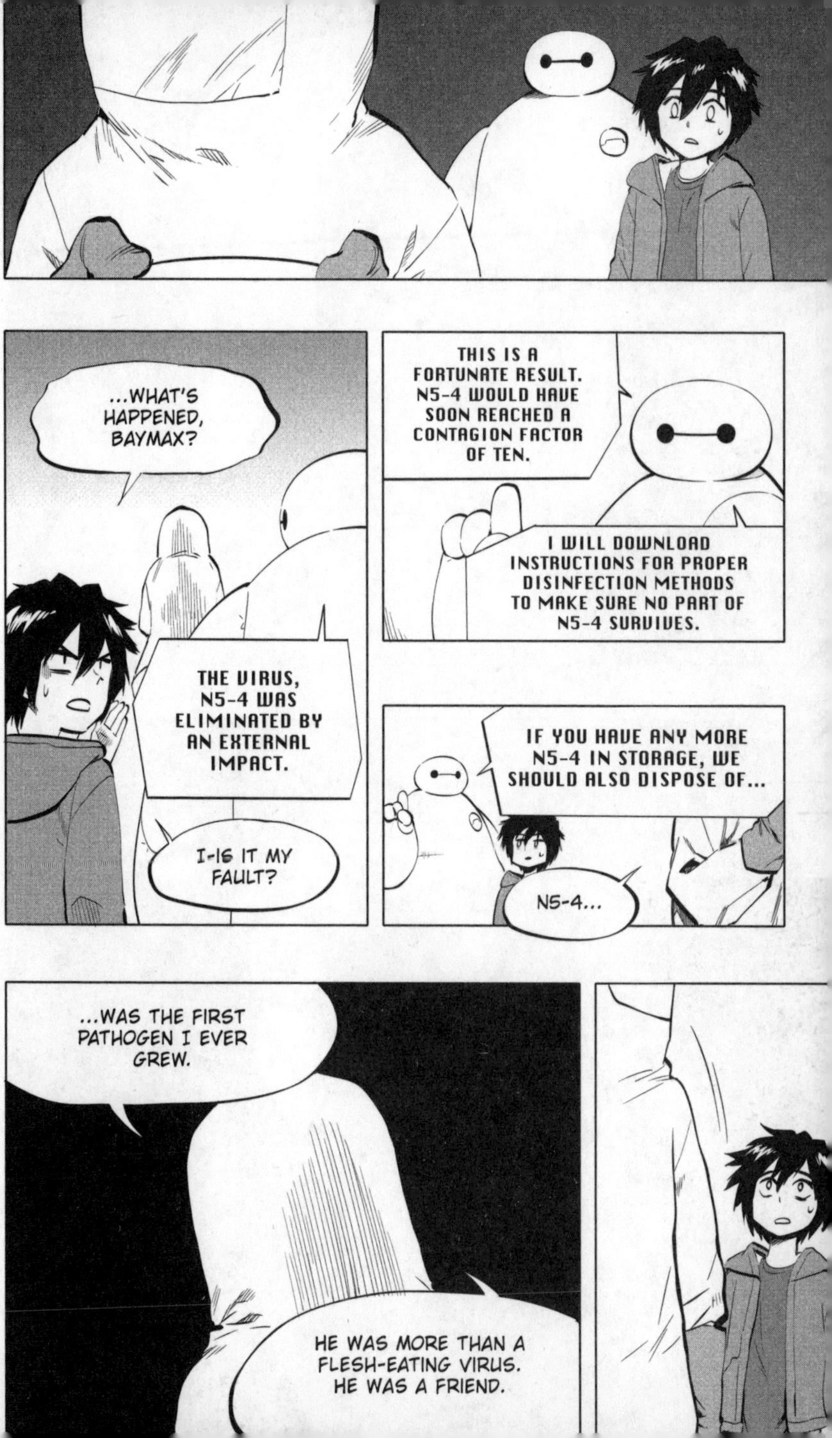
...WHAT'S HAPPENED, BAYMAX?
THE VIRUS, N5-4 WAS ELIMINATED BY AN EXTERNAL IMPACT.
I-IS IT MY FAULT?
THIS IS A FORTUNATE RESULT. N5-4 WOULD HAVE SOON REACHED A CONTAGION FACTOR OF TEN.
I WILL DOWNLOAD INSTRUCTIONS FOR PROPER DISINFECTION METHODS TO MAKE SURE NO PART OF N5-4 SURVIVES.
IF YOU HAVE ANY MORE N5-4 IN STORAGE, WE SHOULD ALSO DISPOSE OF...
N5-4...
...WAS THE FIRST PATHOGEN I EVER GREW.
HE WAS MORE THAN A FLESH-EATING VIRUS. HE WAS A FRIEND.

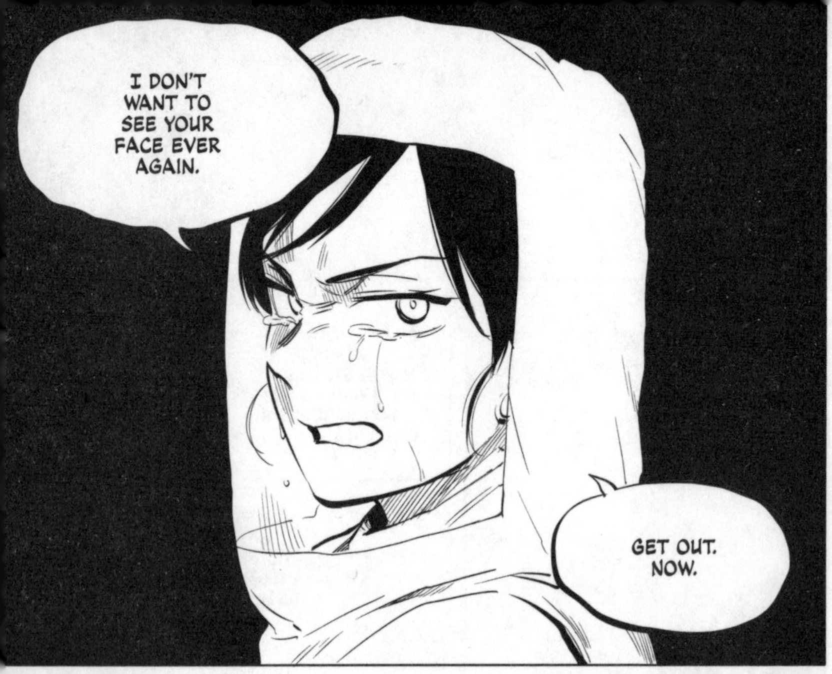
I DON'T WANT TO SEE YOUR FACE EVER AGAIN.
GET OUT. NOW.

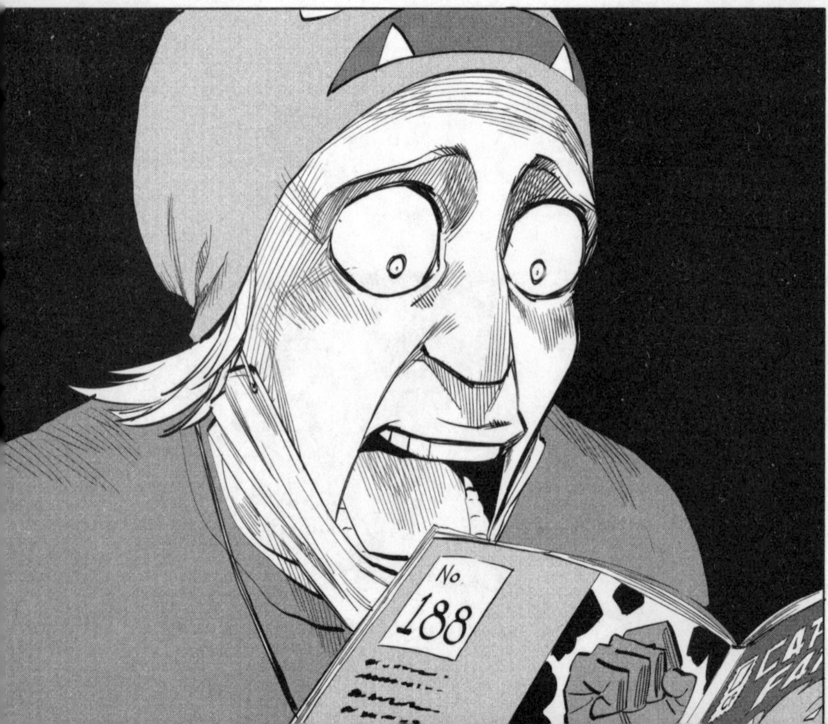
No. 188

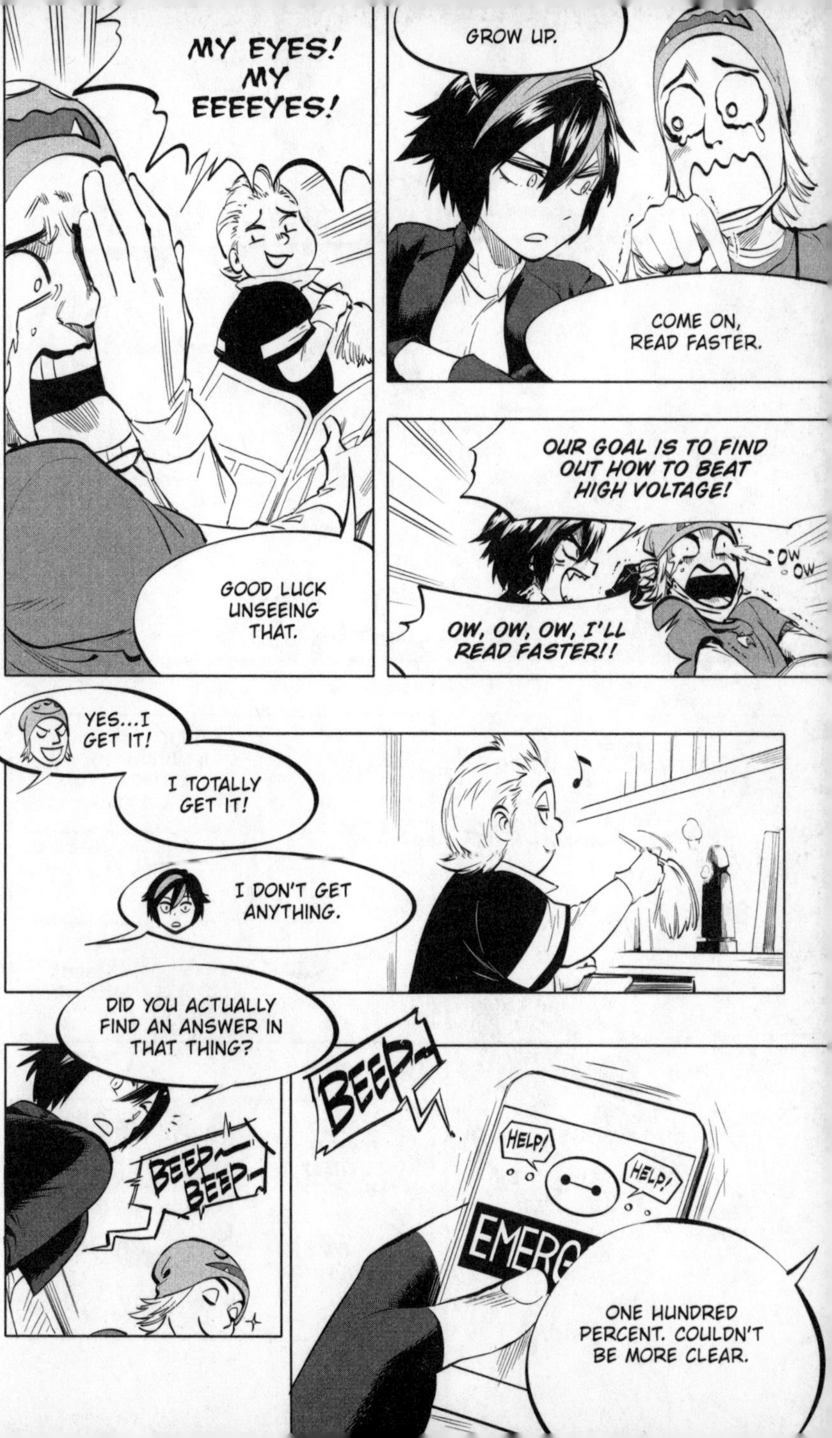
MY EYES! MY EEEEYES!
GOOD LUCK UNSEEING THAT.
GROW UP.
COME ON, READ FASTER.
OUR GOAL IS TO FIND OUT HOW TO BEAT HIGH VOLTAGE!
OW OW
OW, OW, OW, I'LL READ FASTER!!
YES...I GET IT!
I TOTALLY GET IT!
I DON'T GET ANYTHING.
DID YOU ACTUALLY FIND AN ANSWER IN THAT THING?
BEEP BEEP
BEEP
HELP!
HELP!
EMERG
ONE HUNDRED PERCENT. COULDN'T BE MORE CLEAR.

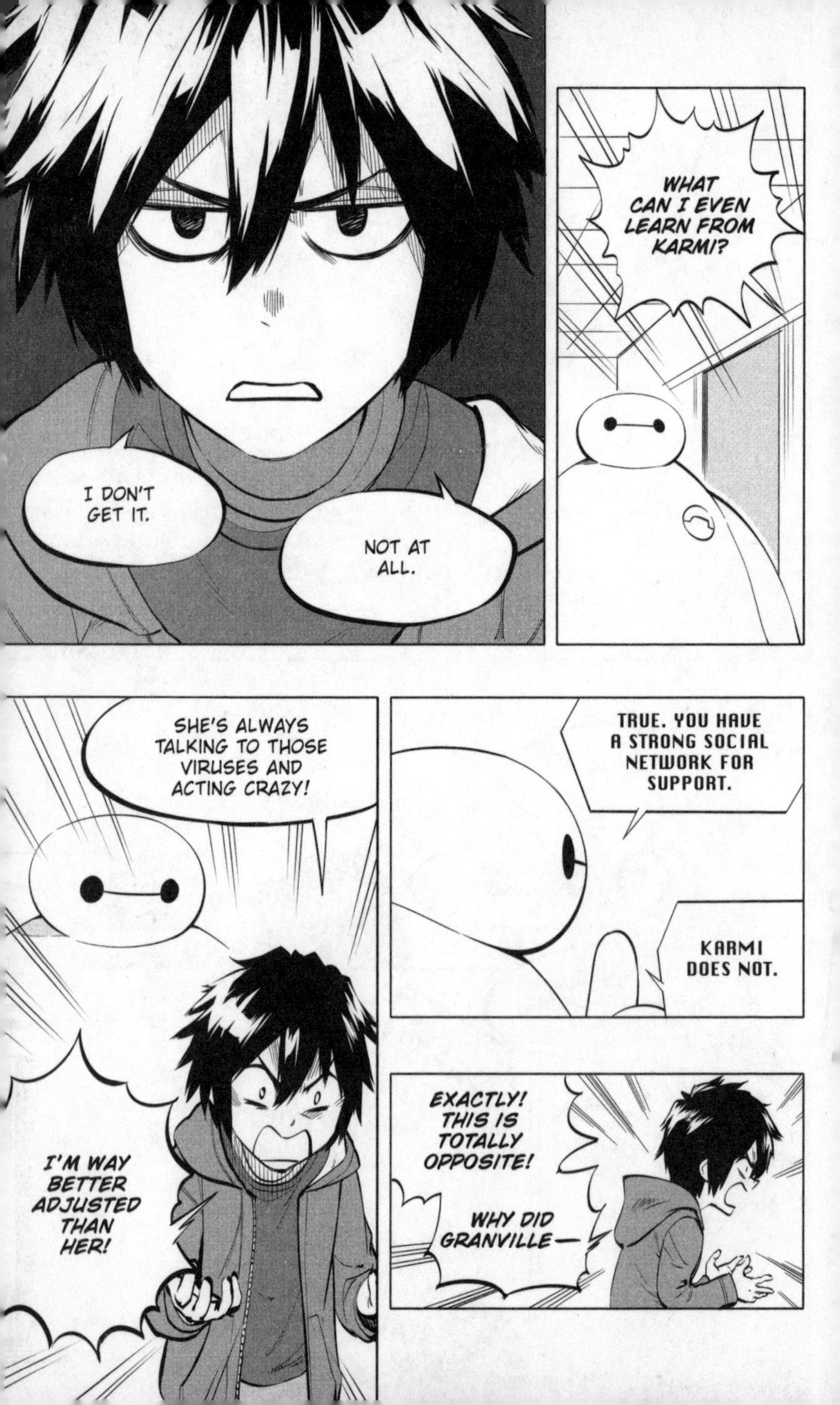

I DON'T GET IT.
NOT AT ALL.
WHAT CAN I EVEN LEARN FROM KARMI?
SHE'S ALWAYS TALKING TO THOSE VIRUSES AND ACTING CRAZY!
I'M WAY BETTER ADJUSTED THAN HER!
TRUE. YOU HAVE A STRONG SOCIAL NETWORK FOR SUPPORT.
KARMI DOES NOT.
EXACTLY! THIS IS TOTALLY OPPOSITE!
WHY DID GRANVILLE—

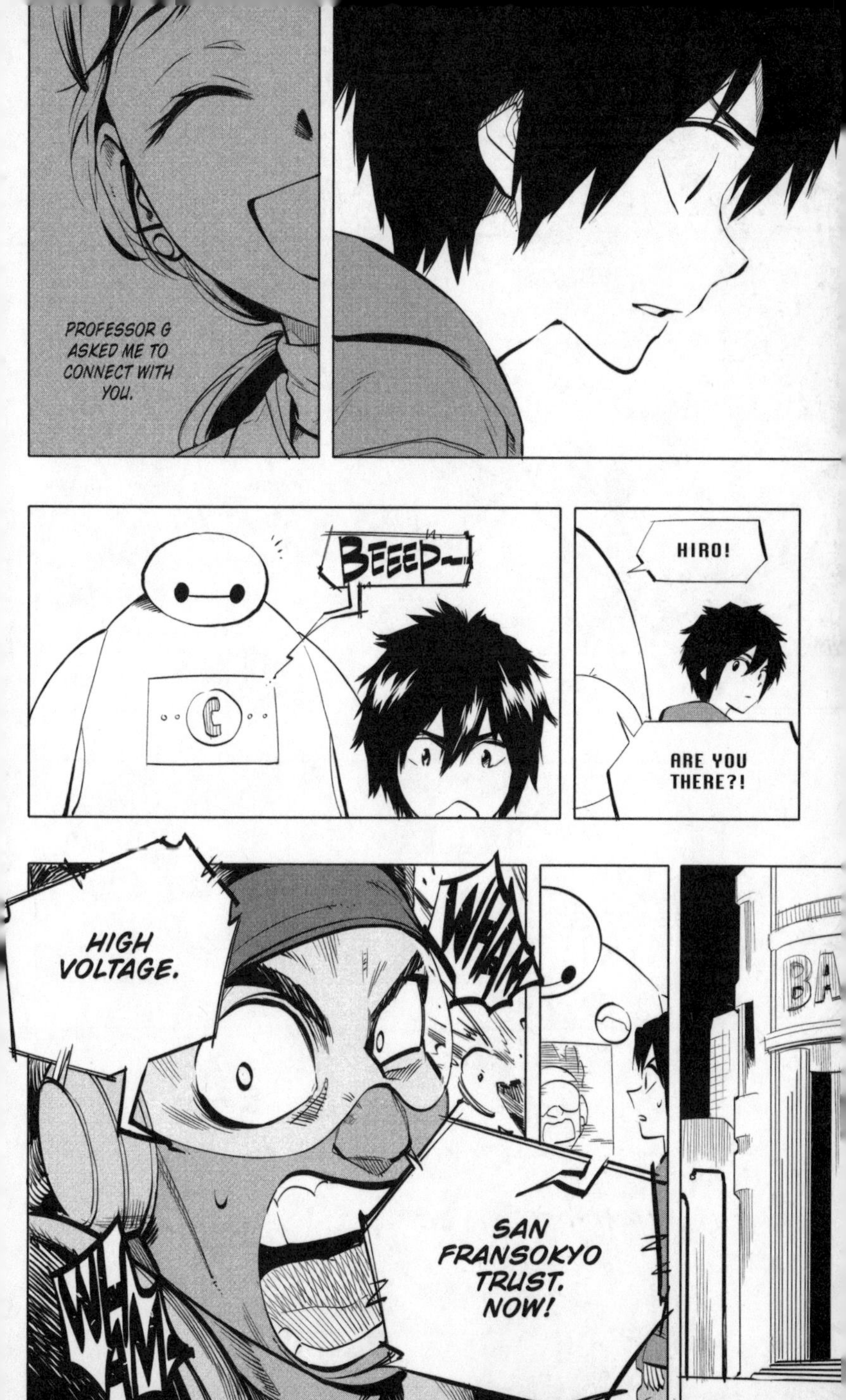

PROFESSOR G ASKED ME TO CONNECT WITH YOU.
BEEEP
HIRO!
ARE YOU THERE?!
HIGH VOLTAGE.
WHAM
WHAM
SAN FRANSOKYO TRUST. NOW!

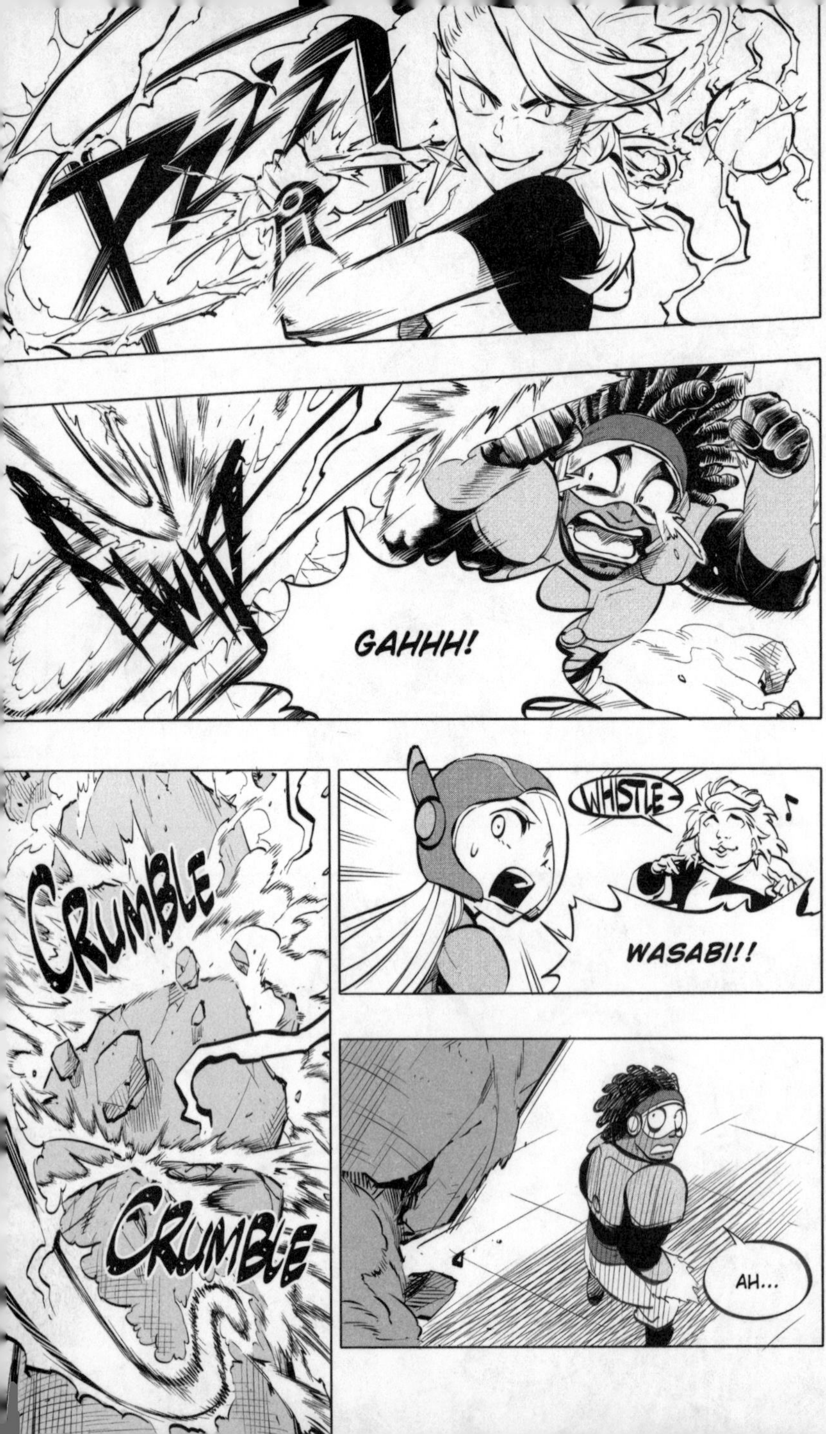
GAHHH!
CRUMBLE
CRUMBLE
WHISTLE
WASABI!!
AH...

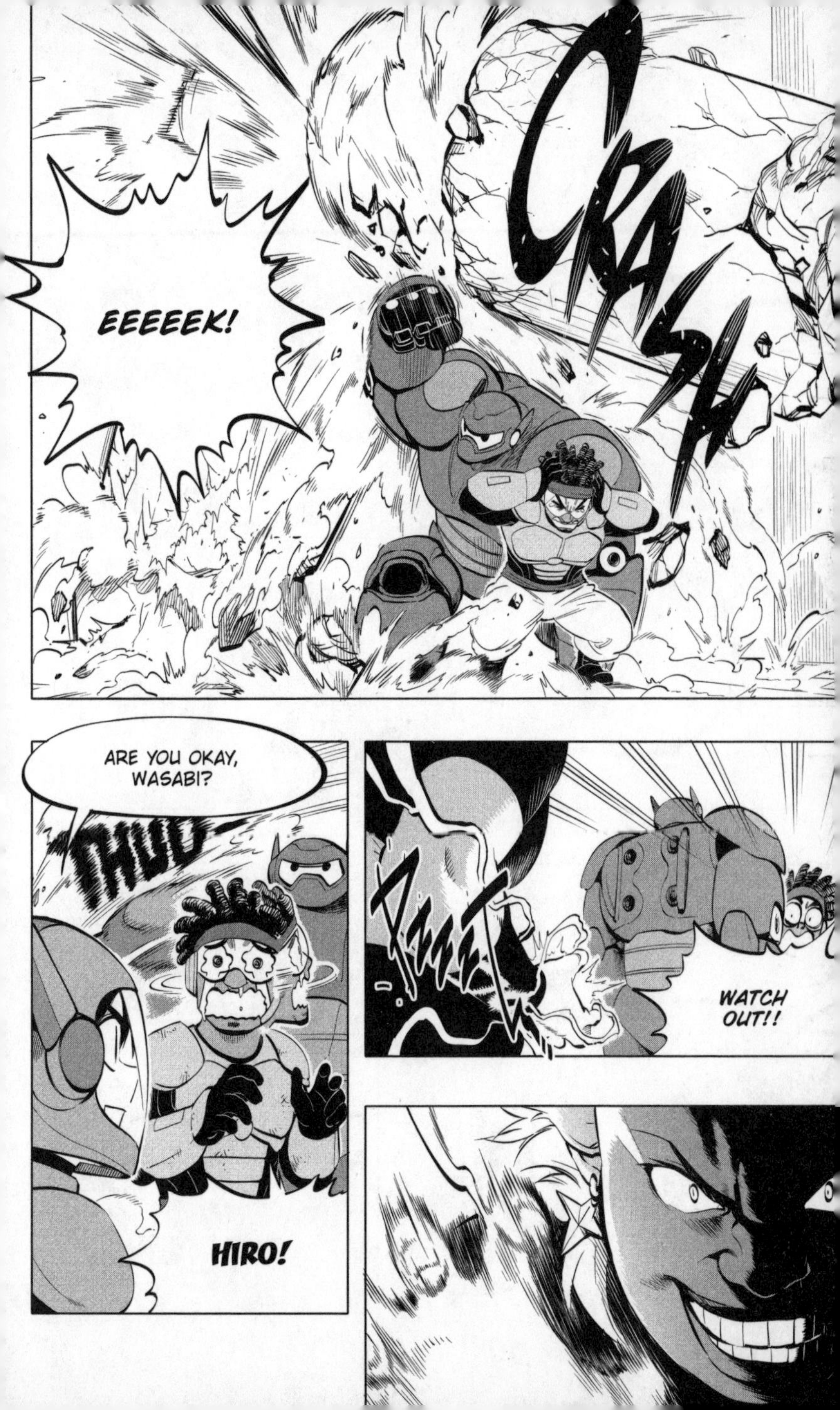
EEEEEK!
CRASH
ARE YOU OKAY, WASABI?
THUD
HIRO!
WATCH OUT!!

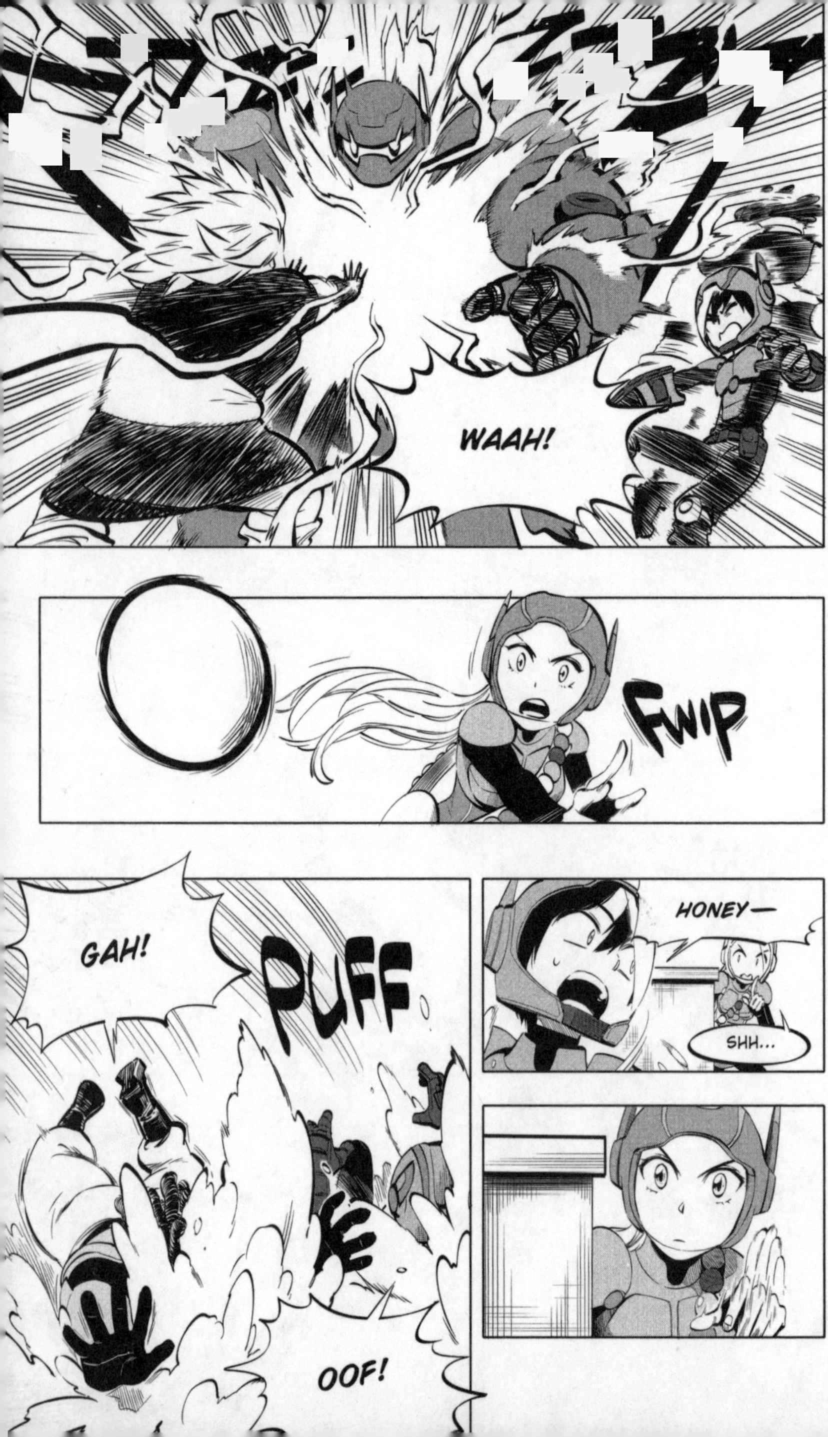
WAAH!
FWIP
GAH!
PUFF
OOF!
HONEY—
SHH...

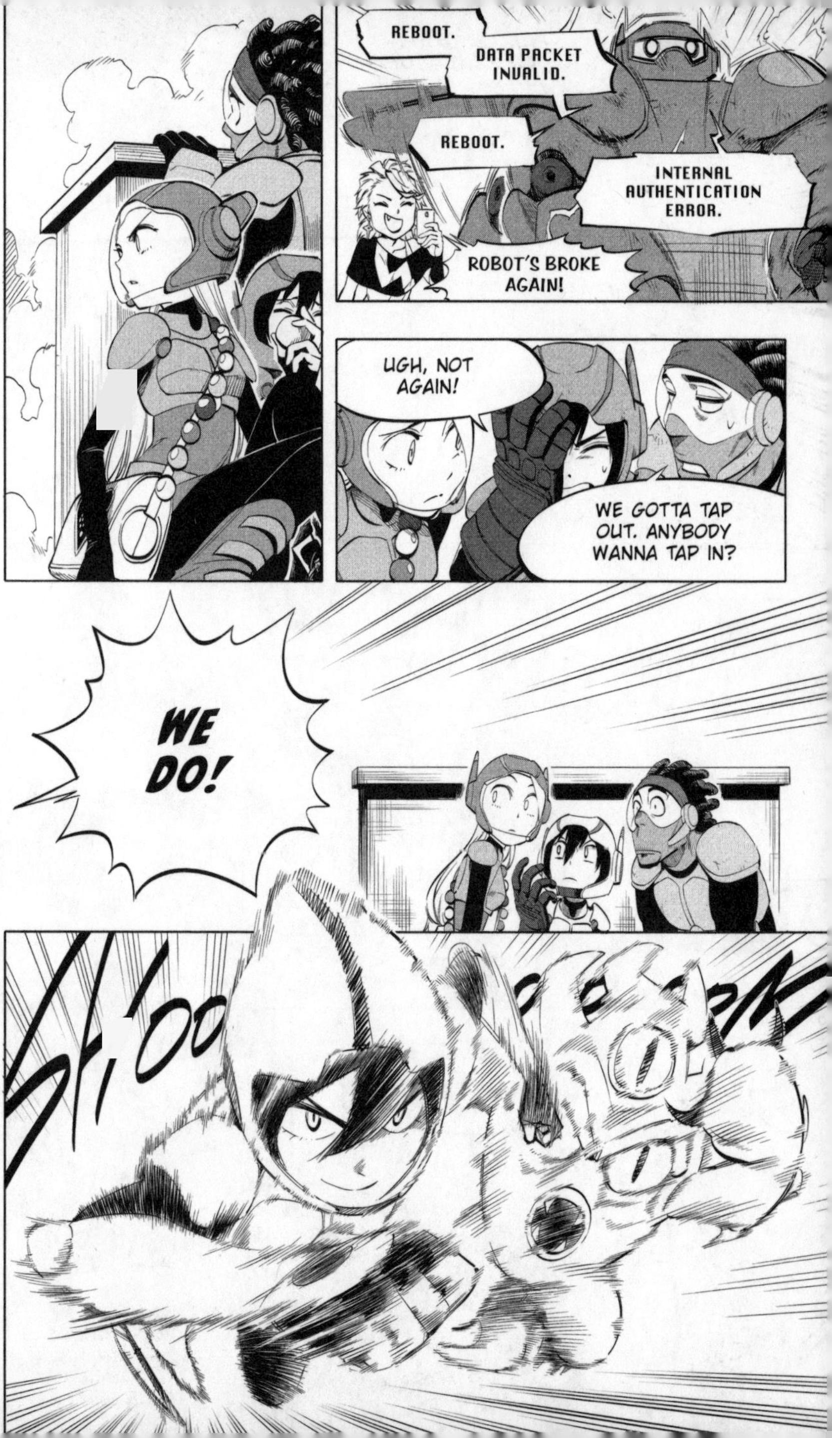
REBOOT.
DATA PACKET INVALID.
REBOOT.
INTERNAL AUTHENTICATION ERROR.
ROBOT'S BROKE AGAIN!
UGH, NOT AGAIN!
WE GOTTA TAP OUT. ANYBODY WANNA TAP IN?
WE DO!

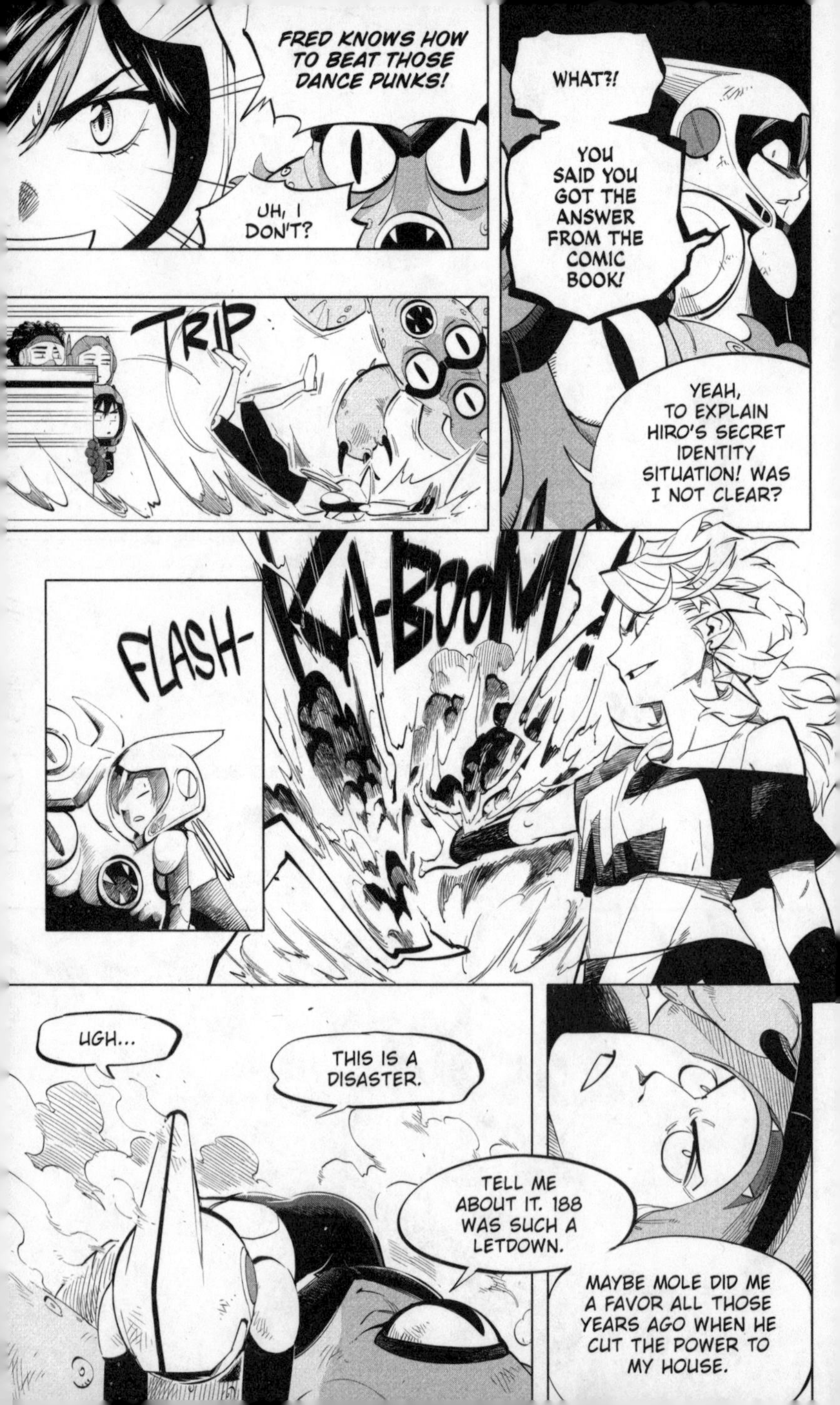
FRED KNOWS HOW TO BEAT THOSE DANCE PUNKS!
UH, I DON'T?
TRIP
WHAT?!
YOU SAID YOU GOT THE ANSWER FROM THE COMIC BOOK!
YEAH, TO EXPLAIN HIRO'S SECRET IDENTITY SITUATION! WAS I NOT CLEAR?
FLASH-
KA-BOOM!
UGH...
THIS IS A DISASTER.
TELL ME ABOUT IT. 188 WAS SUCH A LETDOWN.
MAYBE MOLE DID ME A FAVOR ALL THOSE YEARS AGO WHEN HE CUT THE POWER TO MY HOUSE.

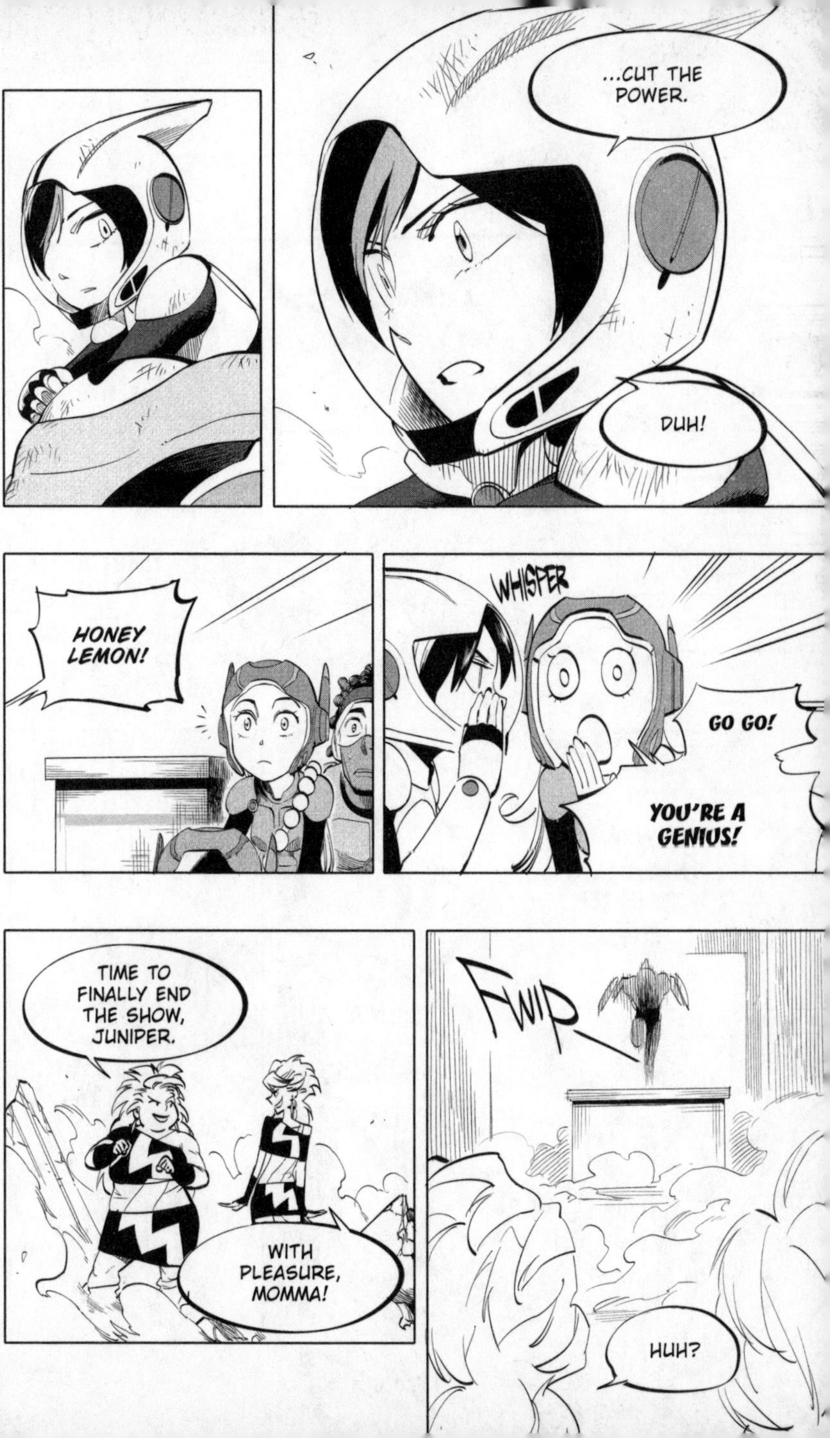
...CUT THE POWER.
DUH!
HONEY LEMON!
WHISPER
GO GO!
YOU'RE A GENIUS!
TIME TO FINALLY END THE SHOW, JUNIPER.
WITH PLEASURE, MOMMA!
FWIP
HUH?

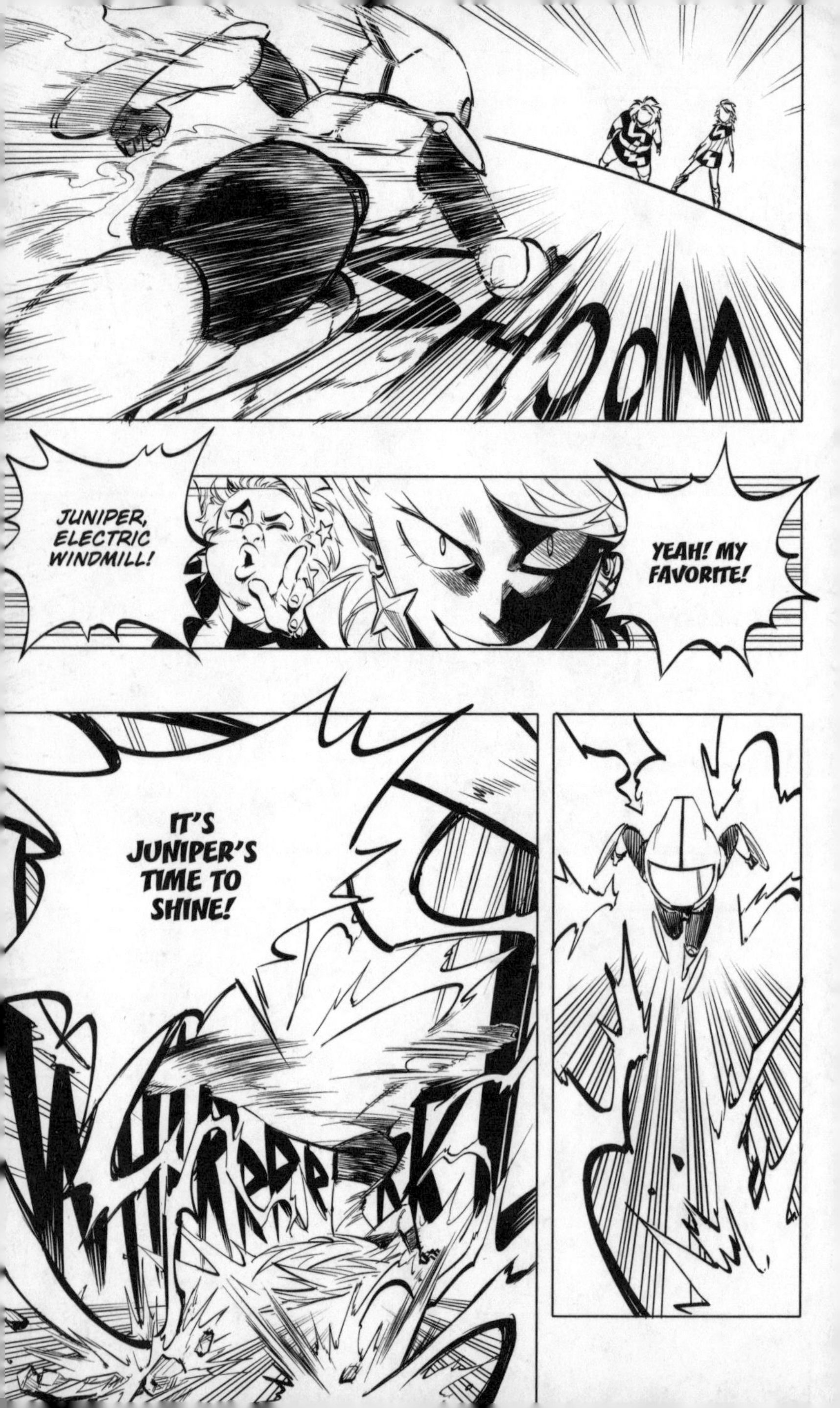
JUNIPER, ELECTRIC WINDMILL!
YEAH! MY FAVORITE!
IT'S JUNIPER'S TIME TO SHINE!

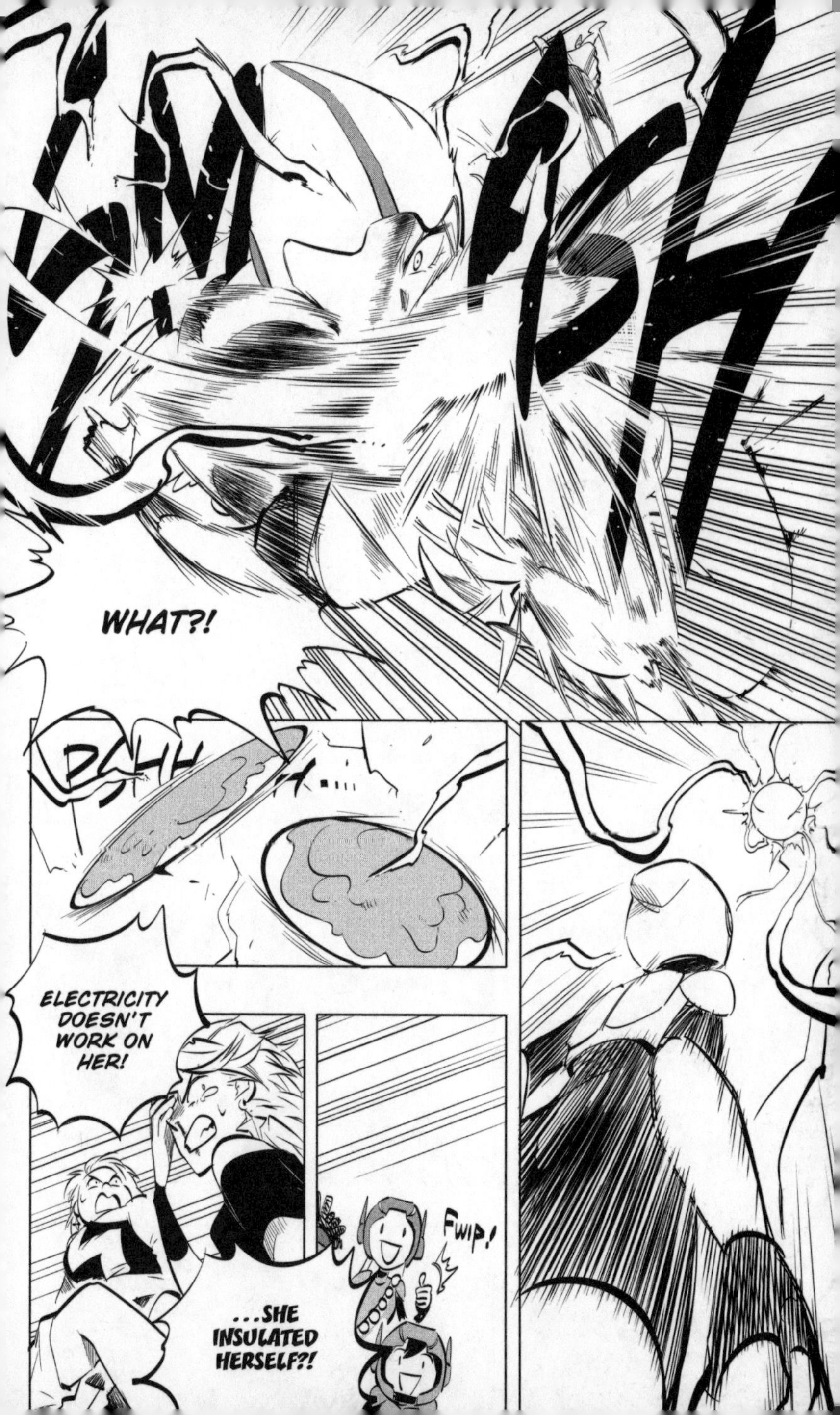
SMASH
WHAT?!
PSHH...
ELECTRICITY DOESN'T WORK ON HER!
...SHE INSULATED HERSELF?!
FWIP!

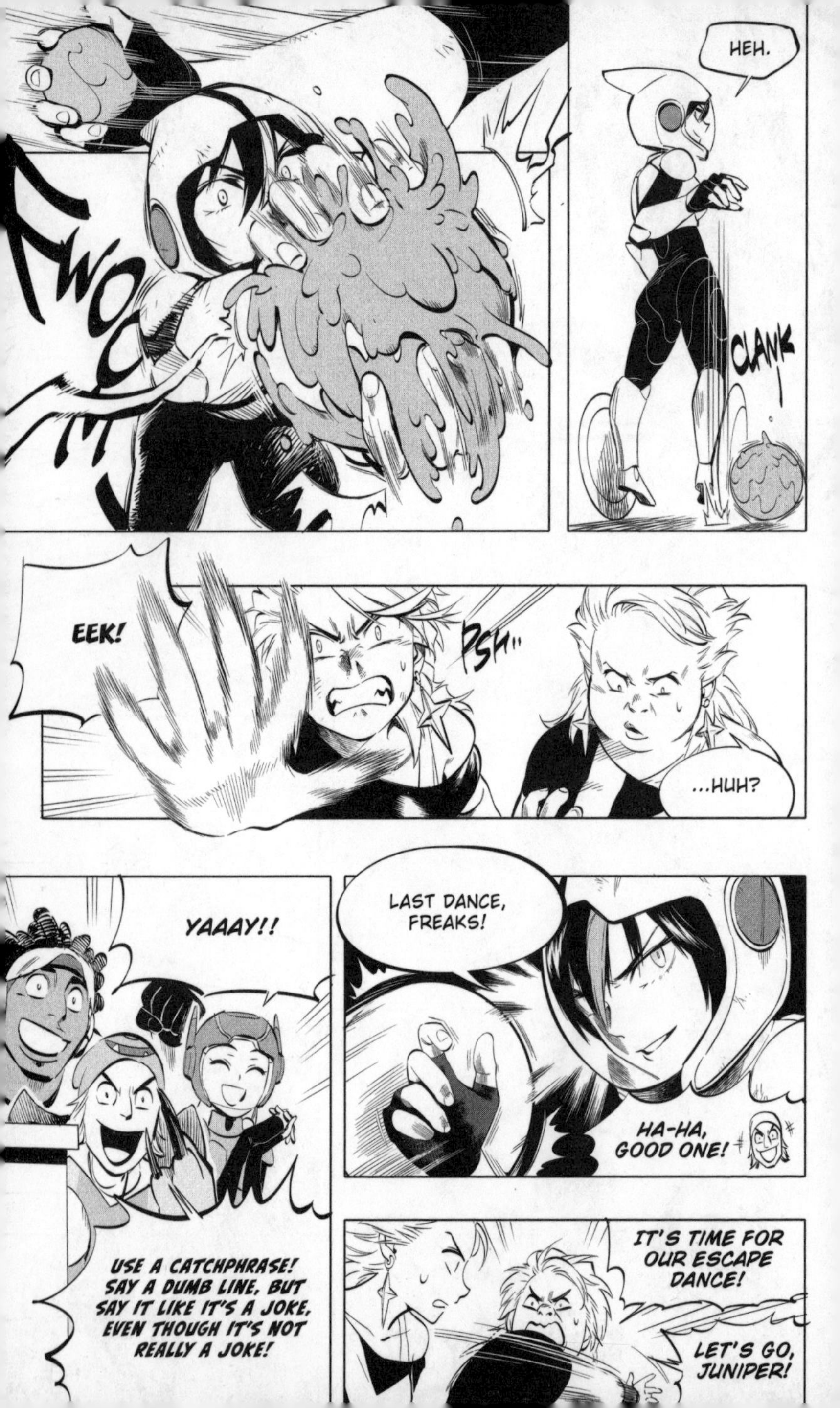
HEH.
CLANK
EEK!
PSH
...HUH?
YAAAY!!
USE A CATCHPHRASE! SAY A DUMB LINE, BUT SAY IT LIKE IT'S A JOKE, EVEN THOUGH IT'S NOT REALLY A JOKE!
LAST DANCE, FREAKS!
HA-HA, GOOD ONE!
IT'S TIME FOR OUR ESCAPE DANCE!
LET'S GO, JUNIPER!

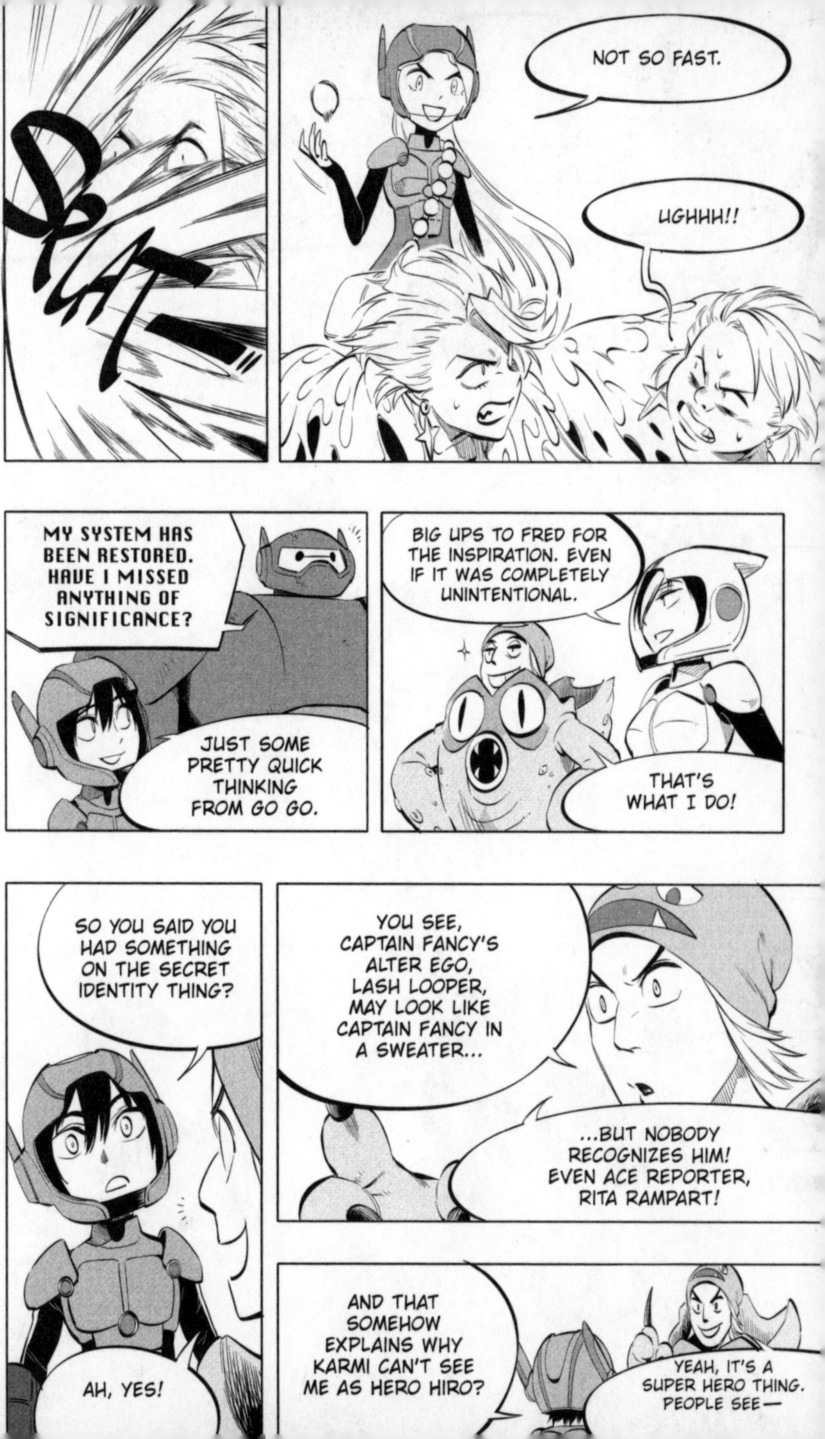
SPLAT
NOT SO FAST.
UGHHH!!
MY SYSTEM HAS BEEN RESTORED. HAVE I MISSED ANYTHING OF SIGNIFICANCE?
JUST SOME PRETTY QUICK THINKING FROM GO GO.
BIG UPS TO FRED FOR THE INSPIRATION. EVEN IF IT WAS COMPLETELY UNINTENTIONAL.
THAT'S WHAT I DO!
SO YOU SAID YOU HAD SOMETHING ON THE SECRET IDENTITY THING?
AH, YES!
YOU SEE, CAPTAIN FANCY'S ALTER EGO, LASH LOOPER, MAY LOOK LIKE CAPTAIN FANCY IN A SWEATER...
...BUT NOBODY RECOGNIZES HIM! EVEN ACE REPORTER, RITA RAMPART!
AND THAT SOMEHOW EXPLAINS WHY KARMI CAN'T SEE ME AS HERO HIRO?
YEAH, IT'S A SUPER HERO THING. PEOPLE SEE—

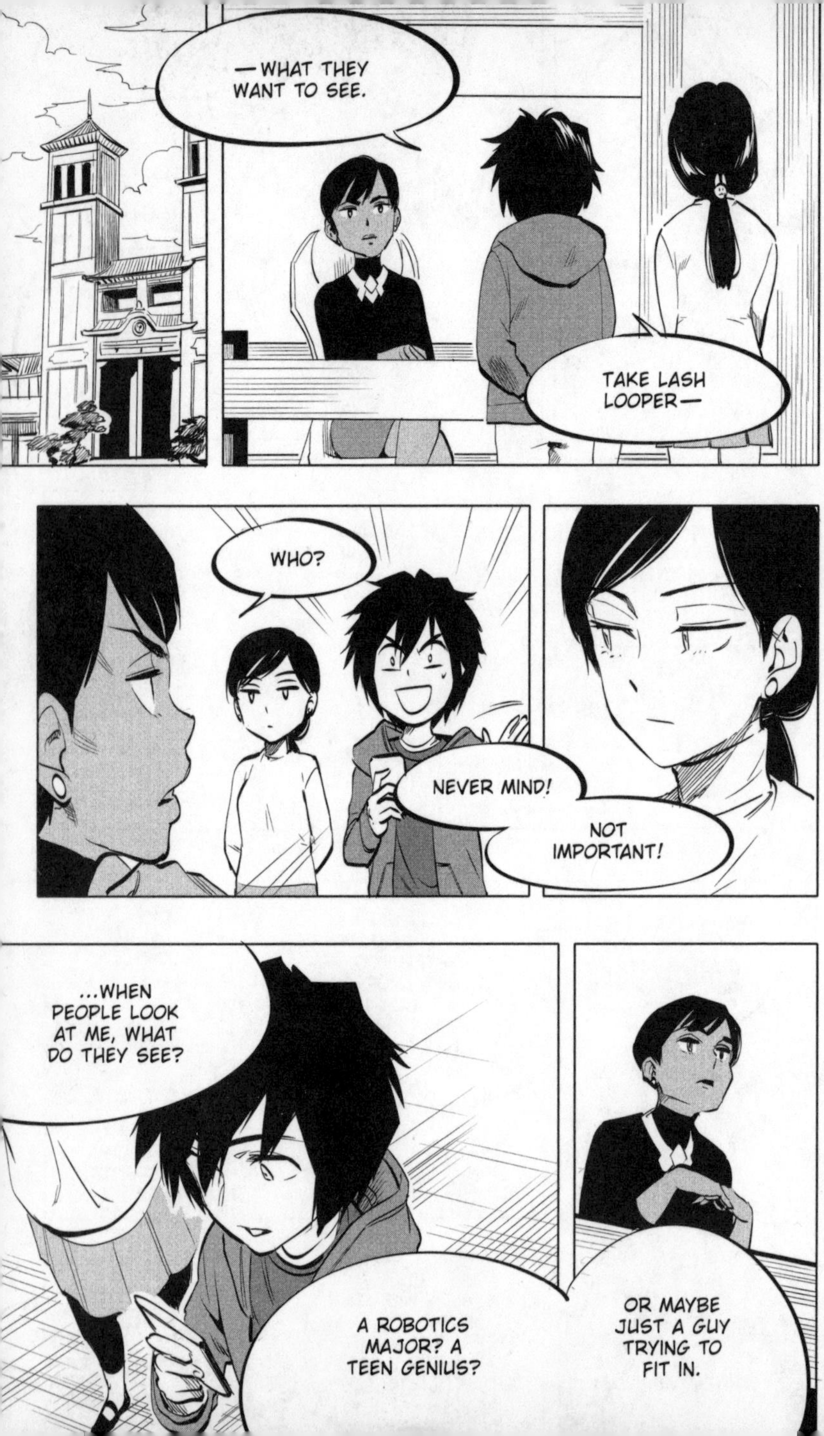
—WHAT THEY WANT TO SEE.
TAKE LASH LOOPER—
WHO?
NEVER MIND!
NOT IMPORTANT!
...WHEN PEOPLE LOOK AT ME, WHAT DO THEY SEE?
A ROBOTICS MAJOR? A TEEN GENIUS?
OR MAYBE JUST A GUY TRYING TO FIT IN.

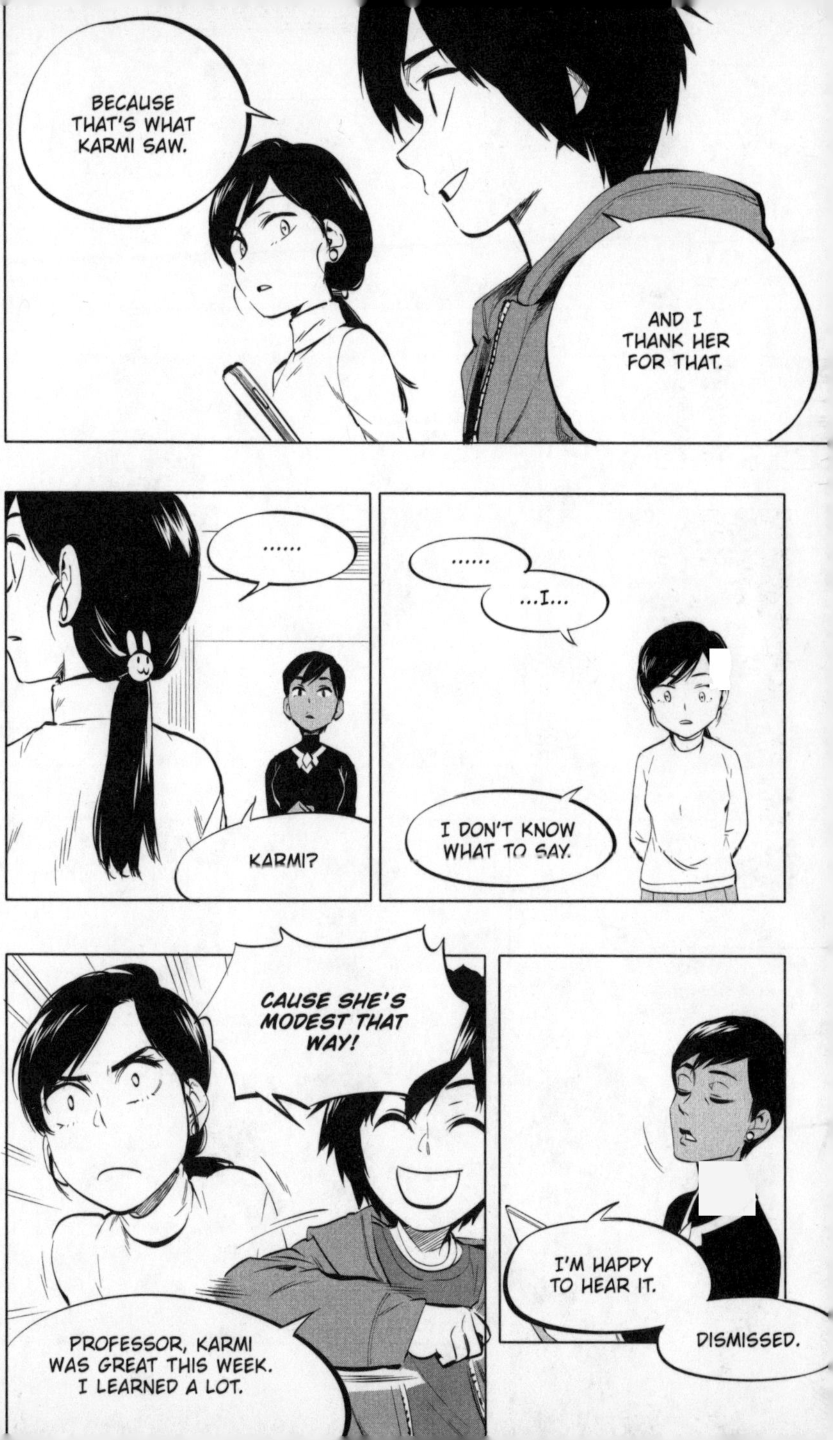
BECAUSE THAT'S WHAT KARMI SAW.
AND I THANK HER FOR THAT.
......
KARMI?
......
...I...
I DON'T KNOW WHAT TO SAY.
CAUSE SHE'S MODEST THAT WAY!
PROFESSOR, KARMI WAS GREAT THIS WEEK. I LEARNED A LOT.
I'M HAPPY TO HEAR IT.
DISMISSED.

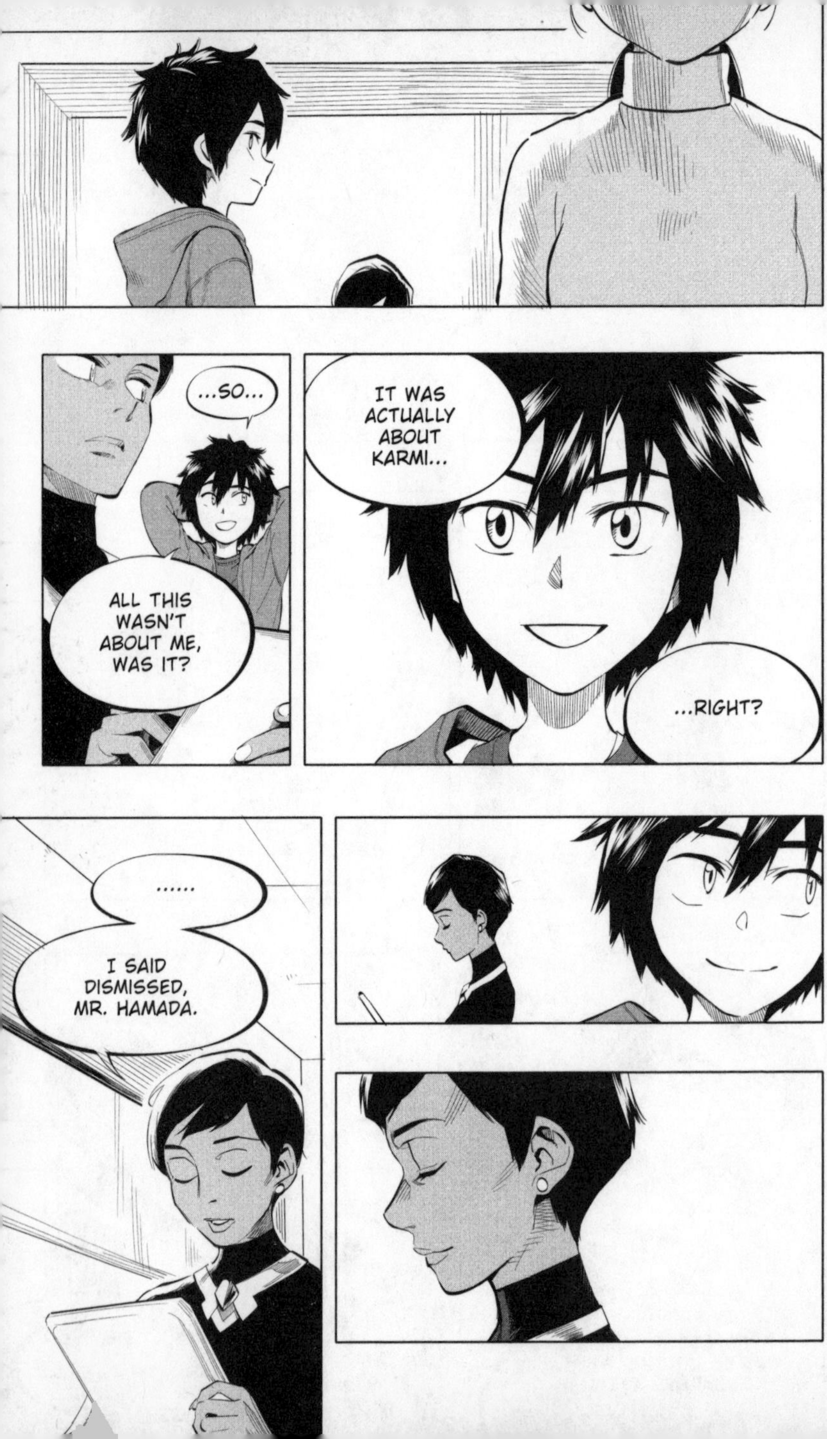

...SO...
ALL THIS WASN'T ABOUT ME, WAS IT?
IT WAS ACTUALLY ABOUT KARMI...
...RIGHT?
......
I SAID DISMISSED, MR. HAMADA.

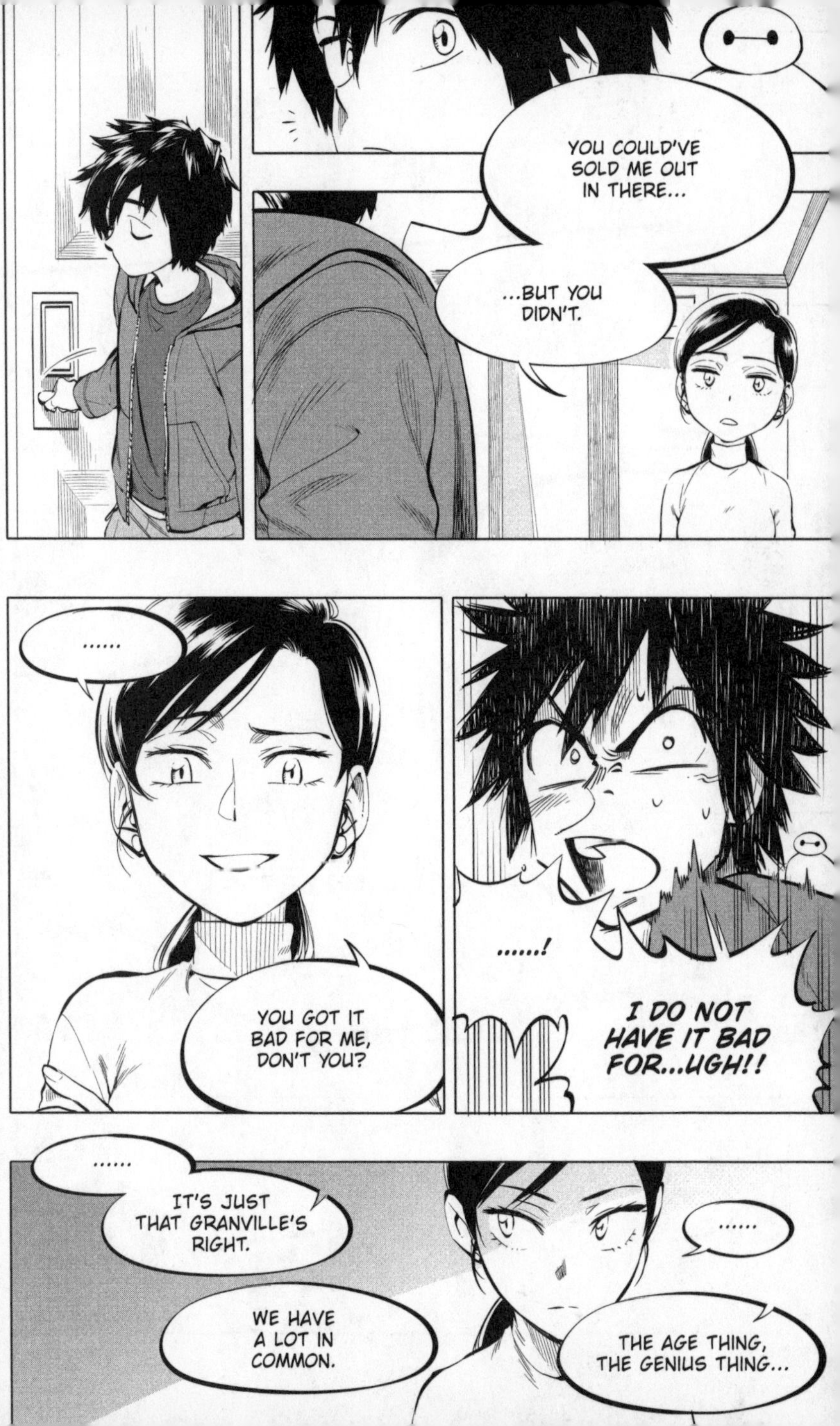
YOU COULD'VE SOLD ME OUT IN THERE...
...BUT YOU DIDN'T.
......
YOU GOT IT BAD FOR ME, DON'T YOU?
......!
I DO NOT HAVE IT BAD FOR...UGH!!
......
IT'S JUST THAT GRANVILLE'S RIGHT.
WE HAVE A LOT IN COMMON.
......
THE AGE THING, THE GENIUS THING...

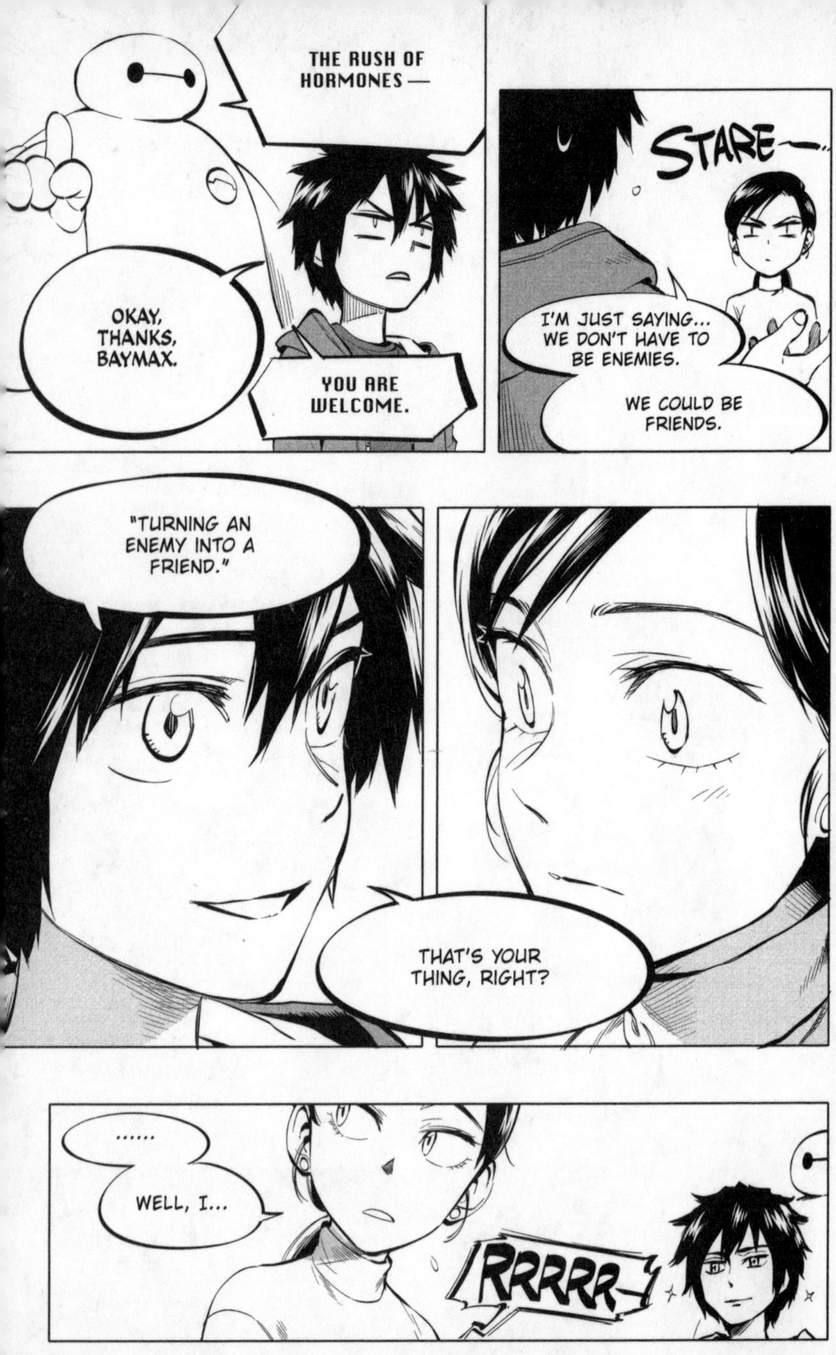
THE RUSH OF HORMONES—
OKAY, THANKS, BAYMAX.
YOU ARE WELCOME.
STARE—...
I'M JUST SAYING... WE DON'T HAVE TO BE ENEMIES.
WE COULD BE FRIENDS.
"TURNING AN ENEMY INTO A FRIEND."
THAT'S YOUR THING, RIGHT?
......
WELL, I...
RRRRR—

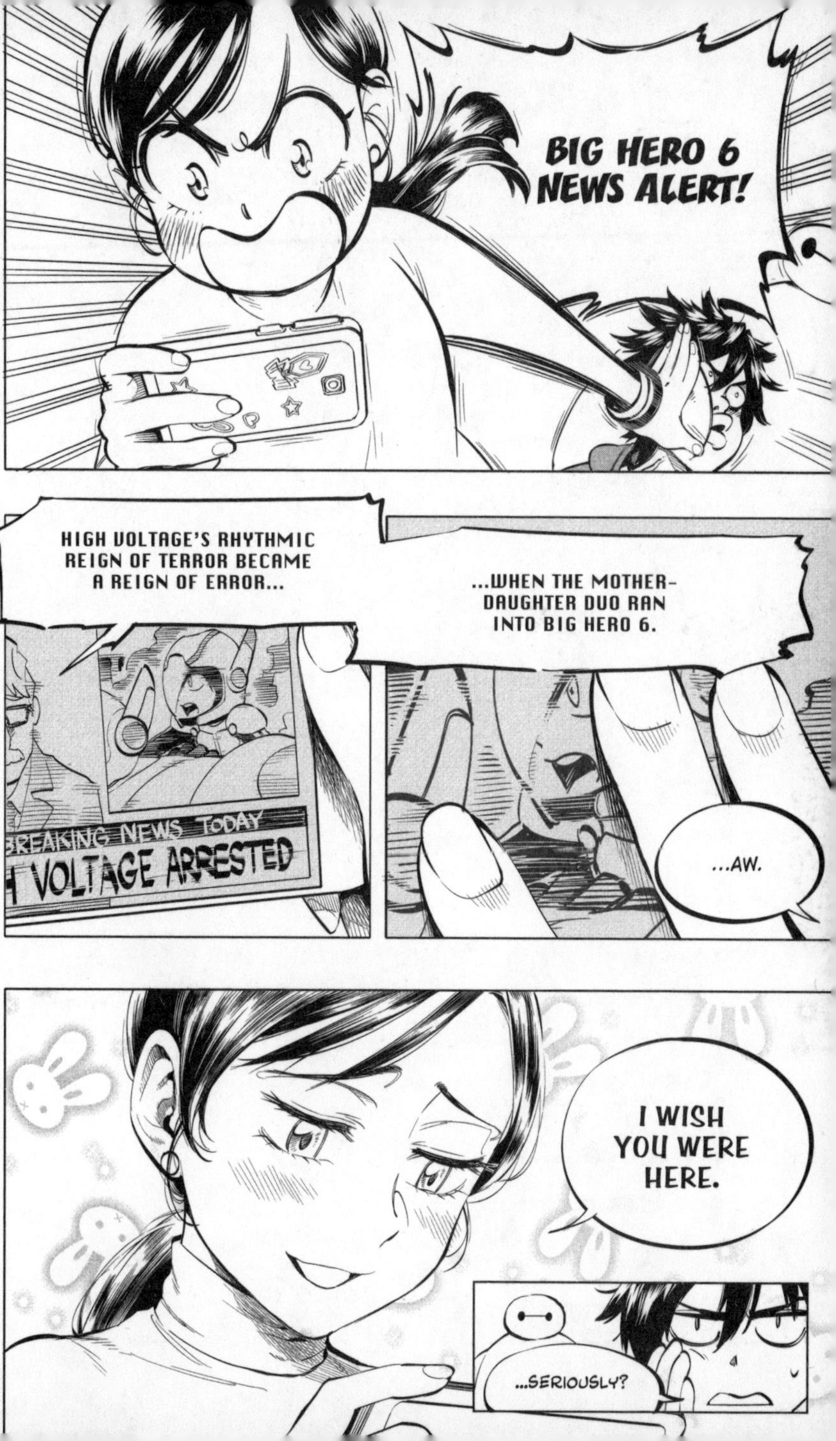
BIG HERO 6 NEWS ALERT!
HIGH VOLTAGE'S RHYTHMIC REIGN OF TERROR BECAME A REIGN OF ERROR...
BREAKING NEWS TODAY
H VOLTAGE ARRESTED
...WHEN THE MOTHER-DAUGHTER DUO RAN INTO BIG HERO 6.
...AW.
I WISH YOU WERE HERE.
...SERIOUSLY?

Disney

BIG HERO 6

THE SERIES

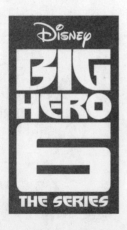

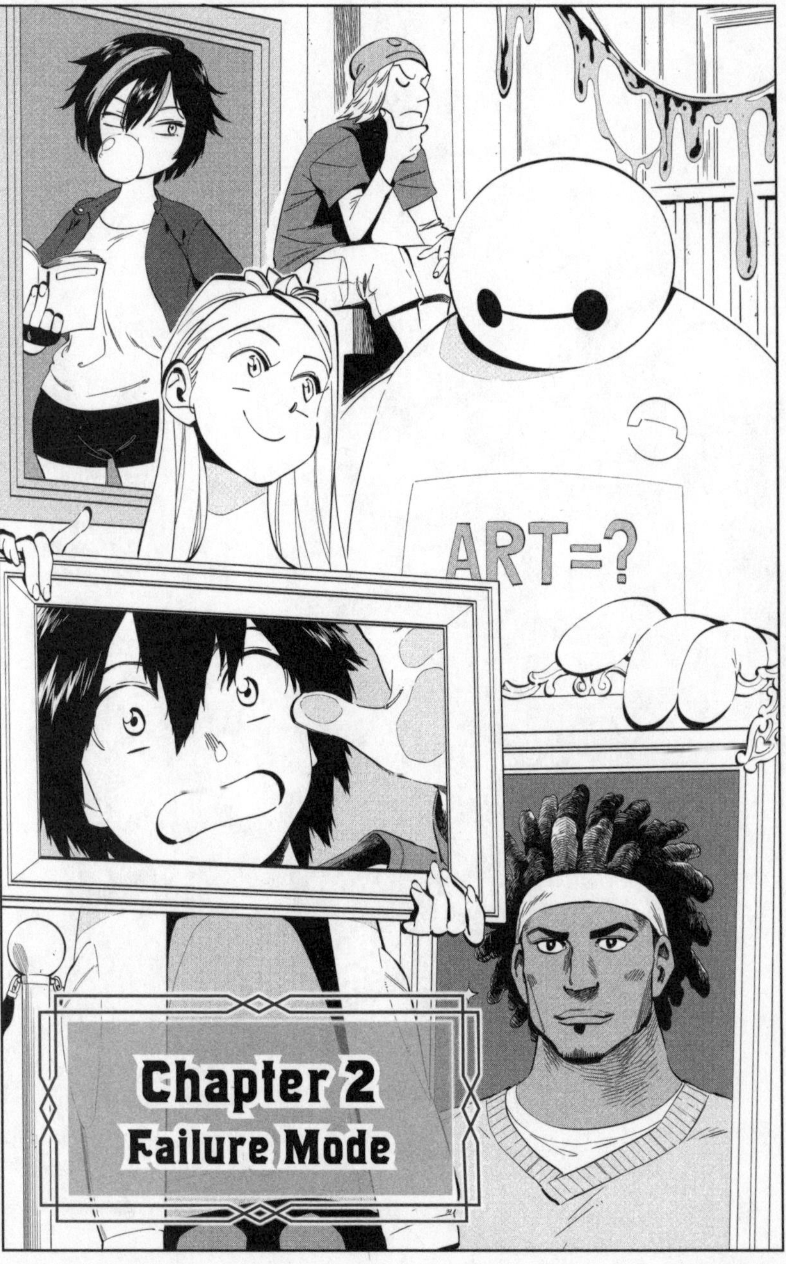
ART=?
Chapter 2
Failure Mode

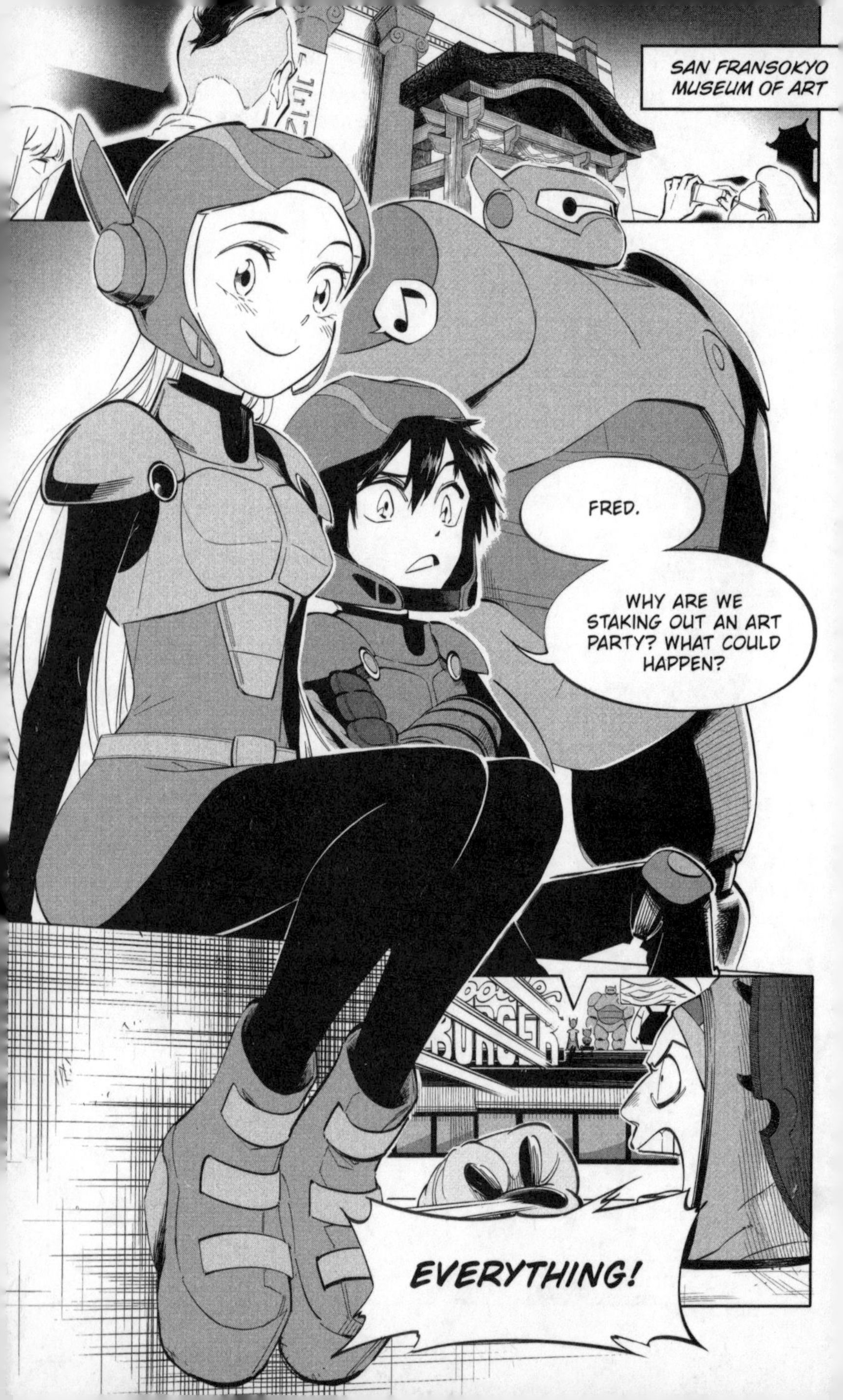
SAN FRANSOKYO MUSEUM OF ART
♪
FRED.
WHY ARE WE STAKING OUT AN ART PARTY? WHAT COULD HAPPEN?
EVERYTHING!

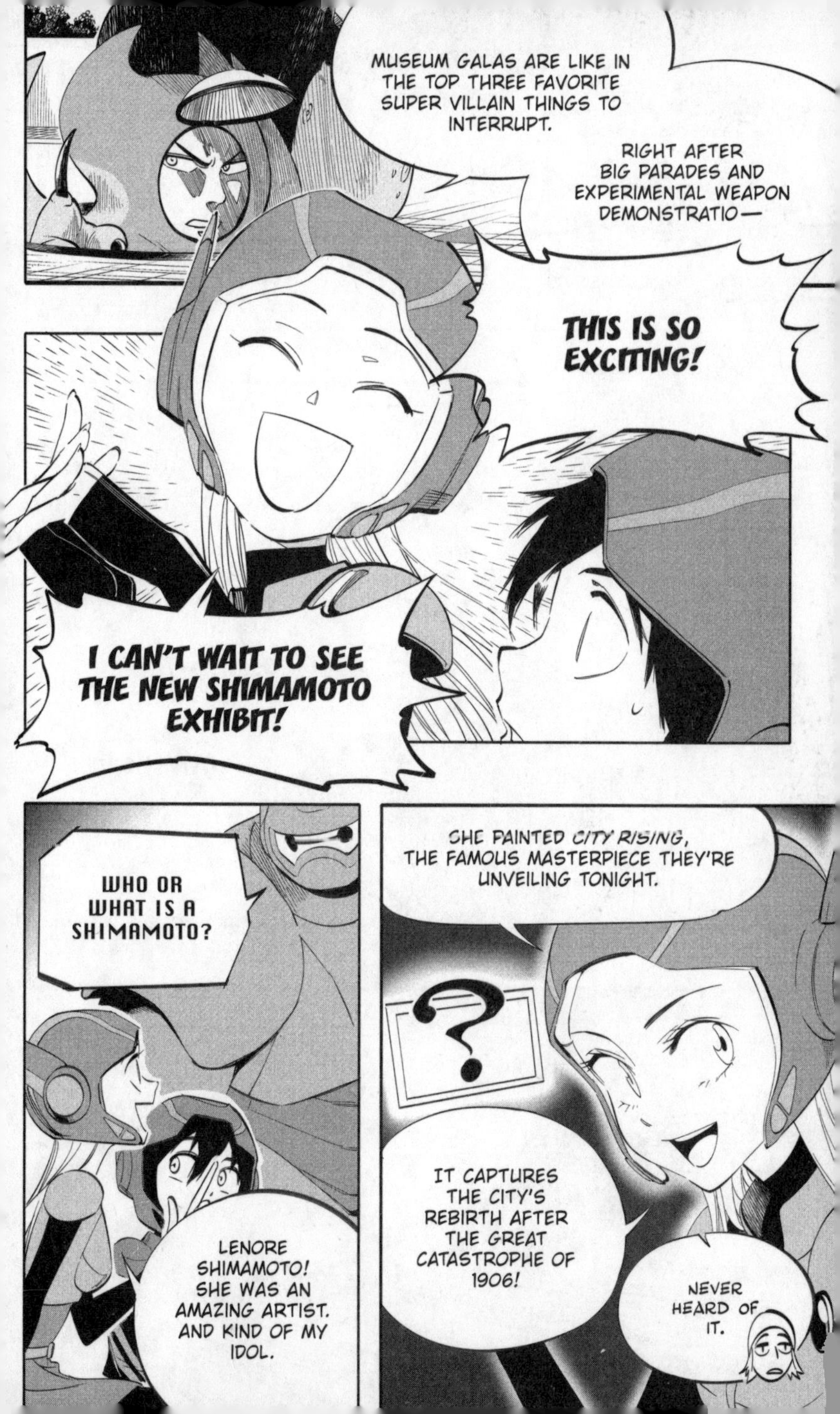
MUSEUM GALAS ARE LIKE IN THE TOP THREE FAVORITE SUPER VILLAIN THINGS TO INTERRUPT.
RIGHT AFTER BIG PARADES AND EXPERIMENTAL WEAPON DEMONSTRATIO—
THIS IS SO EXCITING!
I CAN'T WAIT TO SEE THE NEW SHIMAMOTO EXHIBIT!
WHO OR WHAT IS A SHIMAMOTO?
LENORE SHIMAMOTO! SHE WAS AN AMAZING ARTIST. AND KIND OF MY IDOL.
SHE PAINTED *CITY RISING*, THE FAMOUS MASTERPIECE THEY'RE UNVEILING TONIGHT.
IT CAPTURES THE CITY'S REBIRTH AFTER THE GREAT CATASTROPHE OF 1906!
NEVER HEARD OF IT.

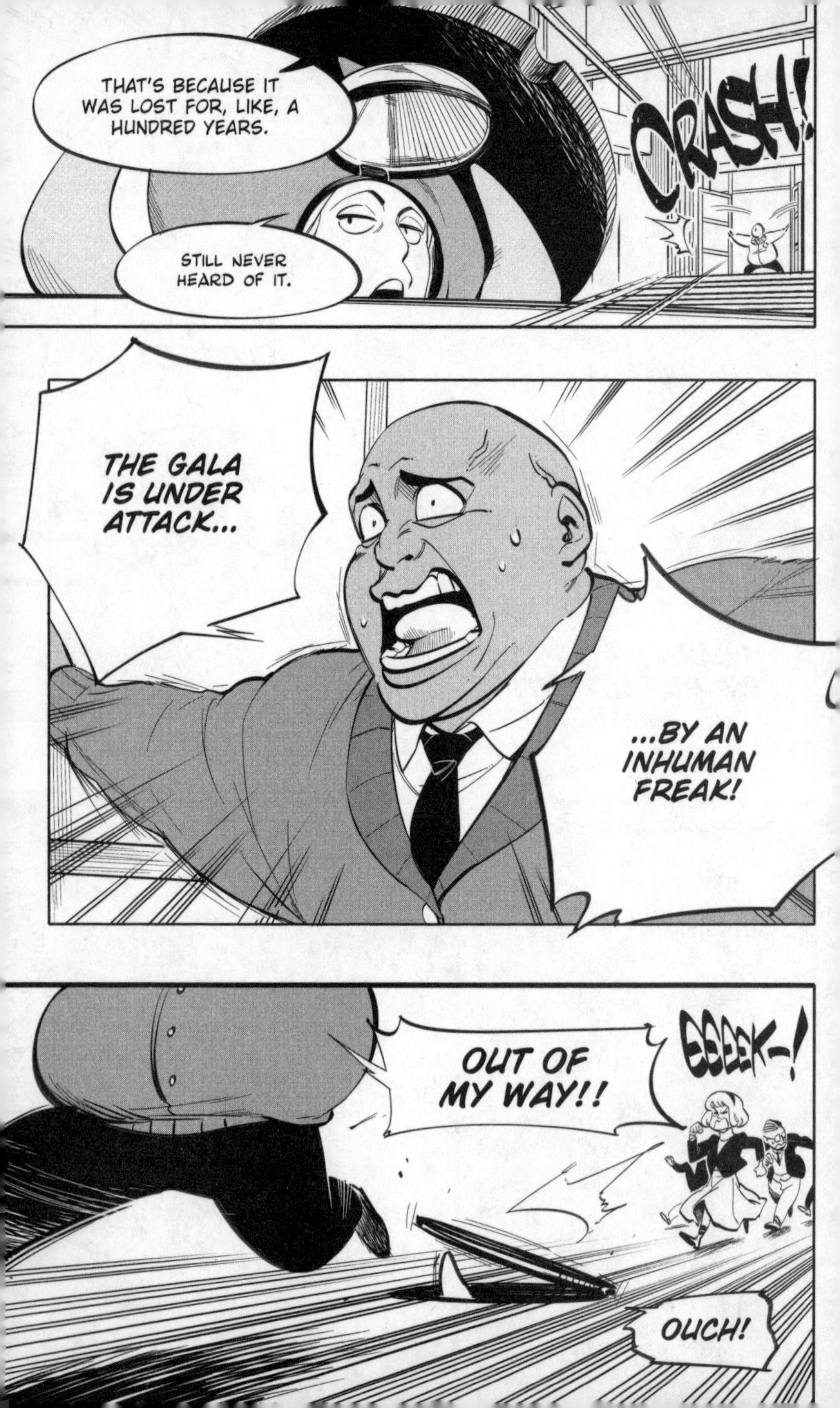
THAT'S BECAUSE IT WAS LOST FOR, LIKE, A HUNDRED YEARS.
STILL NEVER HEARD OF IT.
CRASH!
THE GALA IS UNDER ATTACK...
...BY AN INHUMAN FREAK!
OUT OF MY WAY!!
EEEEK—!
OUCH!

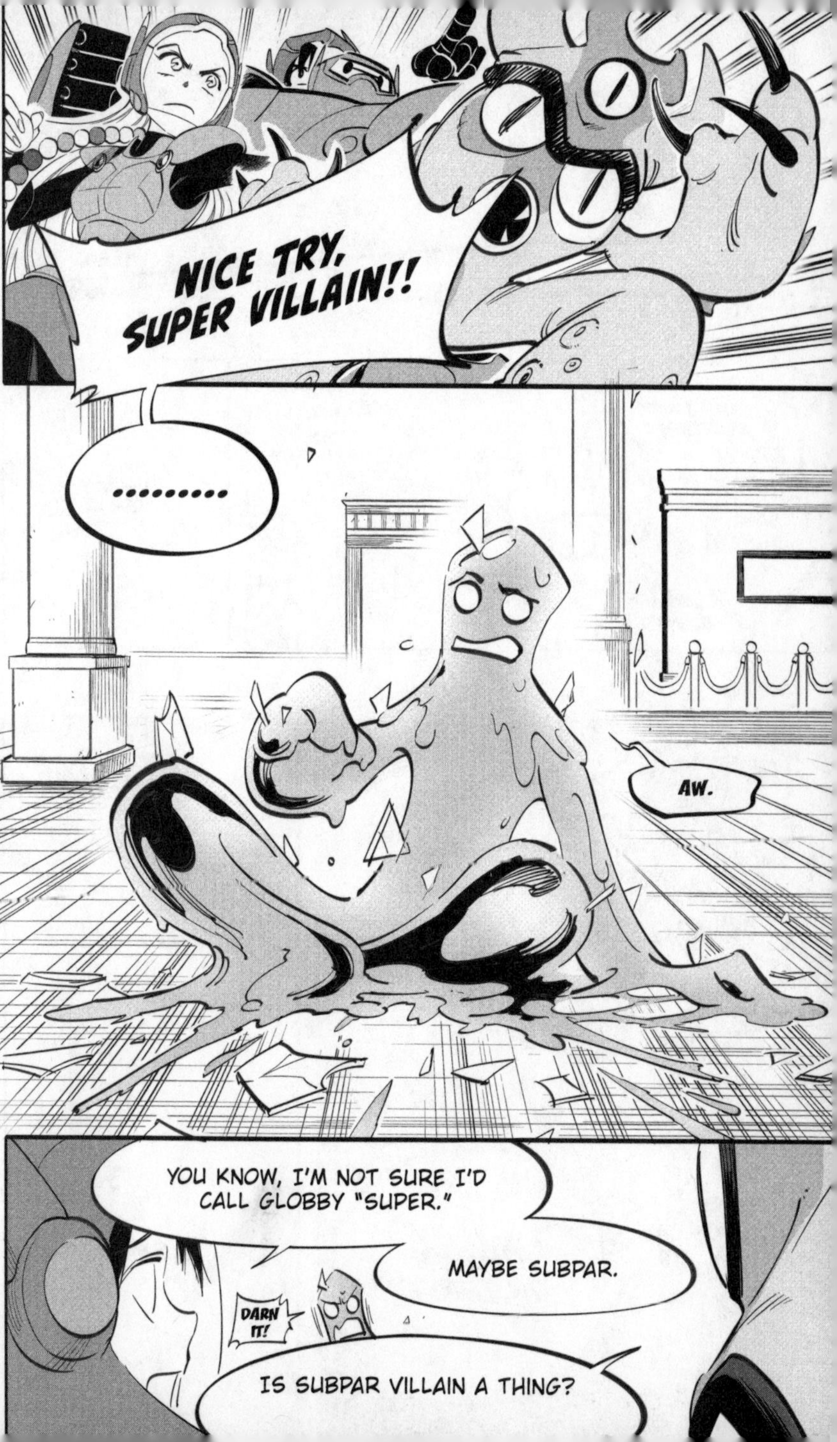

NICE TRY, SUPER VILLAIN!!
....
AW.
YOU KNOW, I'M NOT SURE I'D CALL GLOBBY "SUPER."
MAYBE SUBPAR.
DARN IT!
IS SUBPAR VILLAIN A THING?

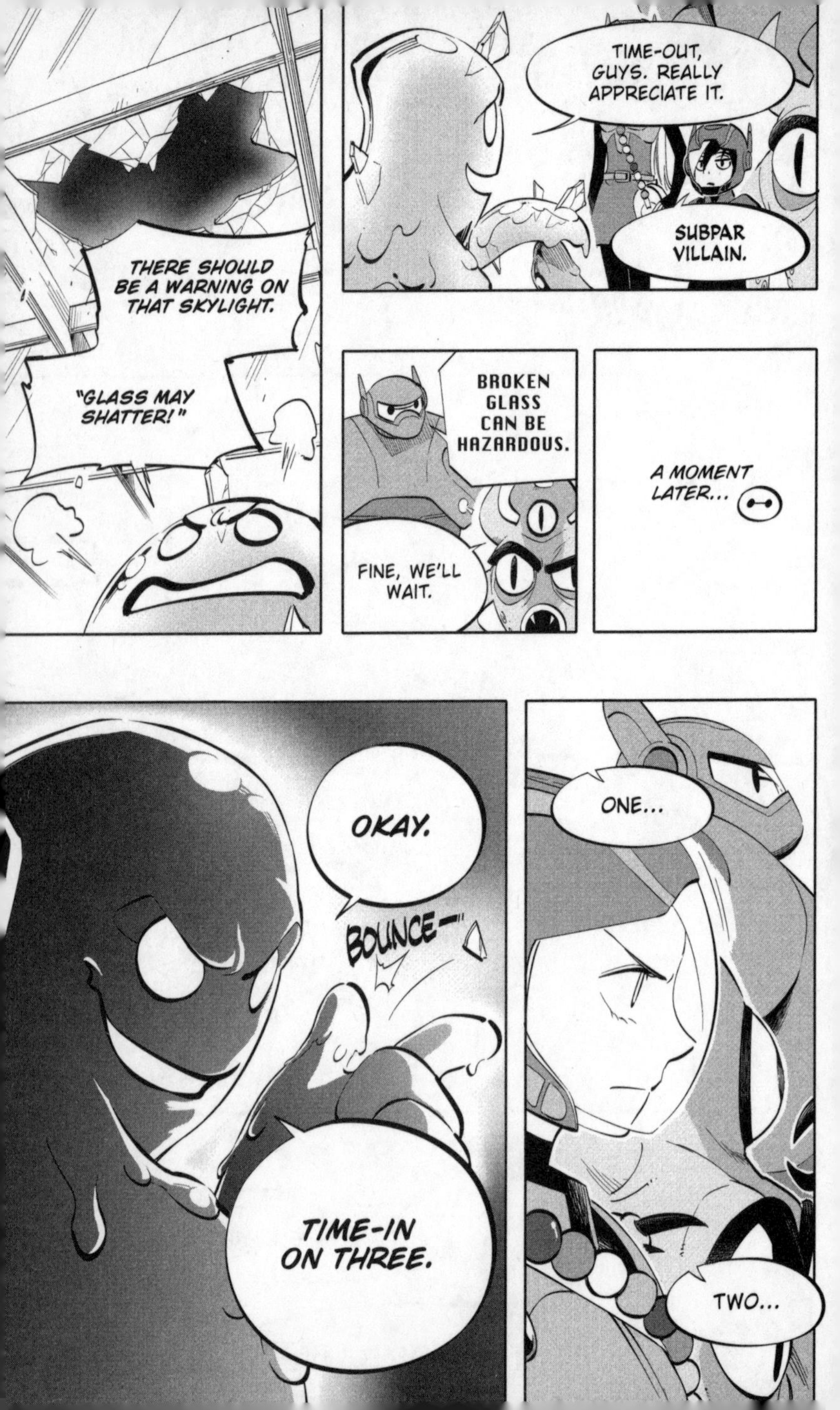
THERE SHOULD BE A WARNING ON THAT SKYLIGHT.
"GLASS MAY SHATTER!"
TIME-OUT, GUYS. REALLY APPRECIATE IT.
SUBPAR VILLAIN.
BROKEN GLASS CAN BE HAZARDOUS.
FINE, WE'LL WAIT.
A MOMENT LATER...
OKAY.
BOUNCE—
TIME-IN ON THREE.
ONE...
TWO...

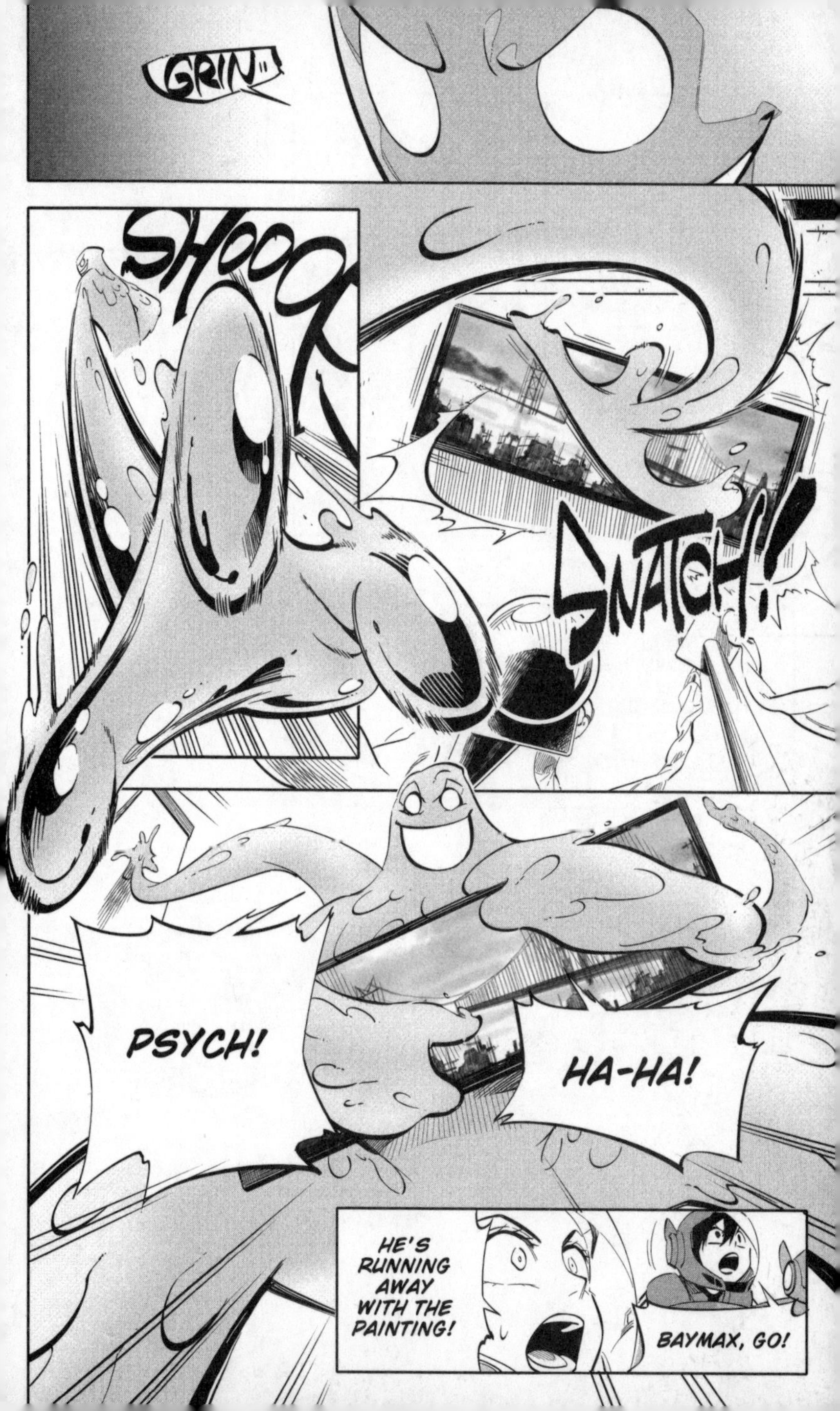
GRIN
SHOOOK
SNATCH!!
PSYCH!
HA-HA!
HE'S RUNNING AWAY WITH THE PAINTING!
BAYMAX, GO!

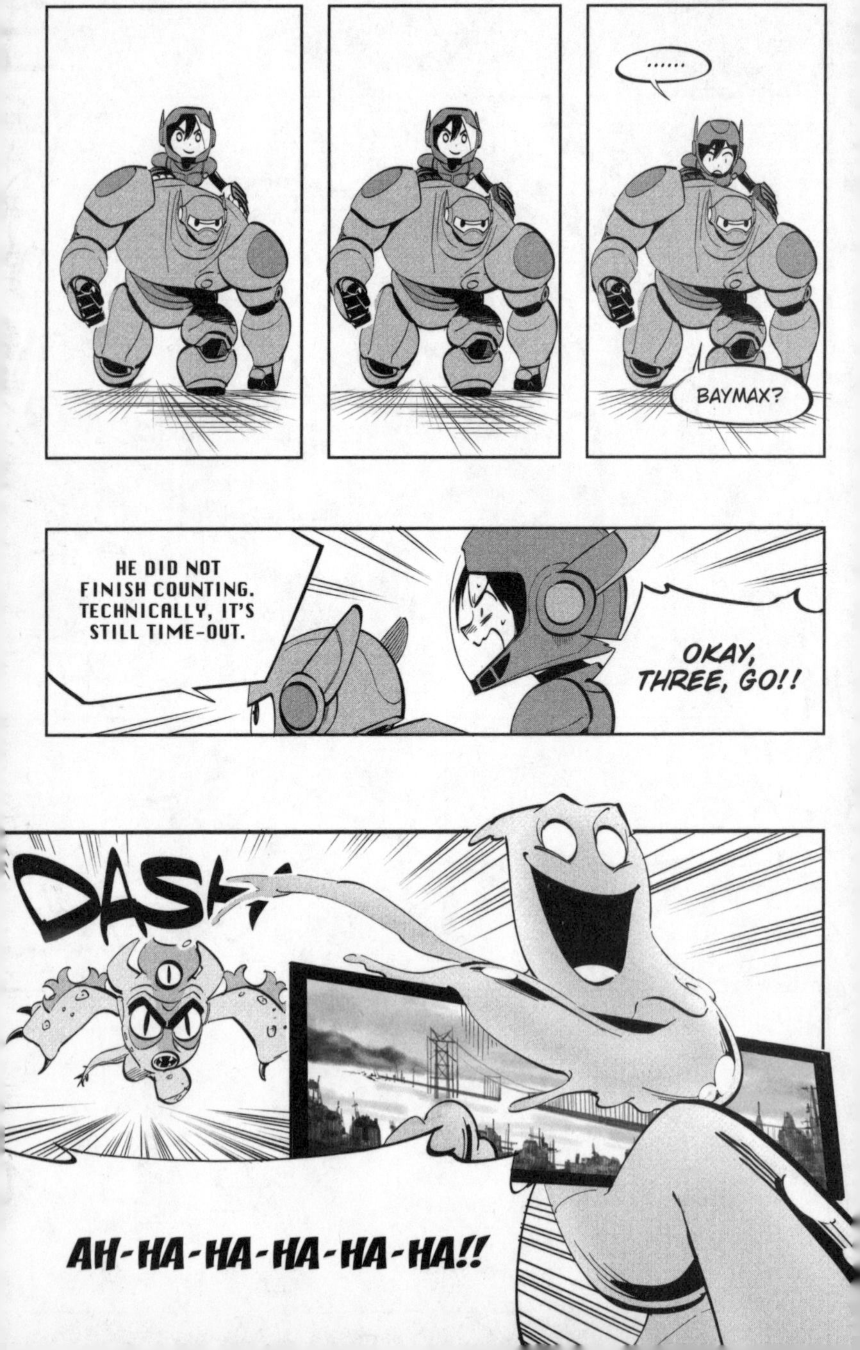

......
BAYMAX?
HE DID NOT FINISH COUNTING. TECHNICALLY, IT'S STILL TIME-OUT.
OKAY, THREE, GO!!
DASH
AH-HA-HA-HA-HA-HA!!

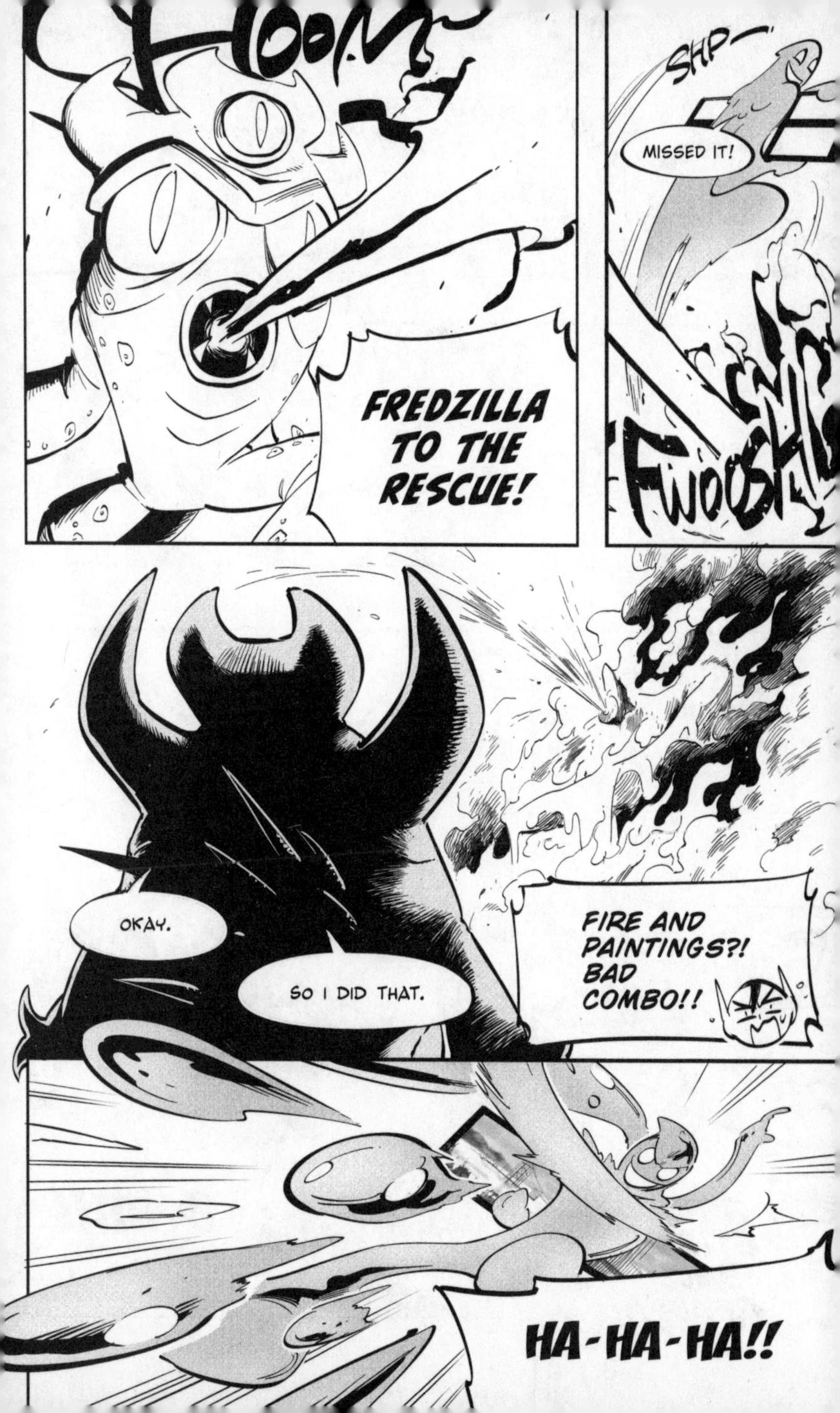
FREDZILLA TO THE RESCUE!
SHP—
MISSED IT!
OKAY.
SO I DID THAT.
FIRE AND PAINTINGS?! BAD COMBO!!
HA-HA-HA!!

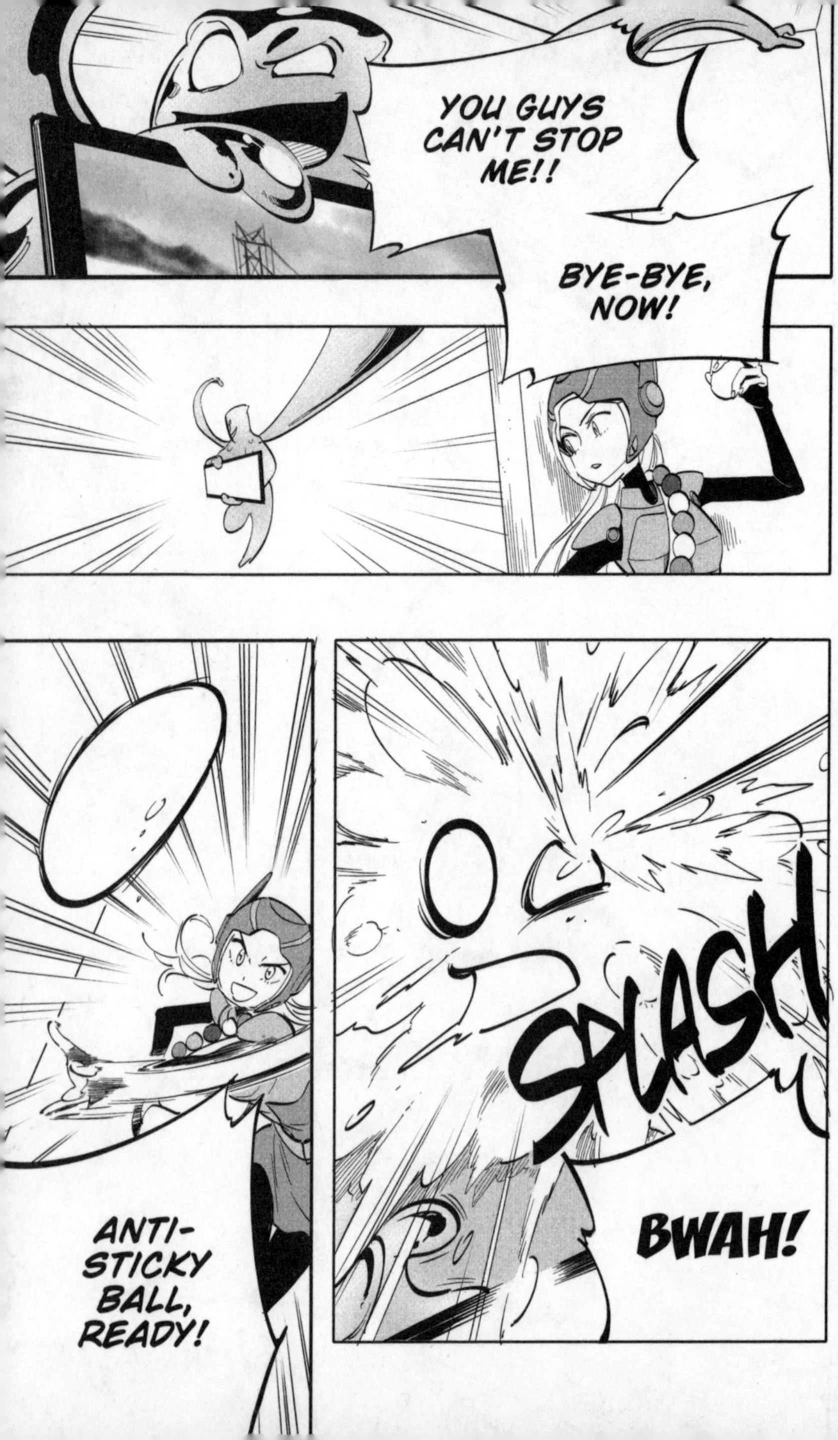
YOU GUYS CAN'T STOP ME!!
BYE-BYE, NOW!
ANTI-STICKY BALL, READY!
SPLASH
BWAH!

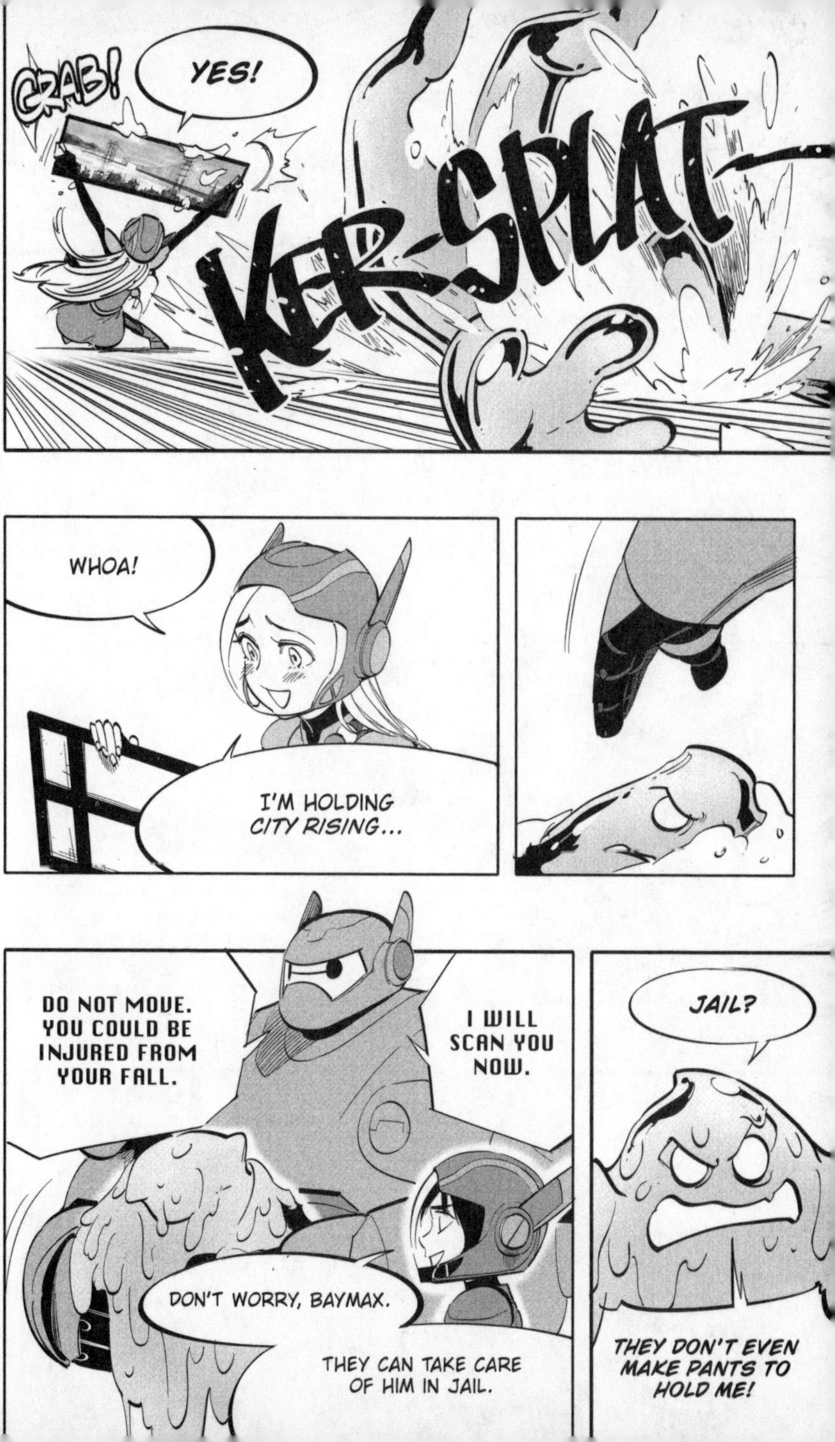

GRAB!
YES!
KER-SPLAT
WHOA!
I'M HOLDING CITY RISING...
DO NOT MOVE. YOU COULD BE INJURED FROM YOUR FALL.
I WILL SCAN YOU NOW.
DON'T WORRY, BAYMAX.
THEY CAN TAKE CARE OF HIM IN JAIL.
JAIL?
THEY DON'T EVEN MAKE PANTS TO HOLD ME!

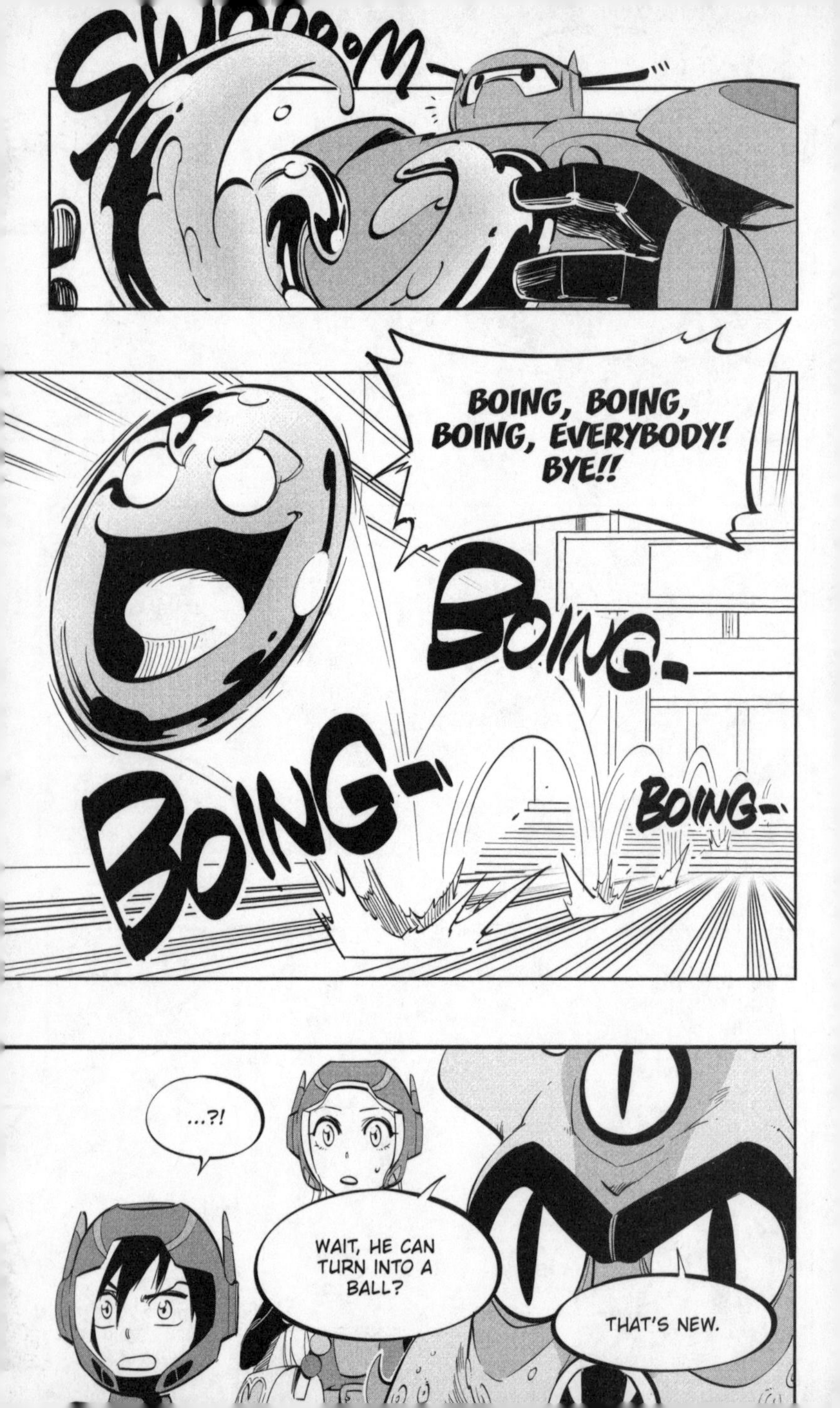
SWOOOOOM
BOING, BOING, BOING, EVERYBODY! BYE!!
BOING-
BOING-
BOING-
...?!
WAIT, HE CAN TURN INTO A BALL?
THAT'S NEW.

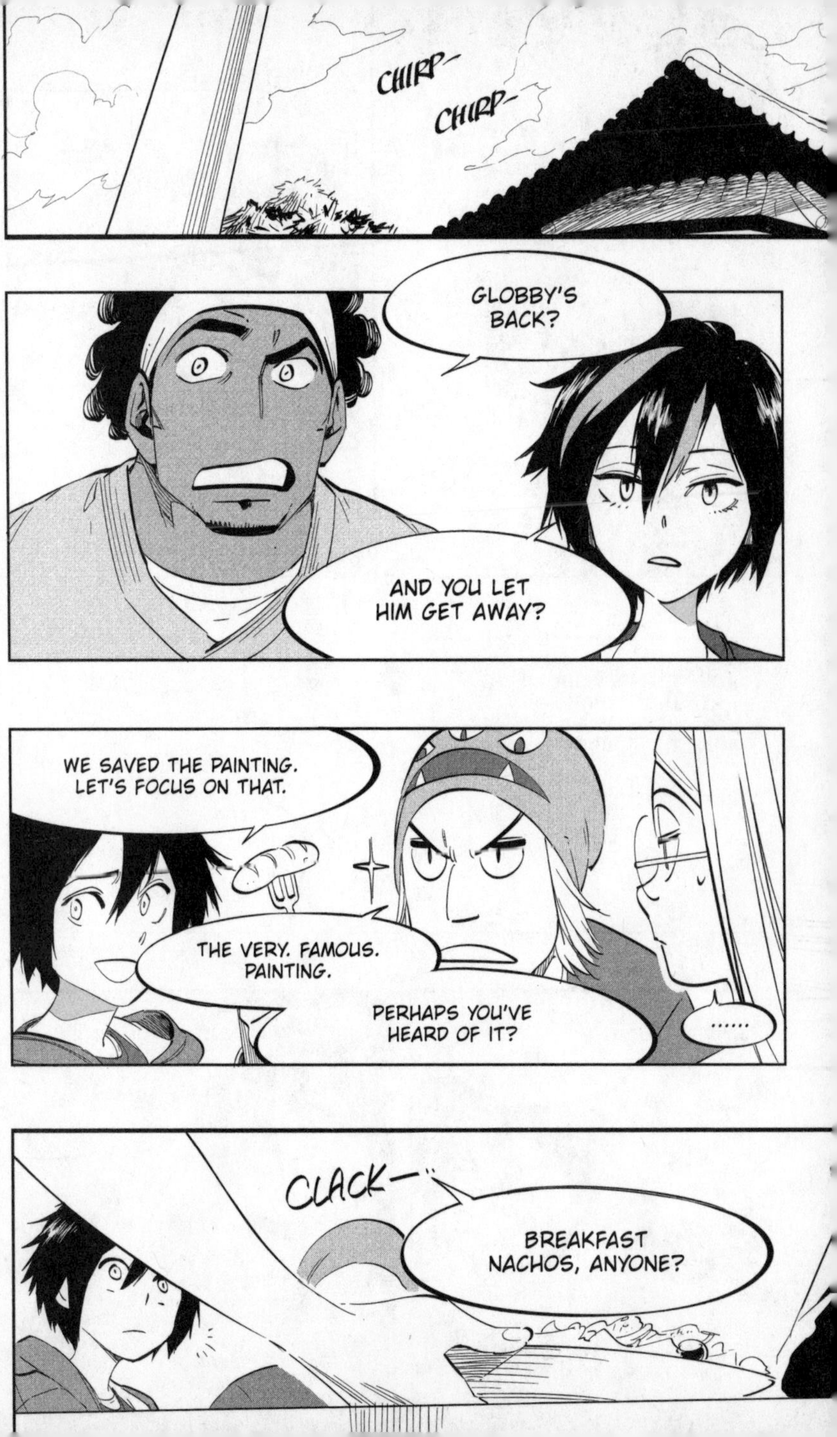
CHIRP-
CHIRP-
GLOBBY'S BACK?
AND YOU LET HIM GET AWAY?
WE SAVED THE PAINTING. LET'S FOCUS ON THAT.
THE VERY. FAMOUS. PAINTING.
PERHAPS YOU'VE HEARD OF IT?
......
CLACK-
BREAKFAST NACHOS, ANYONE?

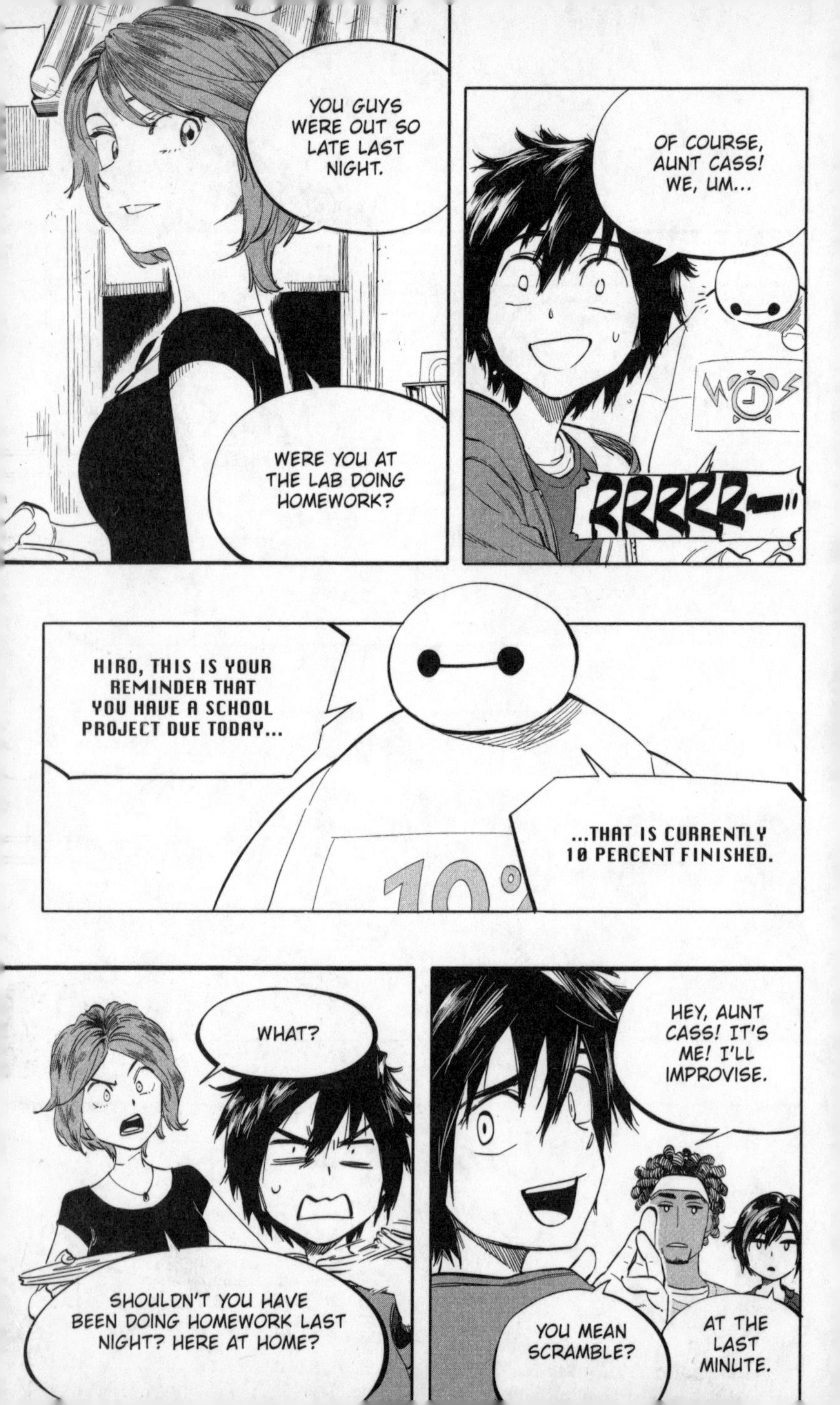
YOU GUYS WERE OUT SO LATE LAST NIGHT.
WERE YOU AT THE LAB DOING HOMEWORK?
OF COURSE, AUNT CASS! WE, UM...
RRRRR—!!
HIRO, THIS IS YOUR REMINDER THAT YOU HAVE A SCHOOL PROJECT DUE TODAY...
...THAT IS CURRENTLY 10 PERCENT FINISHED.
WHAT?
SHOULDN'T YOU HAVE BEEN DOING HOMEWORK LAST NIGHT? HERE AT HOME?
HEY, AUNT CASS! IT'S ME! I'LL IMPROVISE.
YOU MEAN SCRAMBLE?
AT THE LAST MINUTE.

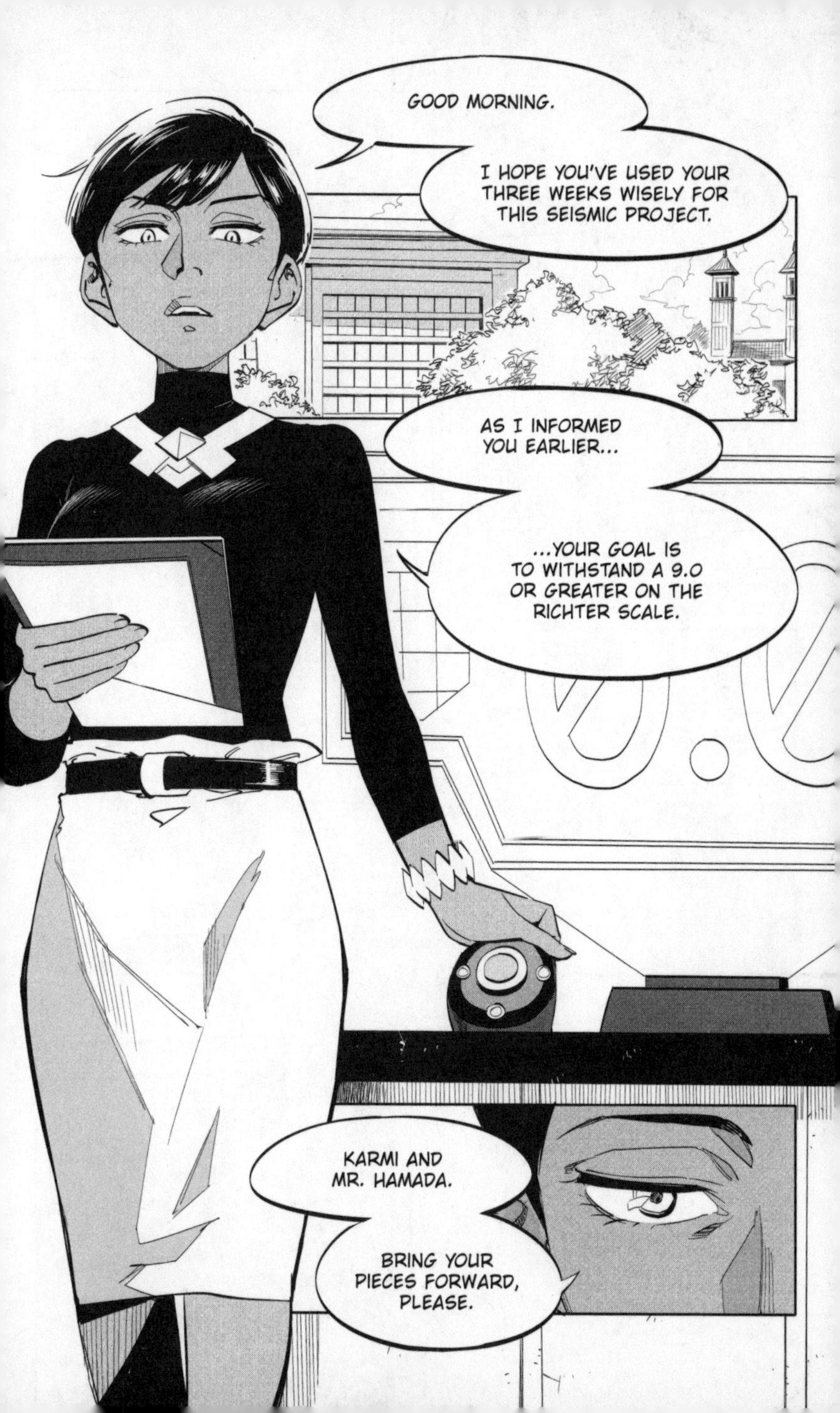
GOOD MORNING.
I HOPE YOU'VE USED YOUR THREE WEEKS WISELY FOR THIS SEISMIC PROJECT.
AS I INFORMED YOU EARLIER...
...YOUR GOAL IS TO WITHSTAND A 9.0 OR GREATER ON THE RICHTER SCALE.
KARMI AND MR. HAMADA.
BRING YOUR PIECES FORWARD, PLEASE.

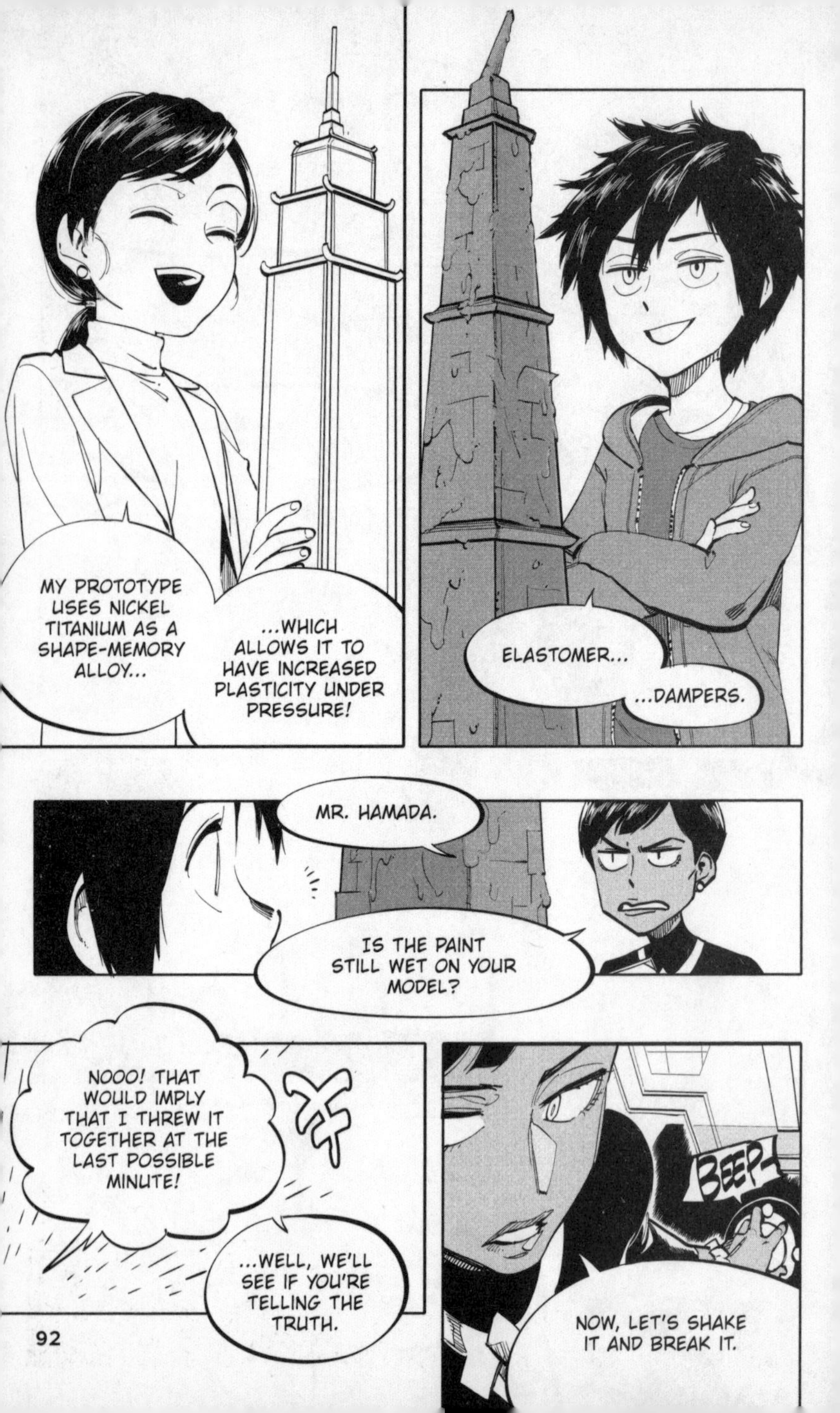

MY PROTOTYPE USES NICKEL TITANIUM AS A SHAPE-MEMORY ALLOY...
...WHICH ALLOWS IT TO HAVE INCREASED PLASTICITY UNDER PRESSURE!
ELASTOMER...
...DAMPERS.
MR. HAMADA.
IS THE PAINT STILL WET ON YOUR MODEL?
NOOO! THAT WOULD IMPLY THAT I THREW IT TOGETHER AT THE LAST POSSIBLE MINUTE!
...WELL, WE'LL SEE IF YOU'RE TELLING THE TRUTH.
BEEP-
NOW, LET'S SHAKE IT AND BREAK IT.

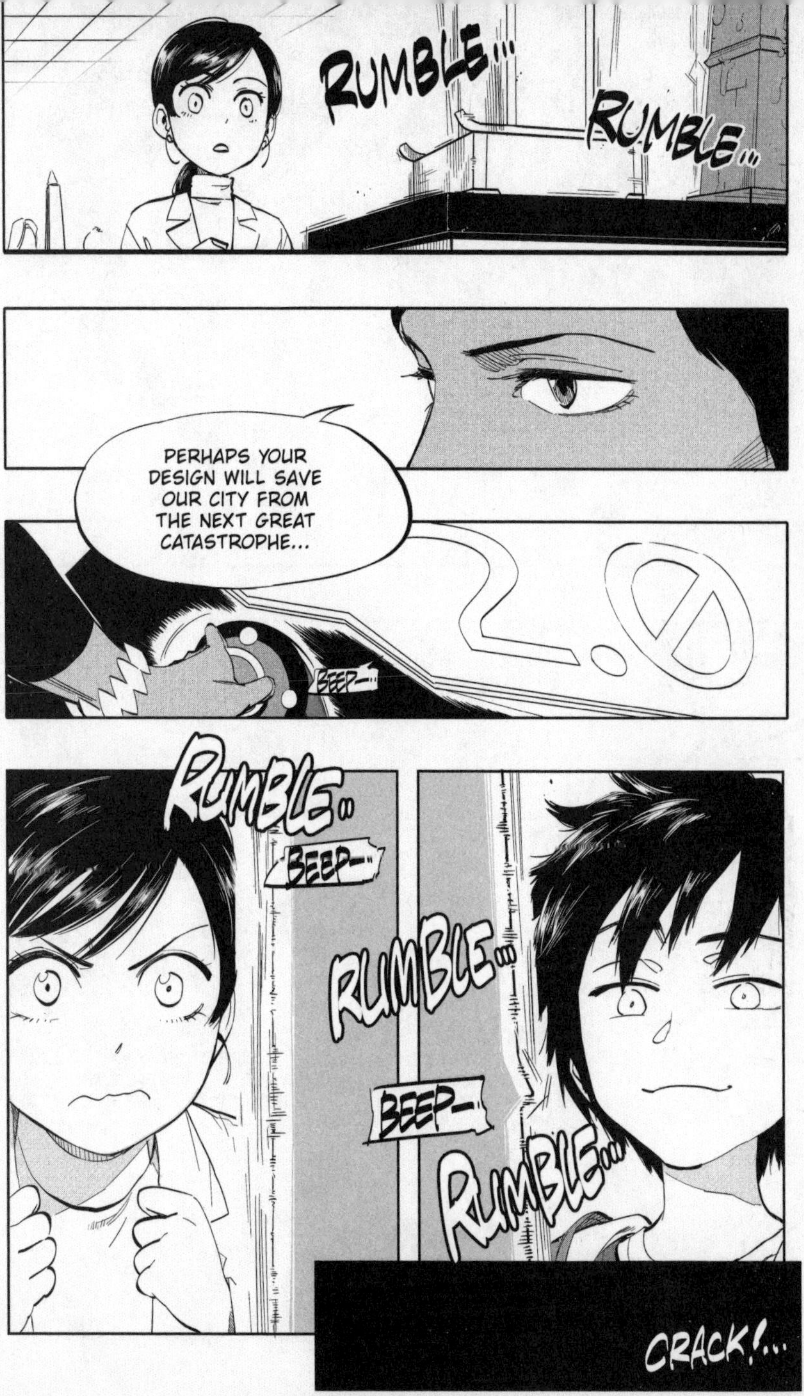
RUMBLE...
RUMBLE...
PERHAPS YOUR DESIGN WILL SAVE OUR CITY FROM THE NEXT GREAT CATASTROPHE...
2.0
BEEP—
RUMBLE..
BEEP—
RUMBLE...
BEEP—
RUMBLE...
CRACK!...

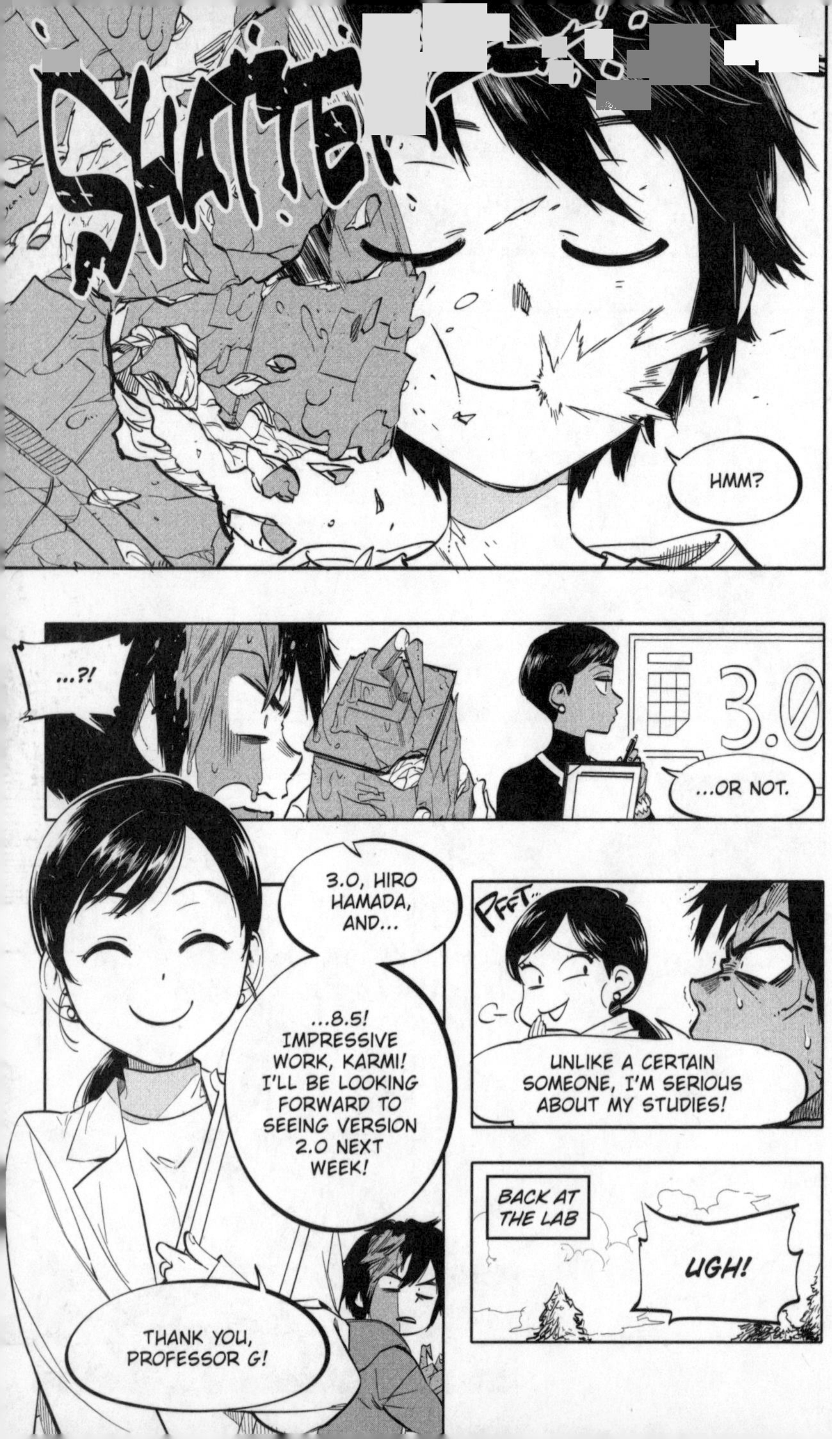
HMM?
...?!
...OR NOT.
3.0, HIRO HAMADA, AND...
...8.5! IMPRESSIVE WORK, KARMI! I'LL BE LOOKING FORWARD TO SEEING VERSION 2.0 NEXT WEEK!
THANK YOU, PROFESSOR G!
PFFT...
UNLIKE A CERTAIN SOMEONE, I'M SERIOUS ABOUT MY STUDIES!
BACK AT THE LAB
UGH!

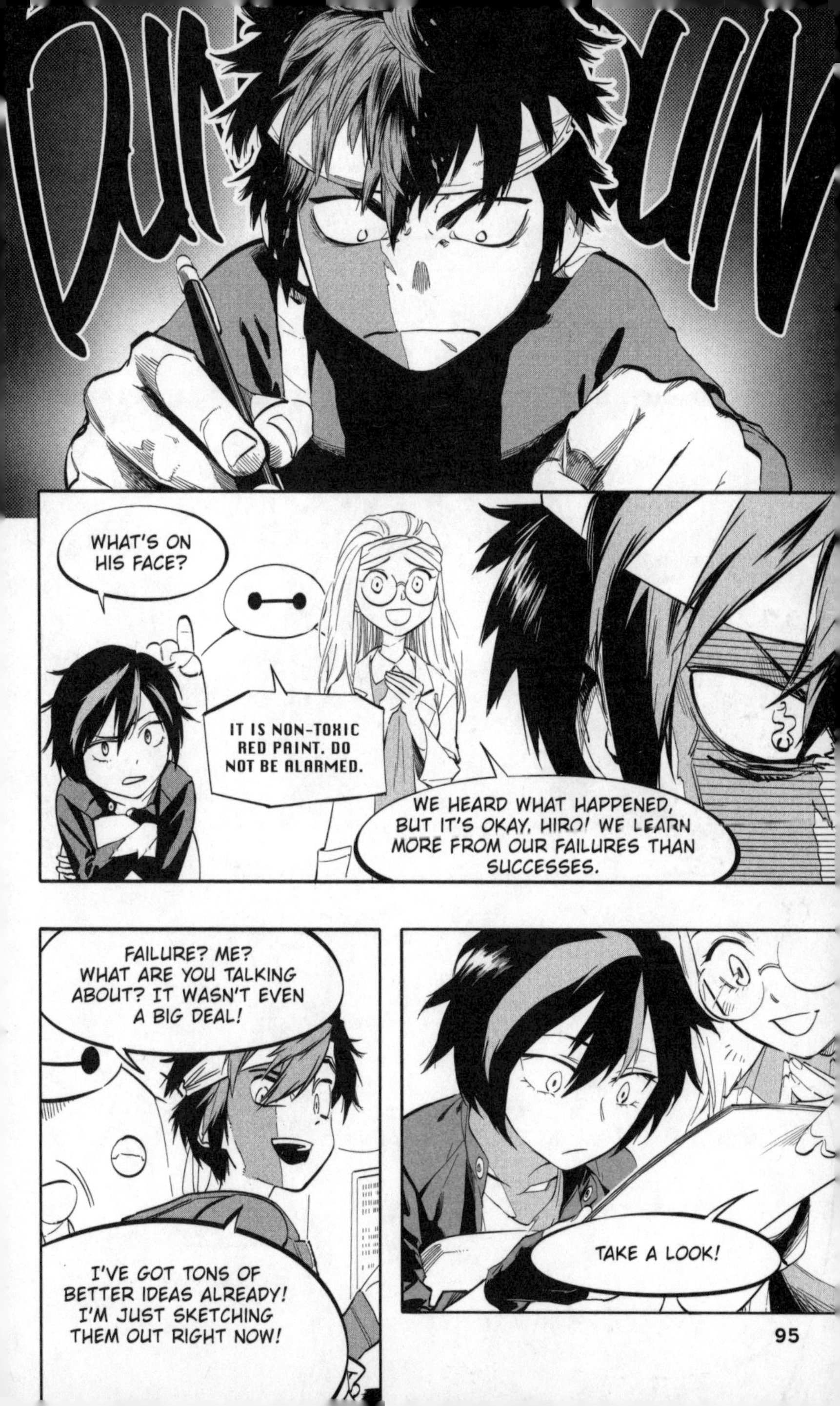
DUN DUN
WHAT'S ON HIS FACE?
IT IS NON-TOXIC RED PAINT. DO NOT BE ALARMED.
WE HEARD WHAT HAPPENED, BUT IT'S OKAY, HIRO! WE LEARN MORE FROM OUR FAILURES THAN SUCCESSES.
FAILURE? ME? WHAT ARE YOU TALKING ABOUT? IT WASN'T EVEN A BIG DEAL!
I'VE GOT TONS OF BETTER IDEAS ALREADY! I'M JUST SKETCHING THEM OUT RIGHT NOW!
TAKE A LOOK!

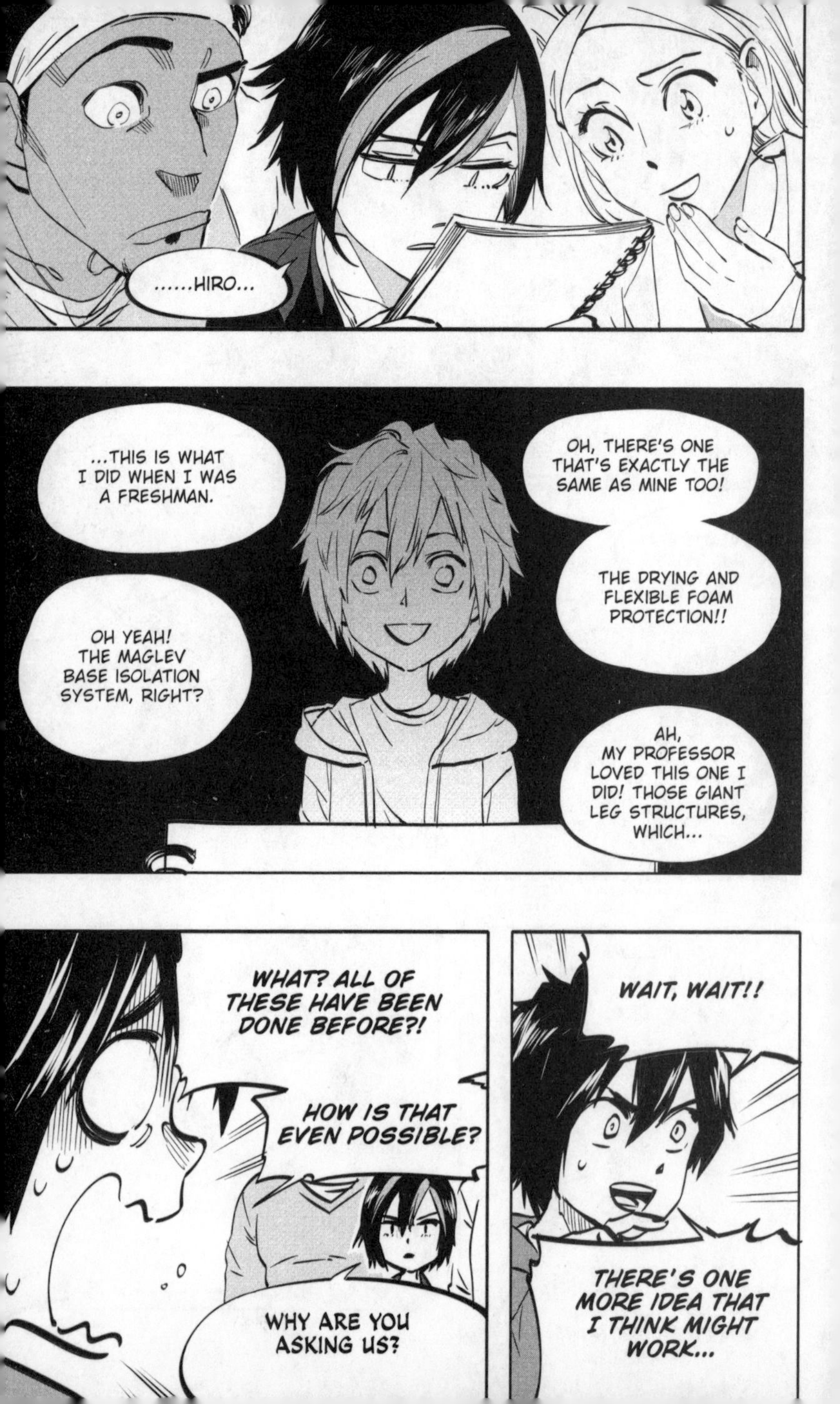
......HIRO...
...THIS IS WHAT I DID WHEN I WAS A FRESHMAN.
OH YEAH! THE MAGLEV BASE ISOLATION SYSTEM, RIGHT?
OH, THERE'S ONE THAT'S EXACTLY THE SAME AS MINE TOO!
THE DRYING AND FLEXIBLE FOAM PROTECTION!!
AH, MY PROFESSOR LOVED THIS ONE I DID! THOSE GIANT LEG STRUCTURES, WHICH...
WHAT? ALL OF THESE HAVE BEEN DONE BEFORE?!
HOW IS THAT EVEN POSSIBLE?
WHY ARE YOU ASKING US?
WAIT, WAIT!!
THERE'S ONE MORE IDEA THAT I THINK MIGHT WORK...

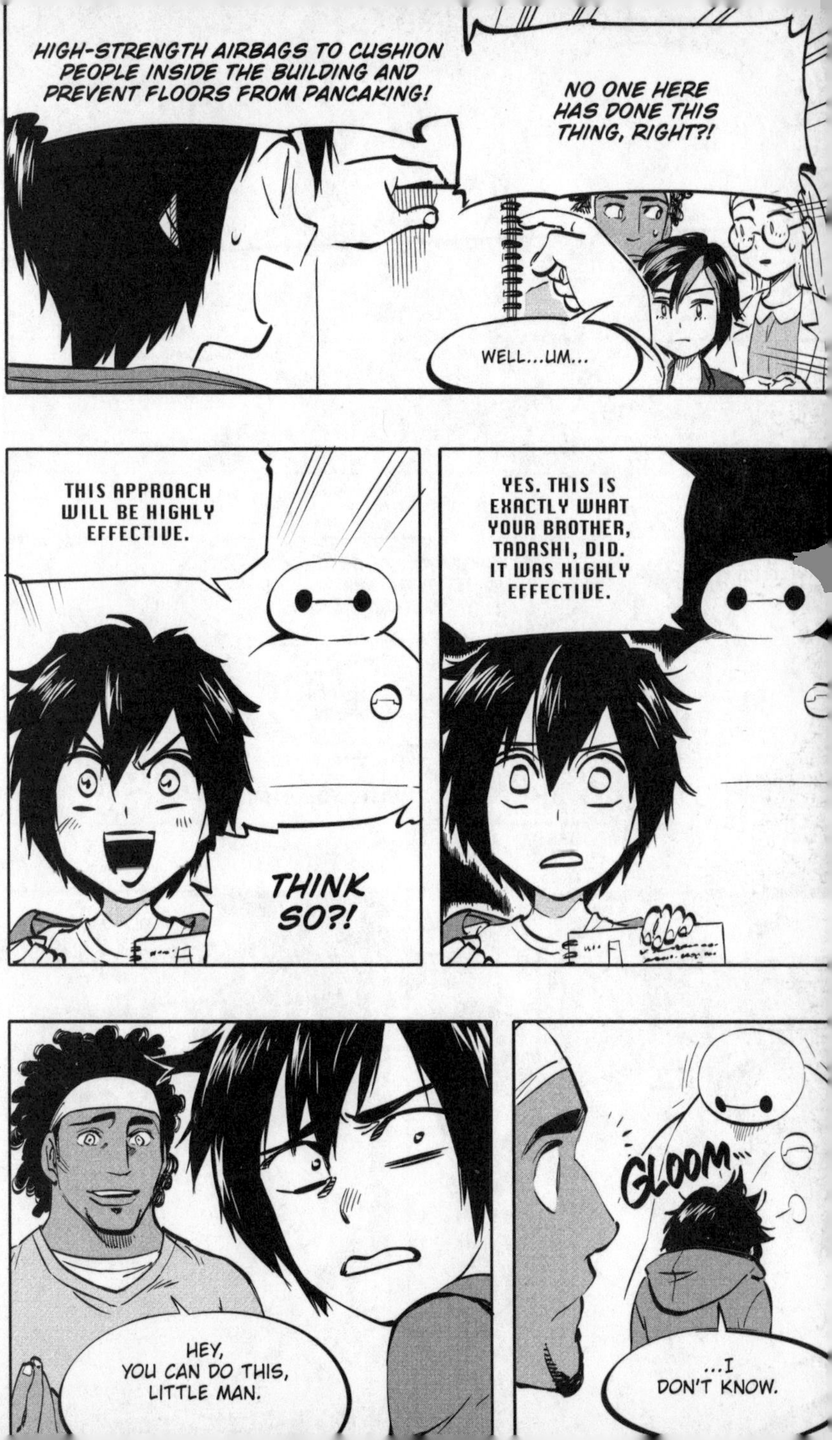
HIGH-STRENGTH AIRBAGS TO CUSHION PEOPLE INSIDE THE BUILDING AND PREVENT FLOORS FROM PANCAKING!
NO ONE HERE HAS DONE THIS THING, RIGHT?!
WELL...UM...
THIS APPROACH WILL BE HIGHLY EFFECTIVE.
THINK SO?!
YES. THIS IS EXACTLY WHAT YOUR BROTHER, TADASHI, DID. IT WAS HIGHLY EFFECTIVE.
HEY, YOU CAN DO THIS, LITTLE MAN.
GLOOM
...I DON'T KNOW.

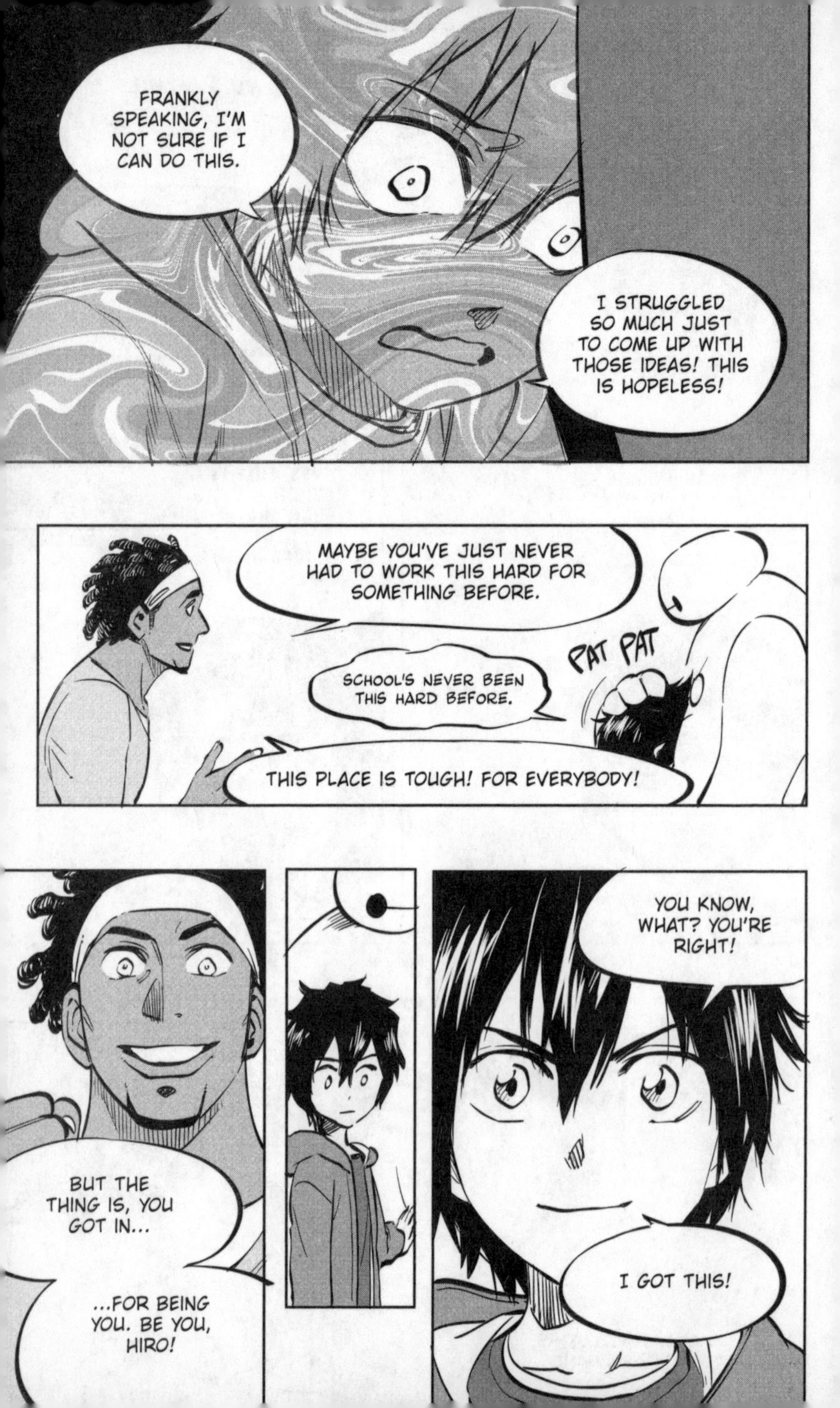
FRANKLY SPEAKING, I'M NOT SURE IF I CAN DO THIS.
I STRUGGLED SO MUCH JUST TO COME UP WITH THOSE IDEAS! THIS IS HOPELESS!
MAYBE YOU'VE JUST NEVER HAD TO WORK THIS HARD FOR SOMETHING BEFORE.
SCHOOL'S NEVER BEEN THIS HARD BEFORE.
PAT PAT
THIS PLACE IS TOUGH! FOR EVERYBODY!
BUT THE THING IS, YOU GOT IN...
...FOR BEING YOU. BE YOU, HIRO!
YOU KNOW, WHAT? YOU'RE RIGHT!
I GOT THIS!

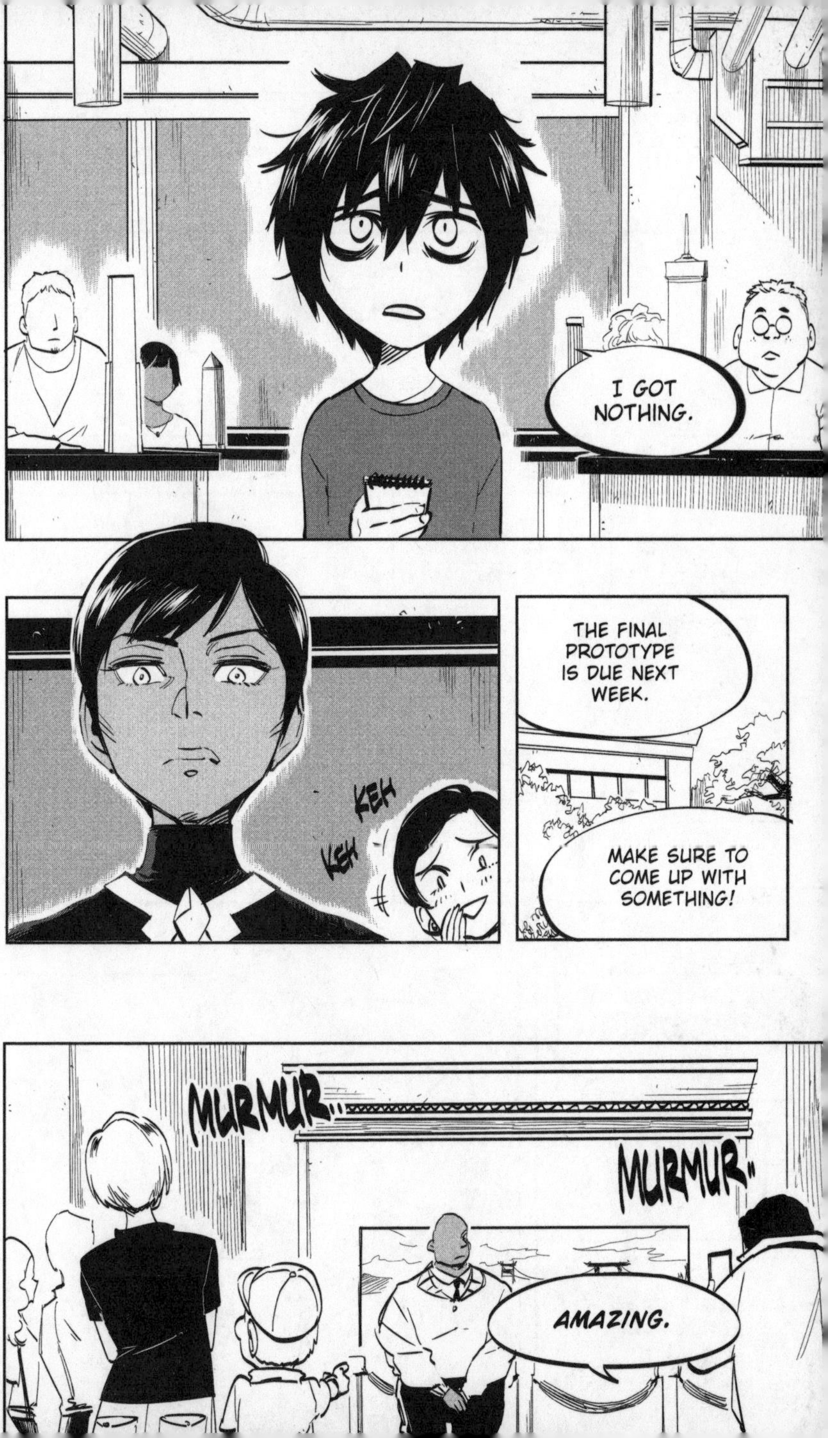
I GOT NOTHING.
KEH
KEH
THE FINAL PROTOTYPE IS DUE NEXT WEEK.
MAKE SURE TO COME UP WITH SOMETHING!
MURMUR..
MURMUR..
AMAZING.

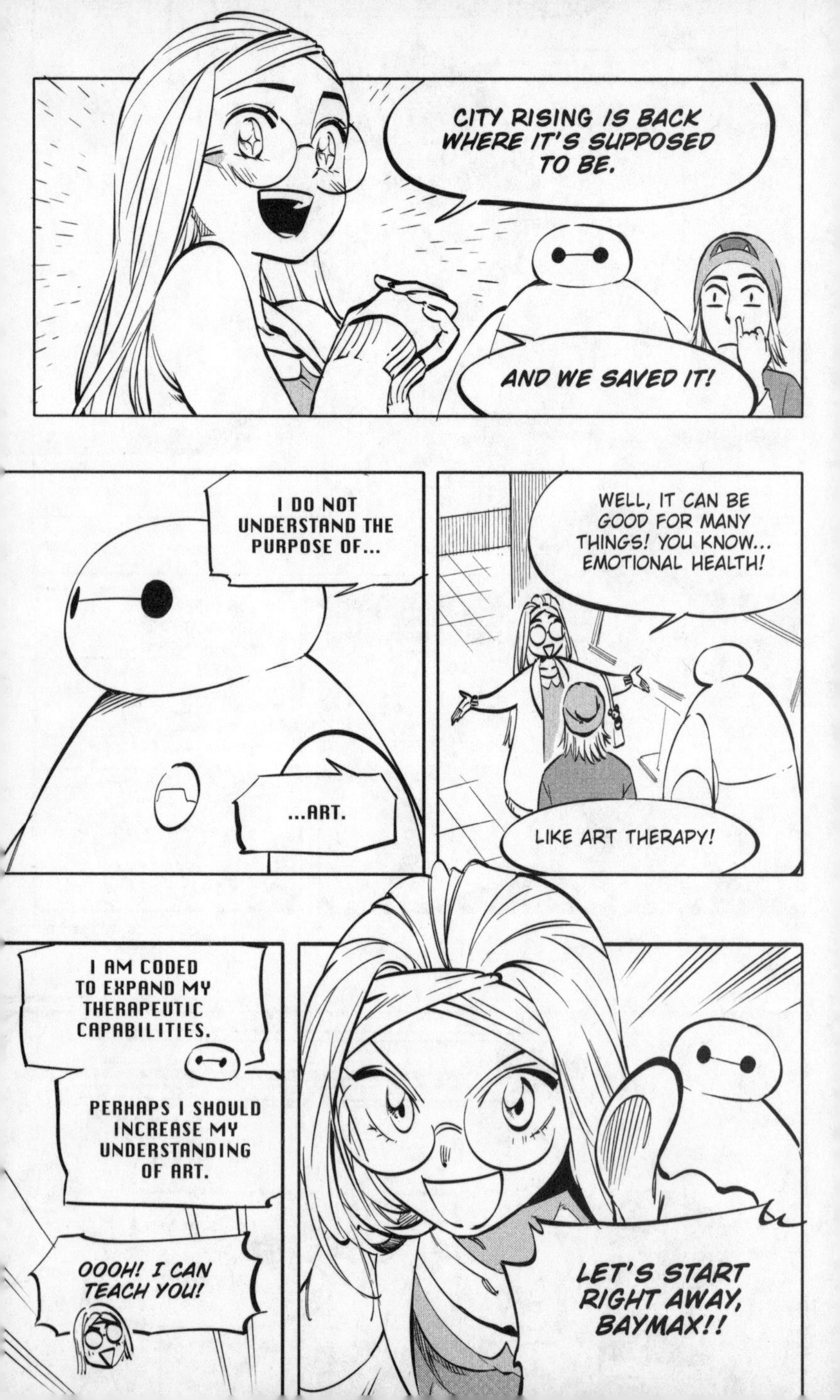
CITY RISING IS BACK WHERE IT'S SUPPOSED TO BE.
AND WE SAVED IT!
I DO NOT UNDERSTAND THE PURPOSE OF...
...ART.
WELL, IT CAN BE GOOD FOR MANY THINGS! YOU KNOW... EMOTIONAL HEALTH!
LIKE ART THERAPY!
I AM CODED TO EXPAND MY THERAPEUTIC CAPABILITIES.
PERHAPS I SHOULD INCREASE MY UNDERSTANDING OF ART.
OOOH! I CAN TEACH YOU!
LET'S START RIGHT AWAY, BAYMAX!!

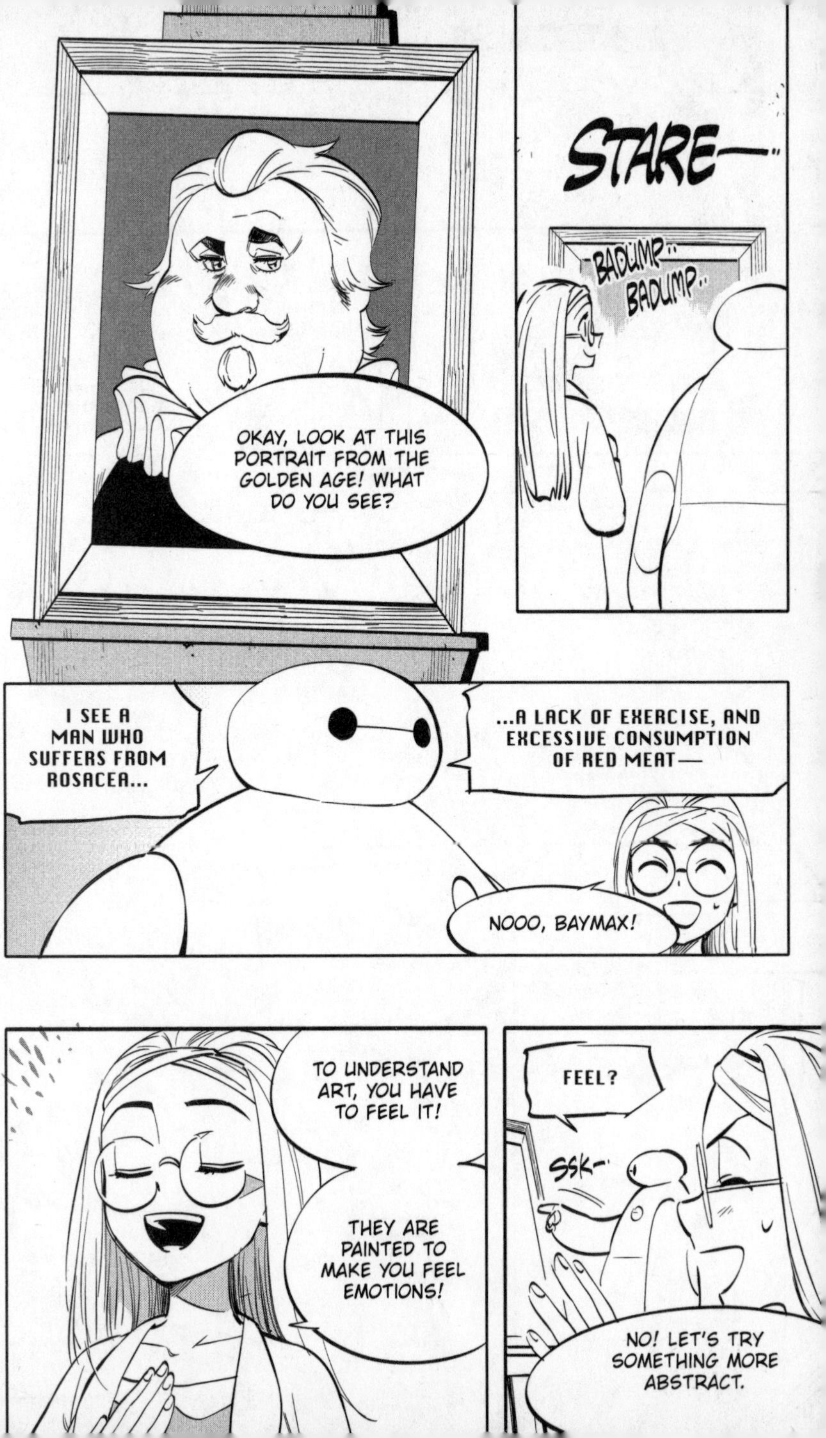
OKAY, LOOK AT THIS PORTRAIT FROM THE GOLDEN AGE! WHAT DO YOU SEE?
STARE—
BADUMP...
BADUMP...
I SEE A MAN WHO SUFFERS FROM ROSACEA...
...A LACK OF EXERCISE, AND EXCESSIVE CONSUMPTION OF RED MEAT—
NOOO, BAYMAX!
TO UNDERSTAND ART, YOU HAVE TO FEEL IT!
THEY ARE PAINTED TO MAKE YOU FEEL EMOTIONS!
FEEL?
SSK-
NO! LET'S TRY SOMETHING MORE ABSTRACT.

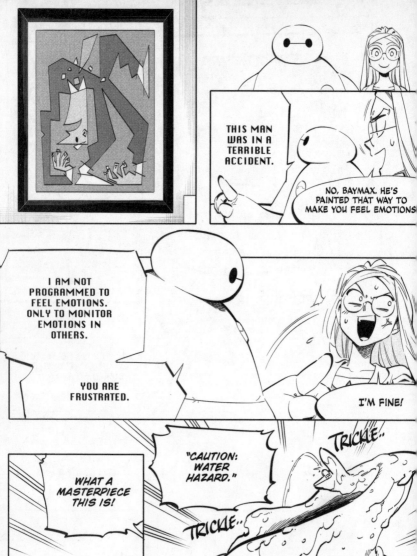

THIS MAN WAS IN A TERRIBLE ACCIDENT.

NO, BAYMAX. HE'S PAINTED THAT WAY TO MAKE YOU FEEL EMOTIONS

I AM NOT PROGRAMMED TO FEEL EMOTIONS. ONLY TO MONITOR EMOTIONS IN OTHERS.

YOU ARE FRUSTRATED.

I'M FINE!

WHAT A MASTERPIECE THIS IS!

"CAUTION: WATER HAZARD."

TRICKLE..

TRICKLE..

SUCH A BOLD STATEMENT ABOUT THE FUTILITY OF EXISTENCE!

CAUTION

WATER HAZARD

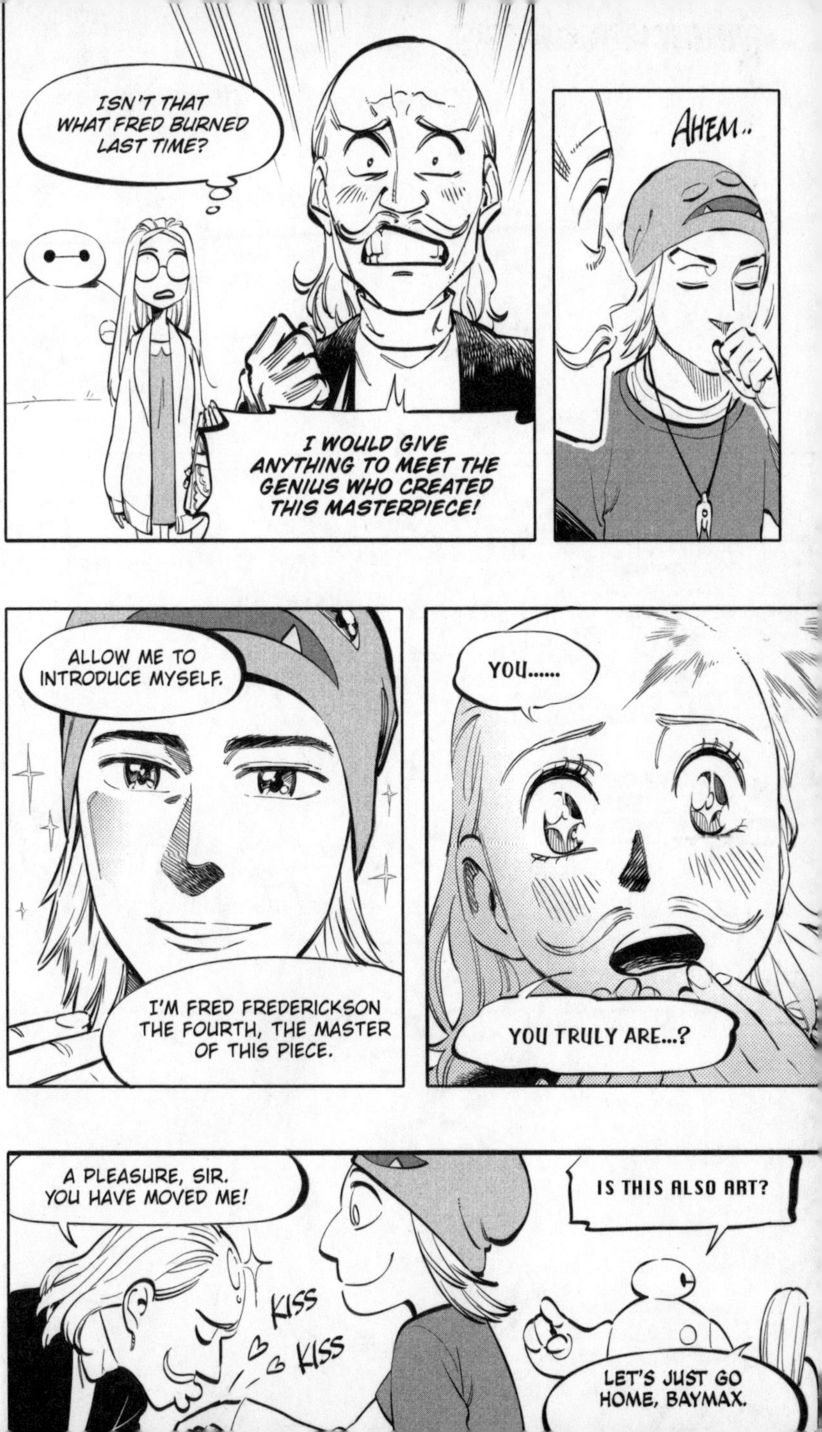
ISN'T THAT WHAT FRED BURNED LAST TIME?
I WOULD GIVE ANYTHING TO MEET THE GENIUS WHO CREATED THIS MASTERPIECE!
AHEM..
ALLOW ME TO INTRODUCE MYSELF.
I'M FRED FREDERICKSON THE FOURTH, THE MASTER OF THIS PIECE.
YOU......
YOU TRULY ARE...?
A PLEASURE, SIR. YOU HAVE MOVED ME!
KISS
KISS
IS THIS ALSO ART?
LET'S JUST GO HOME, BAYMAX.

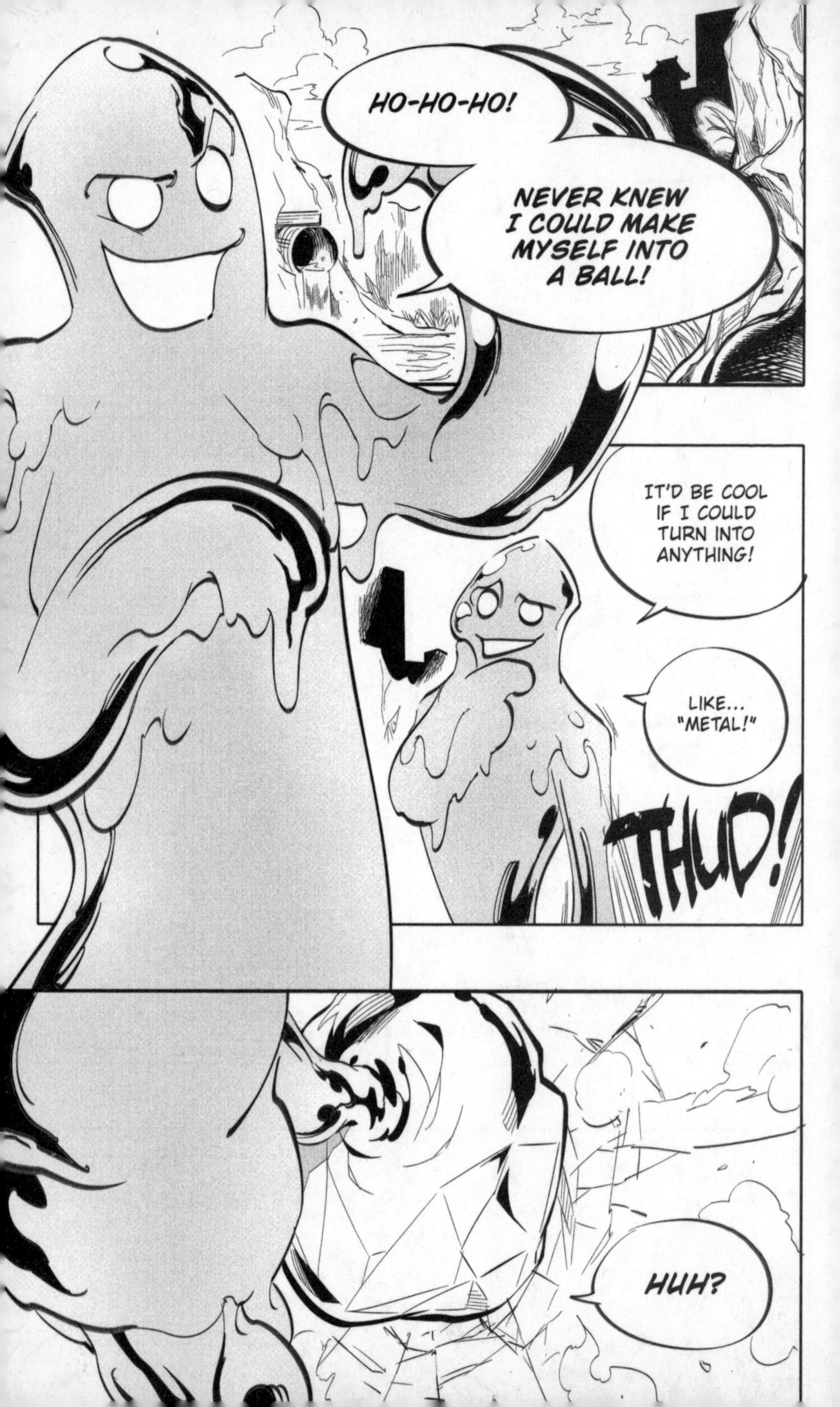
HO-HO-HO!
NEVER KNEW I COULD MAKE MYSELF INTO A BALL!
IT'D BE COOL IF I COULD TURN INTO ANYTHING!
LIKE... "METAL!"
THUD!
HUH?

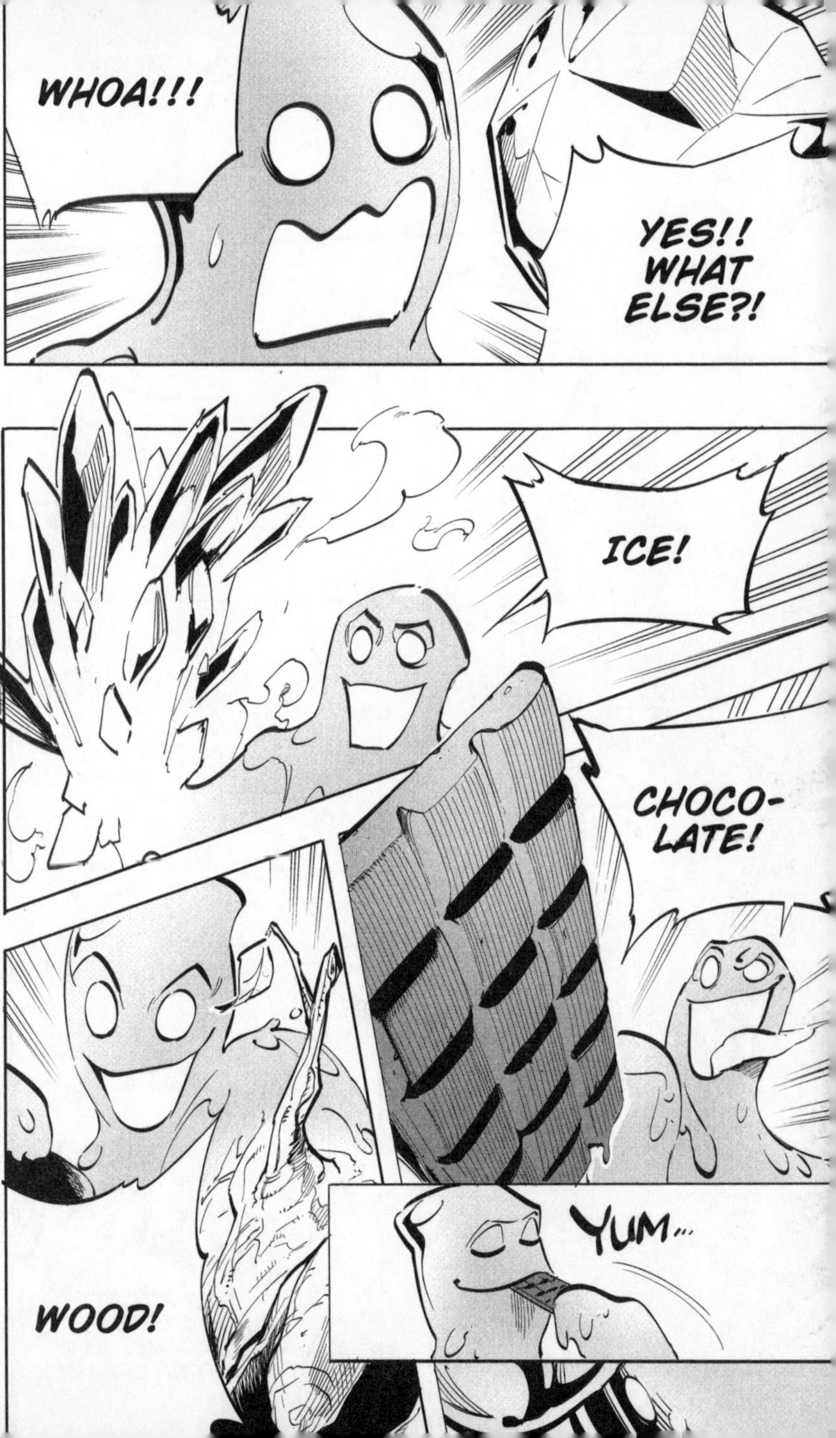
WHOA!!!
YES!! WHAT ELSE?!
ICE!
CHOCO-LATE!
WOOD!
YUM...

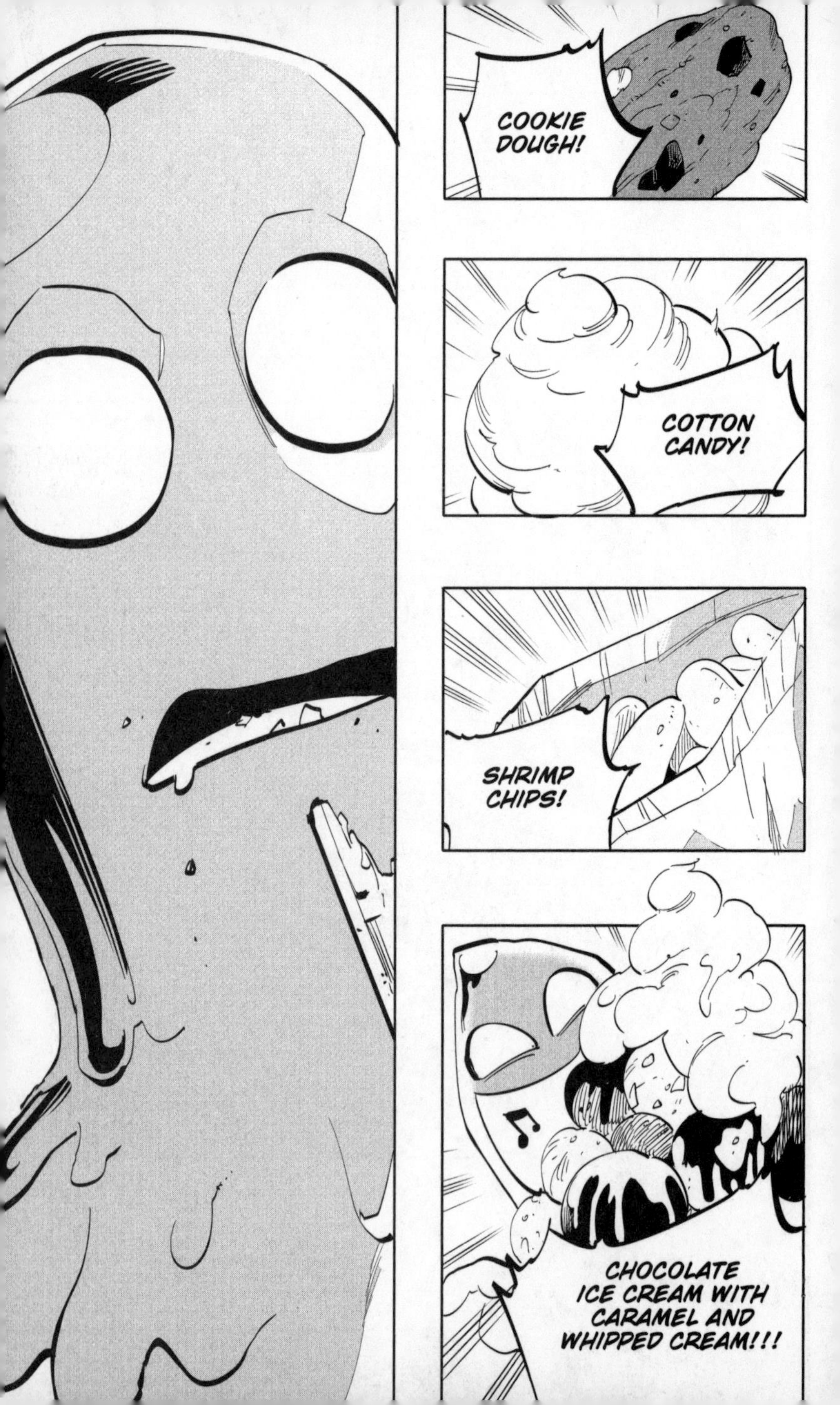
COOKIE DOUGH!
COTTON CANDY!
SHRIMP CHIPS!
CHOCOLATE ICE CREAM WITH CARAMEL AND WHIPPED CREAM!!!

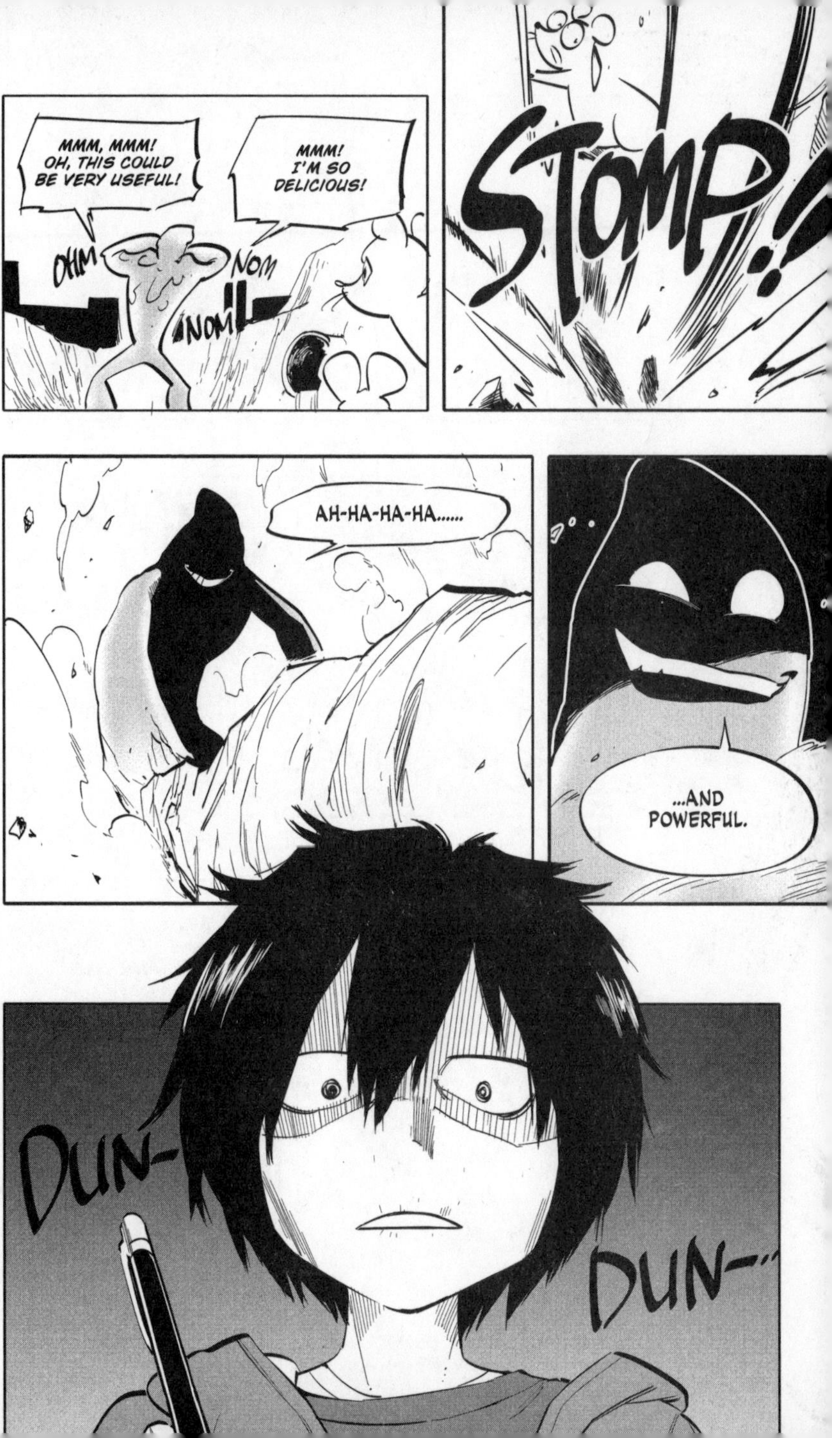
MMM, MMM! OH, THIS COULD BE VERY USEFUL!
MMM! I'M SO DELICIOUS!
OHM
NOM
NOM
STOMP!!
AH-HA-HA-HA......
...AND POWERFUL.
DUN-
DUN-...

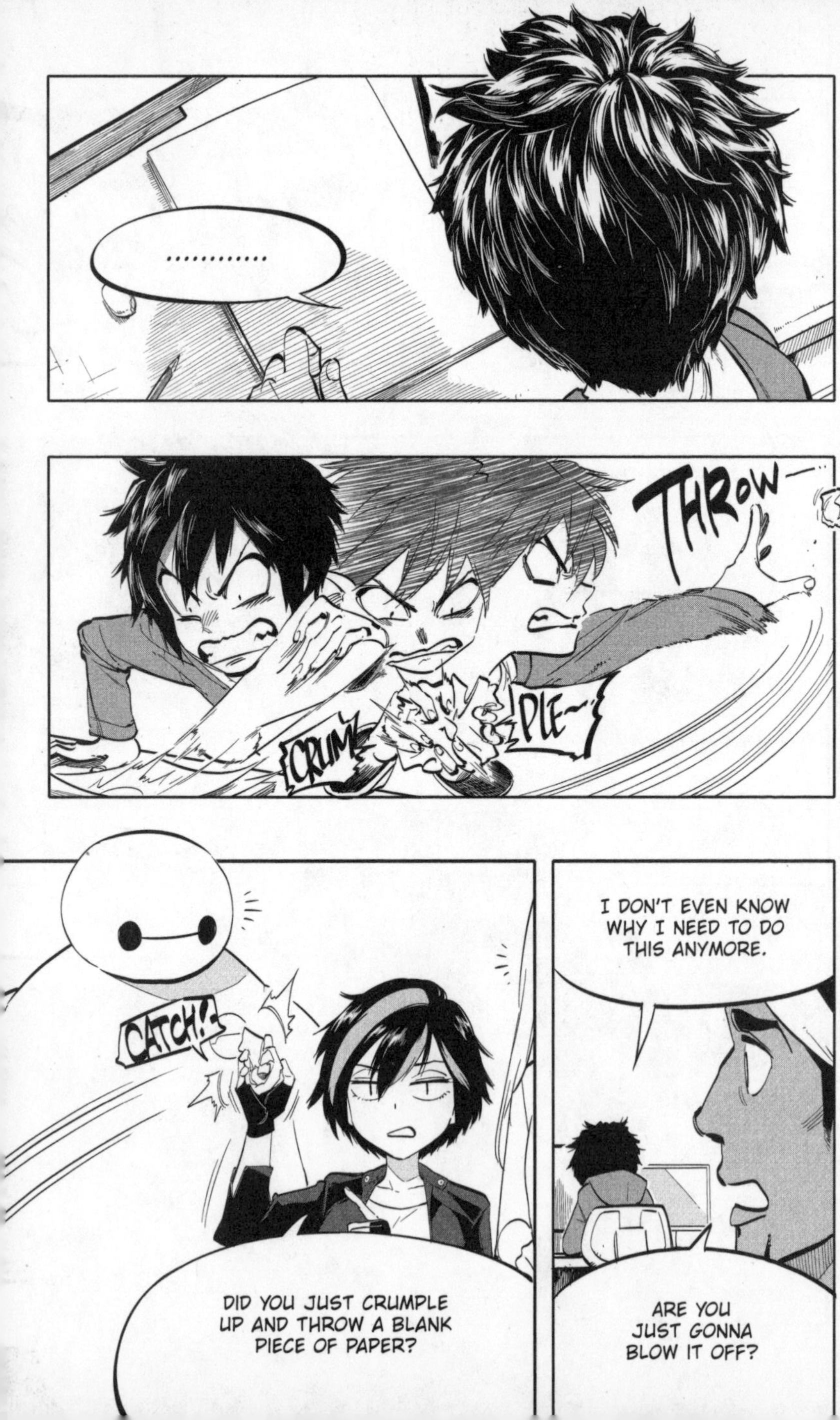

....
THROW
CRUM
PLE
CATCH!
DID YOU JUST CRUMPLE UP AND THROW A BLANK PIECE OF PAPER?
I DON'T EVEN KNOW WHY I NEED TO DO THIS ANYMORE.
ARE YOU JUST GONNA BLOW IT OFF?

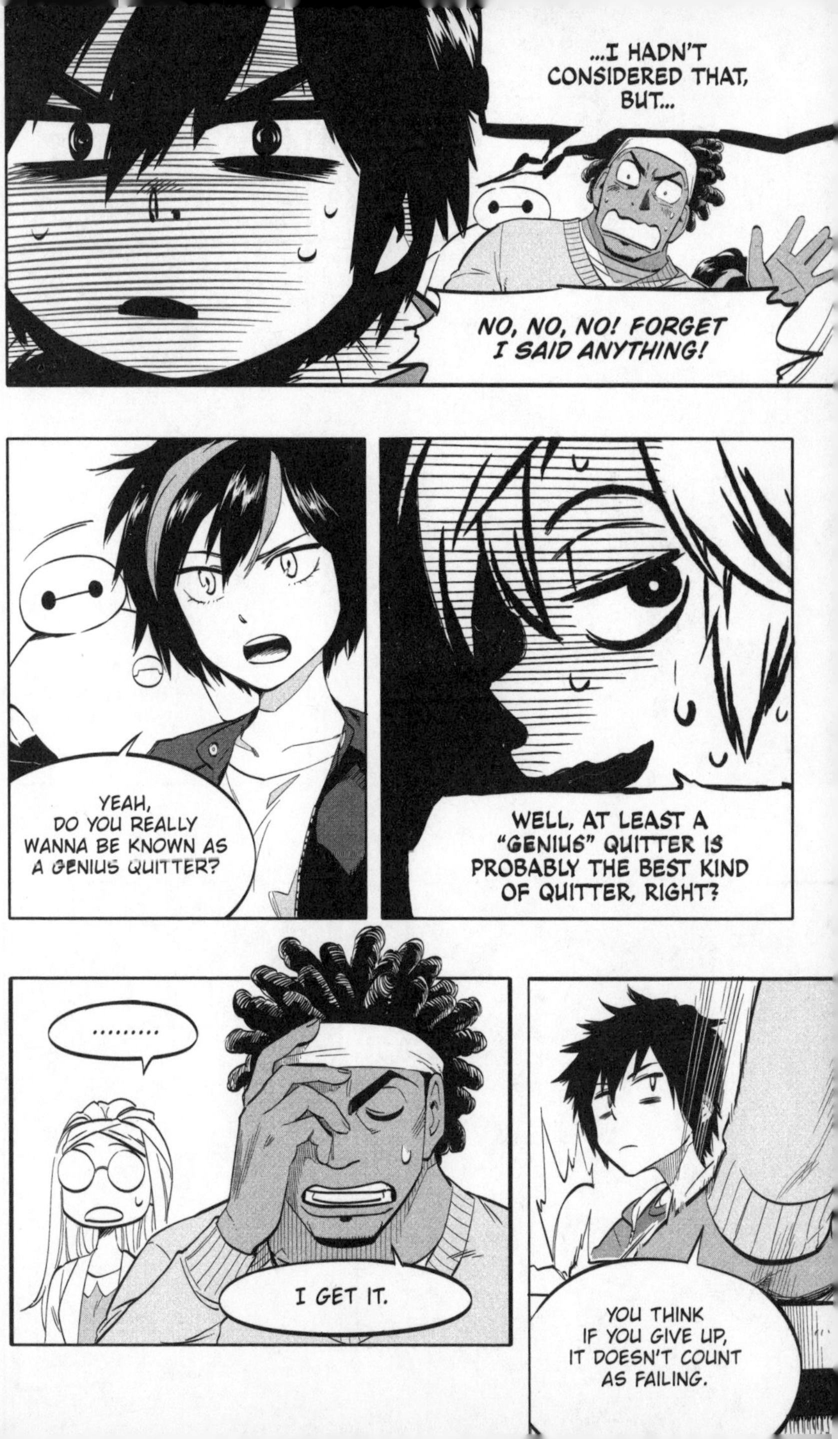
...I HADN'T CONSIDERED THAT, BUT...
NO, NO, NO! FORGET I SAID ANYTHING!
YEAH, DO YOU REALLY WANNA BE KNOWN AS A GENIUS QUITTER?
WELL, AT LEAST A "GENIUS" QUITTER IS PROBABLY THE BEST KIND OF QUITTER, RIGHT?
....
I GET IT.
YOU THINK IF YOU GIVE UP, IT DOESN'T COUNT AS FAILING.

BUT YOU KNOW WHAT?

IT'S ACTUALLY EVEN WORSE!

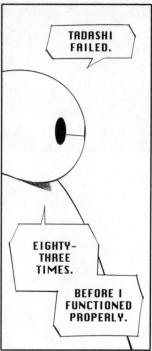

TADASHI FAILED.

EIGHTY-THREE TIMES.

BEFORE I FUNCTIONED PROPERLY.

WELL, MAYBE I'M NOT AS SMART AS TADASHI!

DASH—

HIRO!

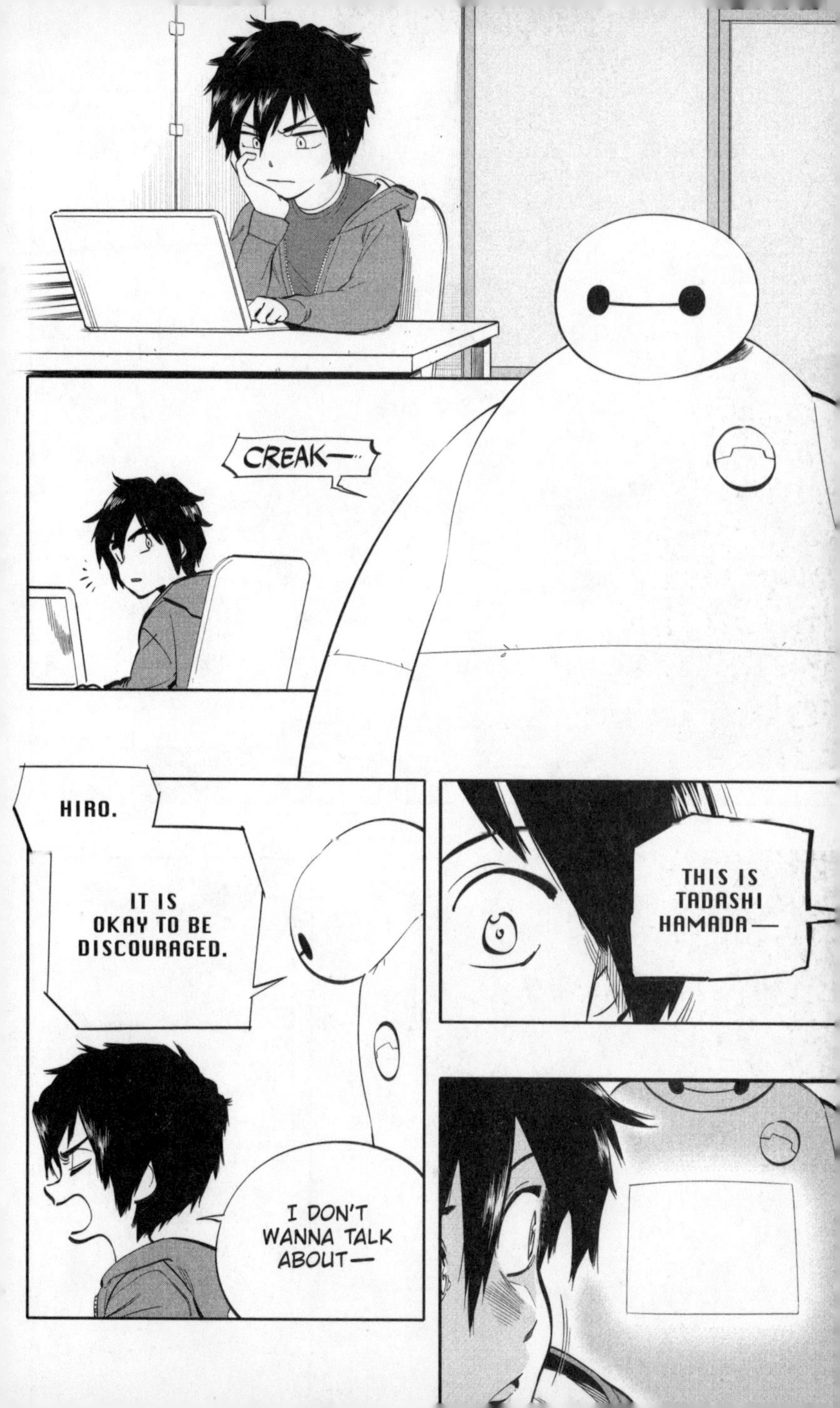
CREAK—
HIRO.
IT IS OKAY TO BE DISCOURAGED.
THIS IS TADASHI HAMADA—
I DON'T WANNA TALK ABOUT—

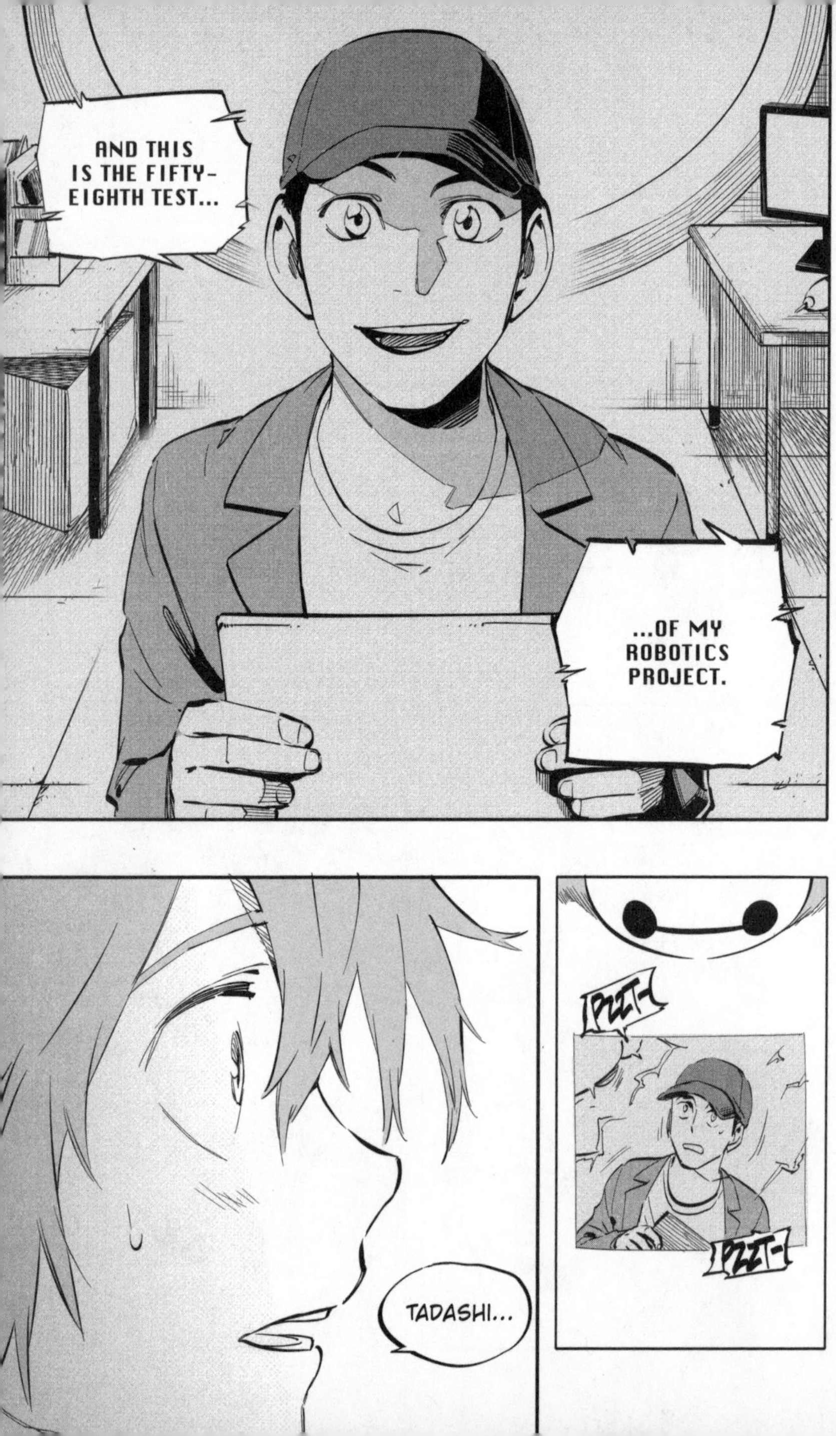
AND THIS IS THE FIFTY-EIGHTH TEST...
...OF MY ROBOTICS PROJECT.
TADASHI...
PZZT-
PZZT-

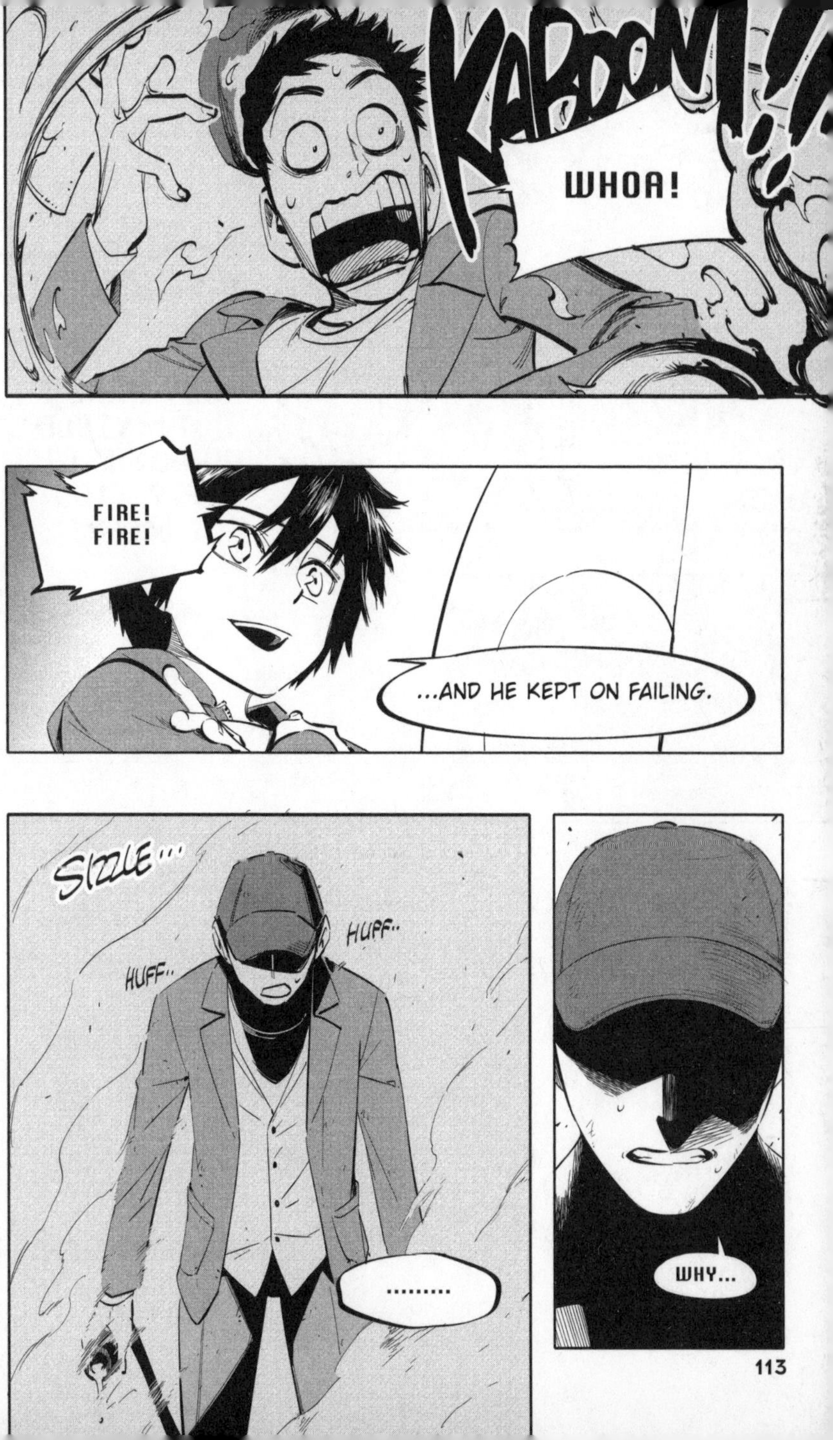
KABOOM!!
WHOA!
FIRE! FIRE!
...AND HE KEPT ON FAILING.
SIZZLE...
HUFF..
HUFF..
....
WHY...

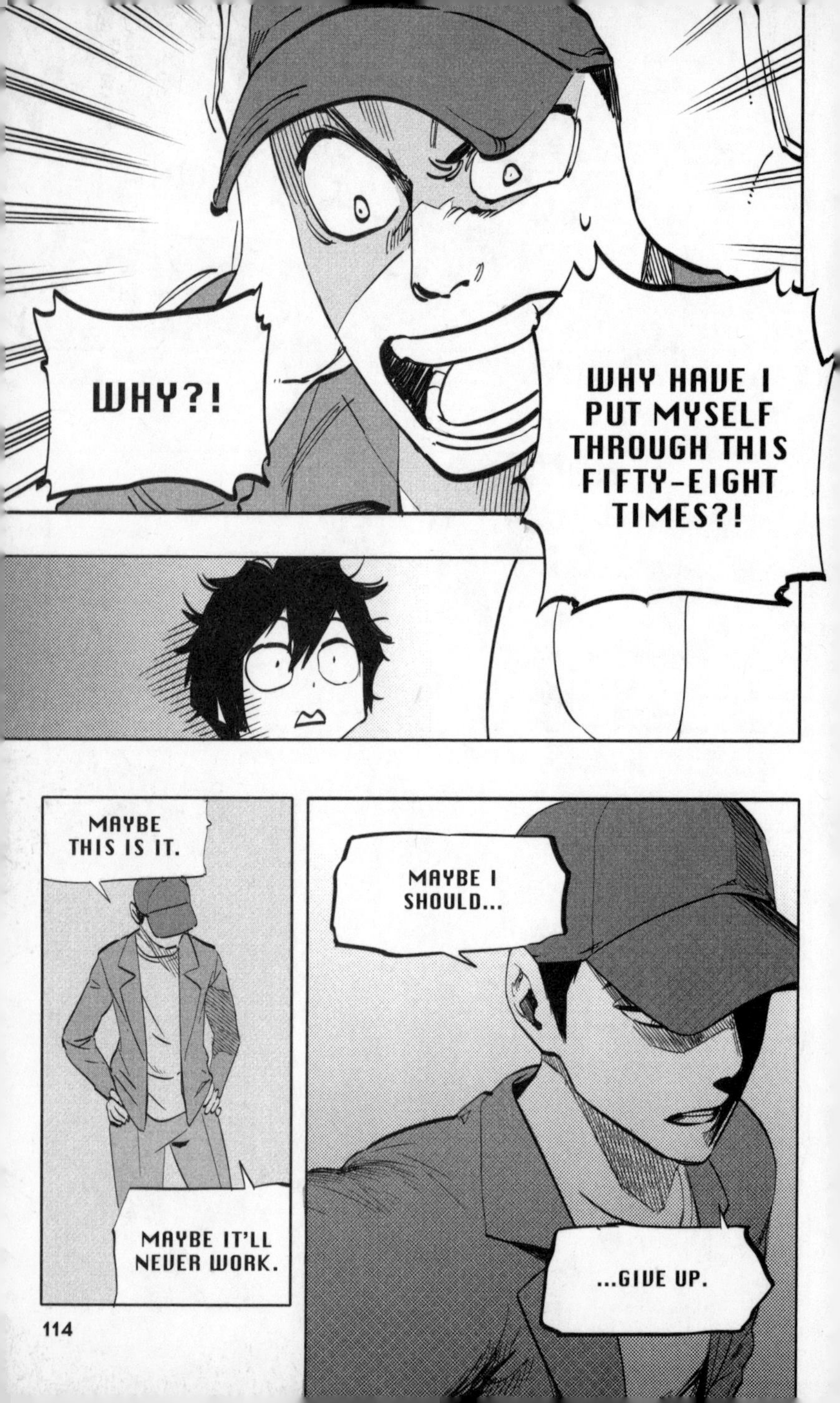
WHY?!
WHY HAVE I PUT MYSELF THROUGH THIS FIFTY-EIGHT TIMES?!
MAYBE THIS IS IT.
MAYBE IT'LL NEVER WORK.
MAYBE I SHOULD...
...GIVE UP.

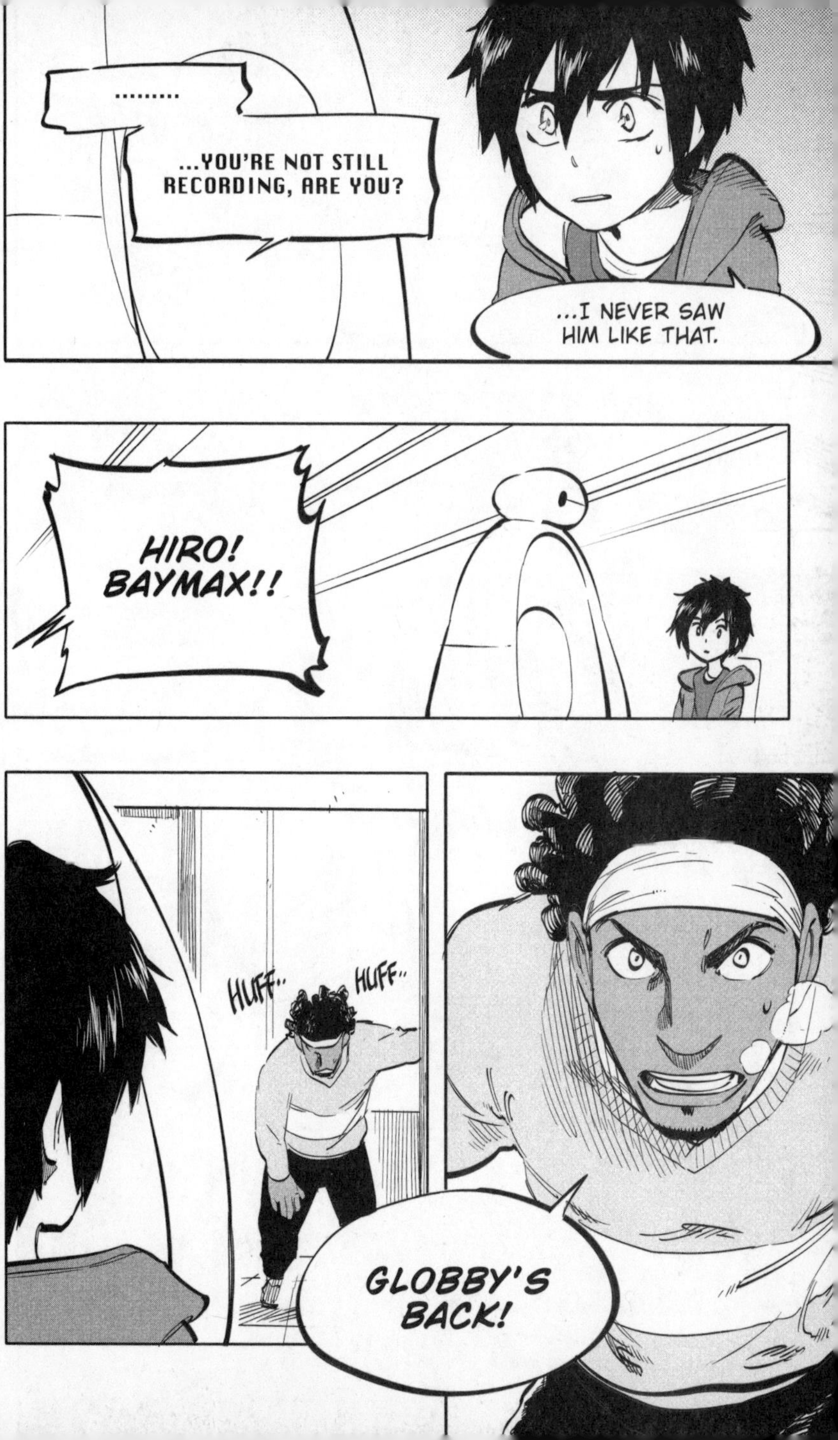
....
...YOU'RE NOT STILL RECORDING, ARE YOU?
...I NEVER SAW HIM LIKE THAT.
HIRO! BAYMAX!!
HUFF.. HUFF..
GLOBBY'S BACK!

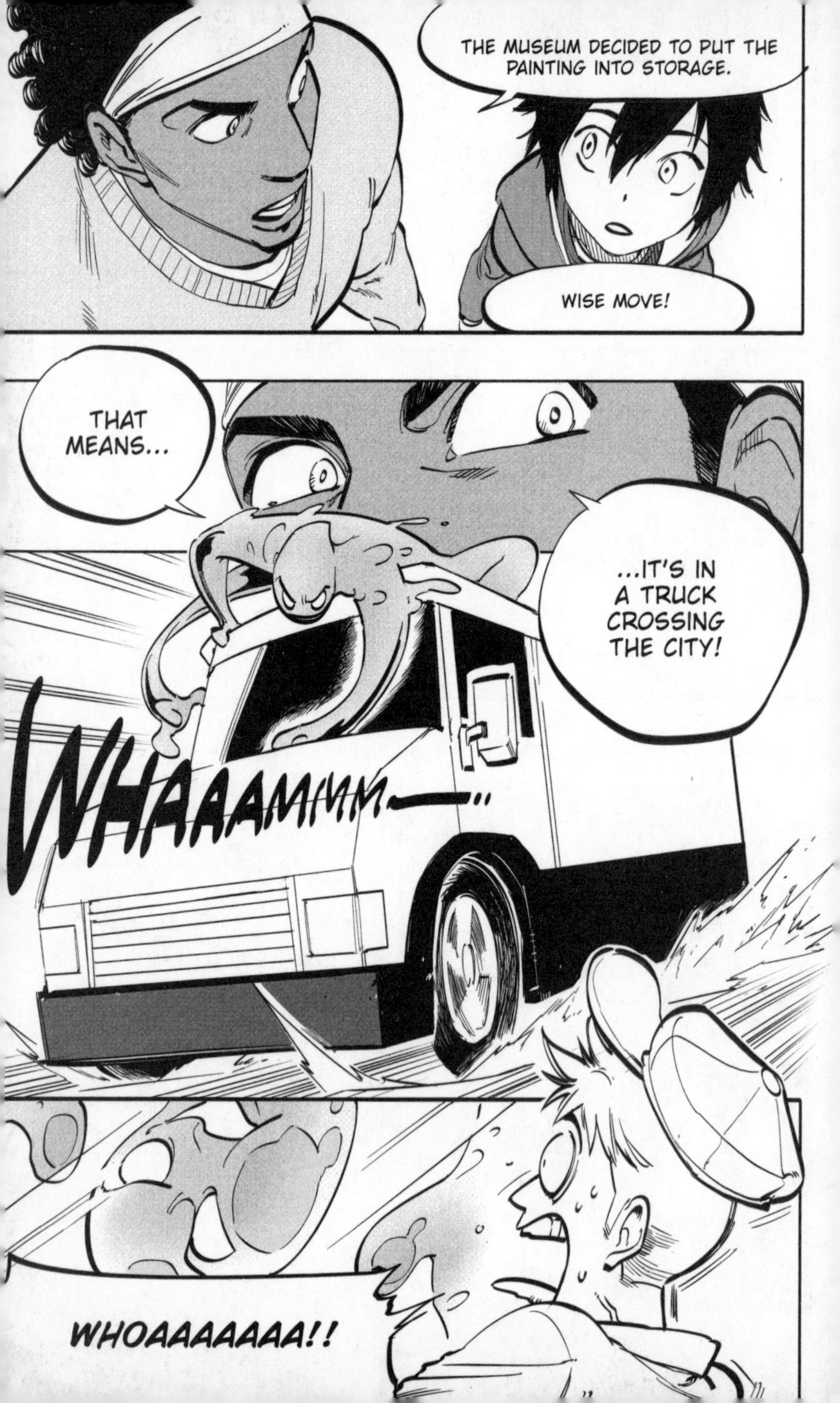
THE MUSEUM DECIDED TO PUT THE PAINTING INTO STORAGE.
WISE MOVE!
THAT MEANS...
...IT'S IN A TRUCK CROSSING THE CITY!
WHAAAMMM—!!
WHOAAAAAAA!!

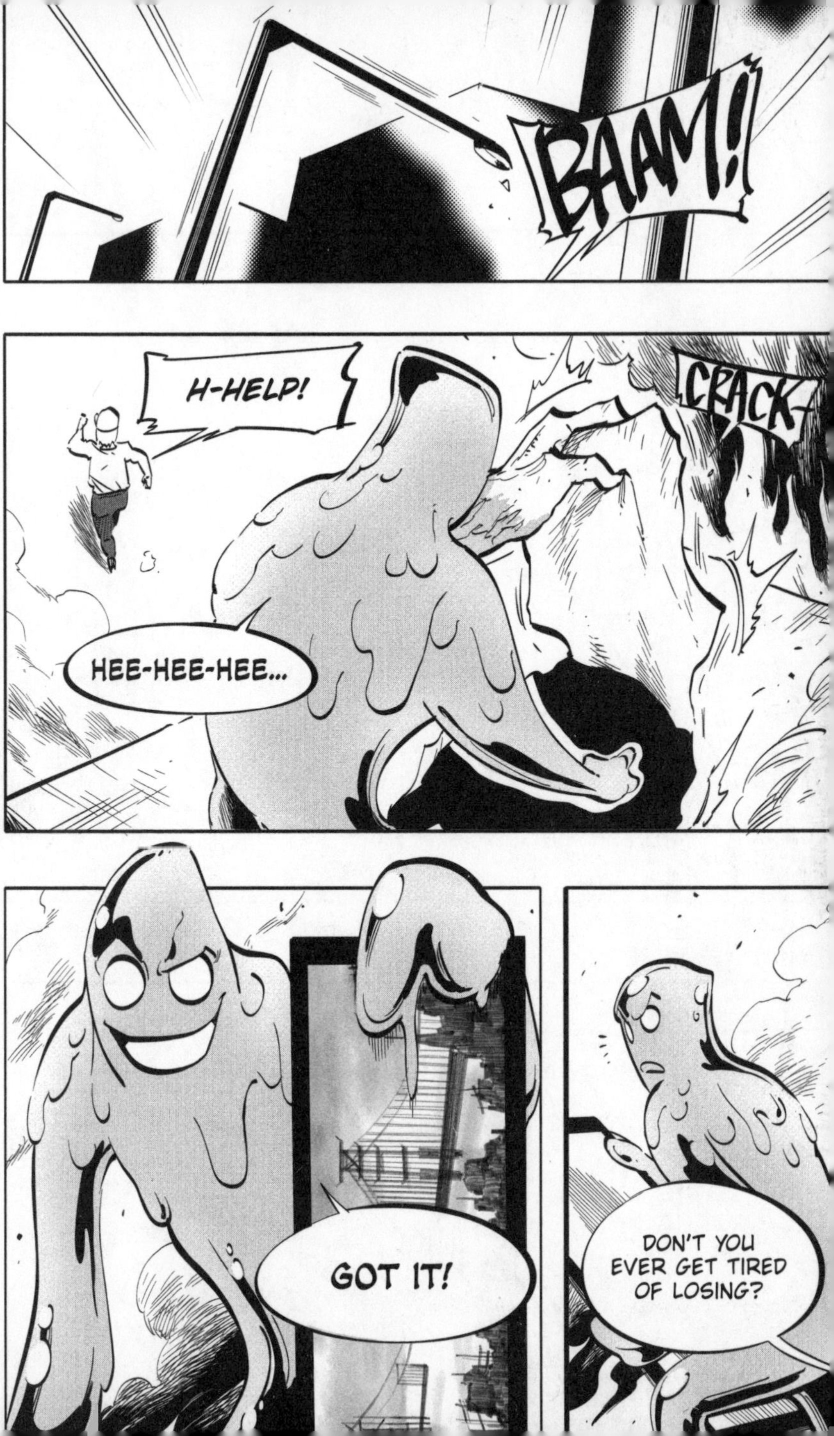
BAAM!
H-HELP!
CRACK
HEE-HEE-HEE...
GOT IT!
DON'T YOU EVER GET TIRED OF LOSING?

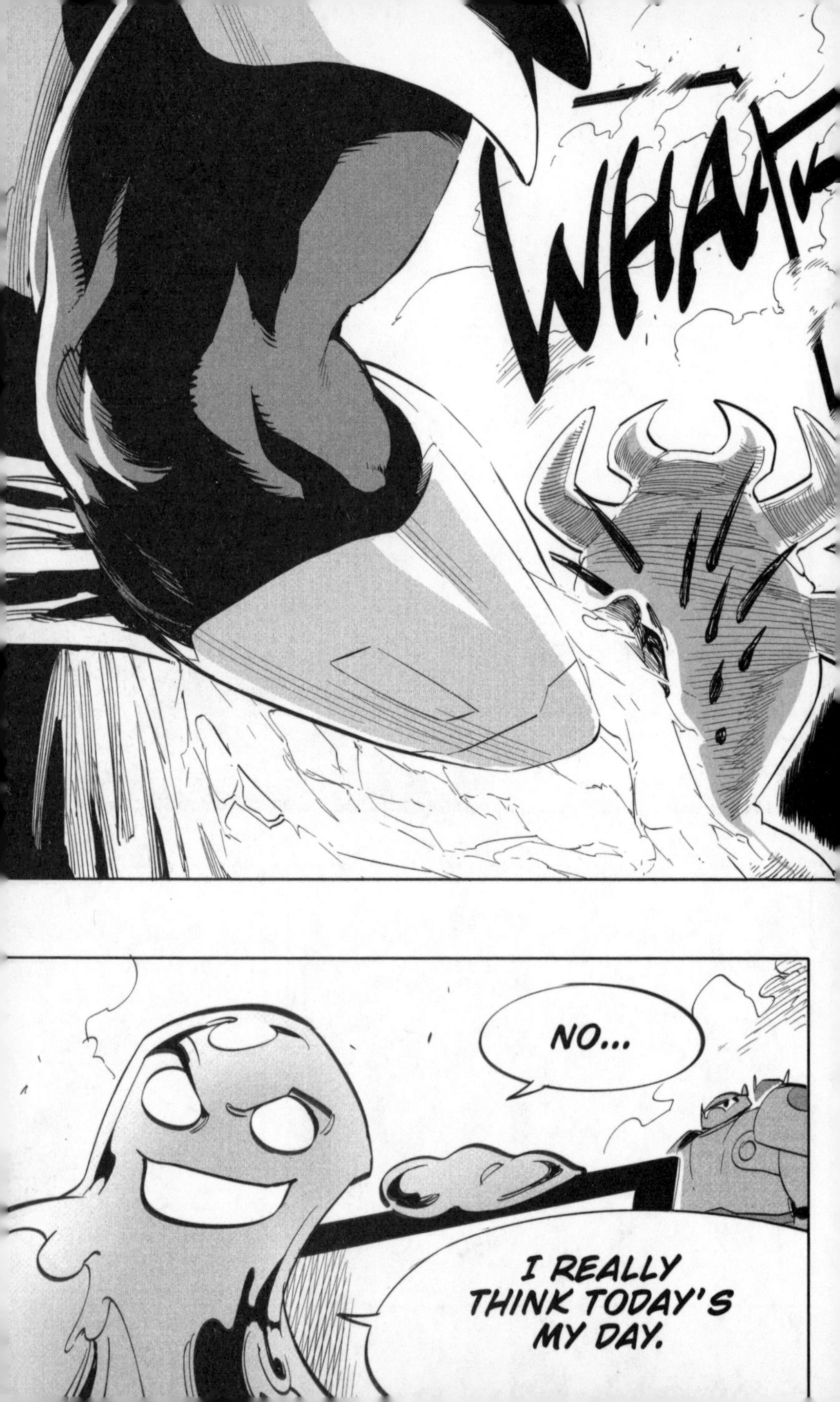
WHAT
NO...
I REALLY THINK TODAY'S MY DAY.

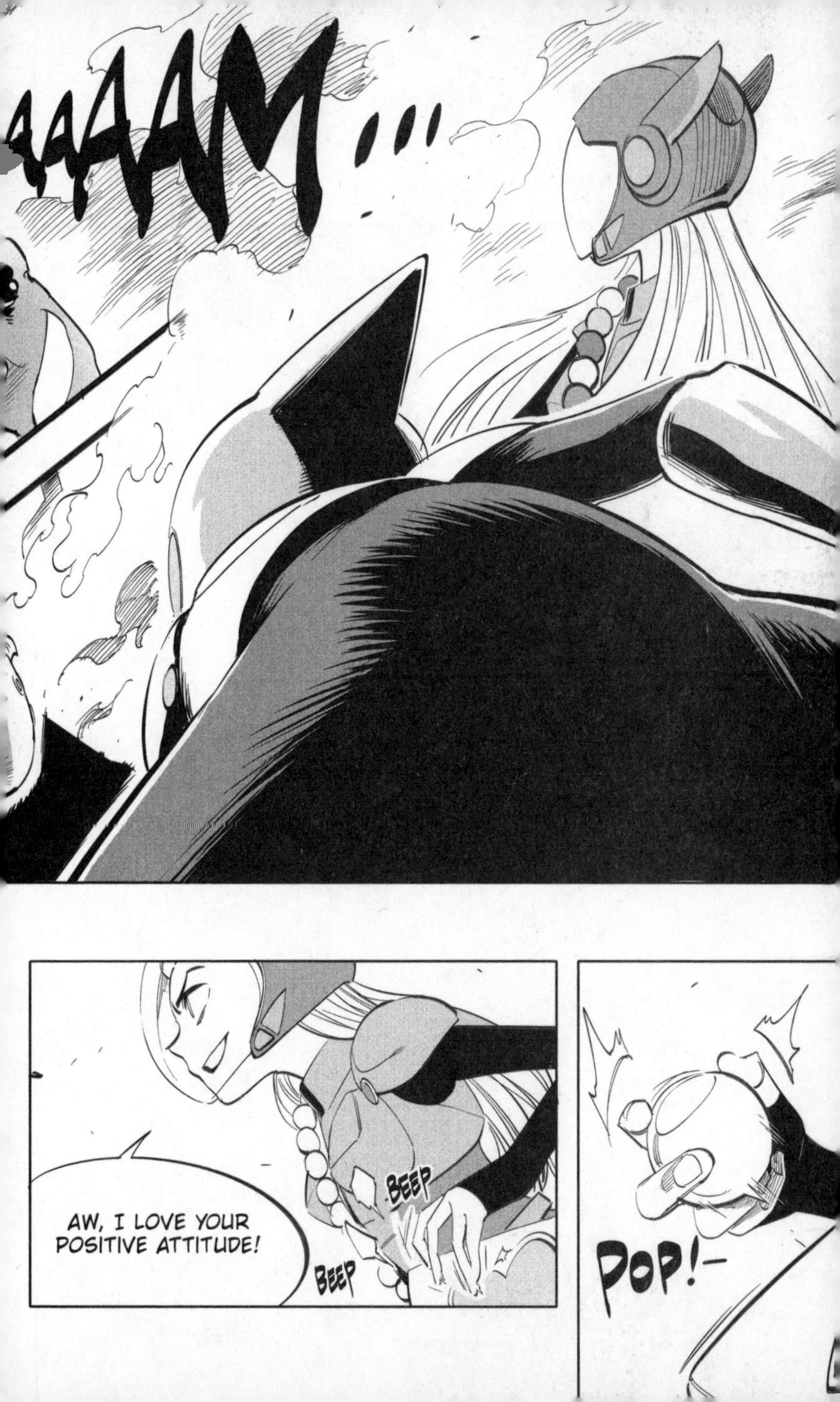
AAAAM...
AW, I LOVE YOUR POSITIVE ATTITUDE!
BEEP
BEEP
POP!

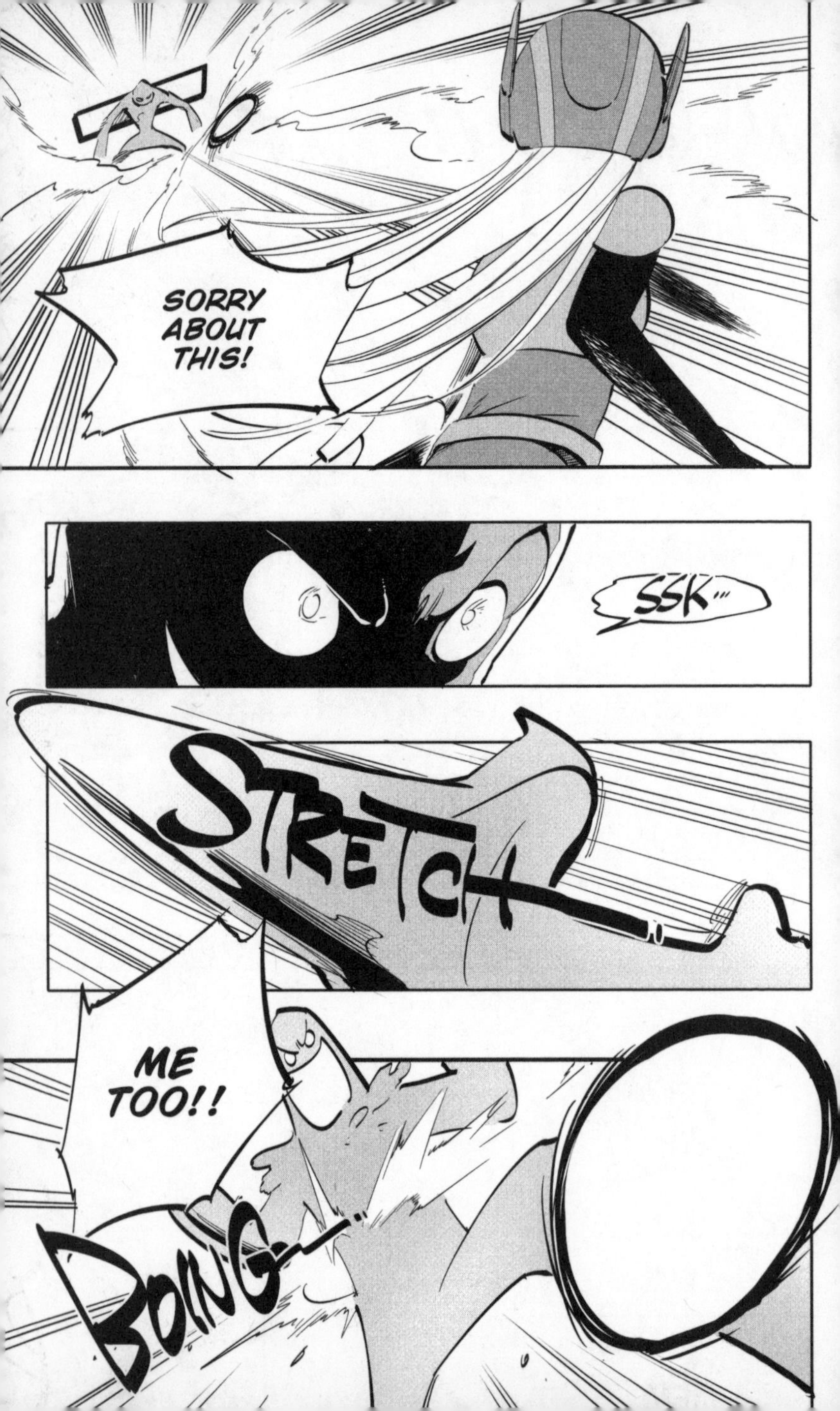
SORRY ABOUT THIS!
SSK...
STRETCH
ME TOO!!
BOING

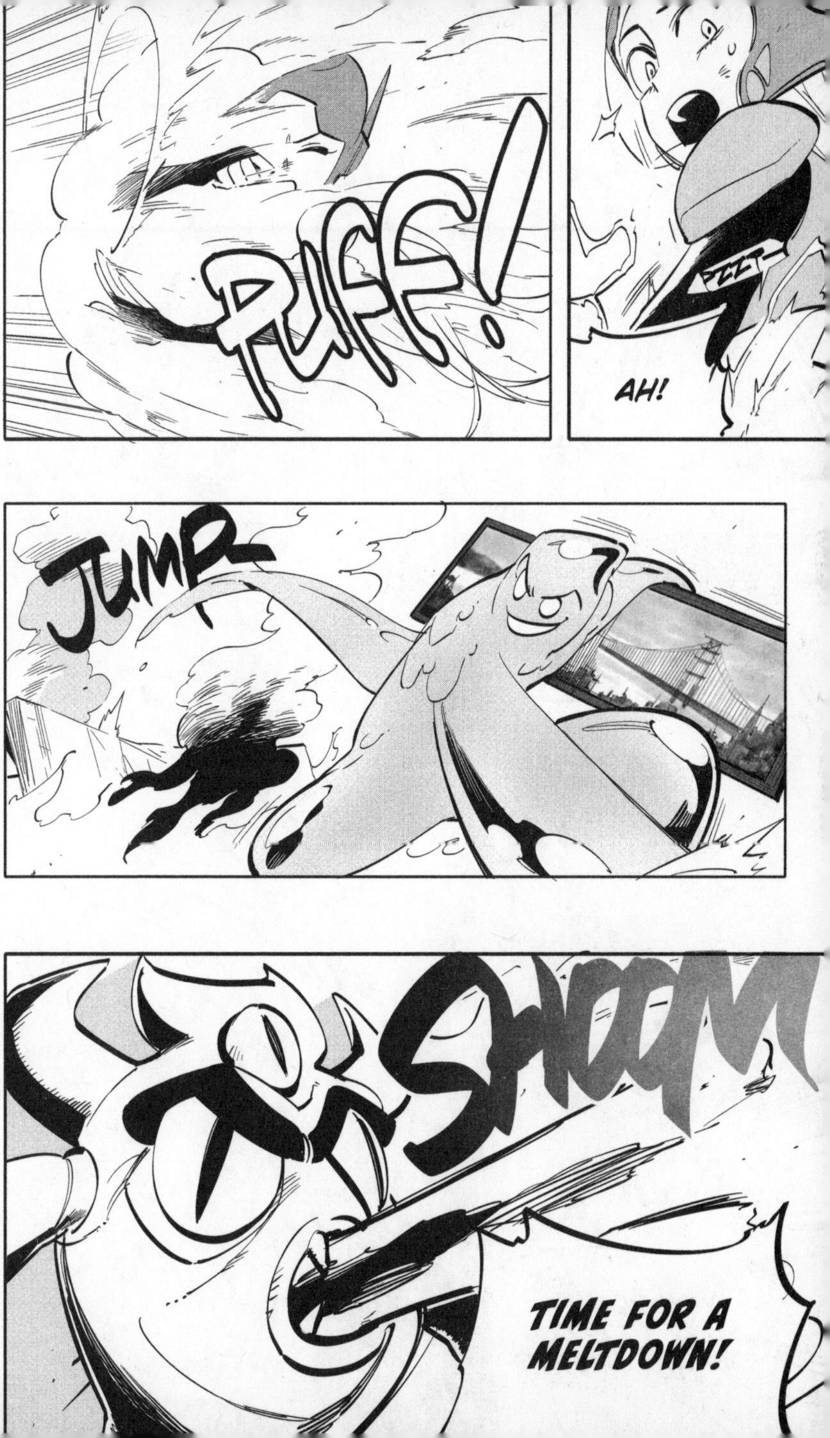
PUFF!
PZZT—
AH!
JUMP
SHOOM
TIME FOR A MELTDOWN!

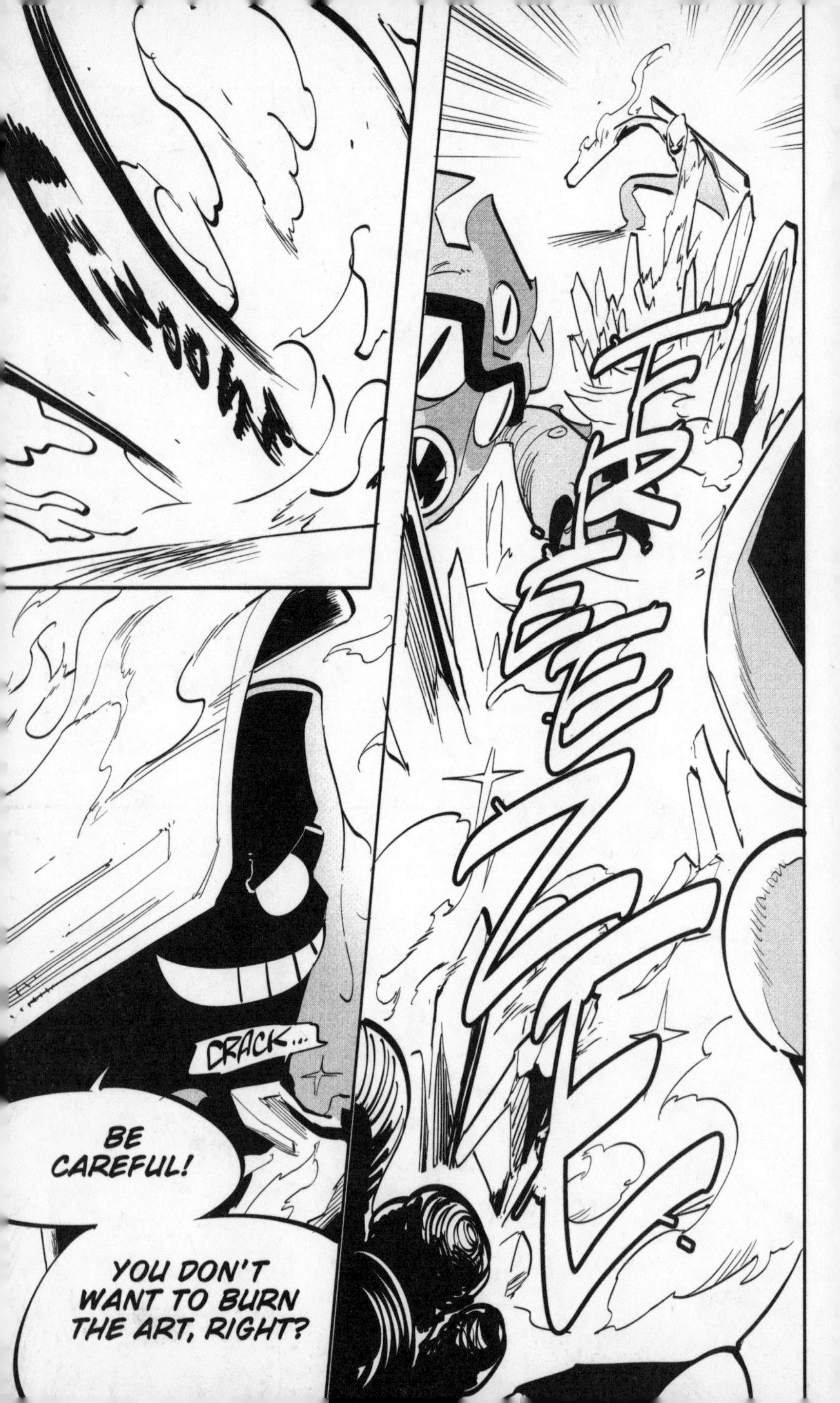
CRACK...
BE CAREFUL!
YOU DON'T WANT TO BURN THE ART, RIGHT?

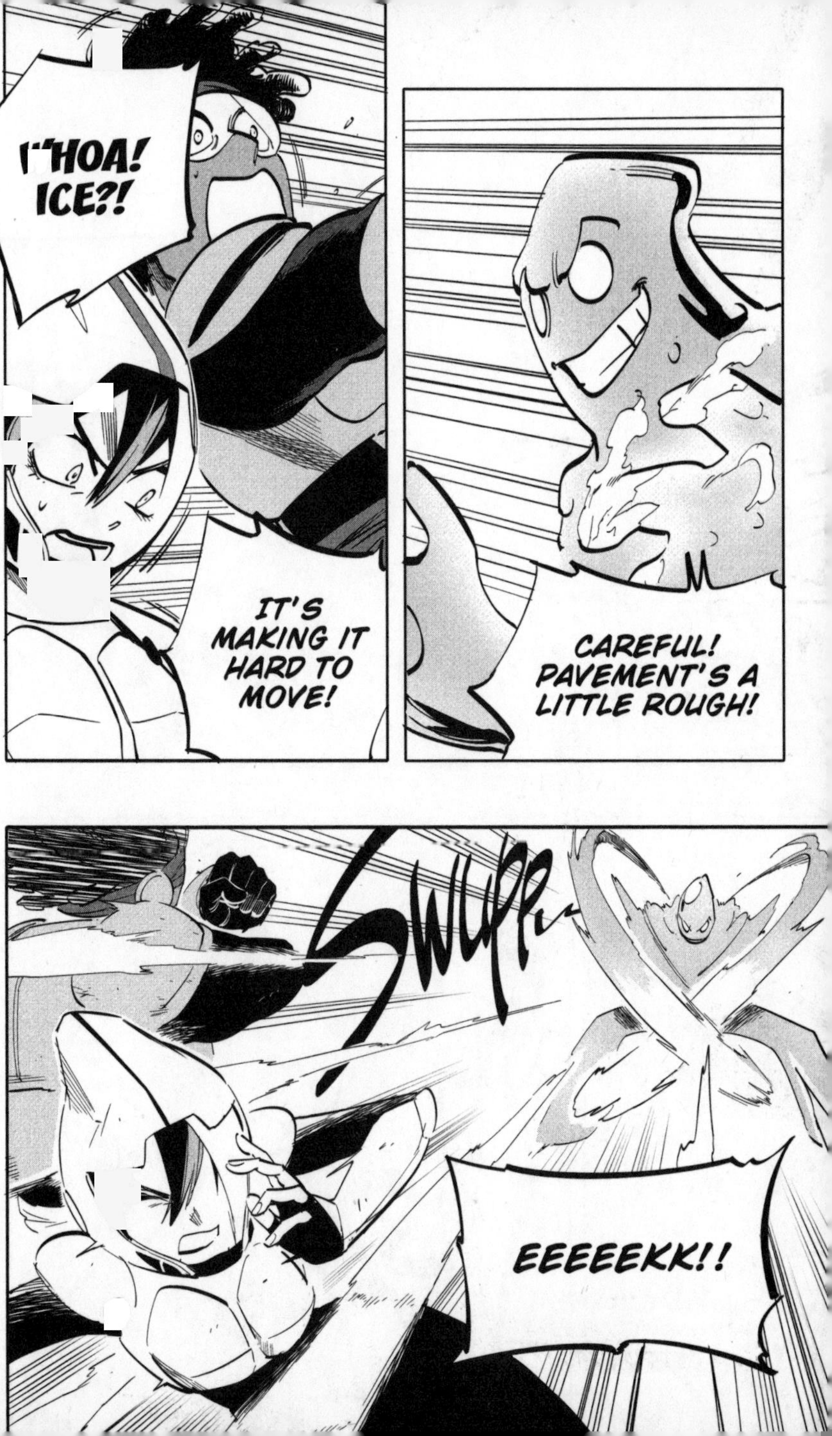
HOA!
ICE?!
IT'S MAKING IT HARD TO MOVE!
CAREFUL! PAVEMENT'S A LITTLE ROUGH!
SWUPP
EEEEEKK!!

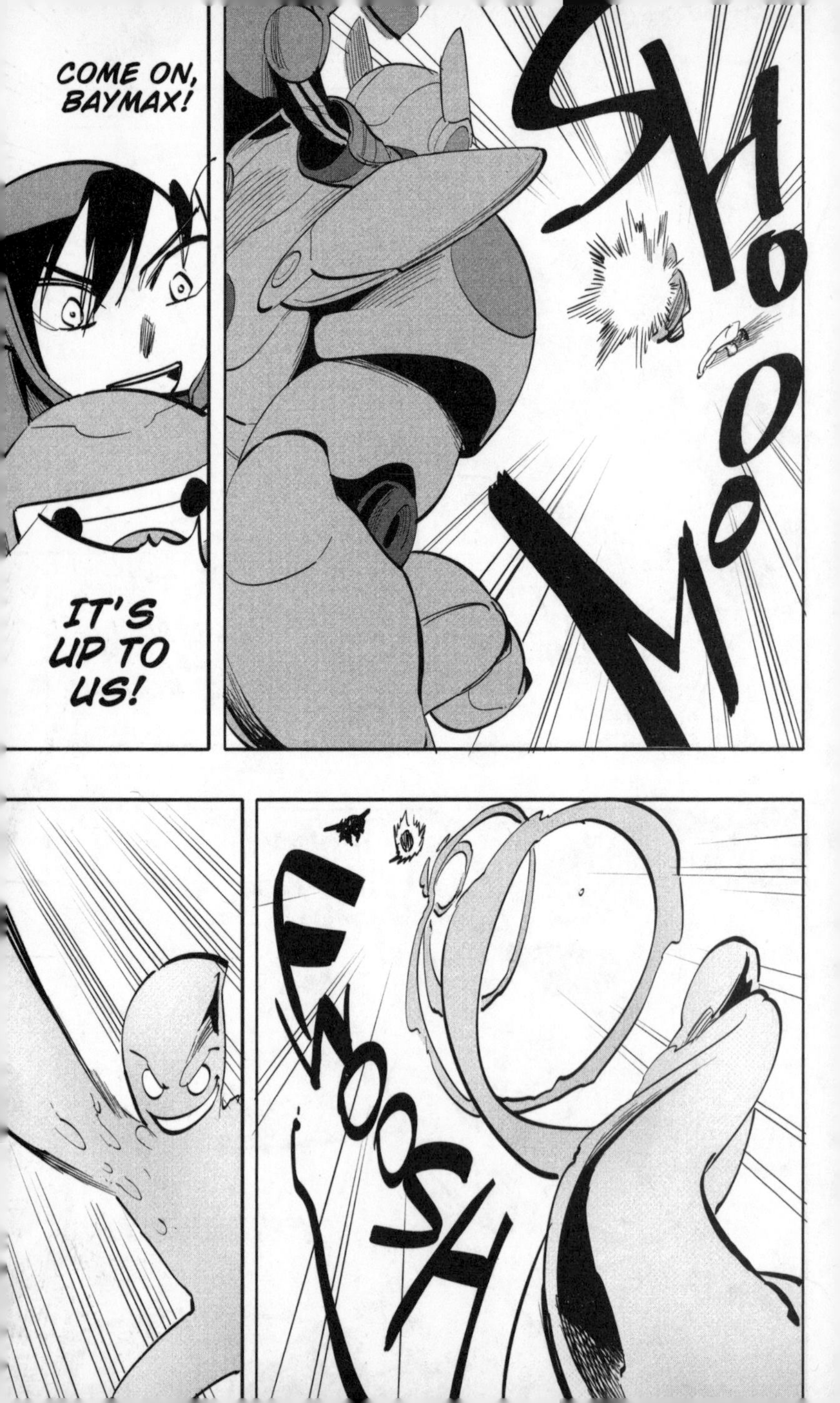
COME ON, BAYMAX!
IT'S UP TO US!
SHOOOOM
WHOOSH

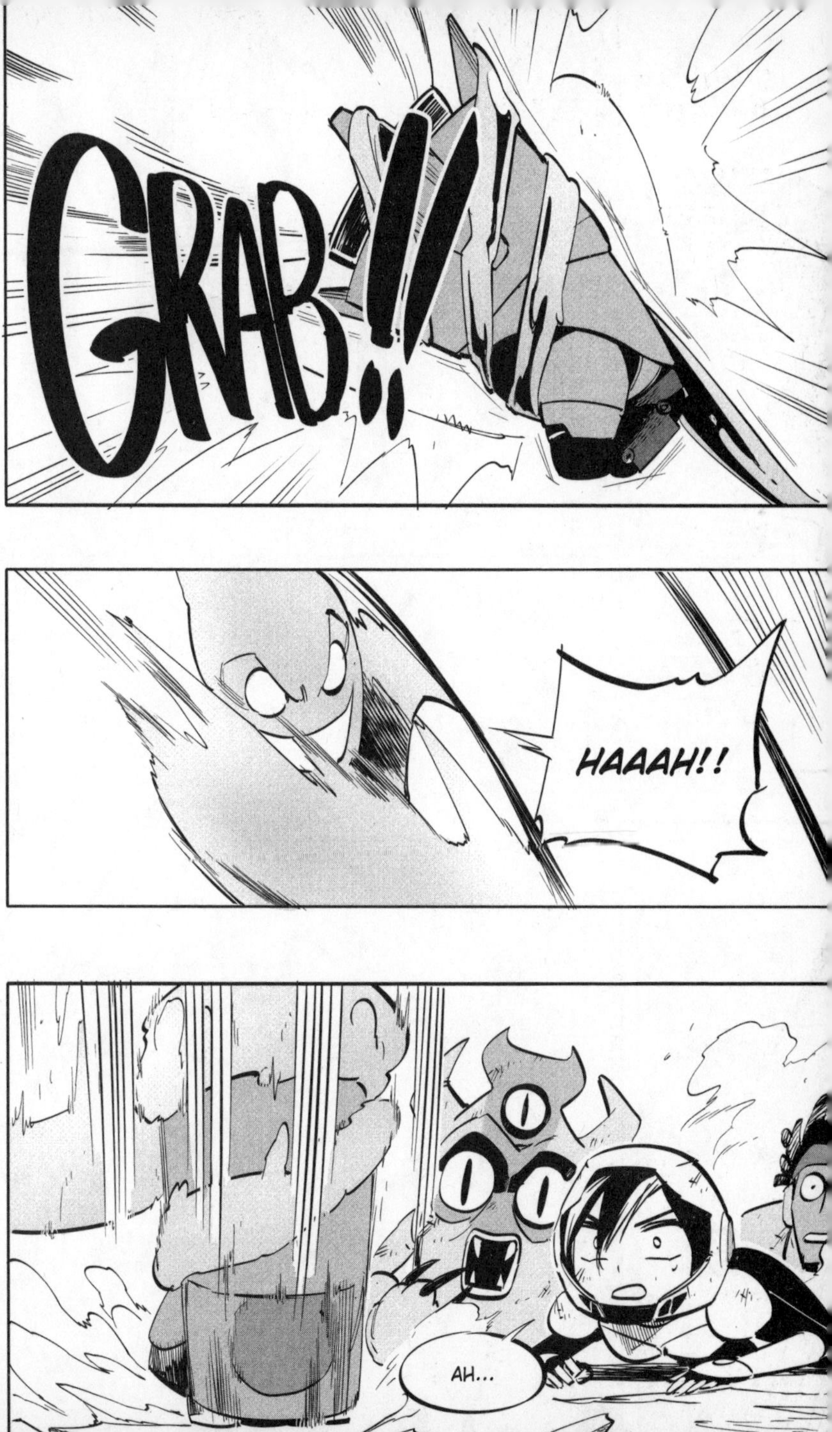

GRAB!!
HAAAH!!
AH...

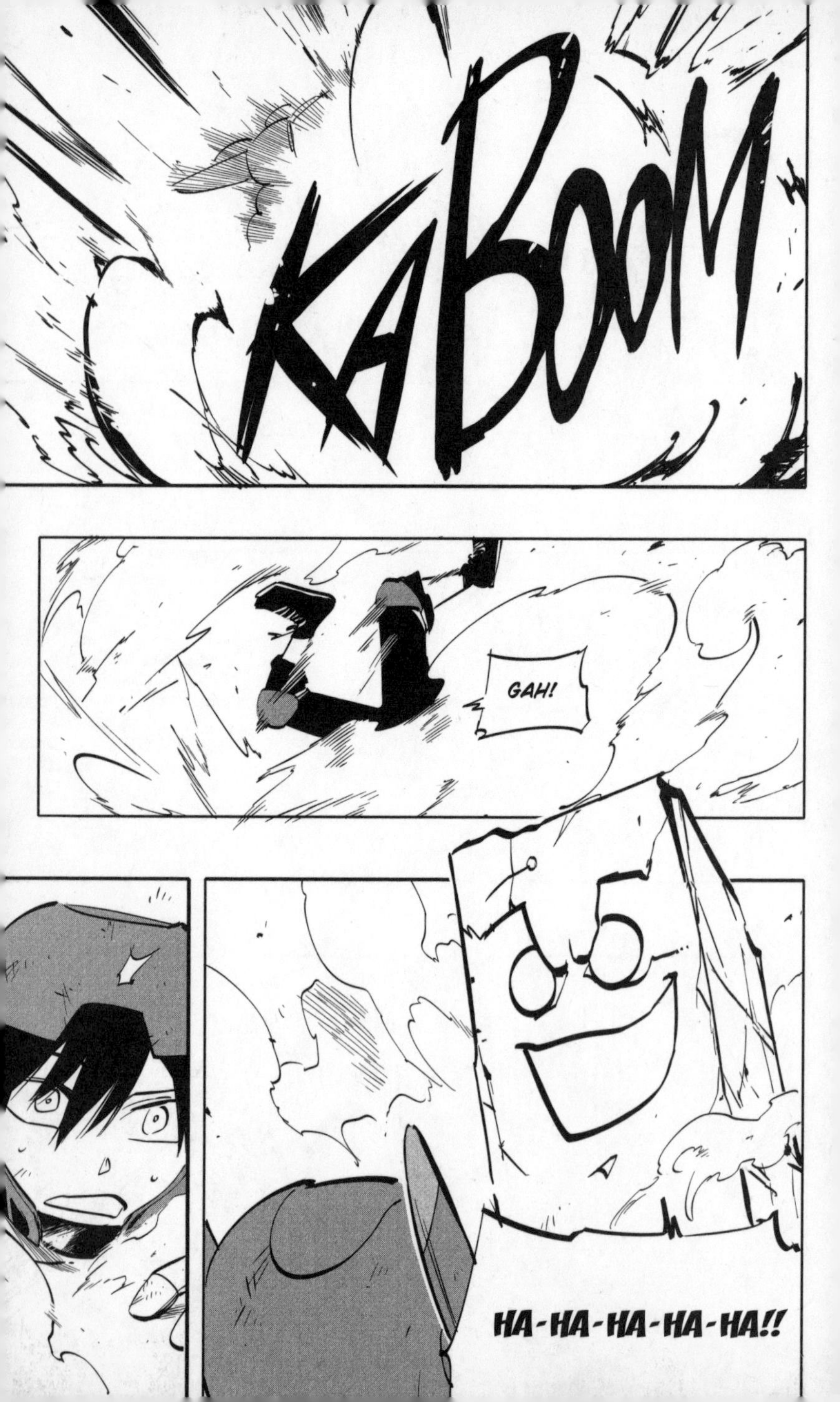
KABOOM
GAH!
HA-HA-HA-HA-HA!!

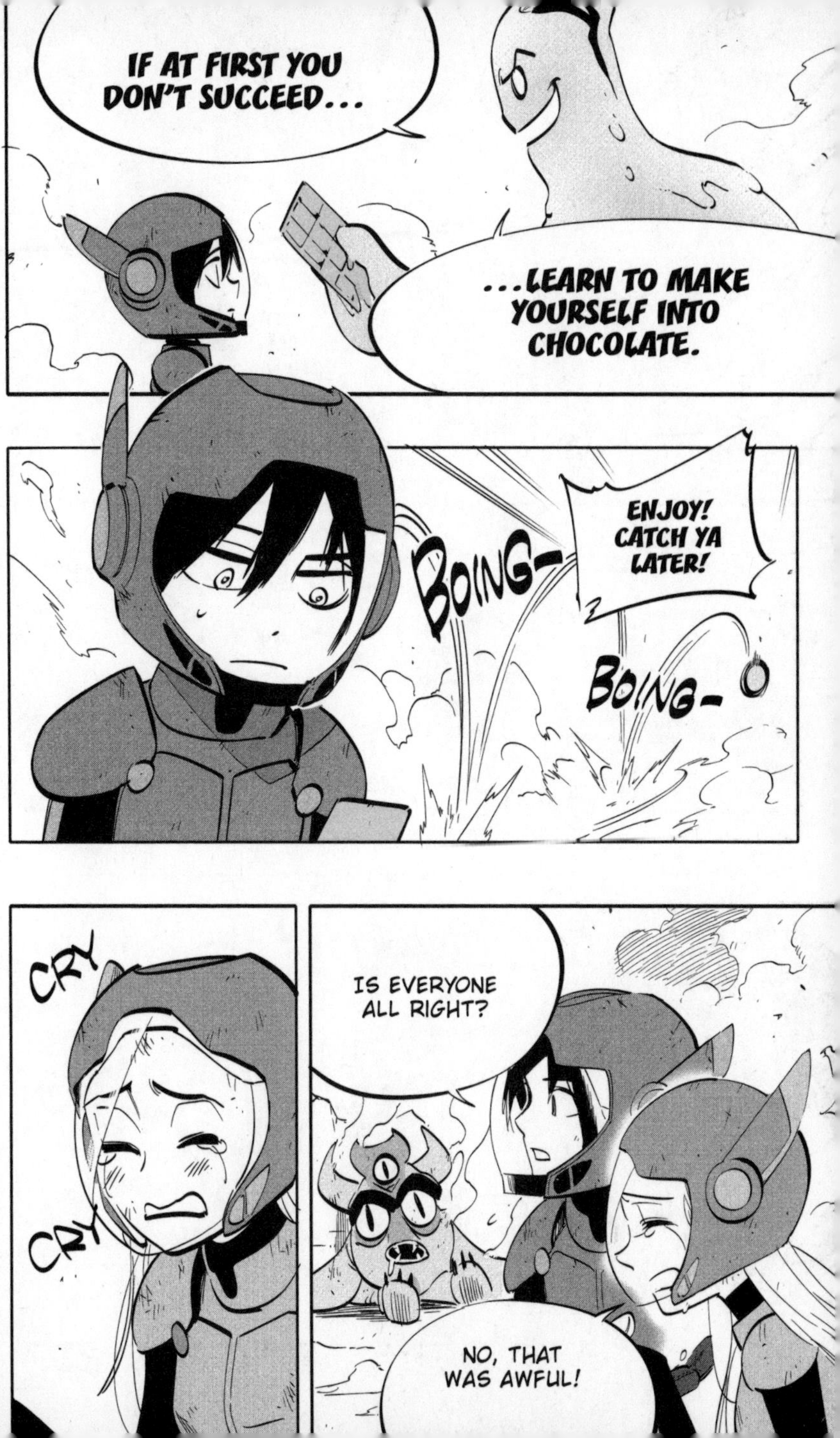
IF AT FIRST YOU DON'T SUCCEED...
...LEARN TO MAKE YOURSELF INTO CHOCOLATE.
BOING-
ENJOY! CATCH YA LATER!
BOING-
CRY
CRY
IS EVERYONE ALL RIGHT?
NO, THAT WAS AWFUL!

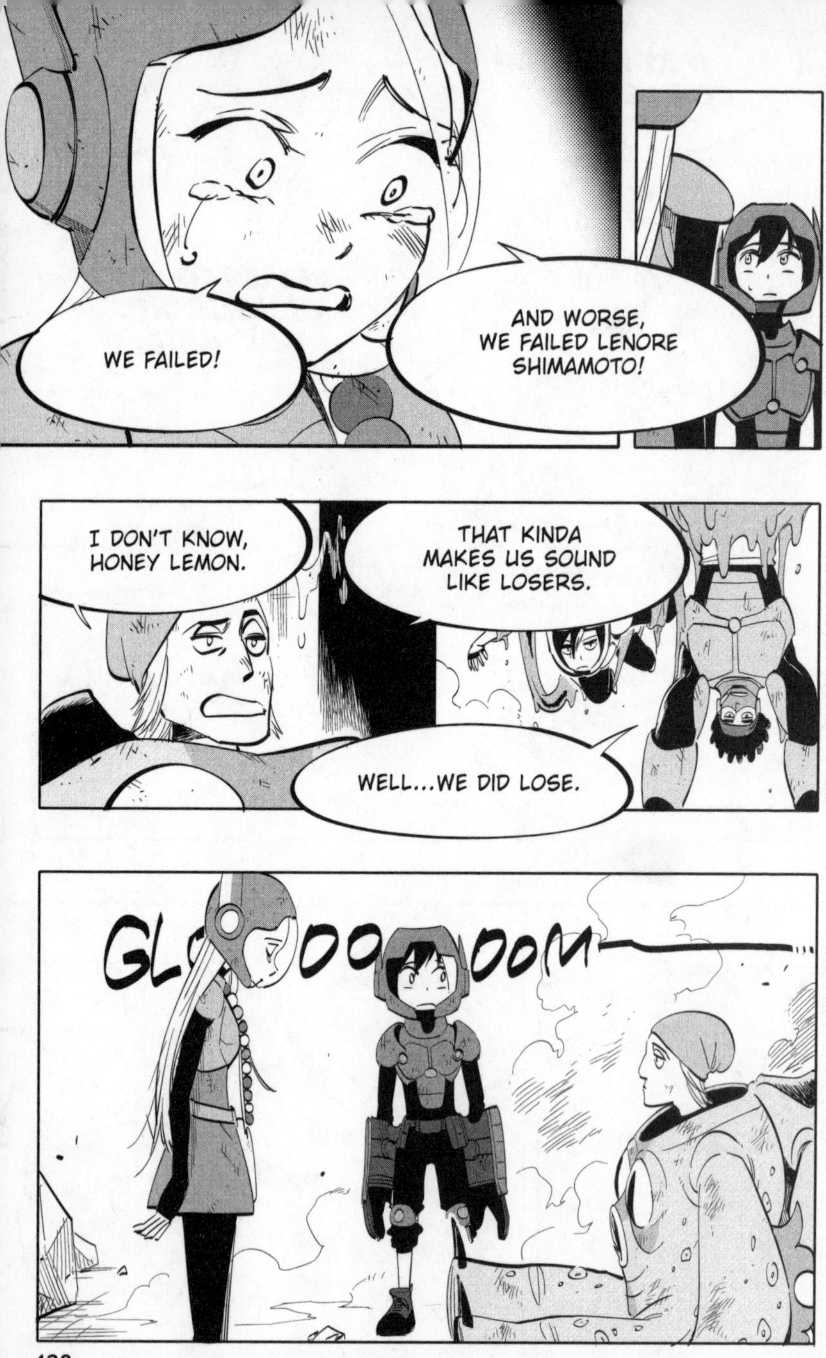
WE FAILED!
AND WORSE, WE FAILED LENORE SHIMAMOTO!
I DON'T KNOW, HONEY LEMON.
THAT KINDA MAKES US SOUND LIKE LOSERS.
WELL...WE DID LOSE.
GLOOOOOOM—

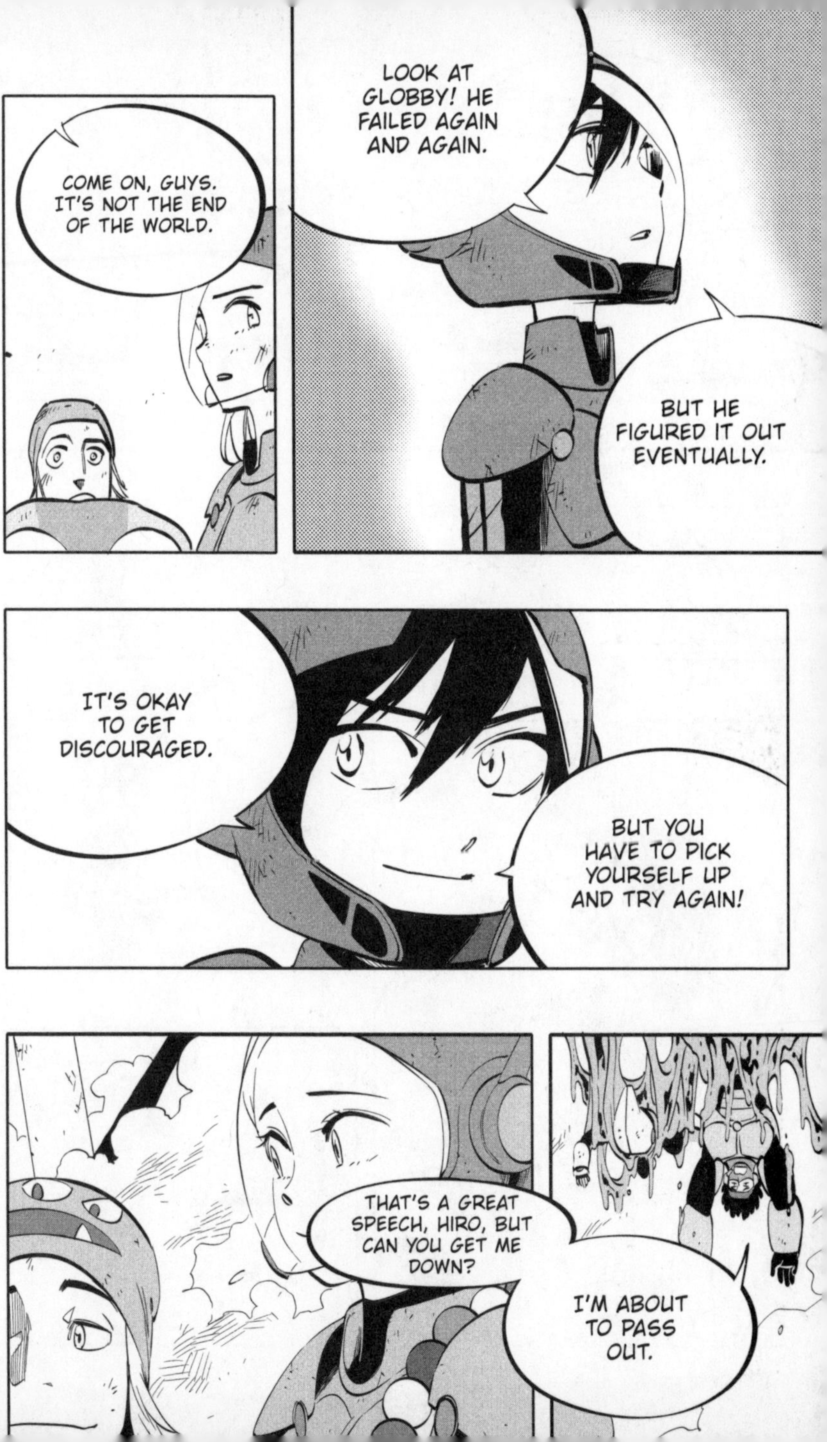
COME ON, GUYS. IT'S NOT THE END OF THE WORLD.
LOOK AT GLOBBY! HE FAILED AGAIN AND AGAIN.
BUT HE FIGURED IT OUT EVENTUALLY.
IT'S OKAY TO GET DISCOURAGED.
BUT YOU HAVE TO PICK YOURSELF UP AND TRY AGAIN!
THAT'S A GREAT SPEECH, HIRO, BUT CAN YOU GET ME DOWN?
I'M ABOUT TO PASS OUT.

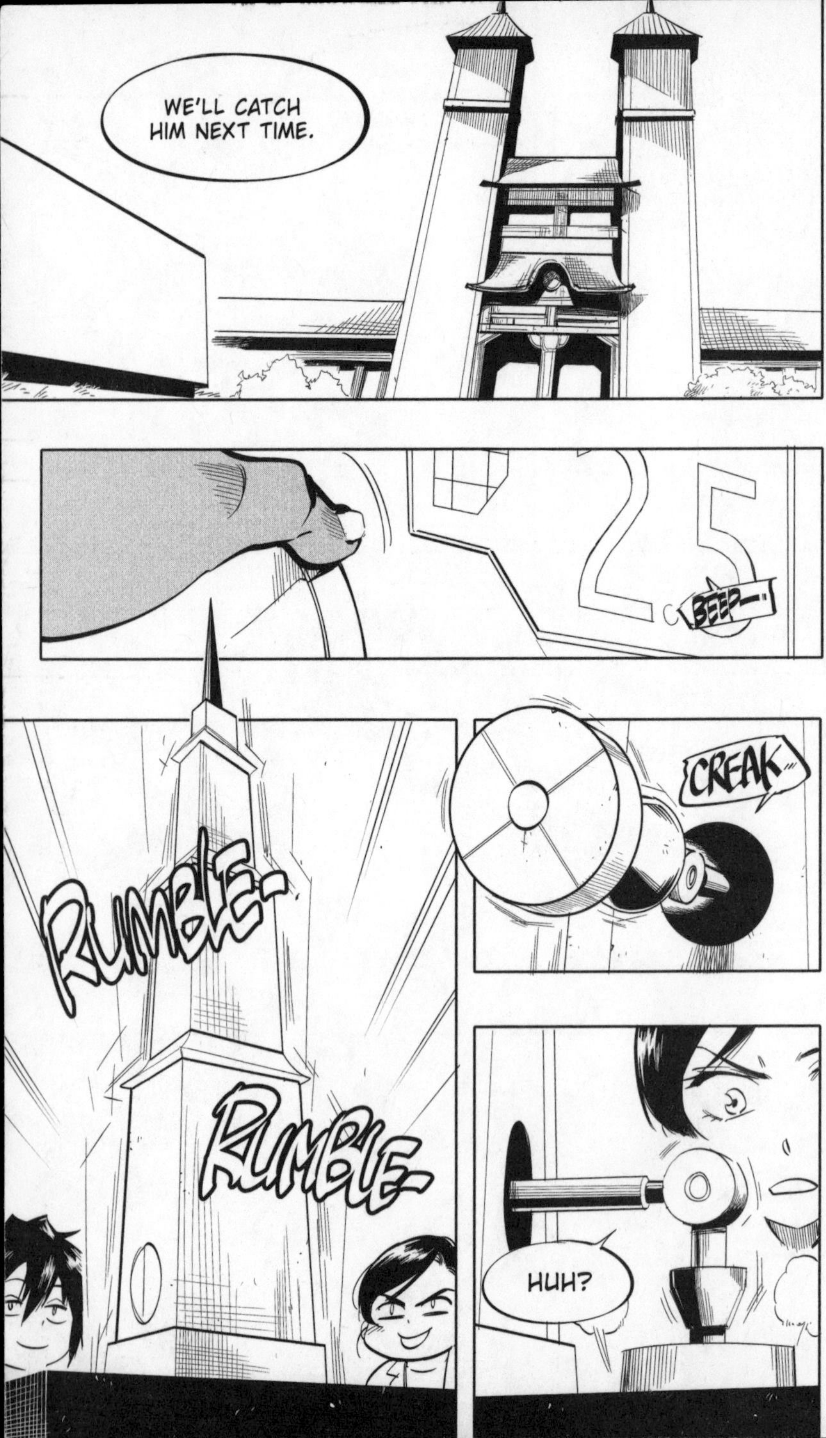
WE'LL CATCH HIM NEXT TIME.
BEEP—
RUMBLE-
RUMBLE-
CREAK
HUH?

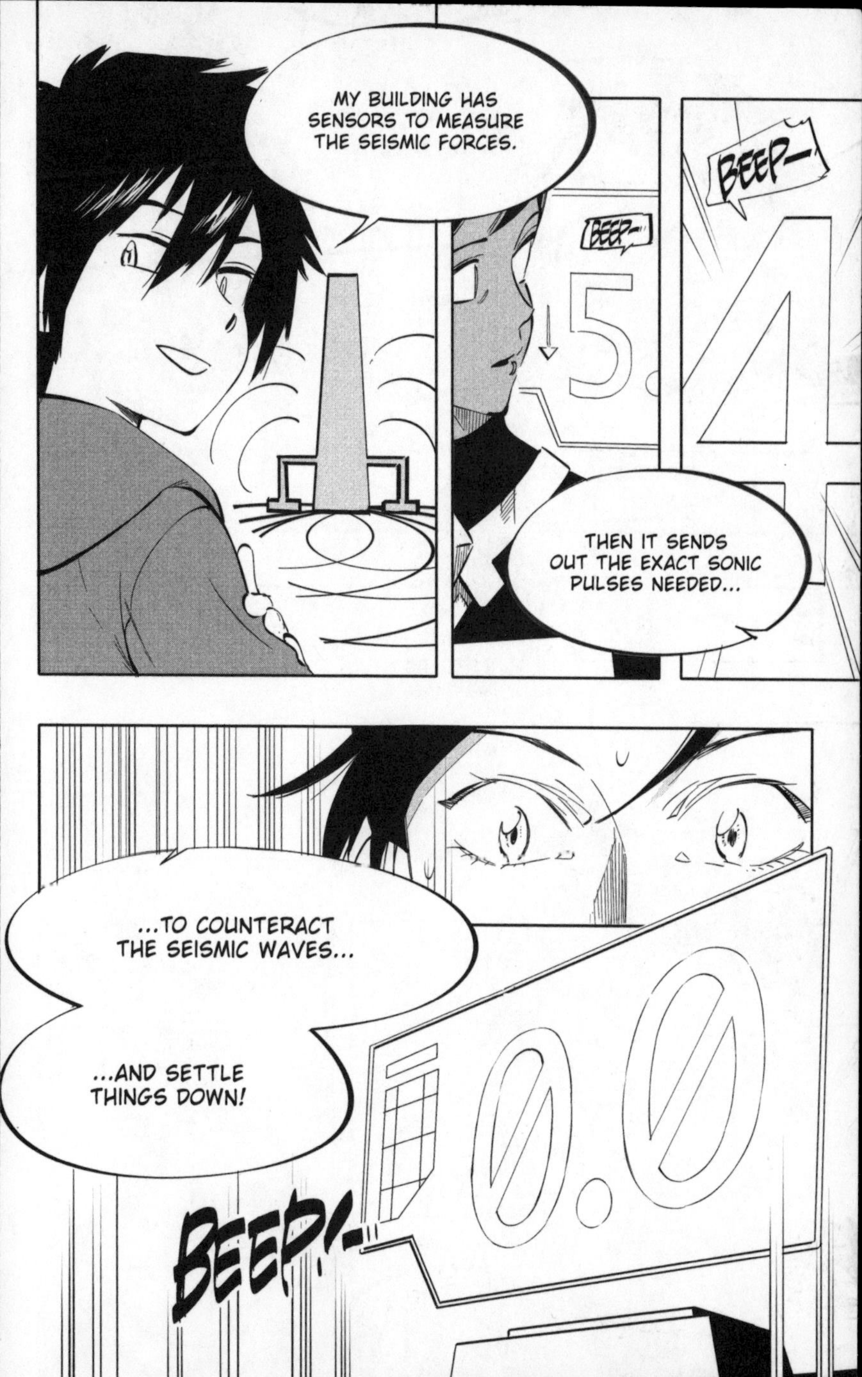
MY BUILDING HAS SENSORS TO MEASURE THE SEISMIC FORCES.
BEEP—
5.
THEN IT SENDS OUT THE EXACT SONIC PULSES NEEDED...
BEEP—
4
...TO COUNTERACT THE SEISMIC WAVES...
...AND SETTLE THINGS DOWN!
0.0
BEEP!—!!

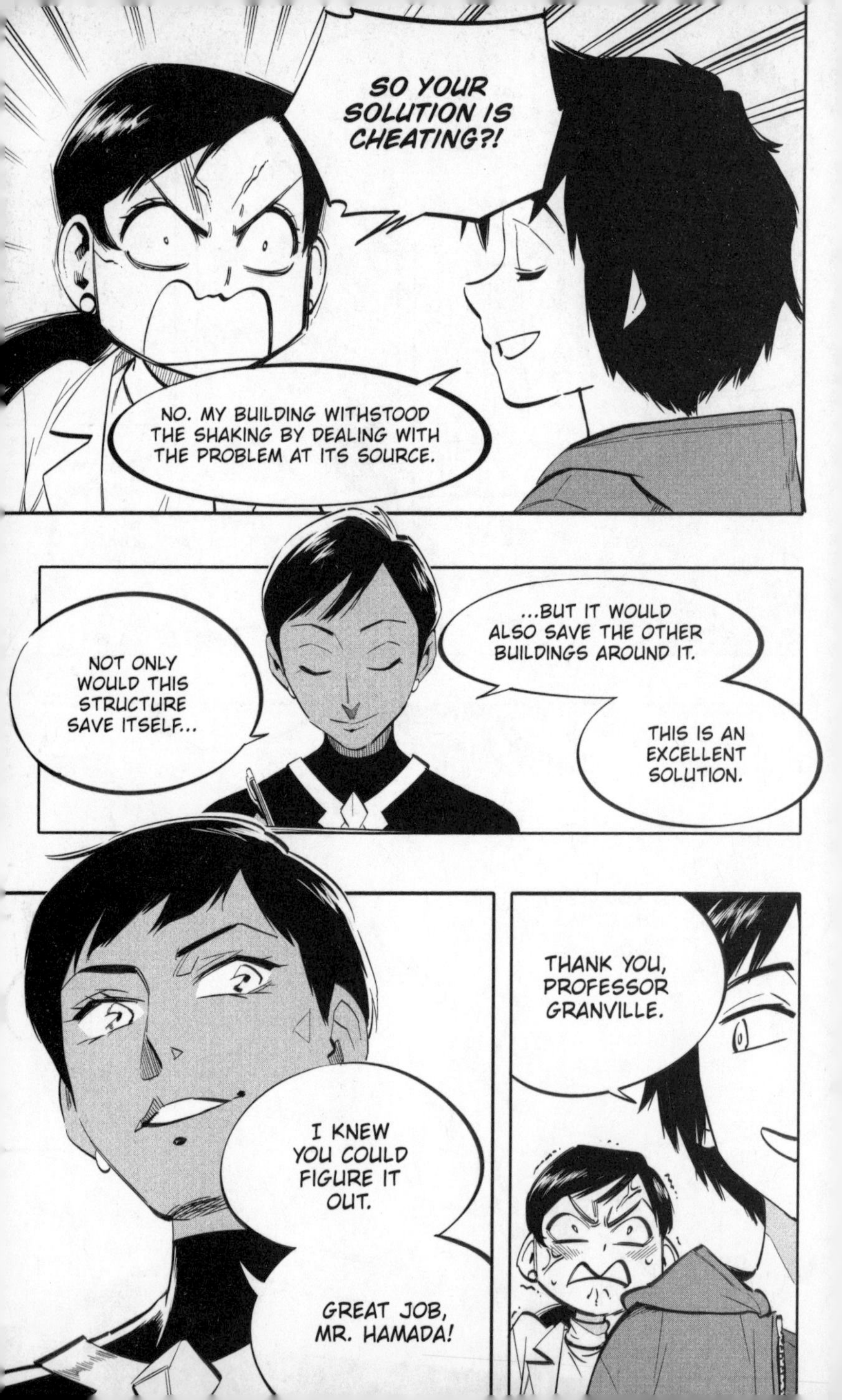
SO YOUR SOLUTION IS CHEATING?!
NO. MY BUILDING WITHSTOOD THE SHAKING BY DEALING WITH THE PROBLEM AT ITS SOURCE.
NOT ONLY WOULD THIS STRUCTURE SAVE ITSELF...
...BUT IT WOULD ALSO SAVE THE OTHER BUILDINGS AROUND IT.
THIS IS AN EXCELLENT SOLUTION.
I KNEW YOU COULD FIGURE IT OUT.
GREAT JOB, MR. HAMADA!
THANK YOU, PROFESSOR GRANVILLE.

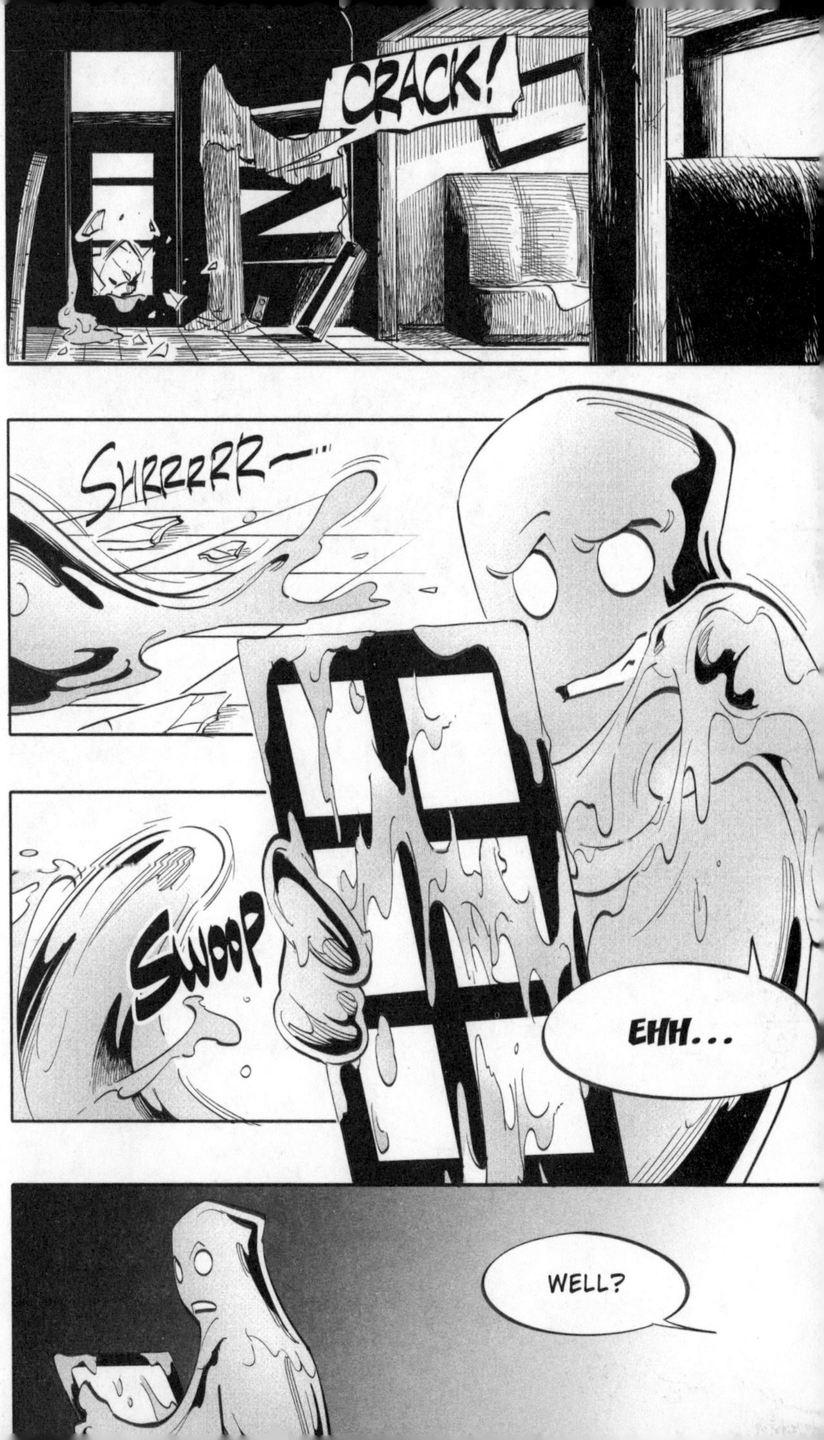
CRACK!
SHRRRRR—
SWOOP
EHH...
WELL?

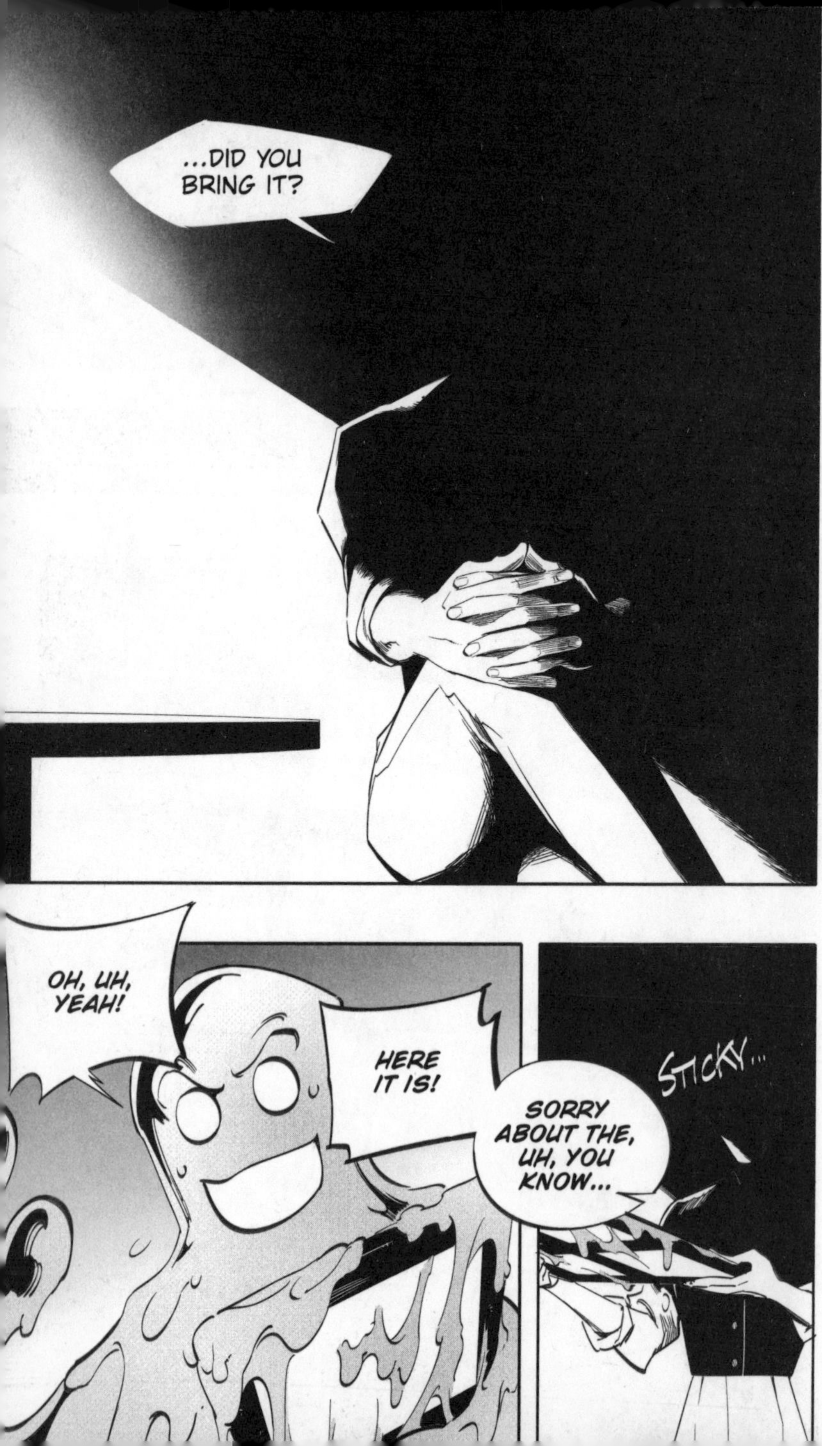
...DID YOU BRING IT?
OH, UH, YEAH!
HERE IT IS!
SORRY ABOUT THE, UH, YOU KNOW...
STICKY...

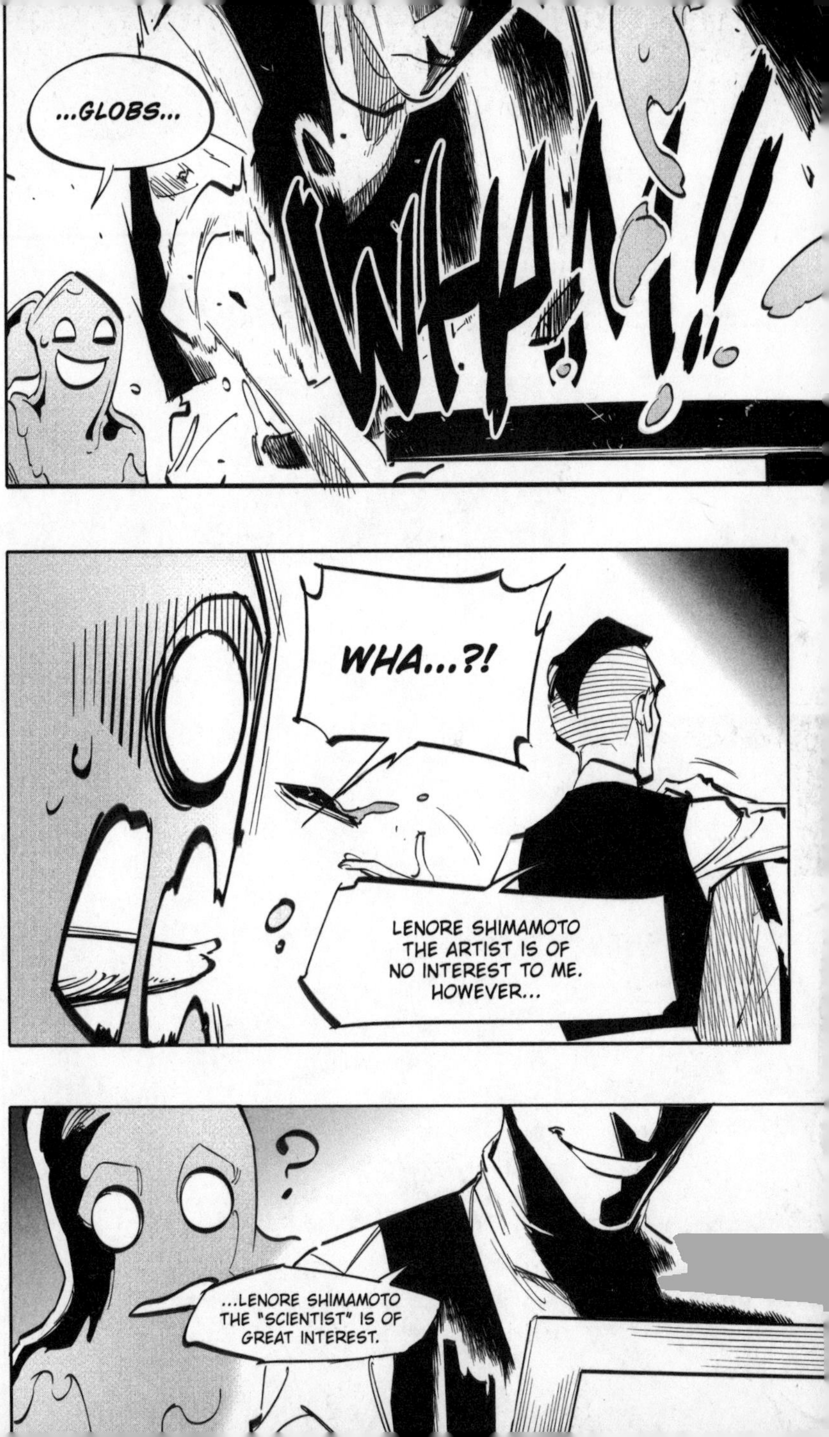
...GLOBS...
WHAM!!
WHA...?!
LENORE SHIMAMOTO THE ARTIST IS OF NO INTEREST TO ME. HOWEVER...
?
...LENORE SHIMAMOTO THE "SCIENTIST" IS OF GREAT INTEREST.

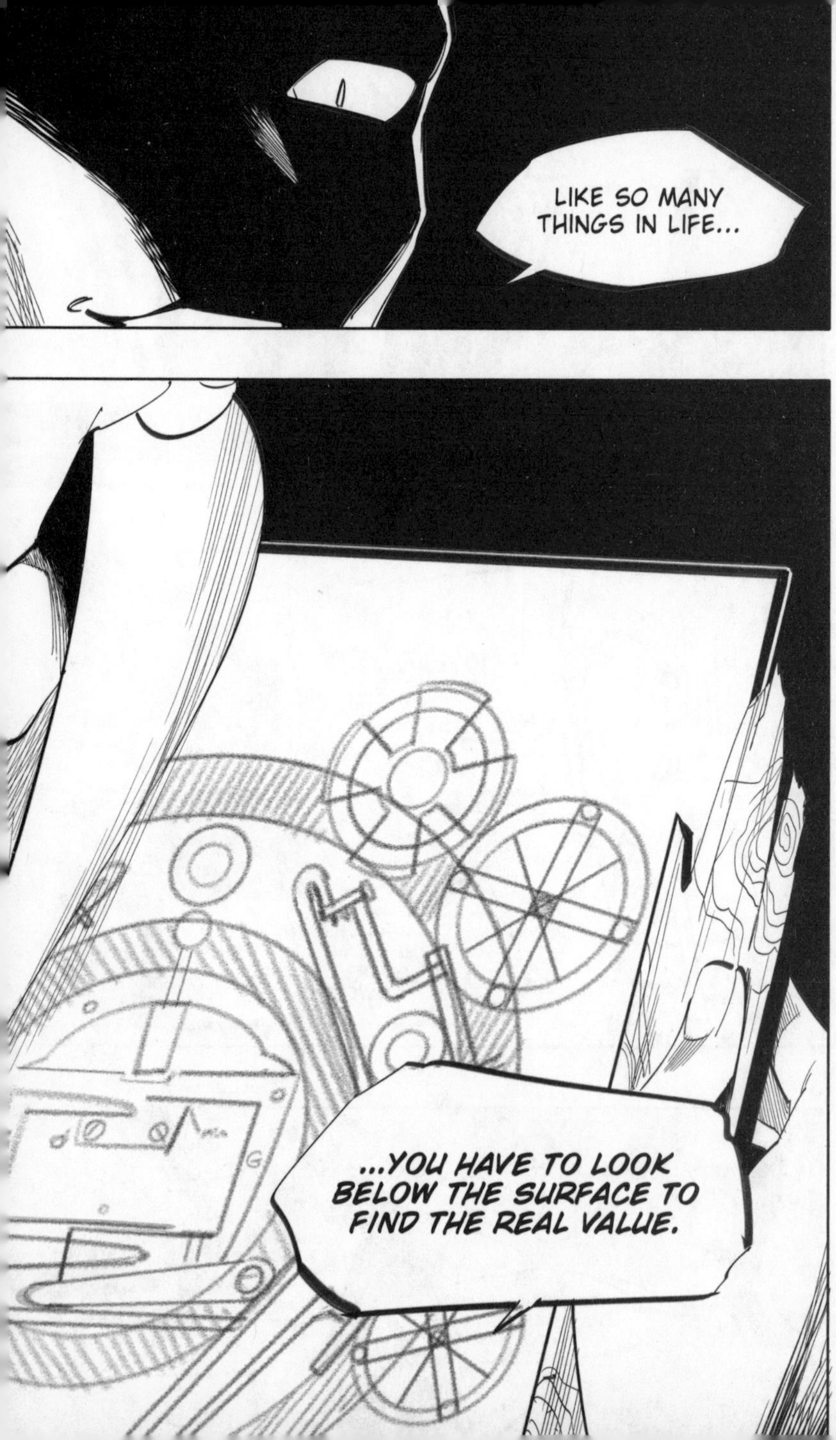
LIKE SO MANY THINGS IN LIFE...
...YOU HAVE TO LOOK BELOW THE SURFACE TO FIND THE REAL VALUE.

Disney

BIG HERO 6

THE SERIES

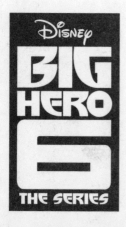

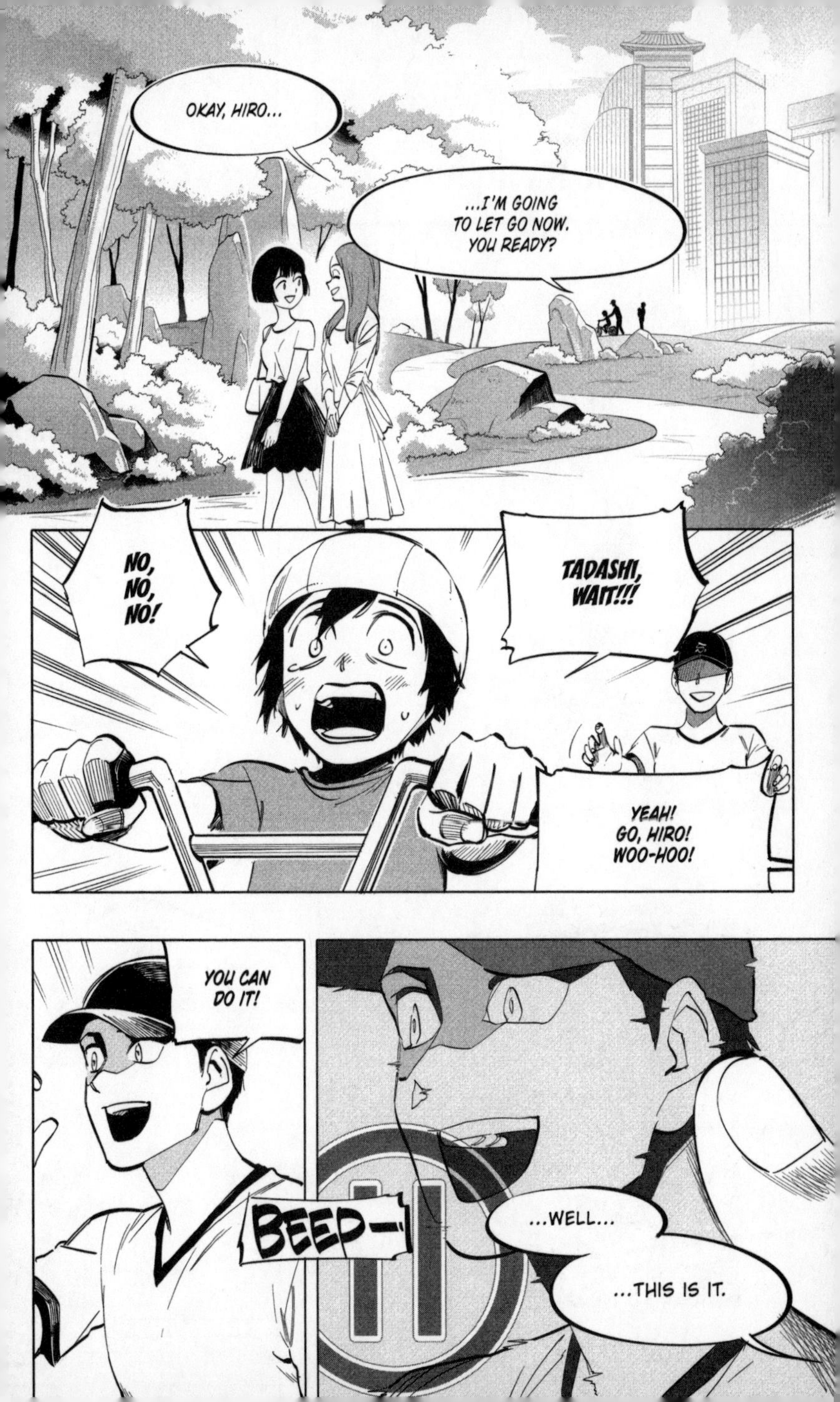
OKAY, HIRO...
...I'M GOING TO LET GO NOW. YOU READY?
NO, NO, NO!
TADASHI, WAIT!!!
YEAH! GO, HIRO! WOO-HOO!
YOU CAN DO IT!
BEEP—
...WELL...
...THIS IS IT.

Chapter 3
Baymax Returns
Part 1

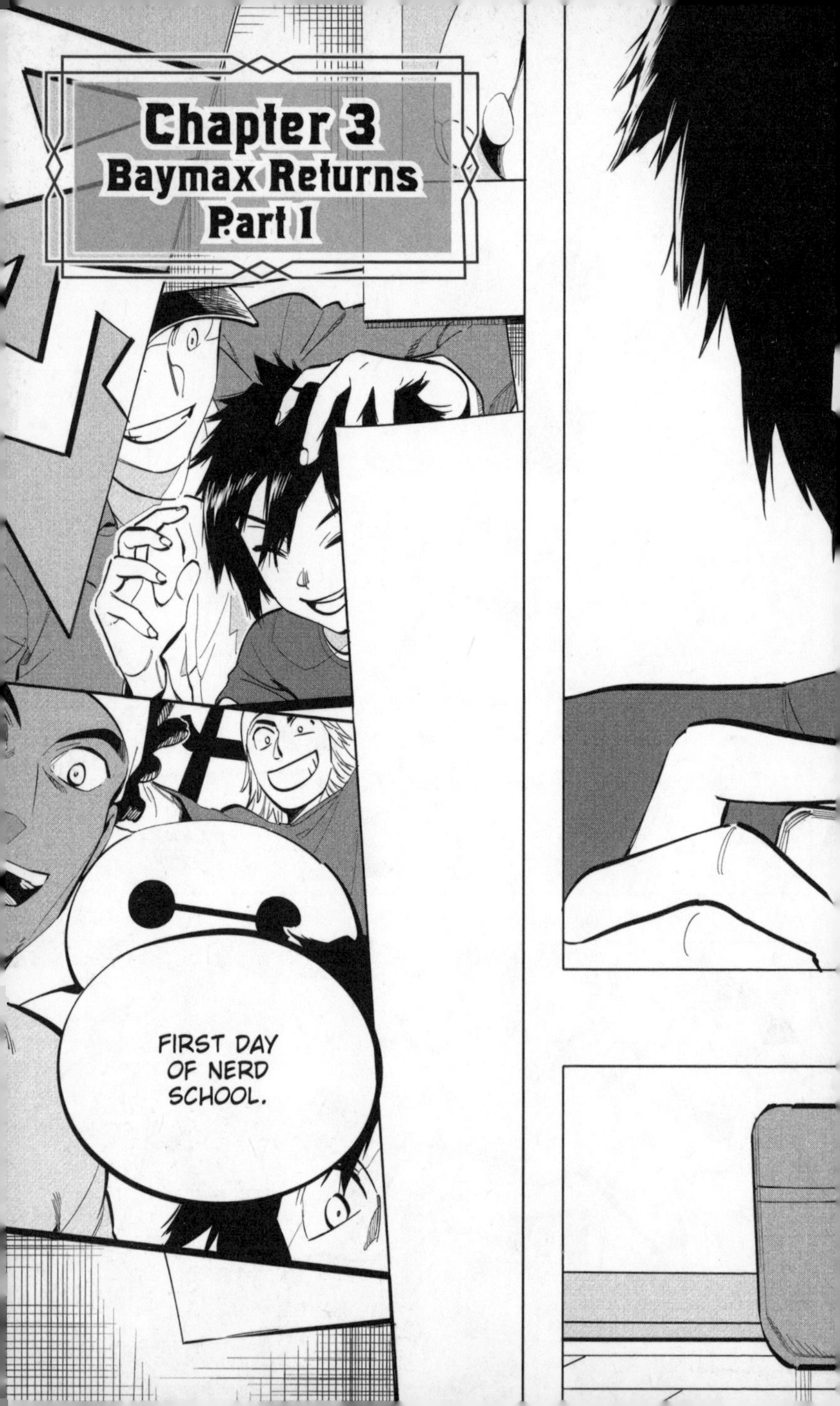
FIRST DAY OF NERD SCHOOL.

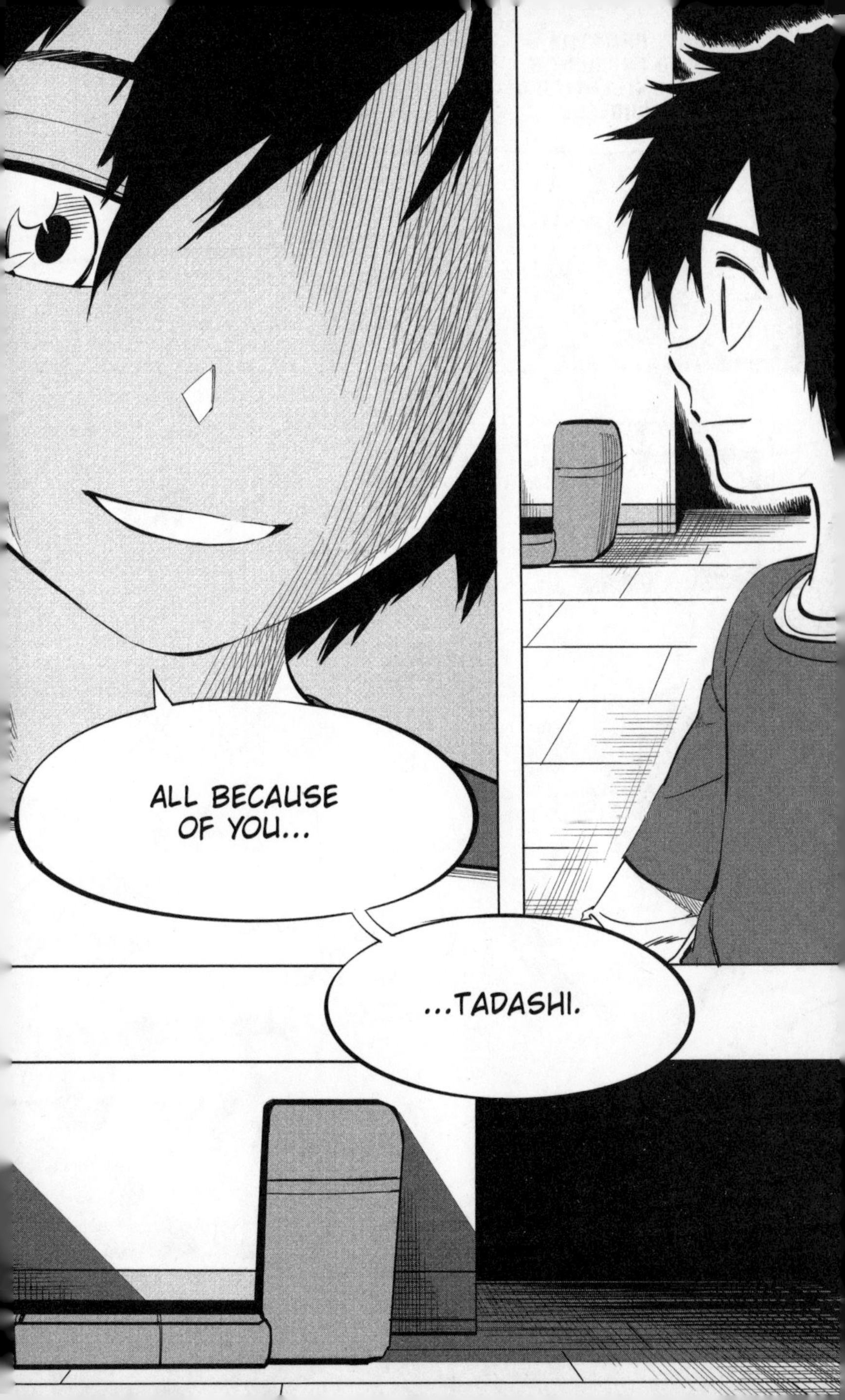
ALL BECAUSE OF YOU...
...TADASHI.

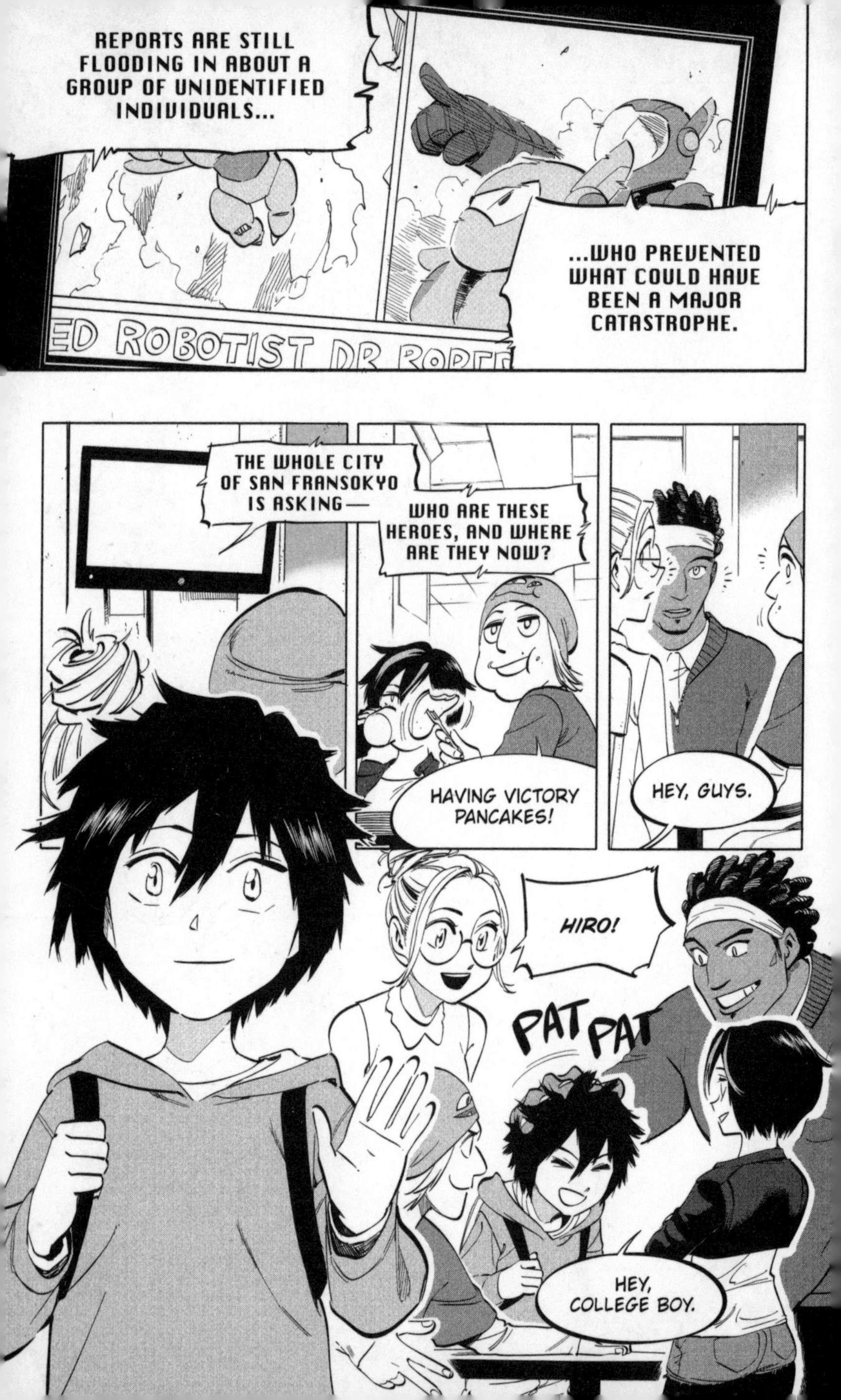
REPORTS ARE STILL FLOODING IN ABOUT A GROUP OF UNIDENTIFIED INDIVIDUALS...
ED ROBOTIST DR ROBE
...WHO PREVENTED WHAT COULD HAVE BEEN A MAJOR CATASTROPHE.
THE WHOLE CITY OF SAN FRANSOKYO IS ASKING—
WHO ARE THESE HEROES, AND WHERE ARE THEY NOW?
HAVING VICTORY PANCAKES!
HEY, GUYS.
HIRO!
PAT PAT
HEY, COLLEGE BOY.

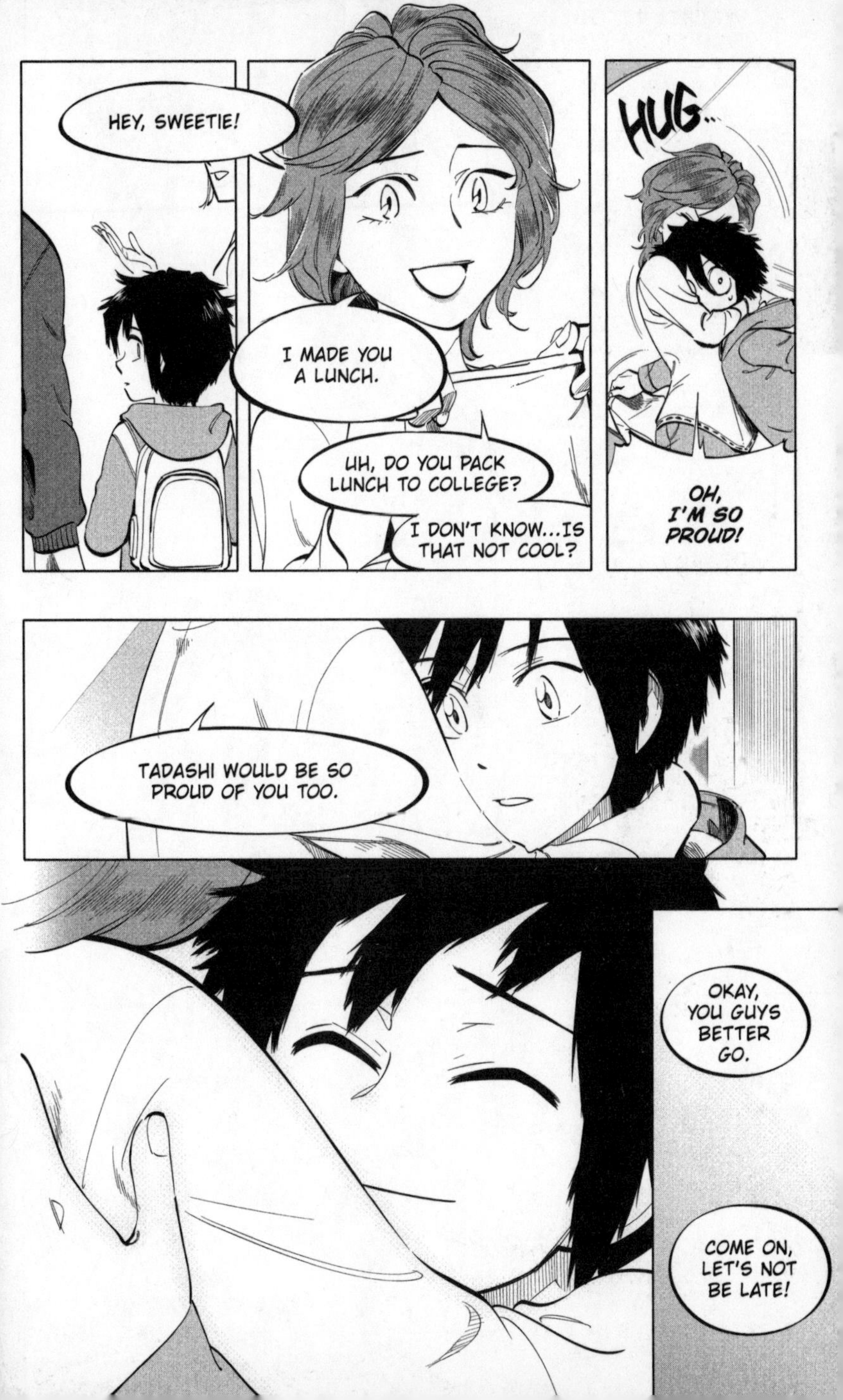
HEY, SWEETIE!
I MADE YOU A LUNCH.
UH, DO YOU PACK LUNCH TO COLLEGE?
I DON'T KNOW...IS THAT NOT COOL?
HUG..
OH, I'M SO PROUD!
TADASHI WOULD BE SO PROUD OF YOU TOO.
OKAY, YOU GUYS BETTER GO.
COME ON, LET'S NOT BE LATE!

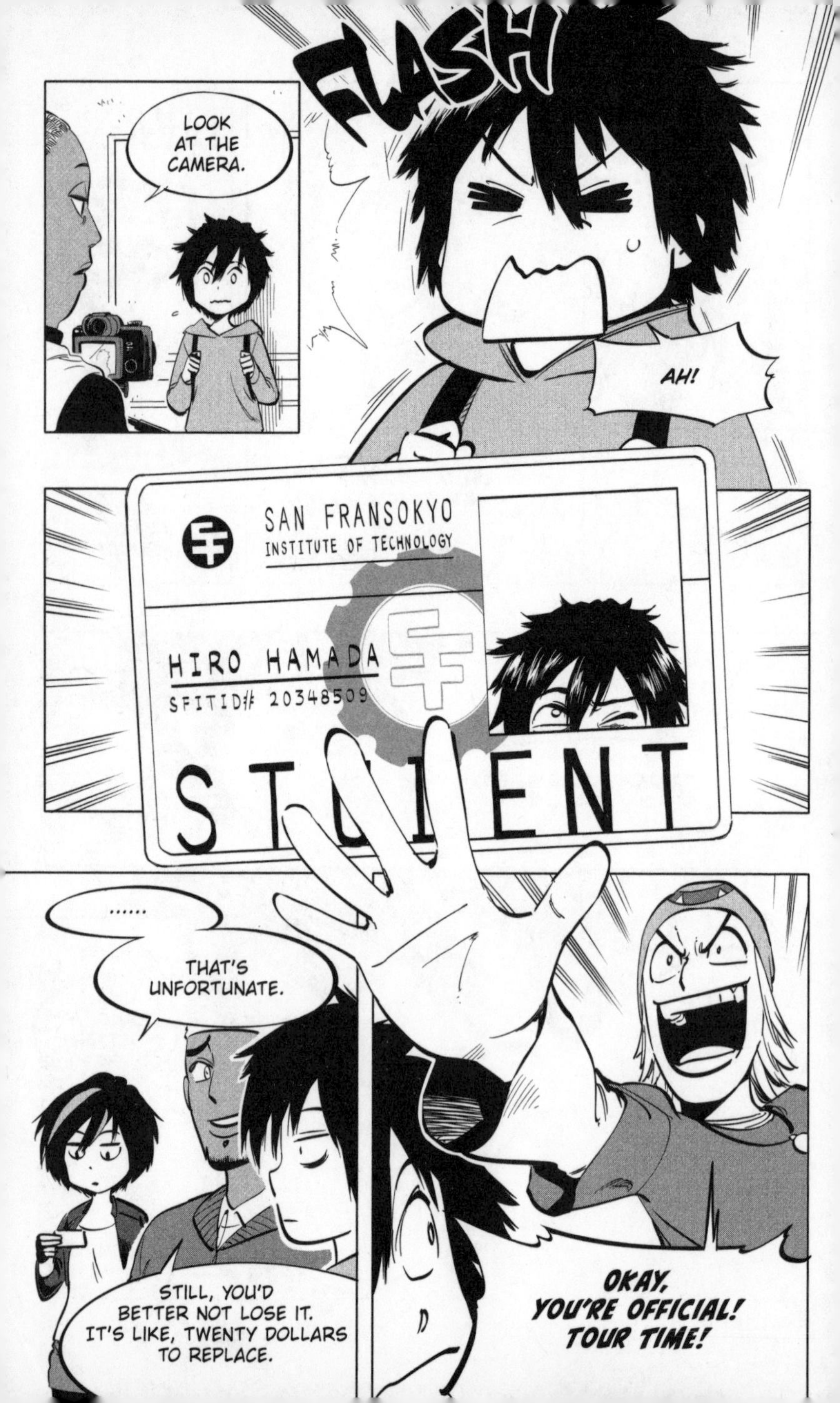
LOOK AT THE CAMERA.
FLASH
AH!
SAN FRANSOKYO INSTITUTE OF TECHNOLOGY
HIRO HAMADA
SFITID# 20348509
STUDENT
......
THAT'S UNFORTUNATE.
STILL, YOU'D BETTER NOT LOSE IT. IT'S LIKE, TWENTY DOLLARS TO REPLACE.
OKAY, YOU'RE OFFICIAL! TOUR TIME!

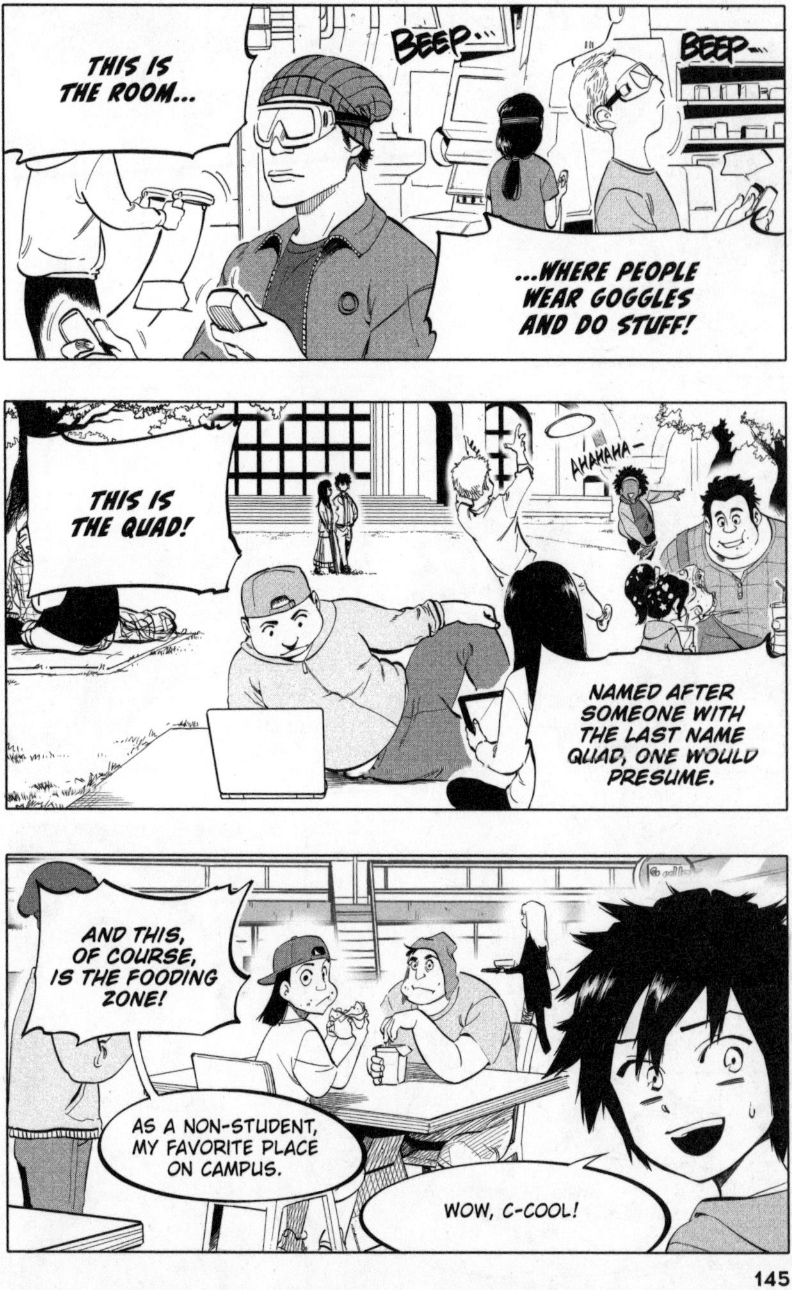
THIS IS THE ROOM...
BEEP...
BEEP...
...WHERE PEOPLE WEAR GOGGLES AND DO STUFF!
THIS IS THE QUAD!
AHAHAHA-
NAMED AFTER SOMEONE WITH THE LAST NAME QUAD, ONE WOULD PRESUME.
AND THIS, OF COURSE, IS THE FOODING ZONE!
AS A NON-STUDENT, MY FAVORITE PLACE ON CAMPUS.
WOW, C-COOL!

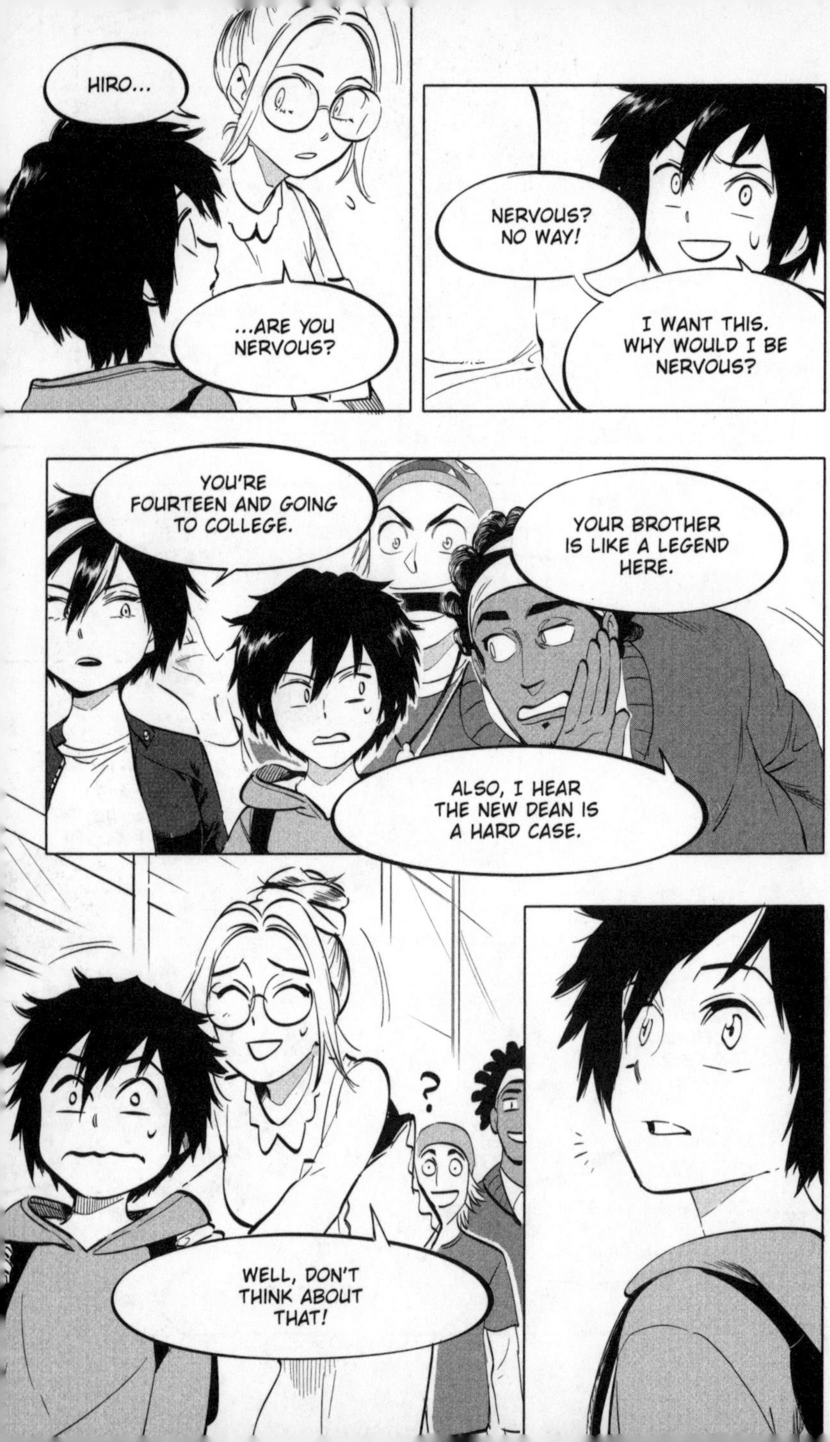
HIRO...
...ARE YOU NERVOUS?
NERVOUS? NO WAY!
I WANT THIS. WHY WOULD I BE NERVOUS?
YOU'RE FOURTEEN AND GOING TO COLLEGE.
YOUR BROTHER IS LIKE A LEGEND HERE.
ALSO, I HEAR THE NEW DEAN IS A HARD CASE.
?
WELL, DON'T THINK ABOUT THAT!

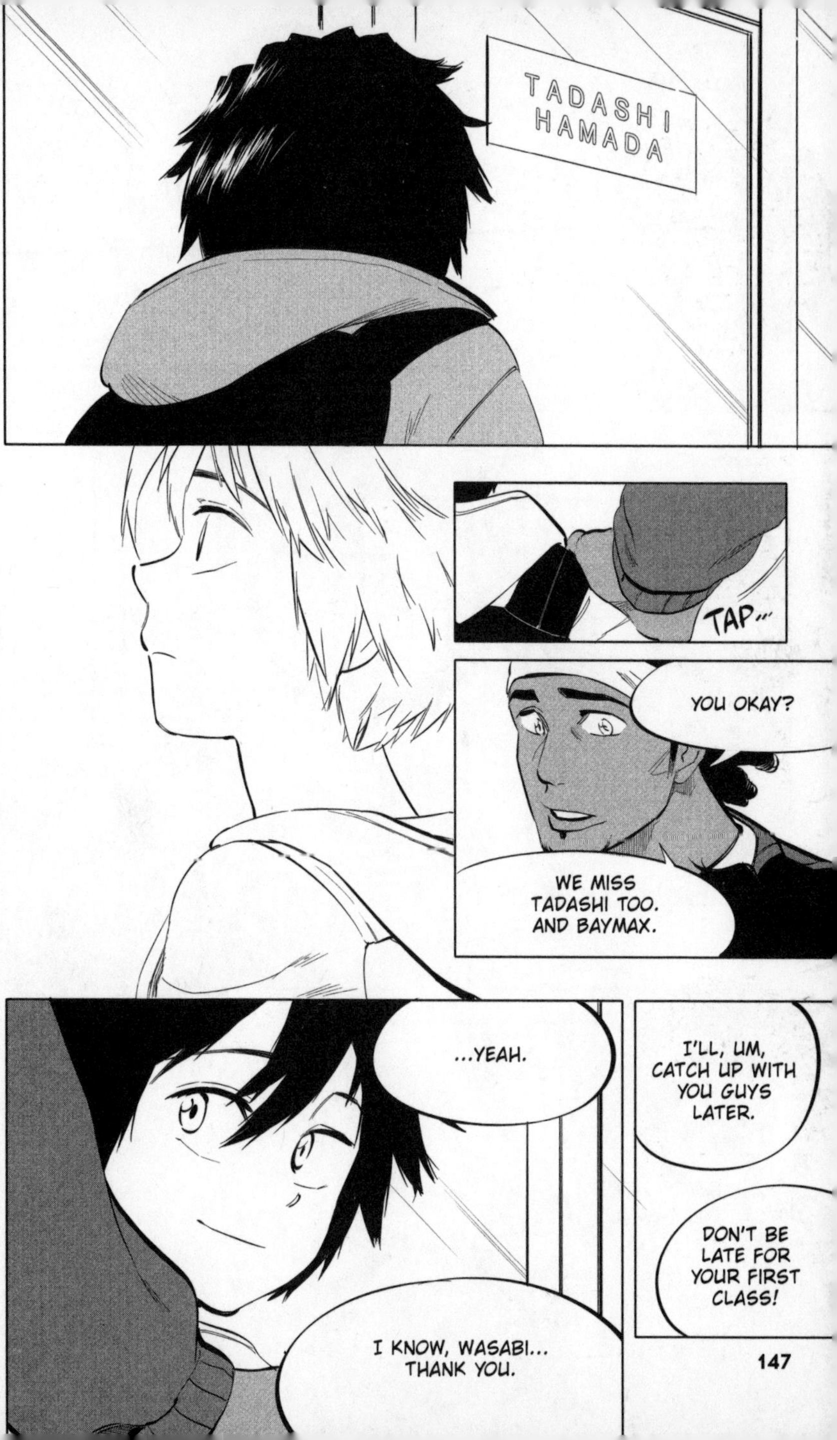
TADASHI HAMADA
TAP...
YOU OKAY?
WE MISS TADASHI TOO. AND BAYMAX.
...YEAH.
I KNOW, WASABI... THANK YOU.
I'LL, UM, CATCH UP WITH YOU GUYS LATER.
DON'T BE LATE FOR YOUR FIRST CLASS!

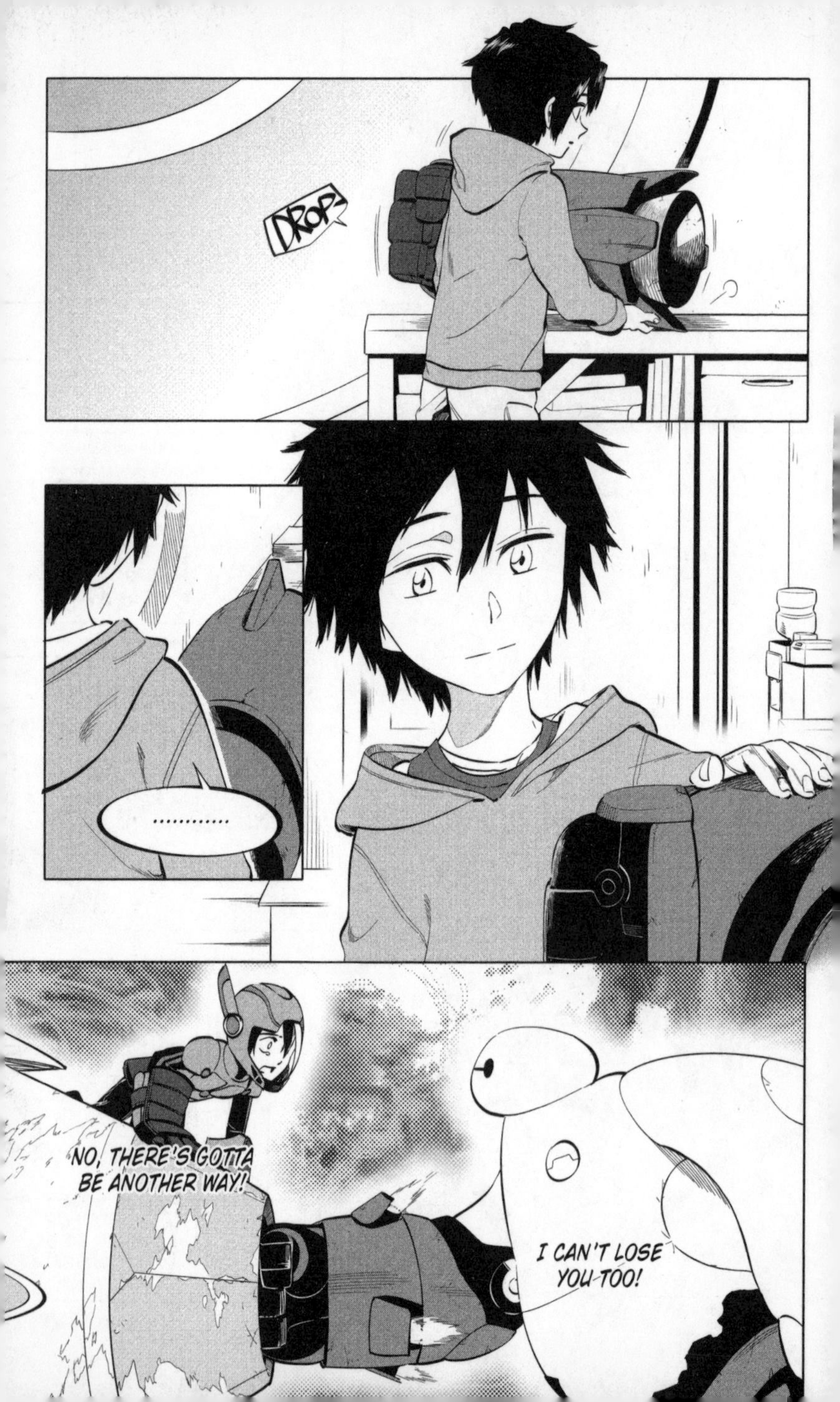
DROP
....
NO, THERE'S GOTTA BE ANOTHER WAY!
I CAN'T LOSE YOU TOO!

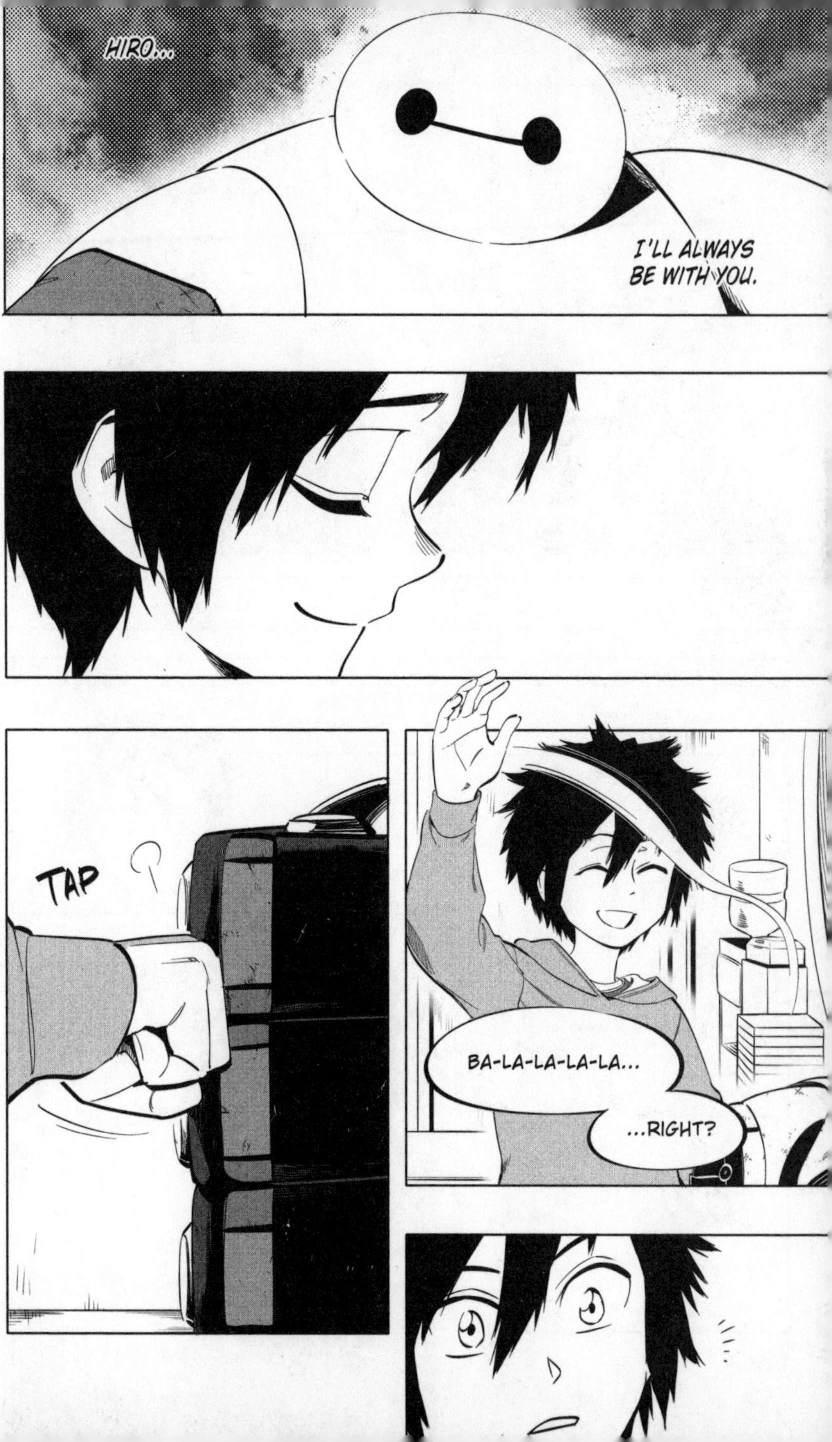
HIRO...
I'LL ALWAYS BE WITH YOU.
TAP
BA-LA-LA-LA-LA...
...RIGHT?

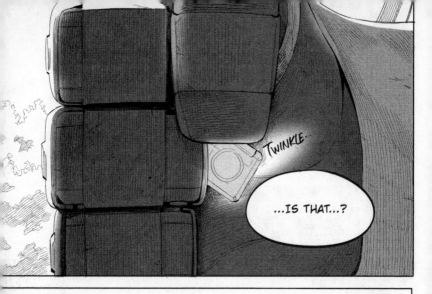

TWINKLE...

...IS THAT...?

HI HAMADA

CLACK—

WHOo~

......

...BAYMAX?

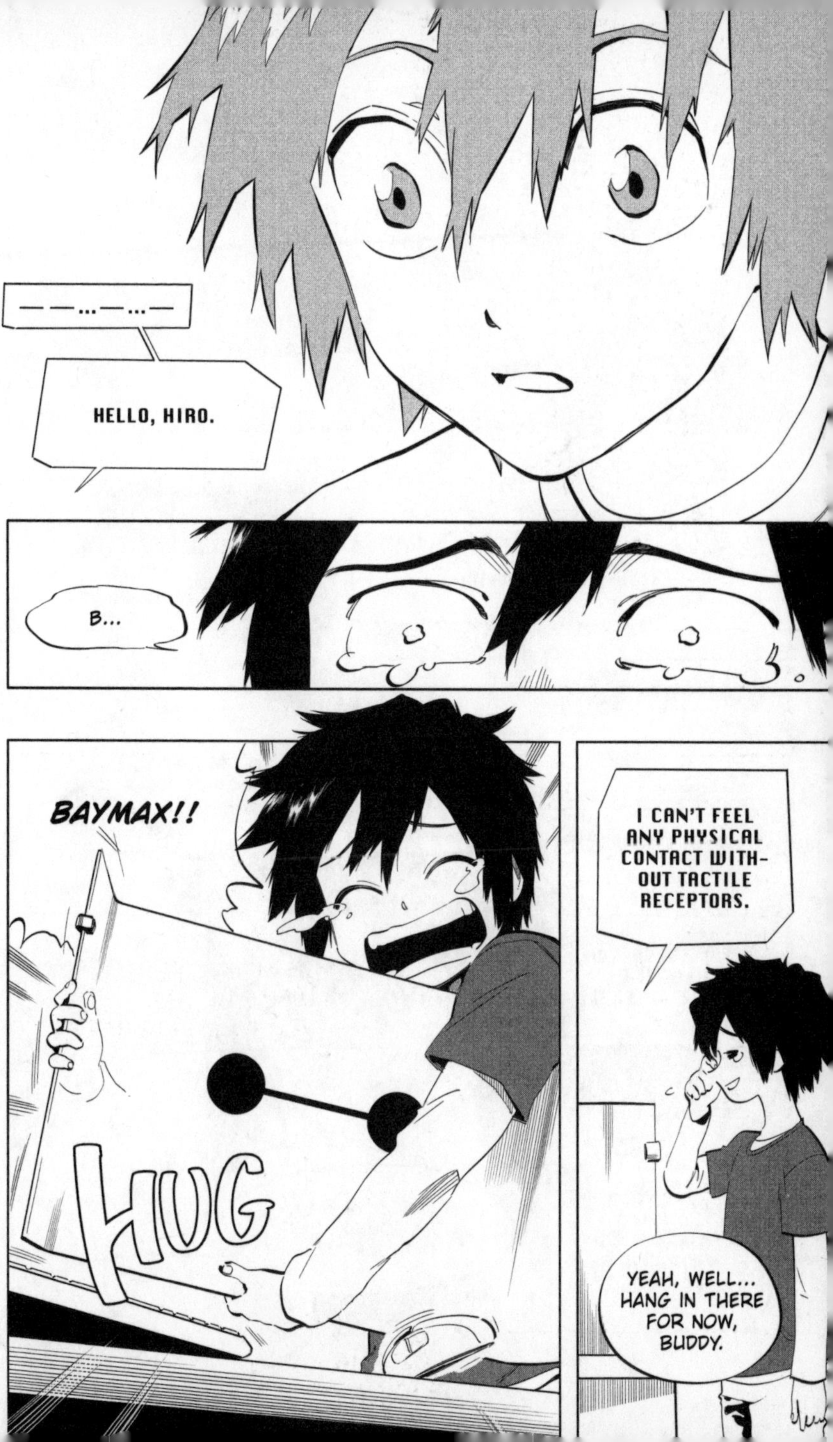
— —...—...—
HELLO, HIRO.
B...
BAYMAX!!
HUG
I CAN'T FEEL ANY PHYSICAL CONTACT WITH-OUT TACTILE RECEPTORS.
YEAH, WELL... HANG IN THERE FOR NOW, BUDDY.

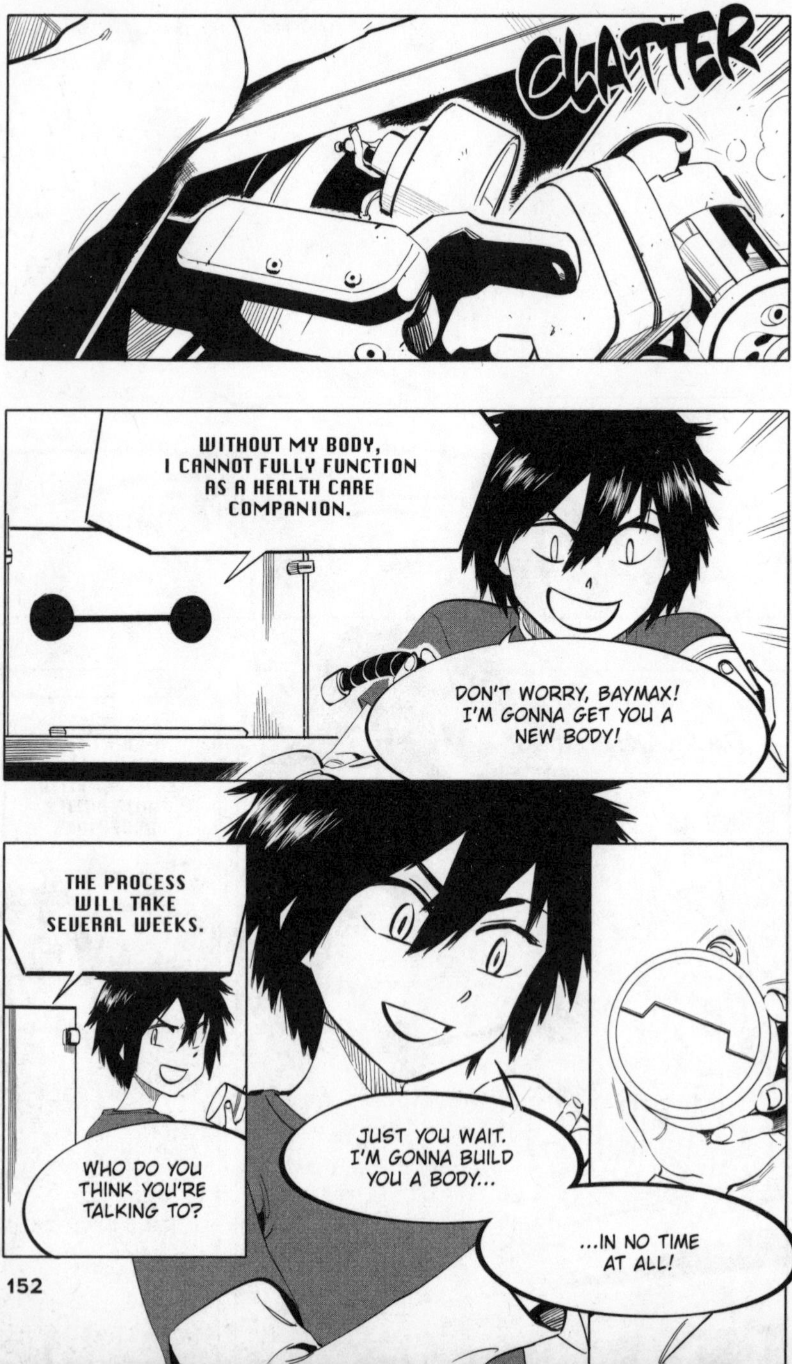
CLATTER
WITHOUT MY BODY, I CANNOT FULLY FUNCTION AS A HEALTH CARE COMPANION.
DON'T WORRY, BAYMAX! I'M GONNA GET YOU A NEW BODY!
THE PROCESS WILL TAKE SEVERAL WEEKS.
WHO DO YOU THINK YOU'RE TALKING TO?
JUST YOU WAIT. I'M GONNA BUILD YOU A BODY...
...IN NO TIME AT ALL!

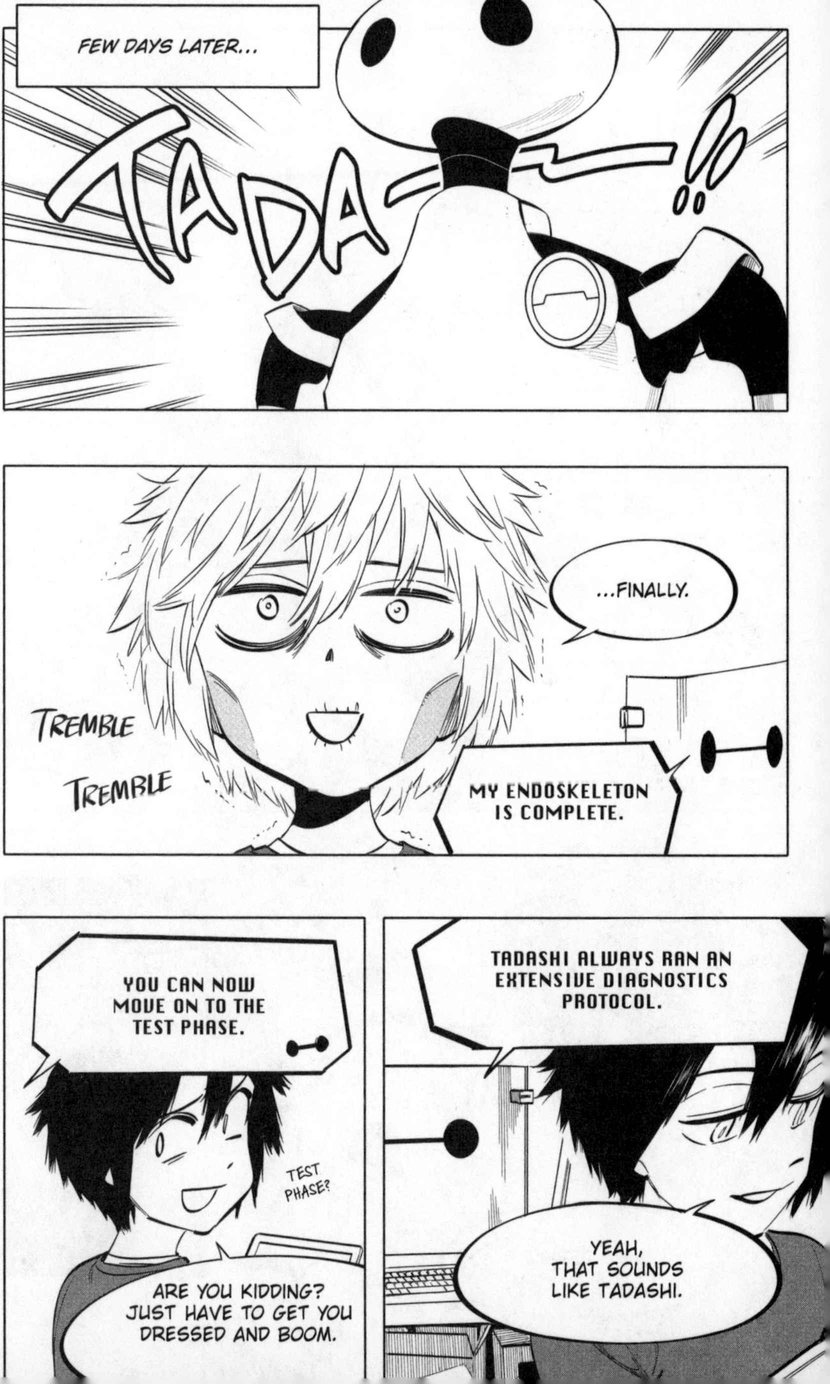
FEW DAYS LATER...
TADA—!!
...FINALLY.
TREMBLE
TREMBLE
MY ENDOSKELETON IS COMPLETE.
YOU CAN NOW MOVE ON TO THE TEST PHASE.
TEST PHASE?
ARE YOU KIDDING? JUST HAVE TO GET YOU DRESSED AND BOOM.
TADASHI ALWAYS RAN AN EXTENSIVE DIAGNOSTICS PROTOCOL.
YEAH, THAT SOUNDS LIKE TADASHI.

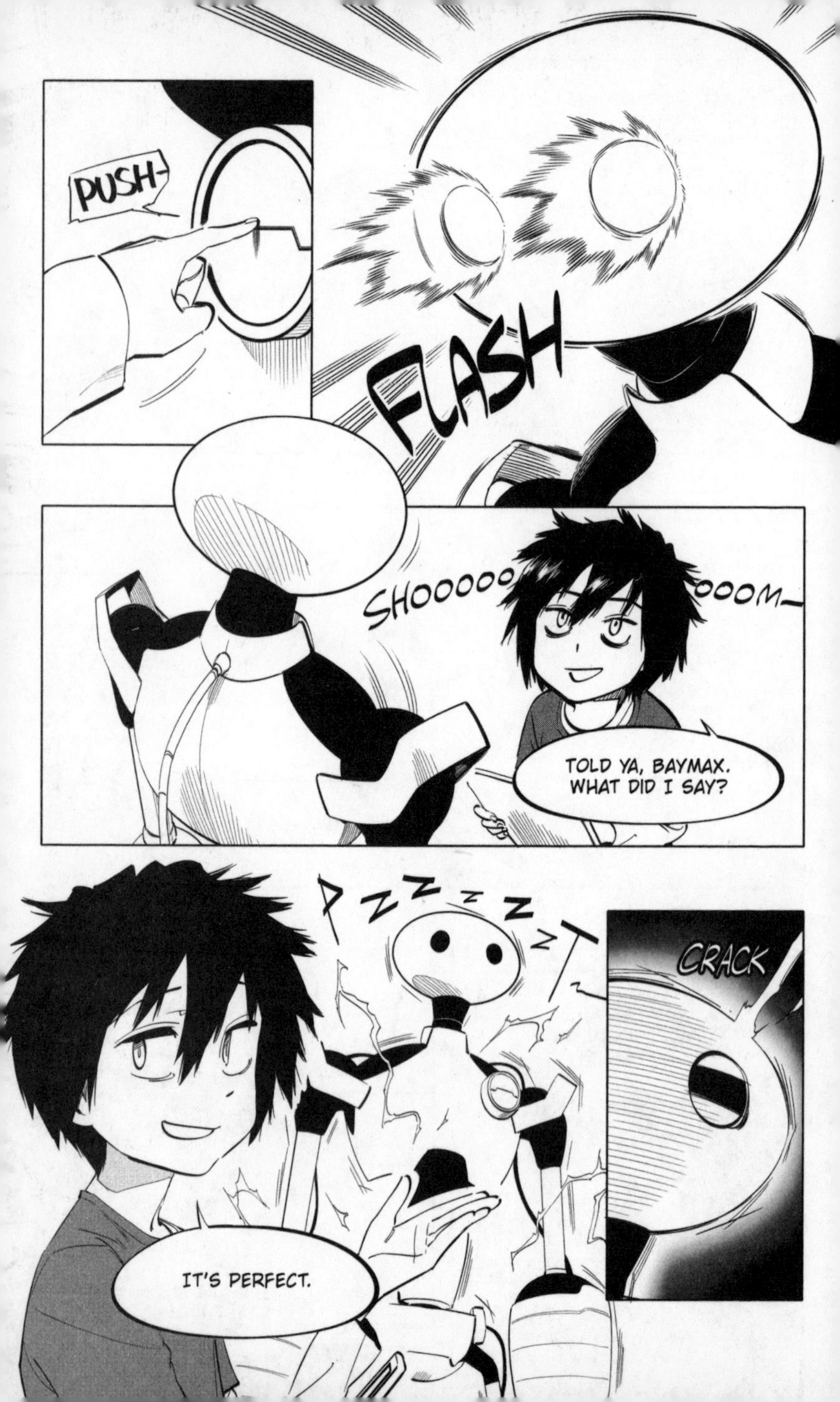
PUSH-
FLASH
SHOOOOO OOOM-
TOLD YA, BAYMAX. WHAT DID I SAY?
PZZZZZT
CRACK
IT'S PERFECT.

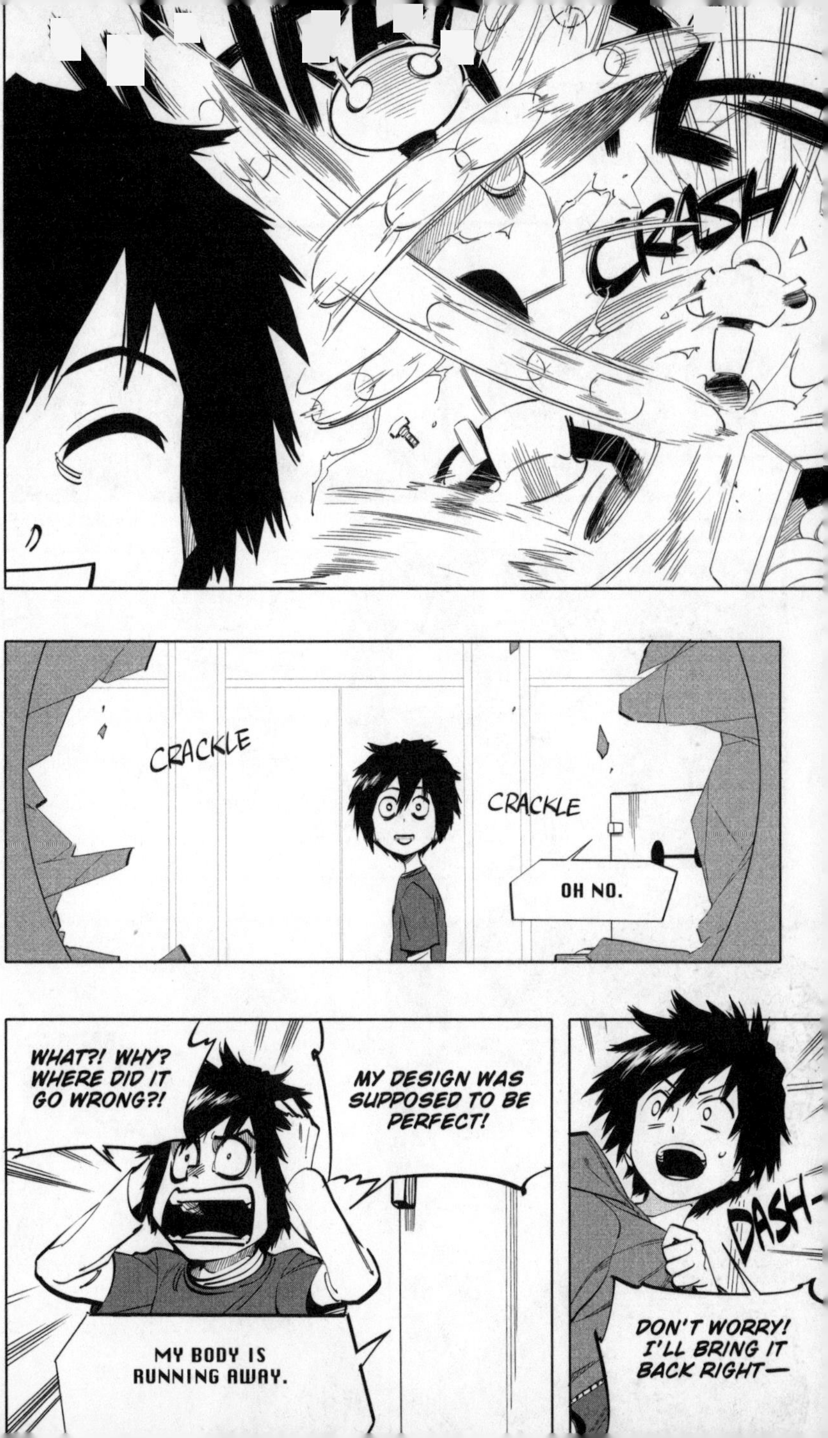
CRASH
CRACKLE
CRACKLE
OH NO.
WHAT?! WHY? WHERE DID IT GO WRONG?!
MY DESIGN WAS SUPPOSED TO BE PERFECT!
MY BODY IS RUNNING AWAY.
DASH-
DON'T WORRY! I'LL BRING IT BACK RIGHT—

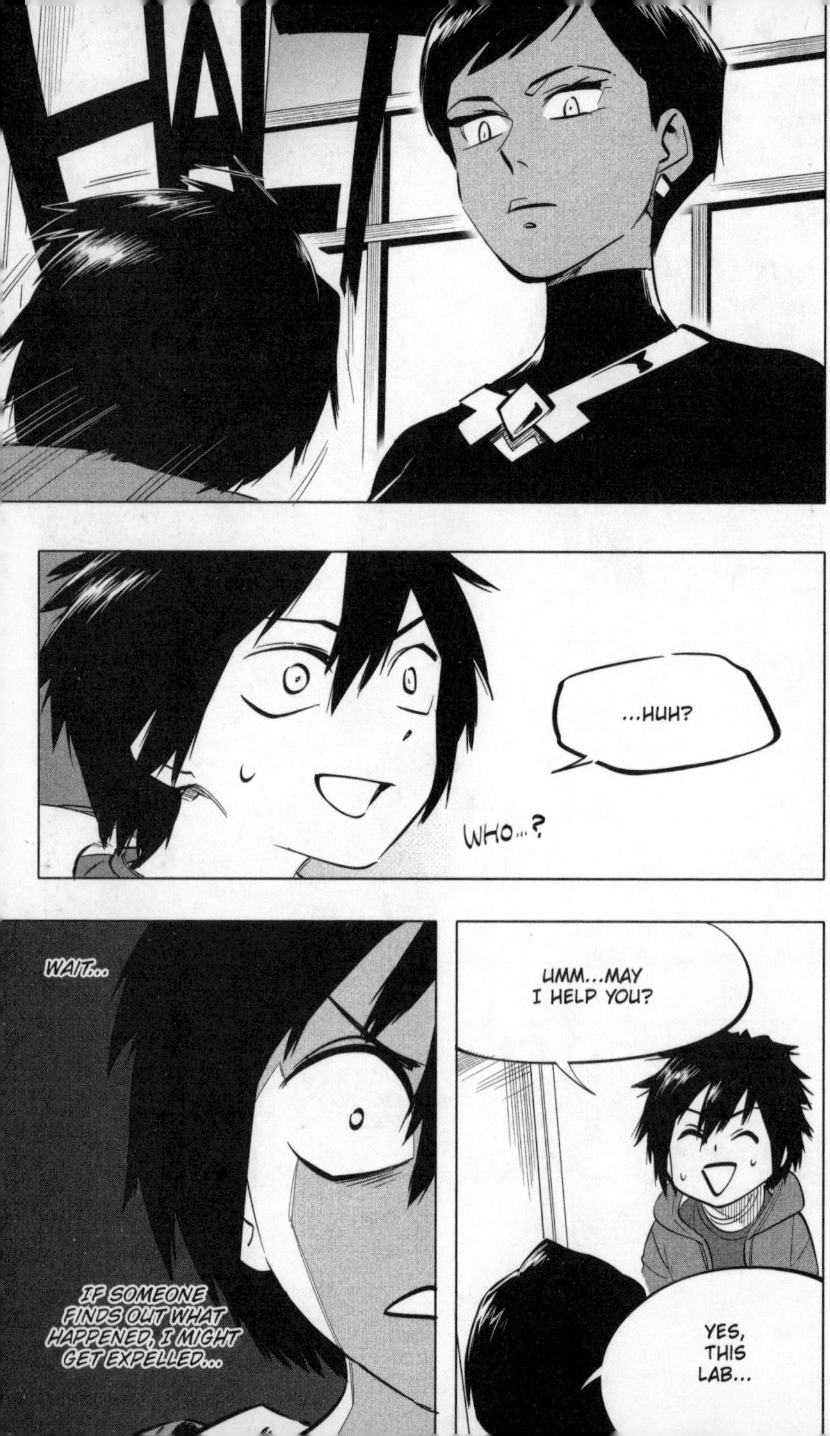
...HUH?
WHO...?
WAIT...
IF SOMEONE FINDS OUT WHAT HAPPENED, I MIGHT GET EXPELLED...
UMM...MAY I HELP YOU?
YES, THIS LAB...

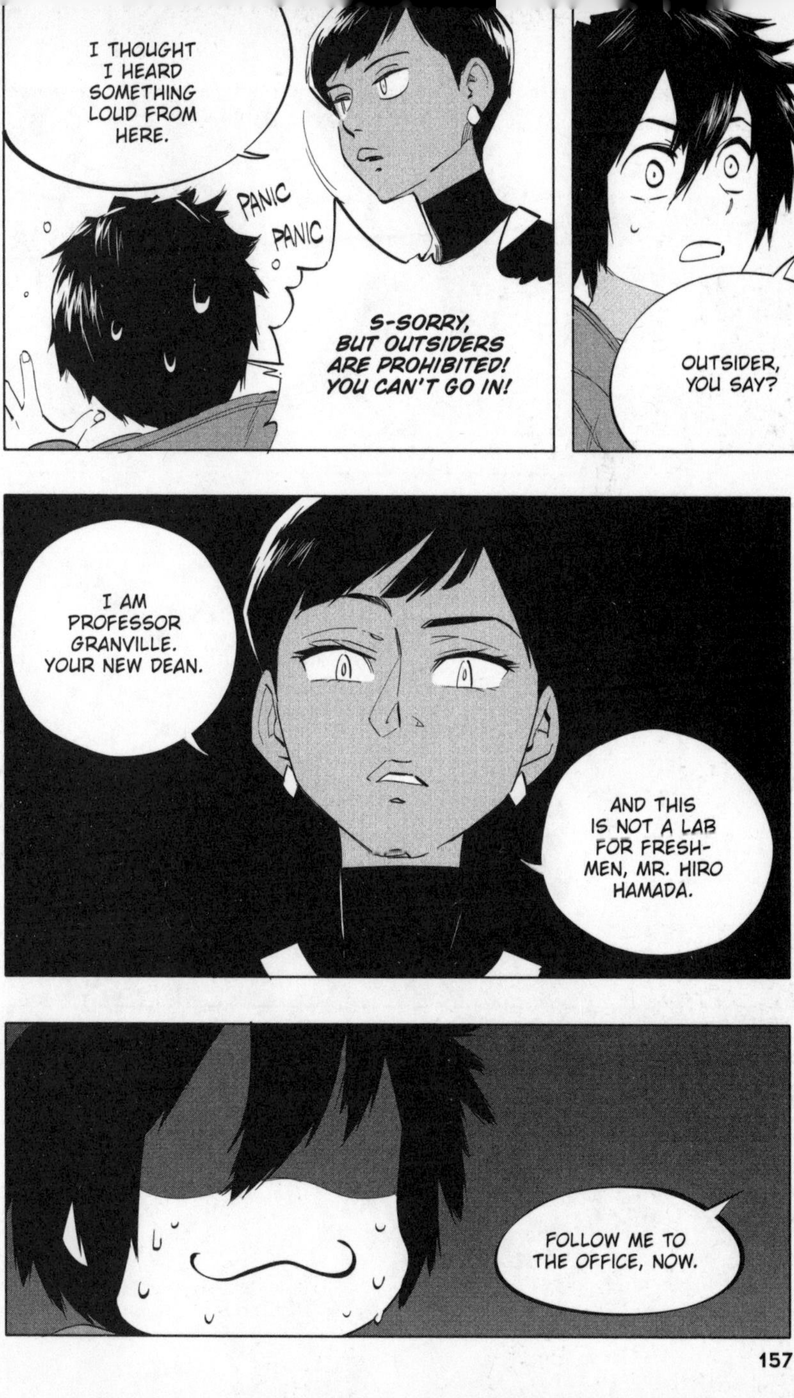
I THOUGHT I HEARD SOMETHING LOUD FROM HERE.
PANIC
PANIC
S-SORRY, BUT OUTSIDERS ARE PROHIBITED! YOU CAN'T GO IN!
OUTSIDER, YOU SAY?
I AM PROFESSOR GRANVILLE. YOUR NEW DEAN.
AND THIS IS NOT A LAB FOR FRESH-MEN, MR. HIRO HAMADA.
FOLLOW ME TO THE OFFICE, NOW.

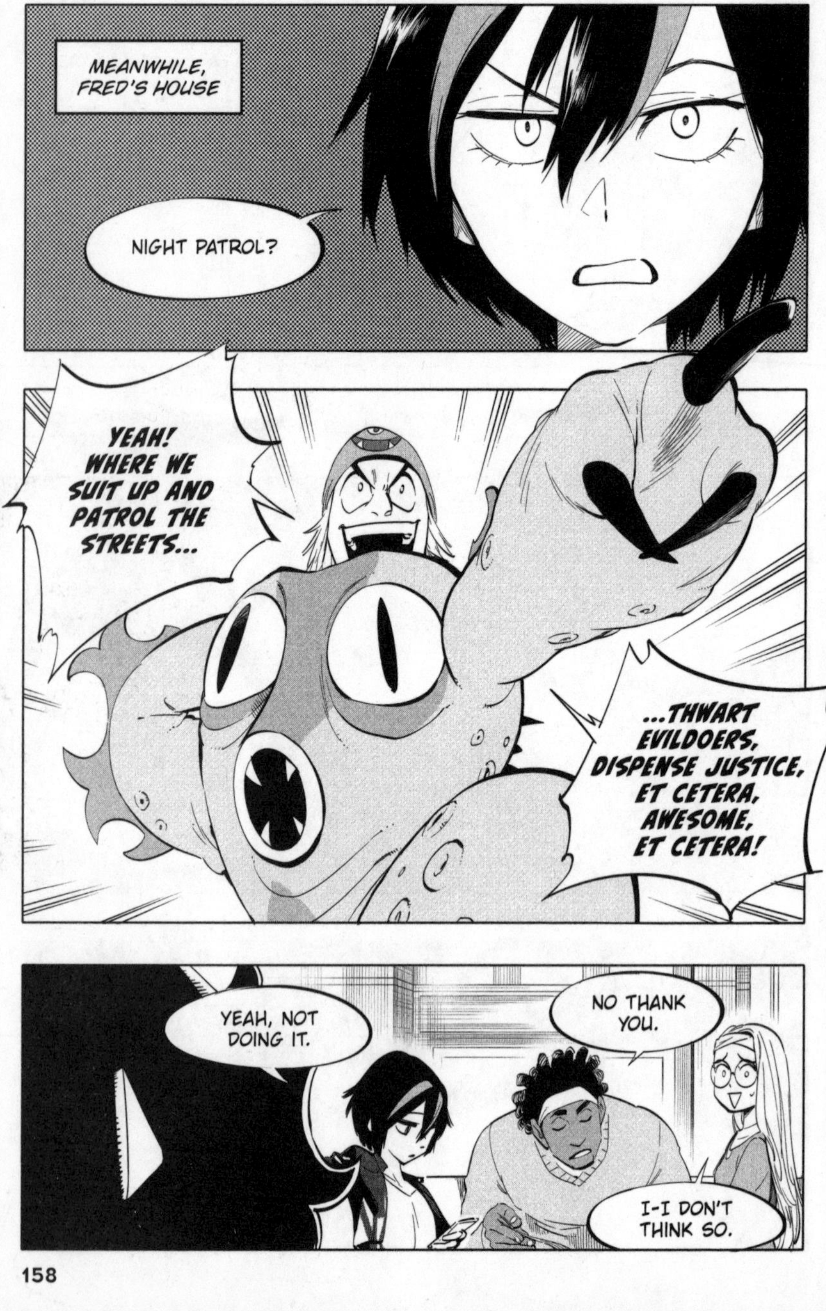
MEANWHILE, FRED'S HOUSE
NIGHT PATROL?
YEAH! WHERE WE SUIT UP AND PATROL THE STREETS...
...THWART EVILDOERS, DISPENSE JUSTICE, ET CETERA, AWESOME, ET CETERA!
YEAH, NOT DOING IT.
NO THANK YOU.
I-I DON'T THINK SO.

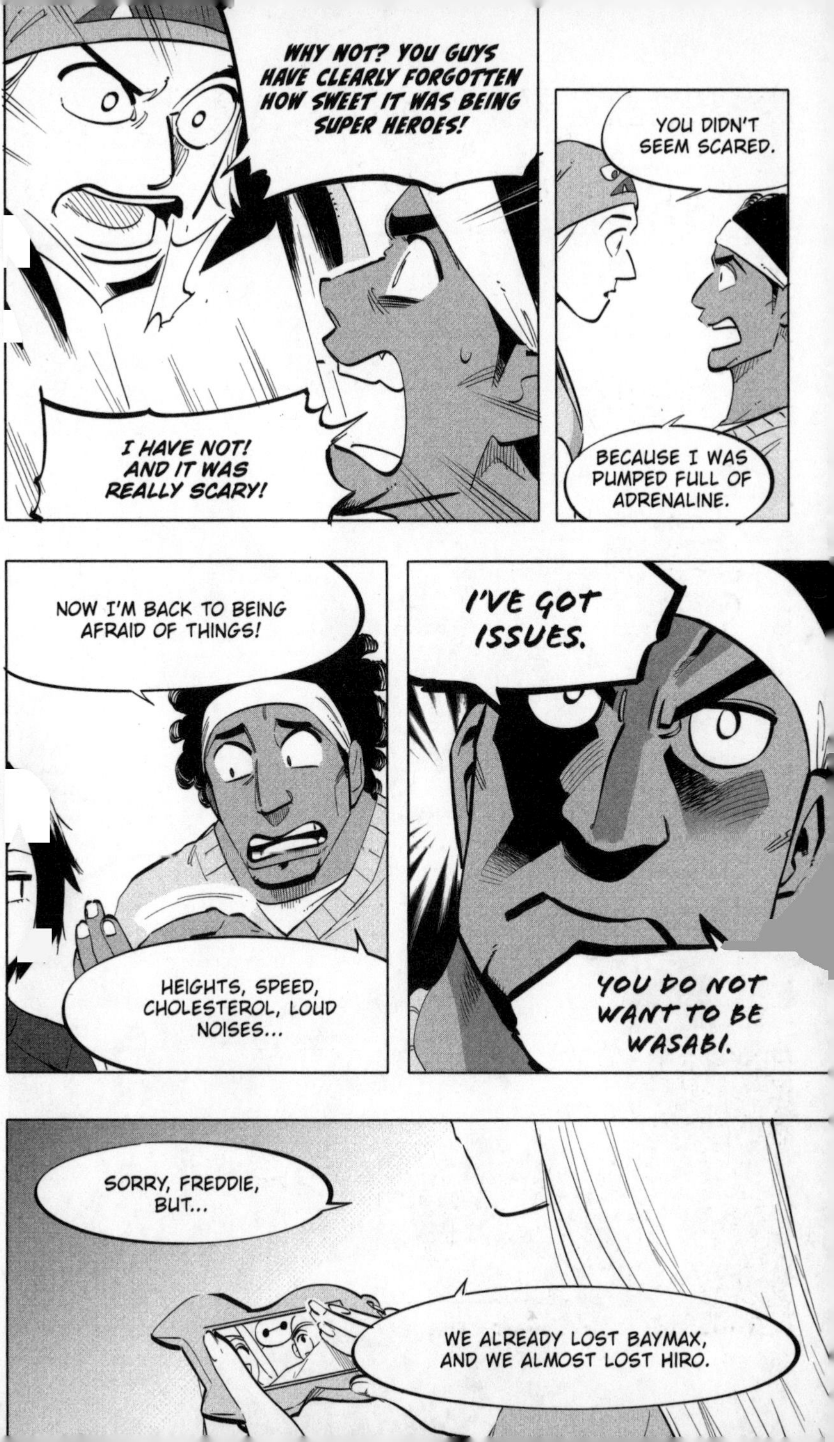
WHY NOT? YOU GUYS HAVE CLEARLY FORGOTTEN HOW SWEET IT WAS BEING SUPER HEROES!
I HAVE NOT! AND IT WAS REALLY SCARY!
YOU DIDN'T SEEM SCARED.
BECAUSE I WAS PUMPED FULL OF ADRENALINE.
NOW I'M BACK TO BEING AFRAID OF THINGS!
HEIGHTS, SPEED, CHOLESTEROL, LOUD NOISES...
I'VE GOT ISSUES.
YOU DO NOT WANT TO BE WASABI.
SORRY, FREDDIE, BUT...
WE ALREADY LOST BAYMAX, AND WE ALMOST LOST HIRO.

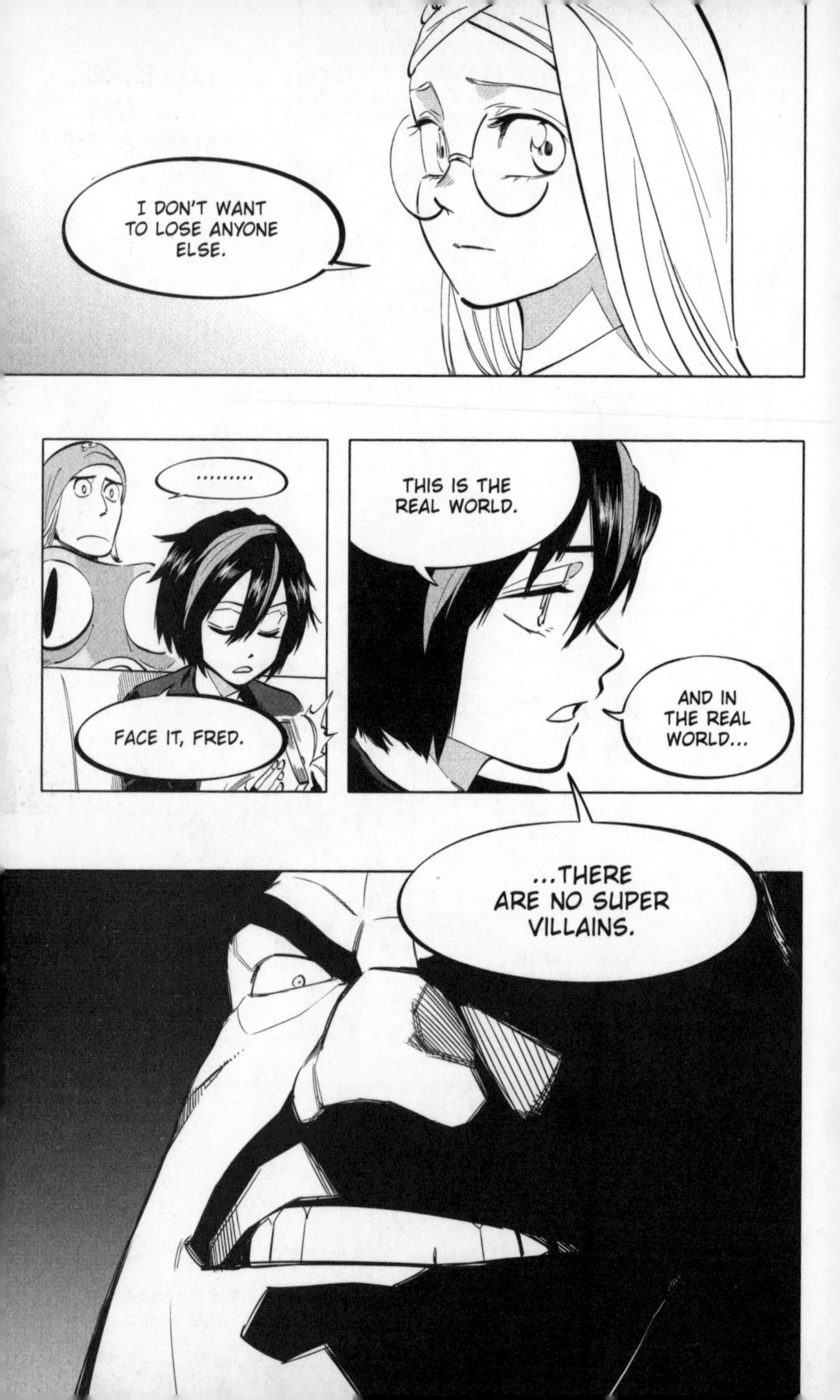
I DON'T WANT TO LOSE ANYONE ELSE.
....
FACE IT, FRED.
THIS IS THE REAL WORLD.
AND IN THE REAL WORLD...
...THERE ARE NO SUPER VILLAINS.

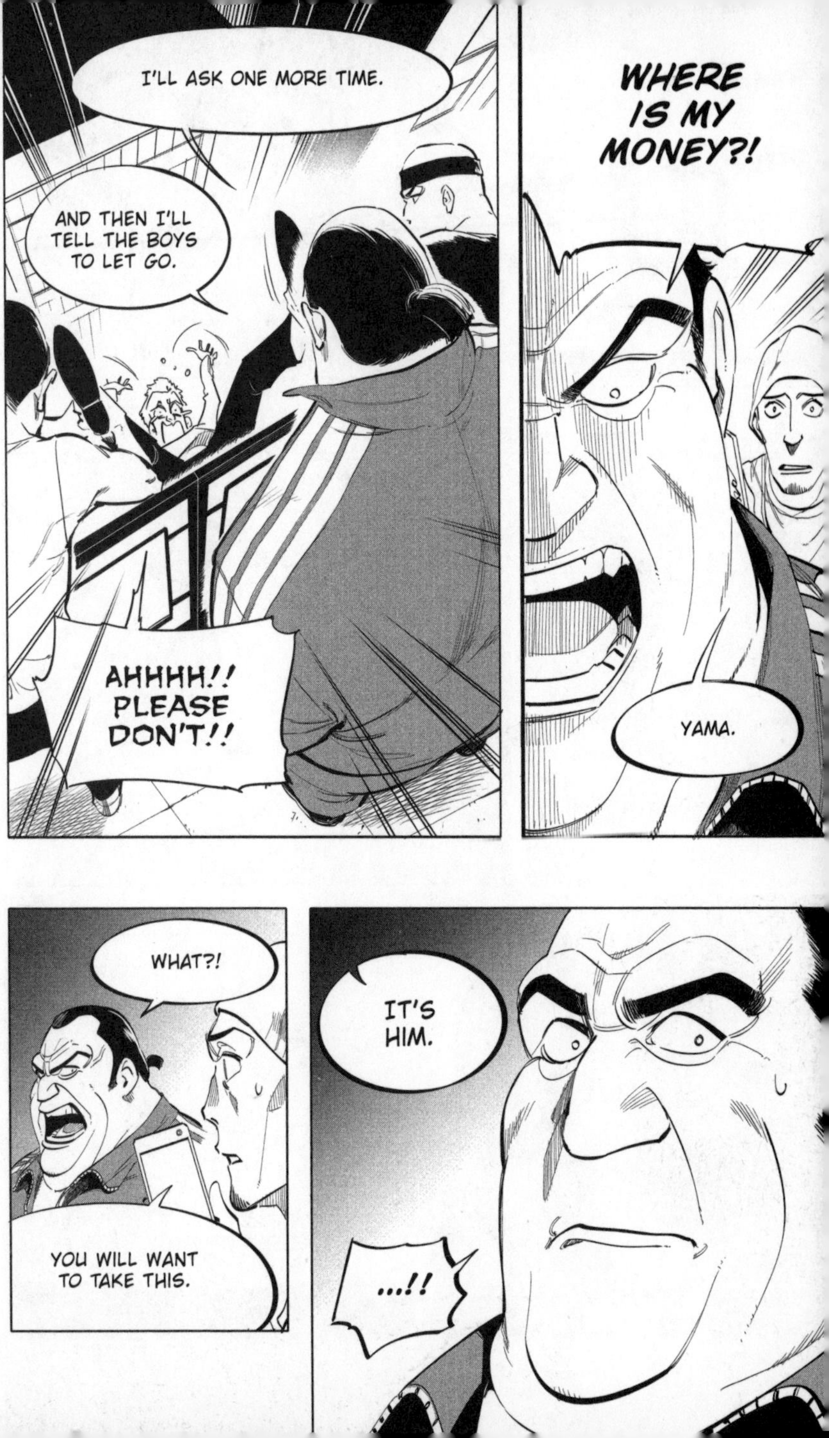
I'LL ASK ONE MORE TIME.
AND THEN I'LL TELL THE BOYS TO LET GO.
AHHHH!! PLEASE DON'T!!
WHERE IS MY MONEY?!
YAMA.
WHAT?!
YOU WILL WANT TO TAKE THIS.
IT'S HIM.
...!!

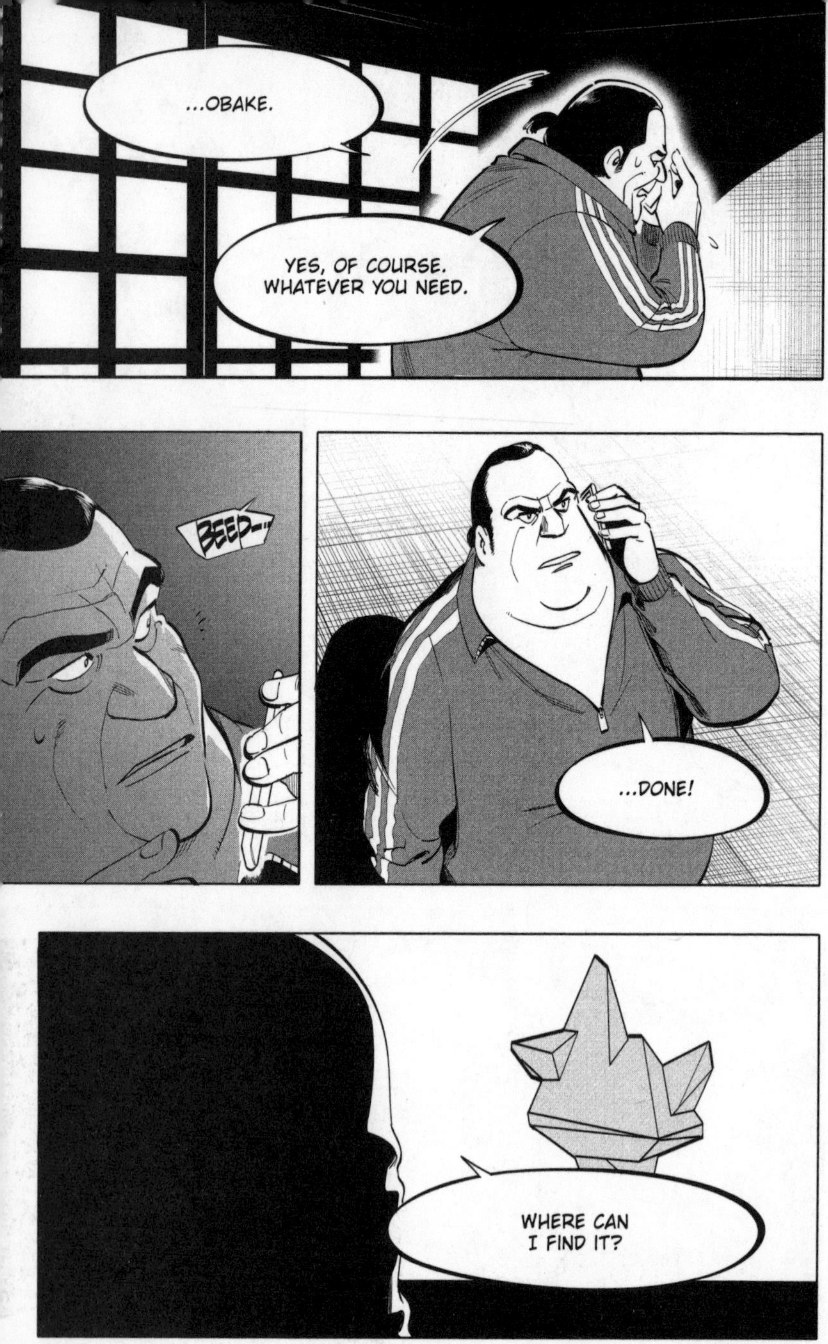
...OBAKE.
YES, OF COURSE. WHATEVER YOU NEED.
BEEP...
...DONE!
WHERE CAN I FIND IT?

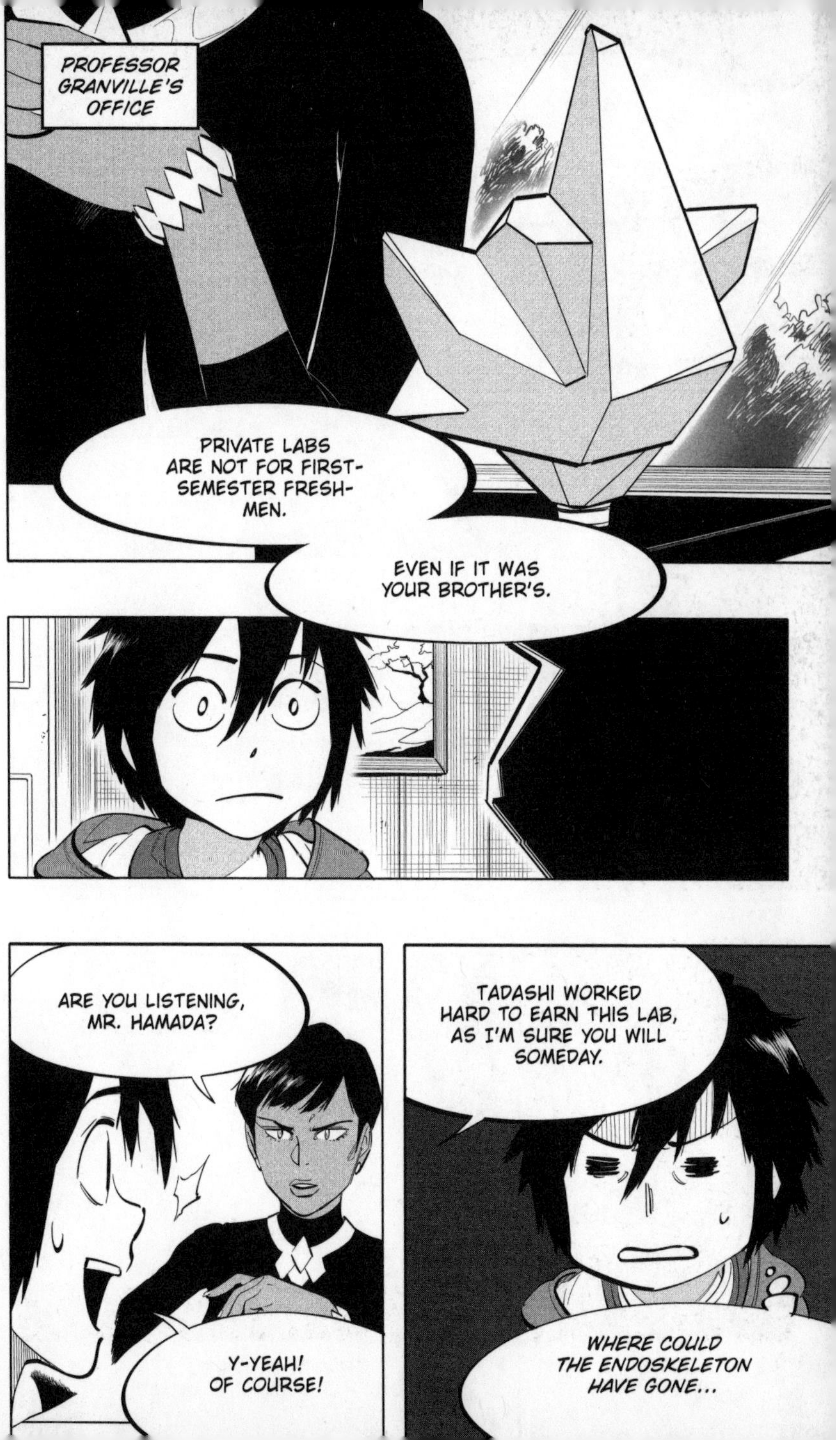
PROFESSOR GRANVILLE'S OFFICE
PRIVATE LABS ARE NOT FOR FIRST-SEMESTER FRESH-MEN.
EVEN IF IT WAS YOUR BROTHER'S.
ARE YOU LISTENING, MR. HAMADA?
Y-YEAH! OF COURSE!
TADASHI WORKED HARD TO EARN THIS LAB, AS I'M SURE YOU WILL SOMEDAY.
WHERE COULD THE ENDOSKELETON HAVE GONE...

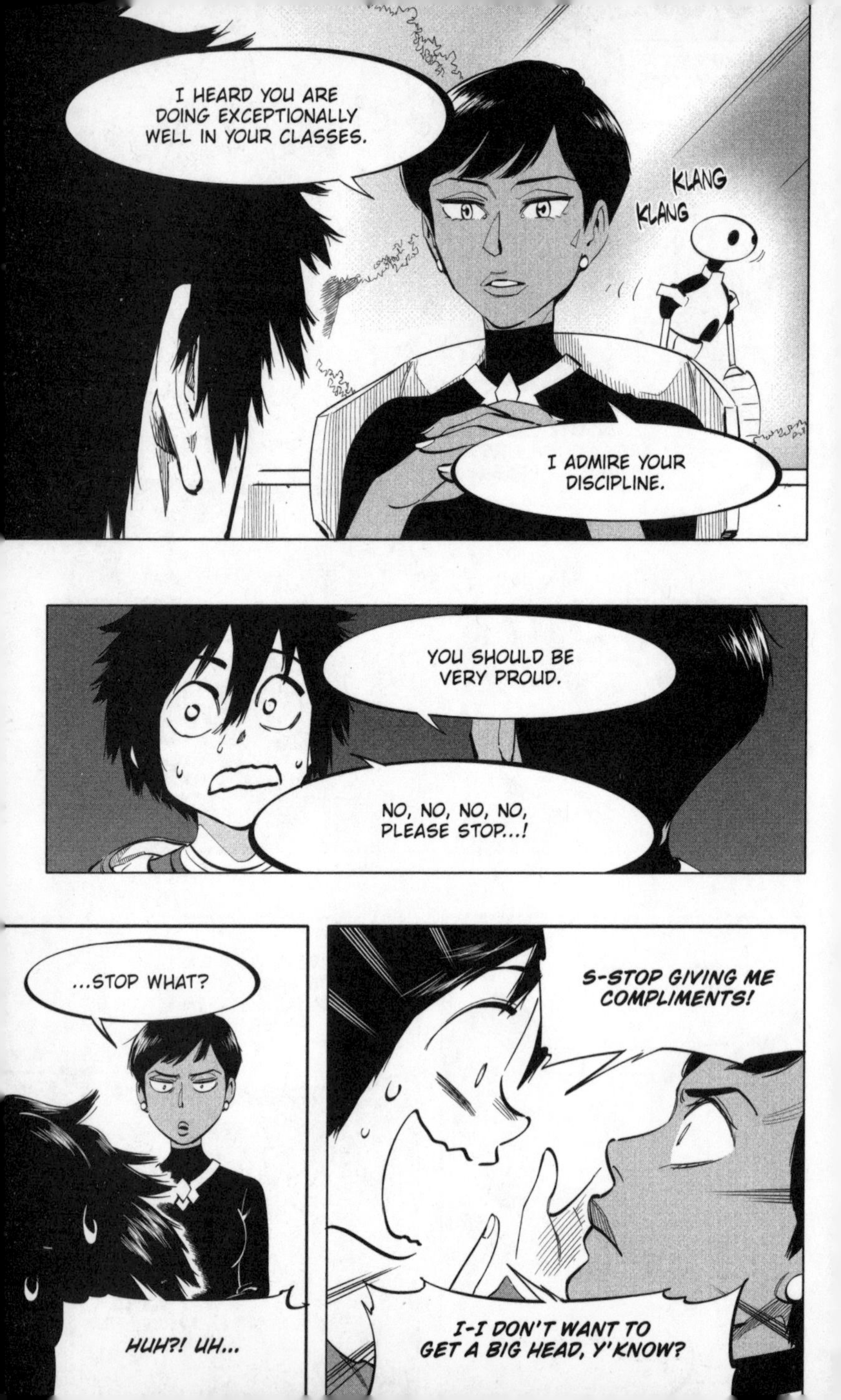
I HEARD YOU ARE DOING EXCEPTIONALLY WELL IN YOUR CLASSES.
KLANG
KLANG
I ADMIRE YOUR DISCIPLINE.
YOU SHOULD BE VERY PROUD.
NO, NO, NO, NO, PLEASE STOP...!
...STOP WHAT?
HUH?! UH...
S-STOP GIVING ME COMPLIMENTS!
I-I DON'T WANT TO GET A BIG HEAD, Y'KNOW?

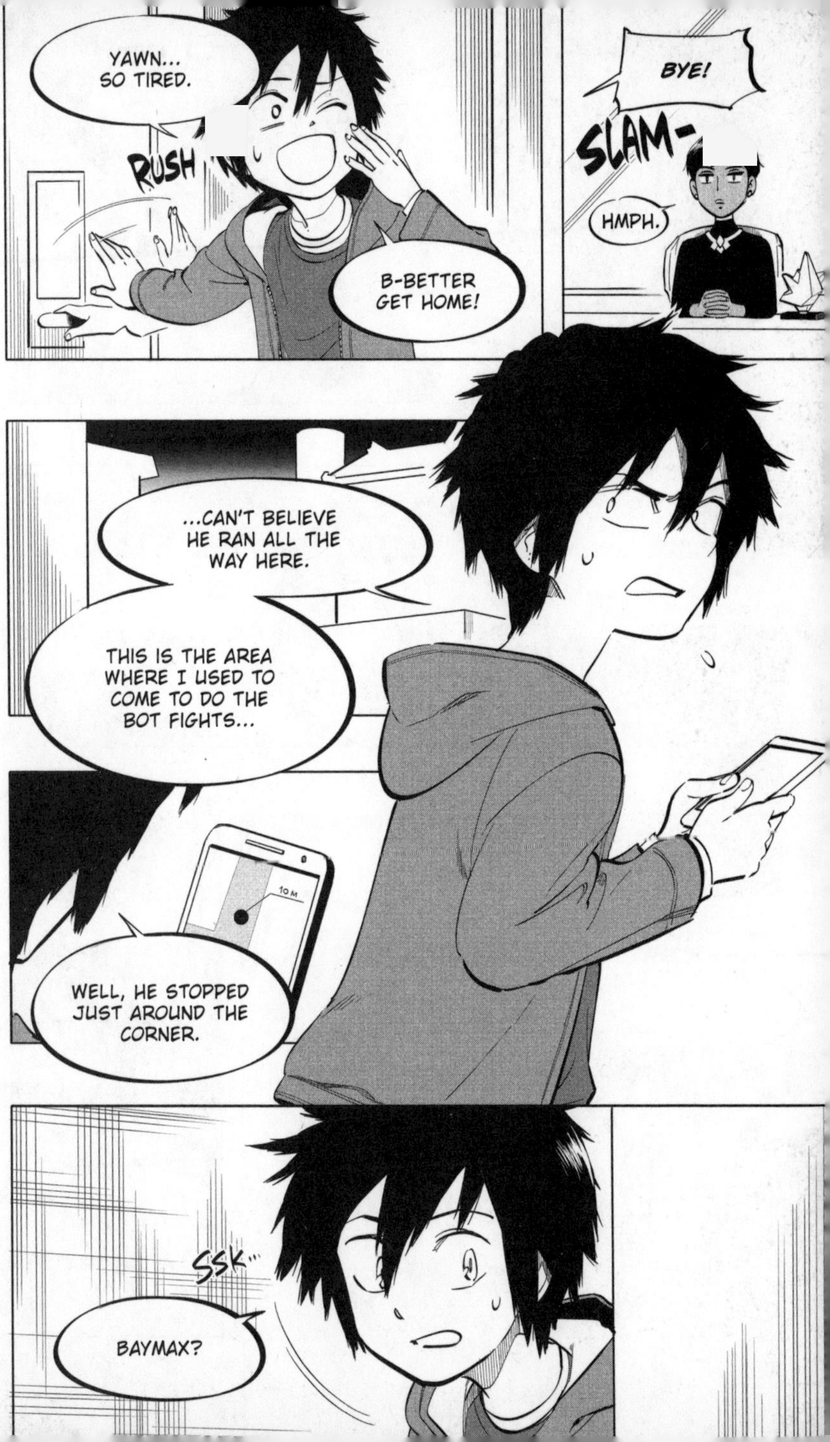
YAWN... SO TIRED.
RUSH
B-BETTER GET HOME!
BYE!
SLAM-
HMPH.
...CAN'T BELIEVE HE RAN ALL THE WAY HERE.
THIS IS THE AREA WHERE I USED TO COME TO DO THE BOT FIGHTS...
10 M
WELL, HE STOPPED JUST AROUND THE CORNER.
SSK
BAYMAX?

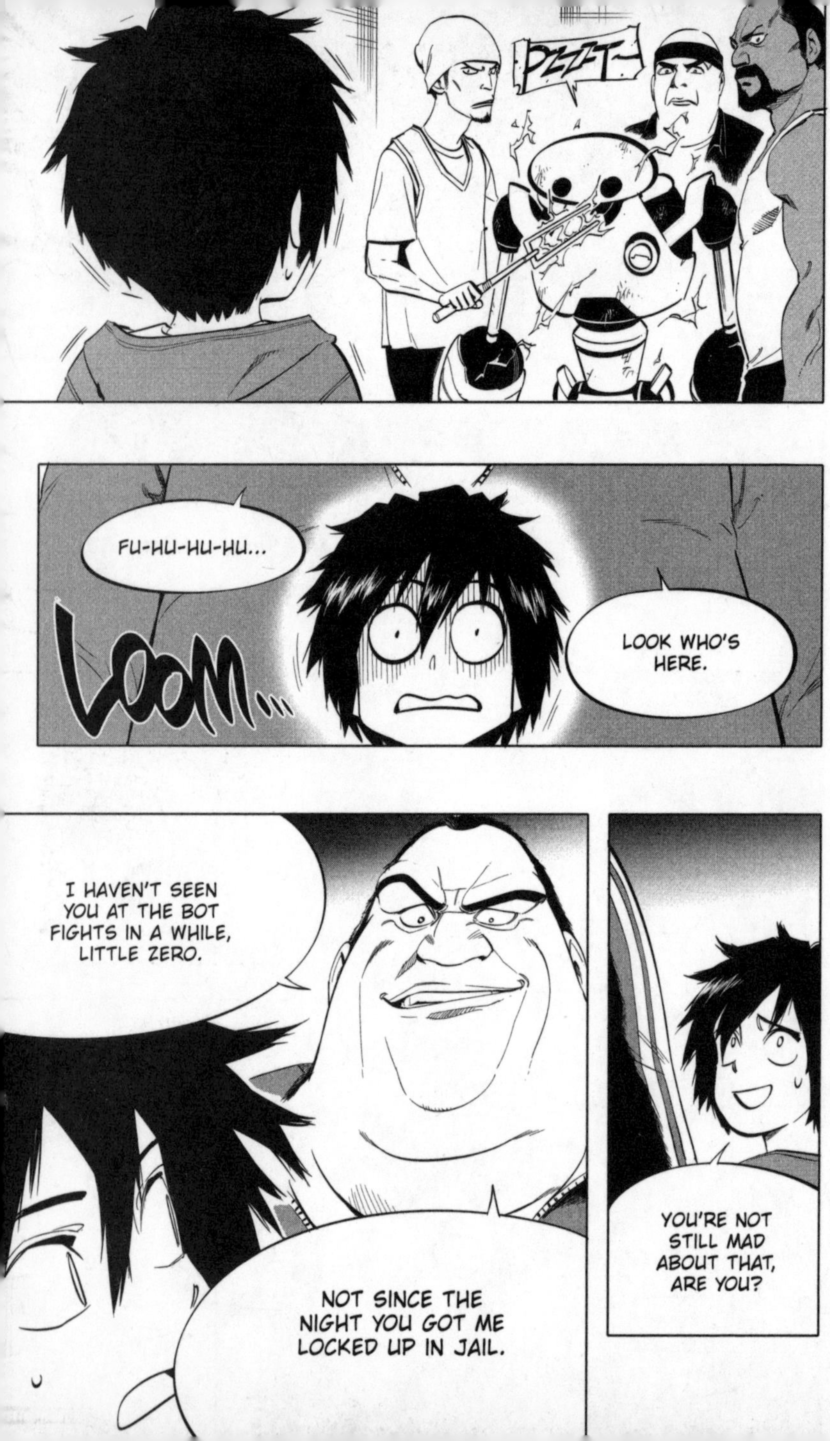
PZZT--
FU-HU-HU-HU...
LOOM...
LOOK WHO'S HERE.
I HAVEN'T SEEN YOU AT THE BOT FIGHTS IN A WHILE, LITTLE ZERO.
NOT SINCE THE NIGHT YOU GOT ME LOCKED UP IN JAIL.
YOU'RE NOT STILL MAD ABOUT THAT, ARE YOU?

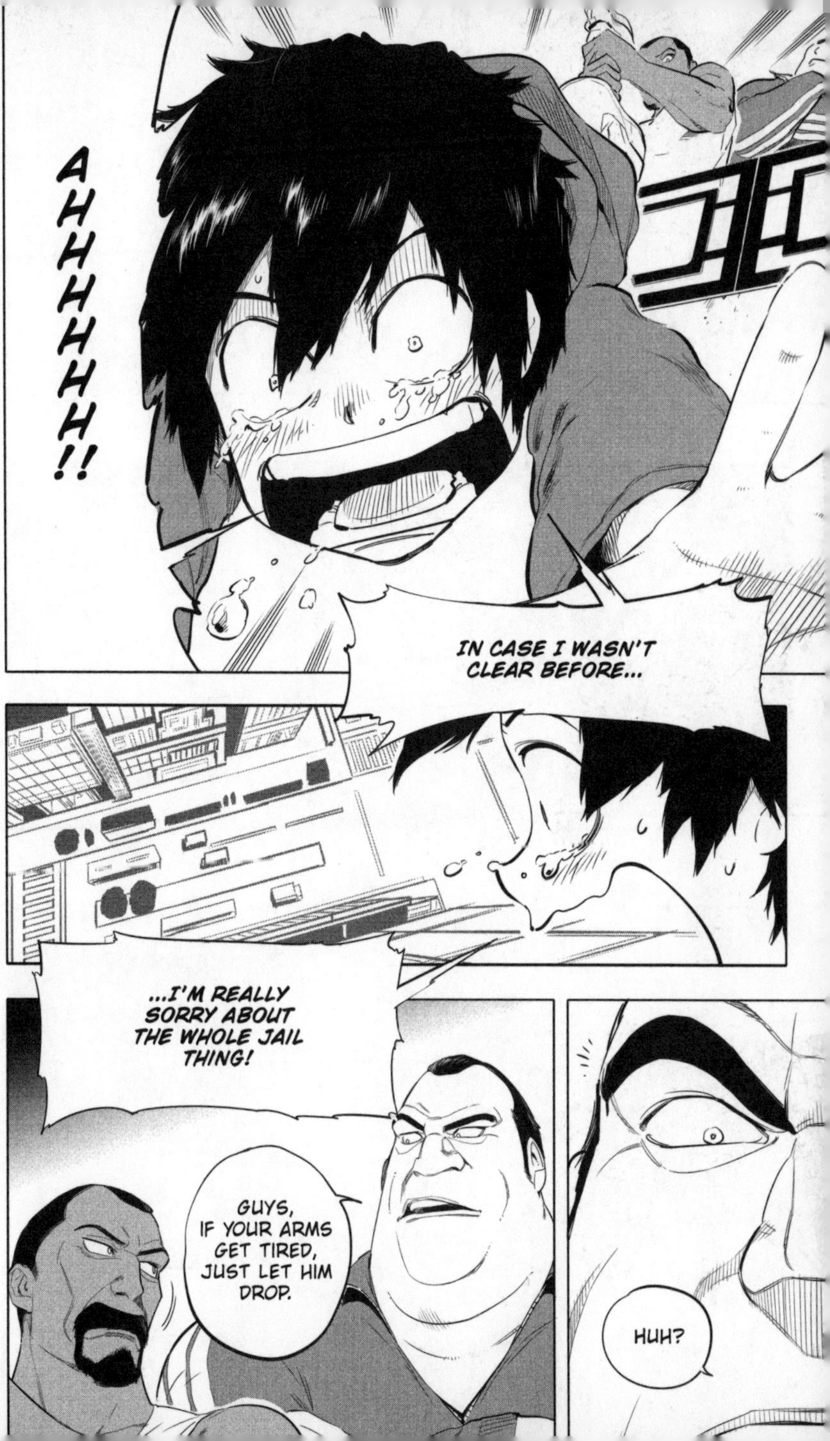
AHHHHHHH!!
IN CASE I WASN'T CLEAR BEFORE...
...I'M REALLY SORRY ABOUT THE WHOLE JAIL THING!
GUYS, IF YOUR ARMS GET TIRED, JUST LET HIM DROP.
HUH?

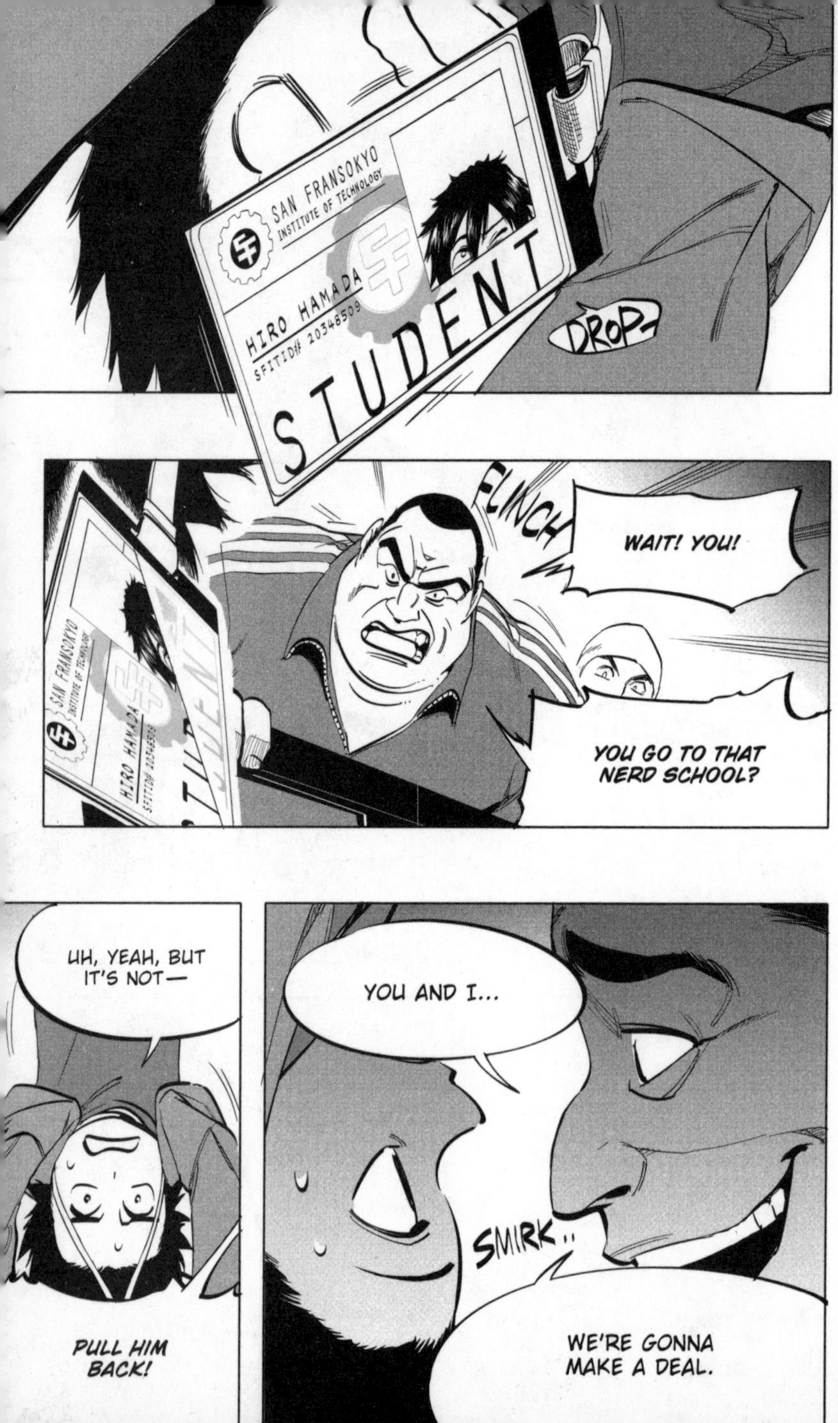
SAN FRANSOKYO
INSTITUTE OF TECHNOLOGY
HIRO HAMADA
SFITID# 20348509
STUDENT
DROP-
FLINCH
WAIT! YOU!
YOU GO TO THAT NERD SCHOOL?
UH, YEAH, BUT IT'S NOT—
PULL HIM BACK!
YOU AND I...
SMIRK..
WE'RE GONNA MAKE A DEAL.

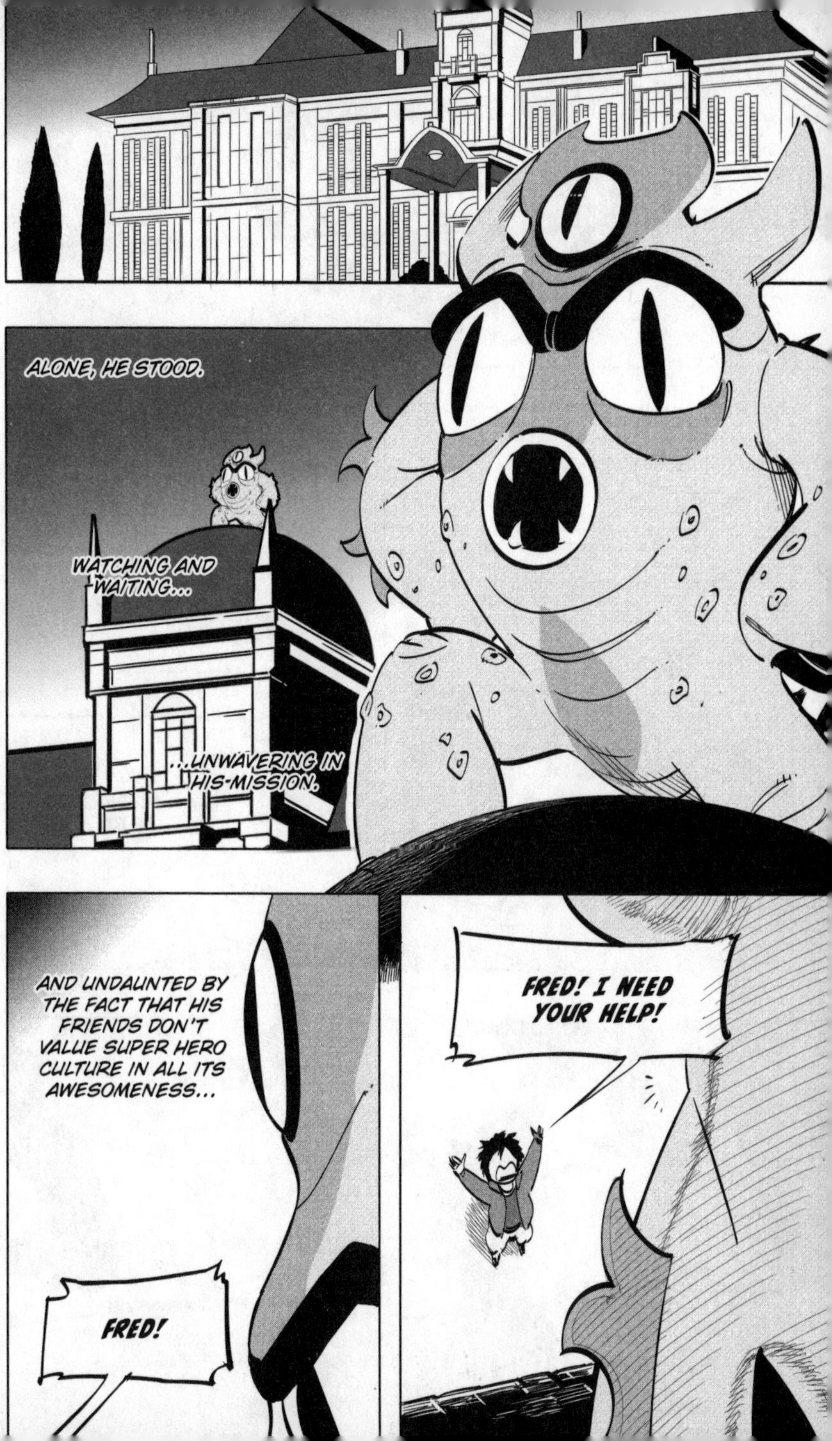
ALONE, HE STOOD.
WATCHING AND WAITING...
...UNWAVERING IN HIS MISSION.
AND UNDAUNTED BY THE FACT THAT HIS FRIENDS DON'T VALUE SUPER HERO CULTURE IN ALL ITS AWESOMENESS...
FRED!
FRED! I NEED YOUR HELP!

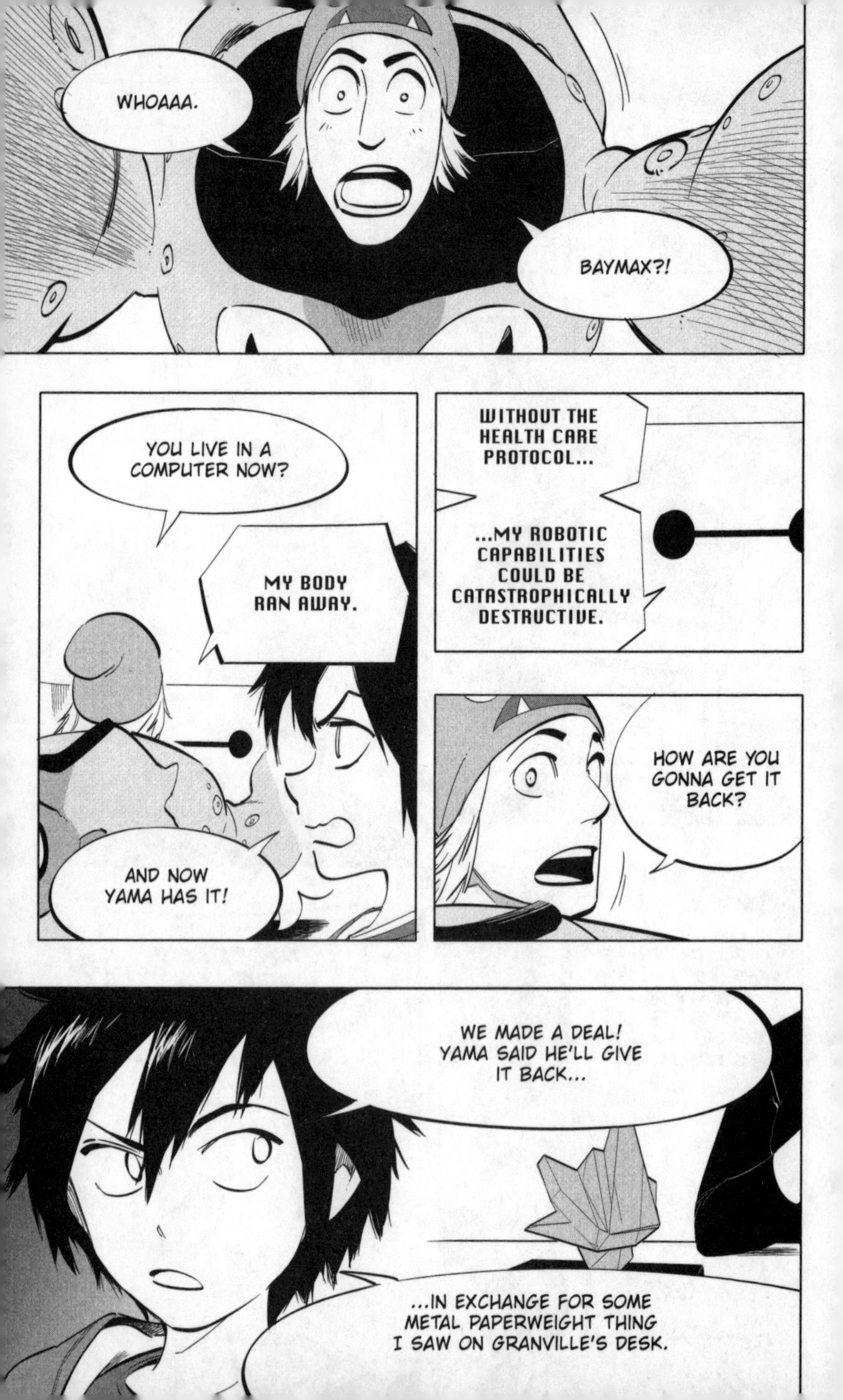
WHOAAA.
BAYMAX?!
YOU LIVE IN A COMPUTER NOW?
MY BODY RAN AWAY.
AND NOW YAMA HAS IT!
WITHOUT THE HEALTH CARE PROTOCOL...
...MY ROBOTIC CAPABILITIES COULD BE CATASTROPHICALLY DESTRUCTIVE.
HOW ARE YOU GONNA GET IT BACK?
WE MADE A DEAL! YAMA SAID HE'LL GIVE IT BACK...
...IN EXCHANGE FOR SOME METAL PAPERWEIGHT THING I SAW ON GRANVILLE'S DESK.

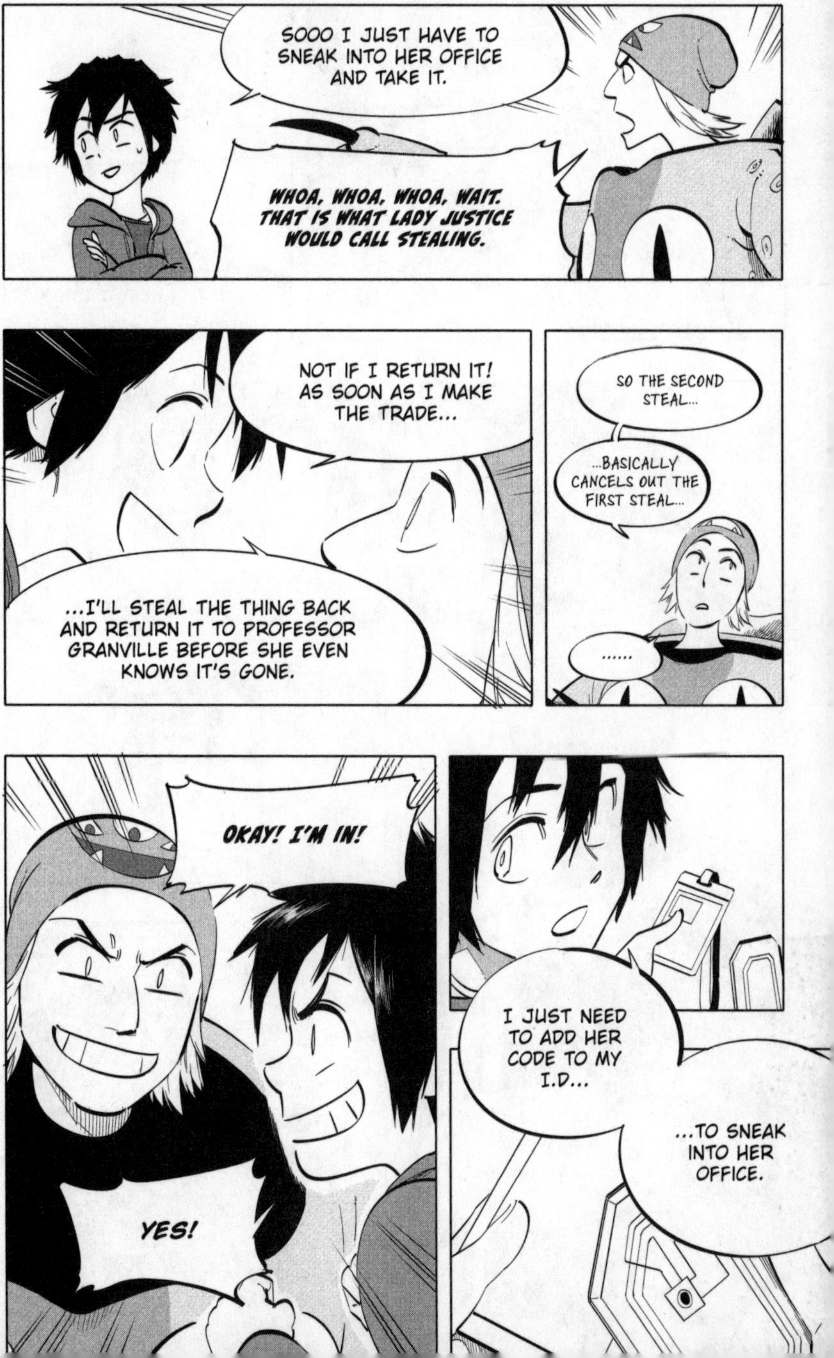
SOOO I JUST HAVE TO SNEAK INTO HER OFFICE AND TAKE IT.
WHOA, WHOA, WHOA, WAIT. THAT IS WHAT LADY JUSTICE WOULD CALL STEALING.
NOT IF I RETURN IT! AS SOON AS I MAKE THE TRADE...
...I'LL STEAL THE THING BACK AND RETURN IT TO PROFESSOR GRANVILLE BEFORE SHE EVEN KNOWS IT'S GONE.
SO THE SECOND STEAL...
...BASICALLY CANCELS OUT THE FIRST STEAL...
......
OKAY! I'M IN!
YES!
I JUST NEED TO ADD HER CODE TO MY I.D...
...TO SNEAK INTO HER OFFICE.

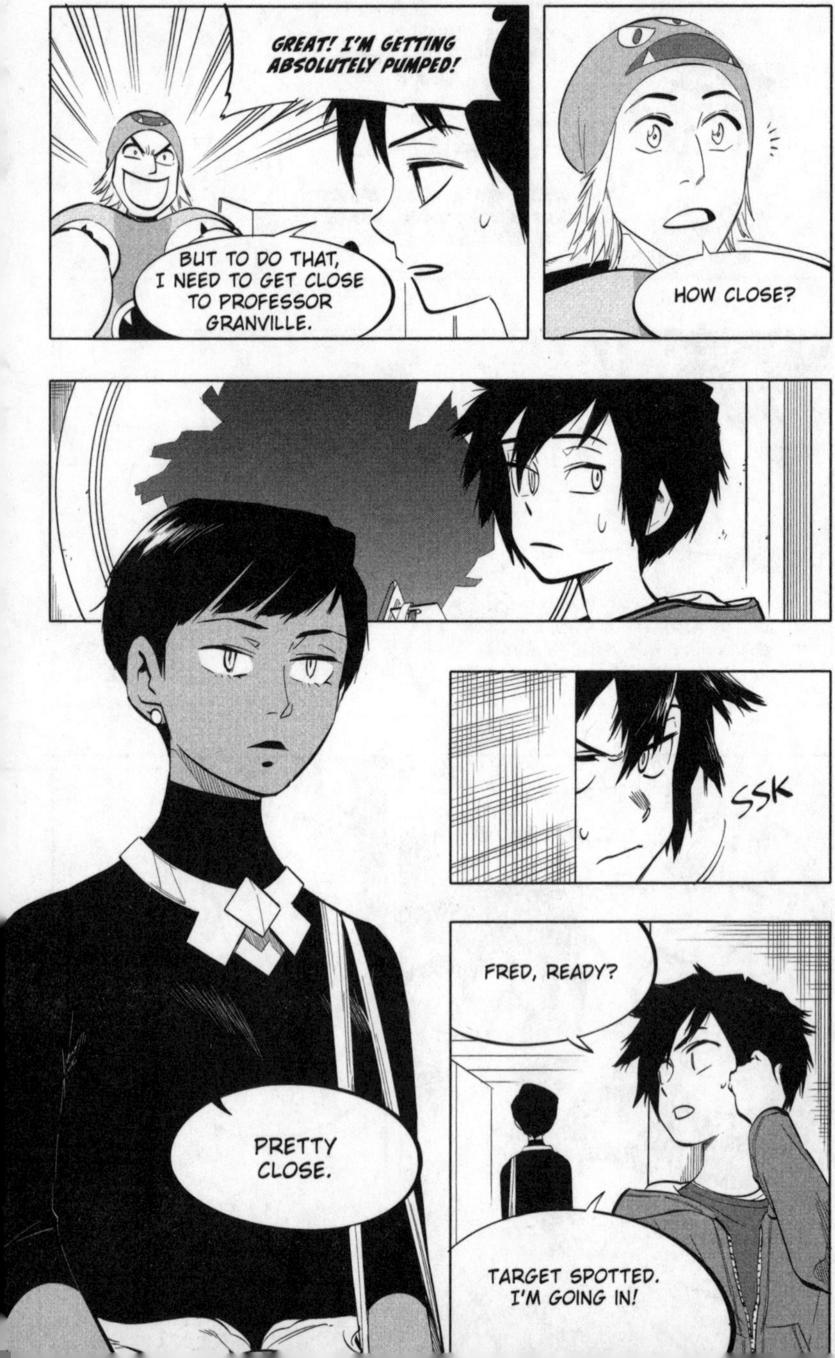

GREAT! I'M GETTING ABSOLUTELY PUMPED!
BUT TO DO THAT, I NEED TO GET CLOSE TO PROFESSOR GRANVILLE.
HOW CLOSE?
PRETTY CLOSE.
SSK
FRED, READY?
TARGET SPOTTED. I'M GOING IN!

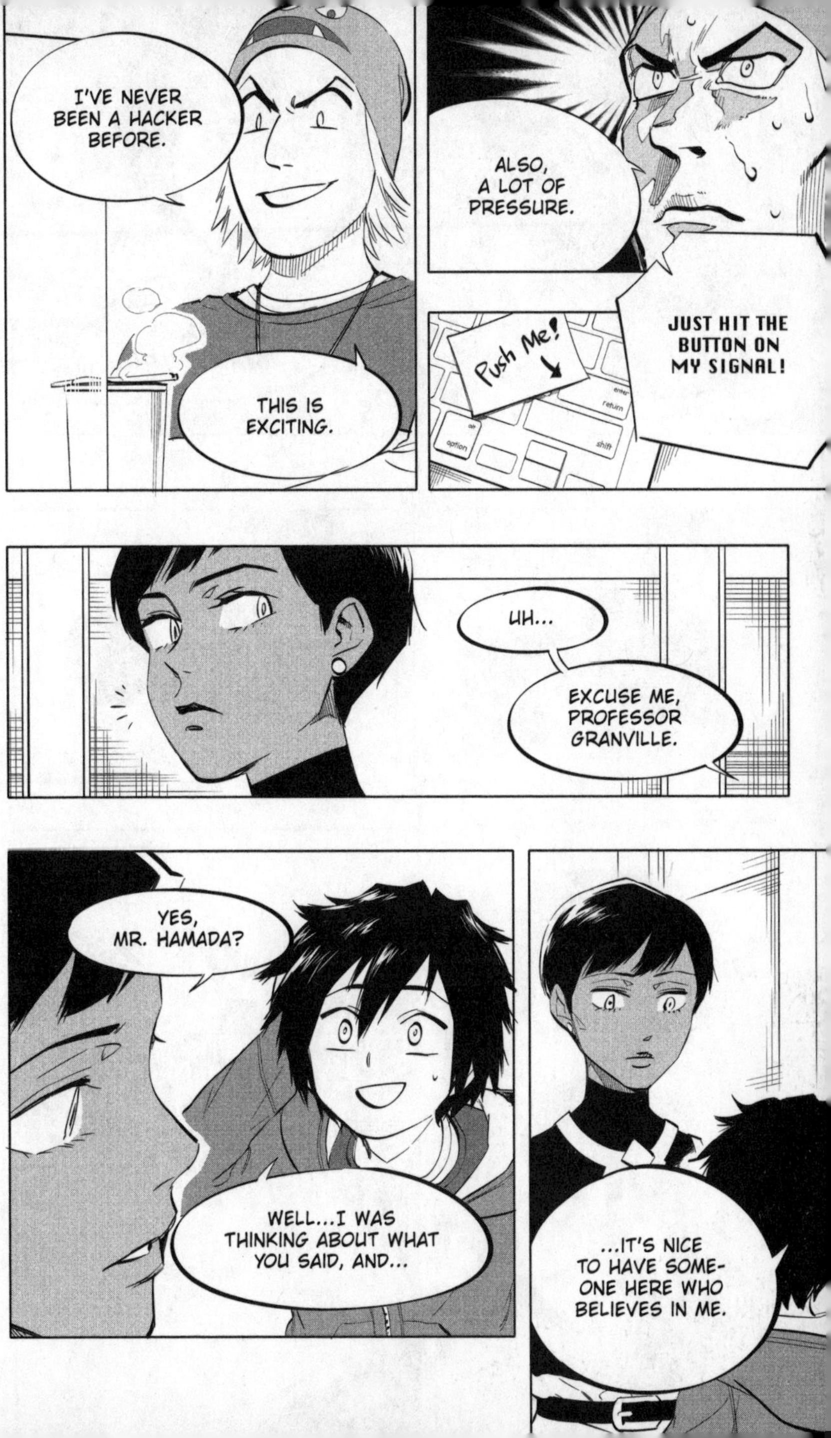
I'VE NEVER BEEN A HACKER BEFORE.
THIS IS EXCITING.
ALSO, A LOT OF PRESSURE.
Push Me!
JUST HIT THE BUTTON ON MY SIGNAL!
UH...
EXCUSE ME, PROFESSOR GRANVILLE.
YES, MR. HAMADA?
WELL...I WAS THINKING ABOUT WHAT YOU SAID, AND...
...IT'S NICE TO HAVE SOME-ONE HERE WHO BELIEVES IN ME.

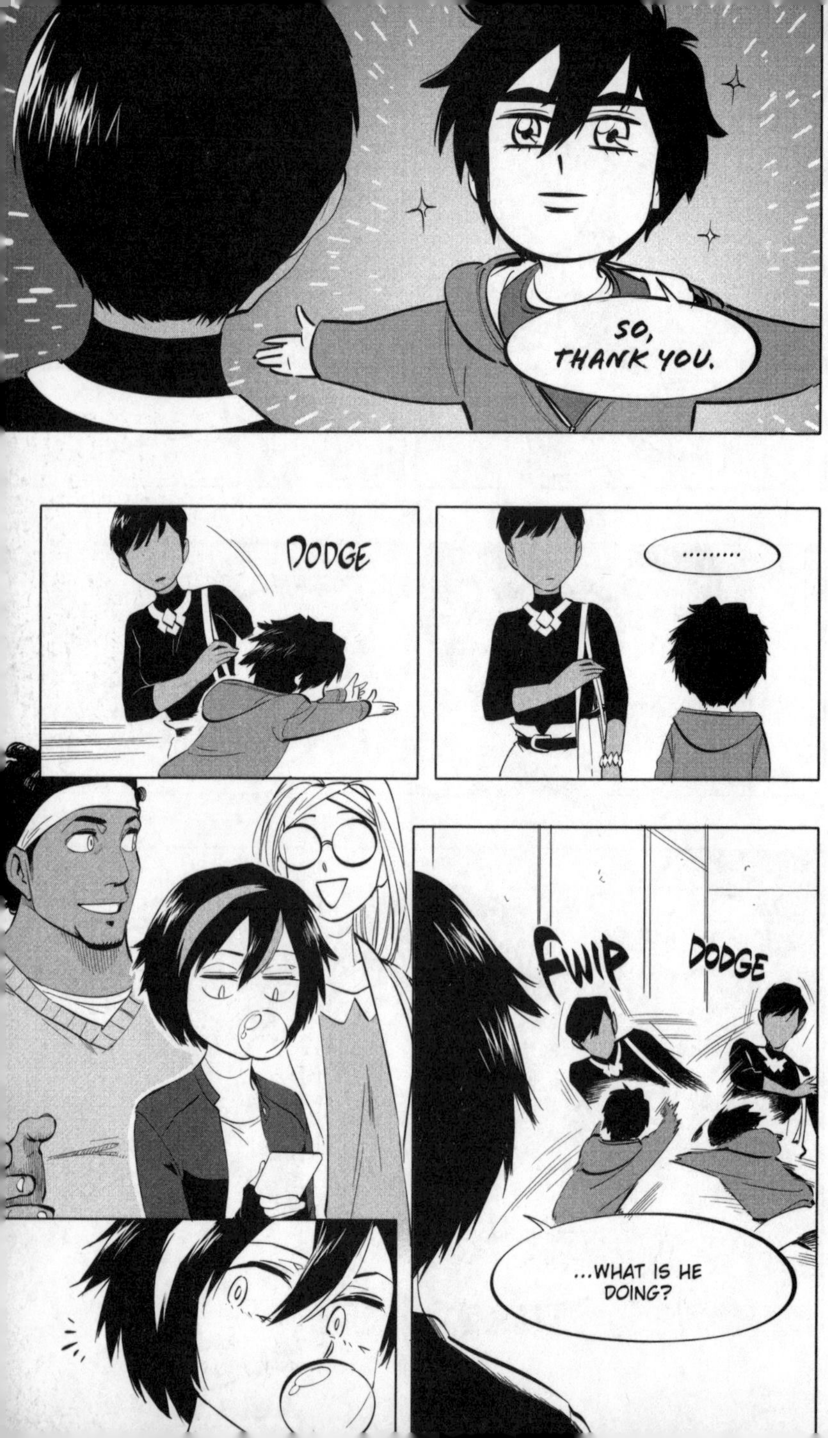
SO, THANK YOU.
DODGE
....
FWIP
DODGE
...WHAT IS HE DOING?

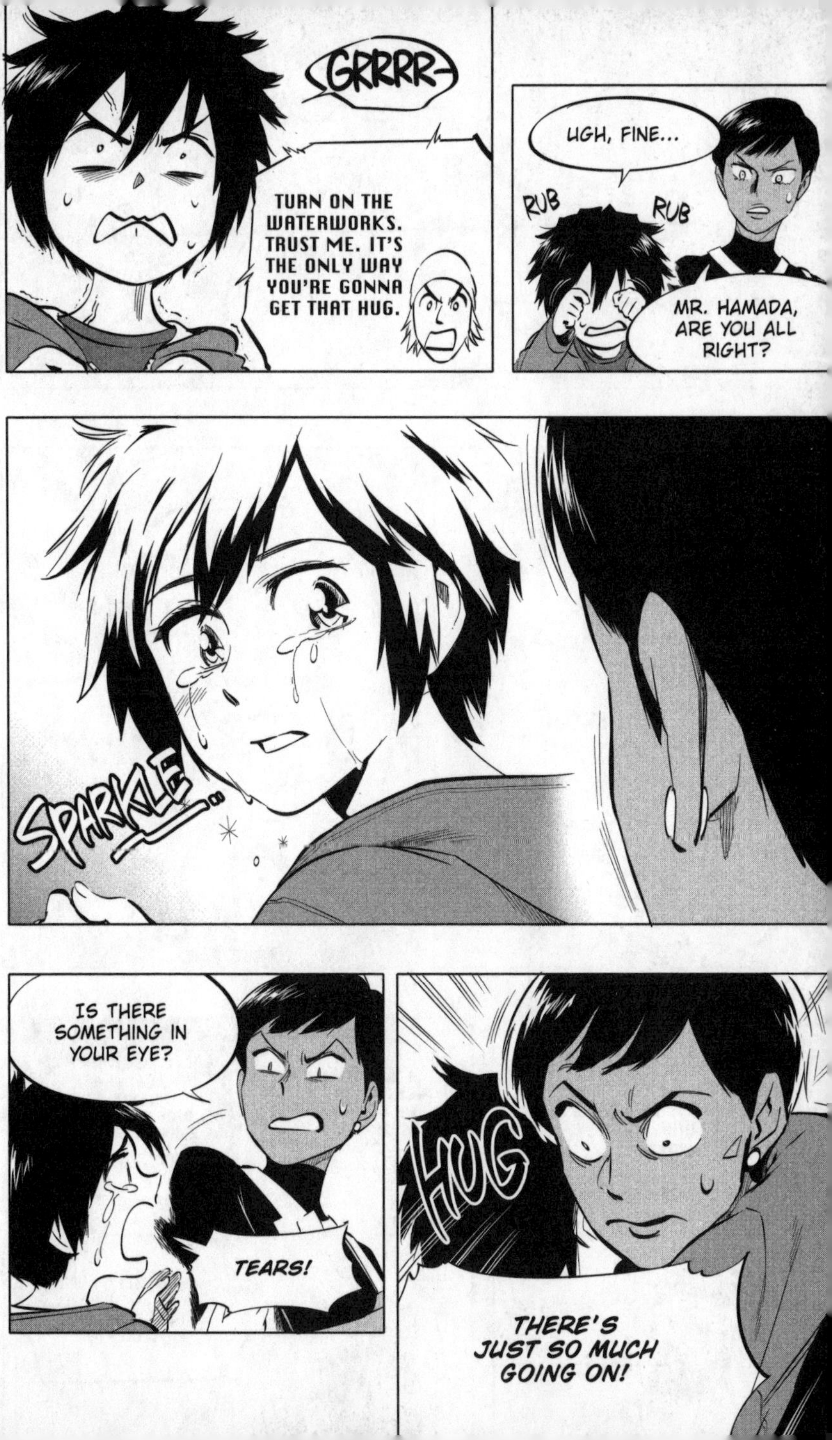
GRRRR-
TURN ON THE WATERWORKS. TRUST ME. IT'S THE ONLY WAY YOU'RE GONNA GET THAT HUG.
UGH, FINE...
RUB
RUB
MR. HAMADA, ARE YOU ALL RIGHT?
SPARKLE
IS THERE SOMETHING IN YOUR EYE?
TEARS!
HUG
THERE'S JUST SO MUCH GOING ON!

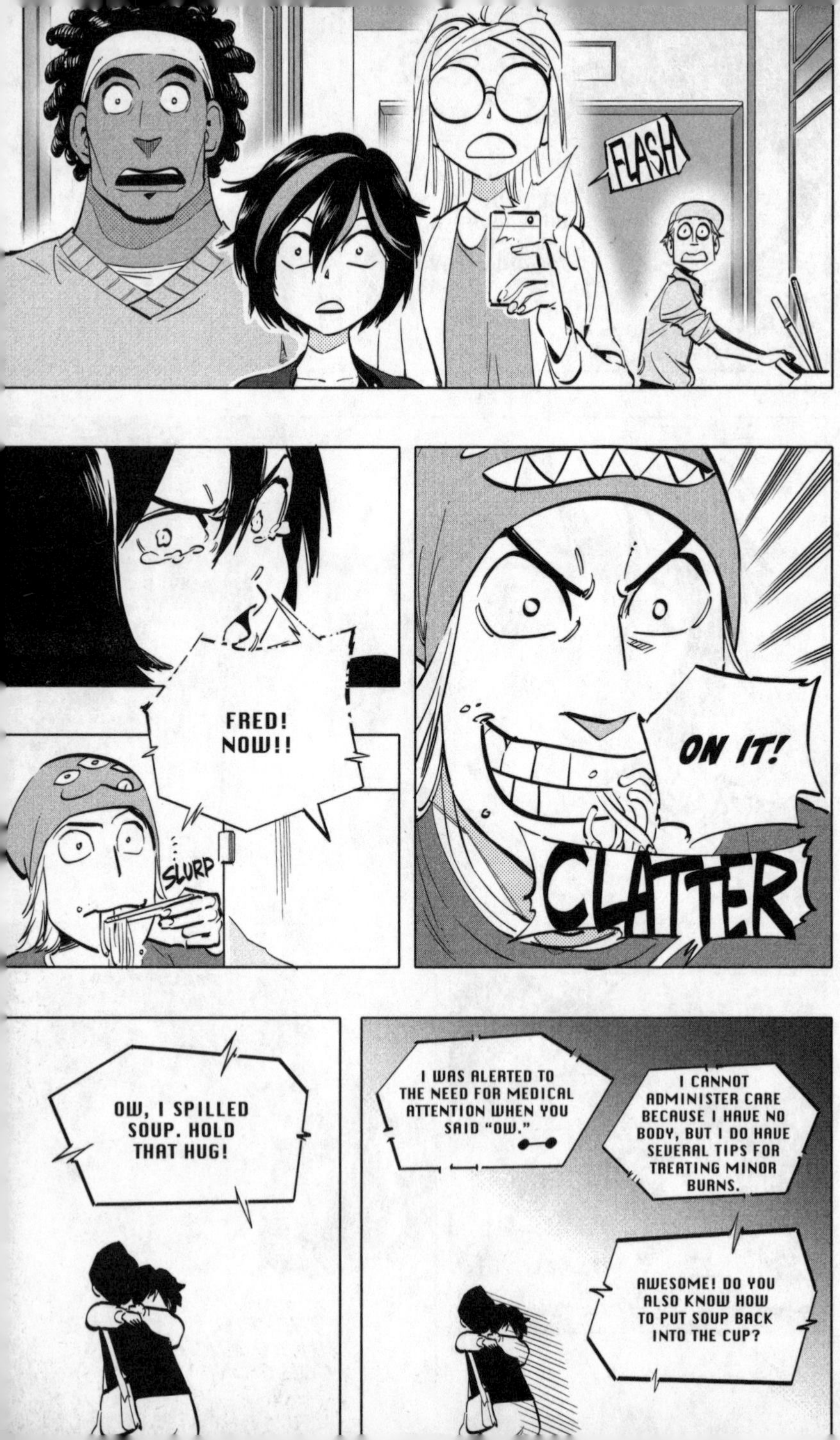
FLASH
FRED! NOW!!
SLURP
ON IT!
CLATTER
OW, I SPILLED SOUP. HOLD THAT HUG!
I WAS ALERTED TO THE NEED FOR MEDICAL ATTENTION WHEN YOU SAID "OW."
I CANNOT ADMINISTER CARE BECAUSE I HAVE NO BODY, BUT I DO HAVE SEVERAL TIPS FOR TREATING MINOR BURNS.
AWESOME! DO YOU ALSO KNOW HOW TO PUT SOUP BACK INTO THE CUP?

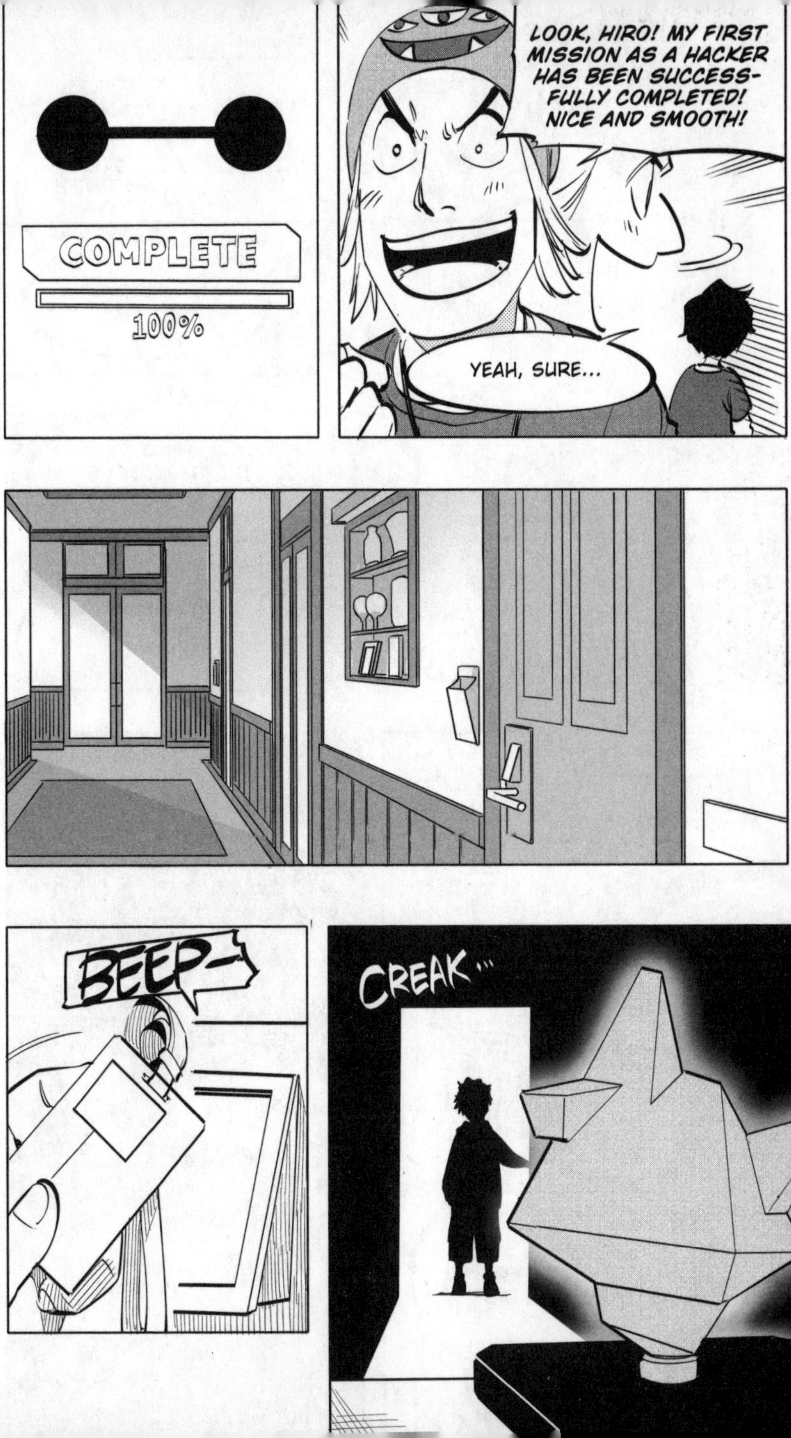
COMPLETE
100%
LOOK, HIRO! MY FIRST MISSION AS A HACKER HAS BEEN SUCCESS-FULLY COMPLETED! NICE AND SMOOTH!
YEAH, SURE...
BEEP-
CREAK

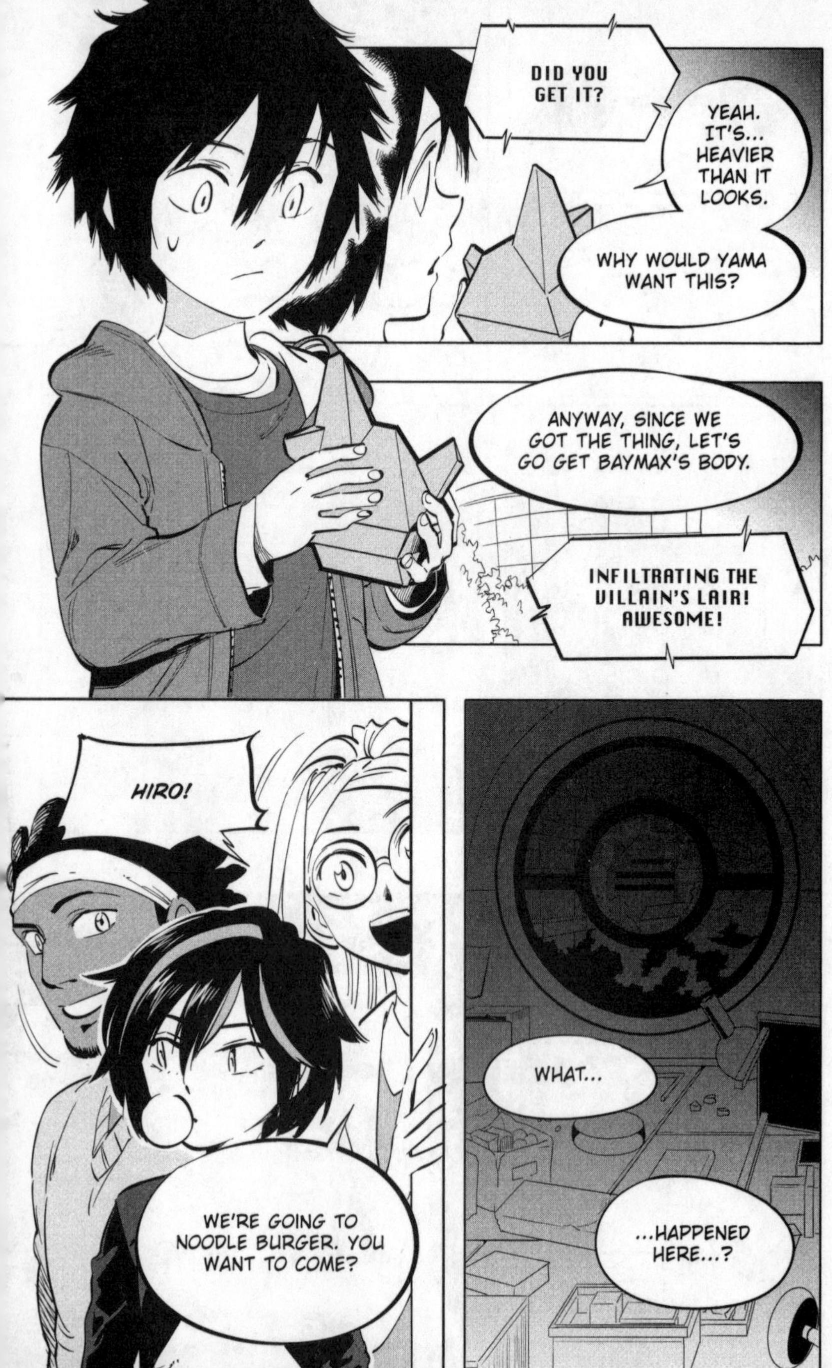
DID YOU GET IT?
YEAH. IT'S... HEAVIER THAN IT LOOKS.
WHY WOULD YAMA WANT THIS?
ANYWAY, SINCE WE GOT THE THING, LET'S GO GET BAYMAX'S BODY.
INFILTRATING THE VILLAIN'S LAIR! AWESOME!
HIRO!
WE'RE GOING TO NOODLE BURGER. YOU WANT TO COME?
WHAT...
...HAPPENED HERE...?

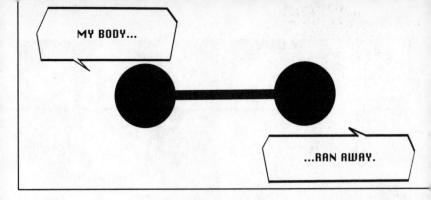

MY BODY...

...RAN AWAY.

BAYMAX?!

YOU'RE BACK!

WAIT, WHY ARE YOU IN A COMPUTER? WHERE'S HIRO?

HIRO CAN BE FOUND...

...HERE.

BEEP—

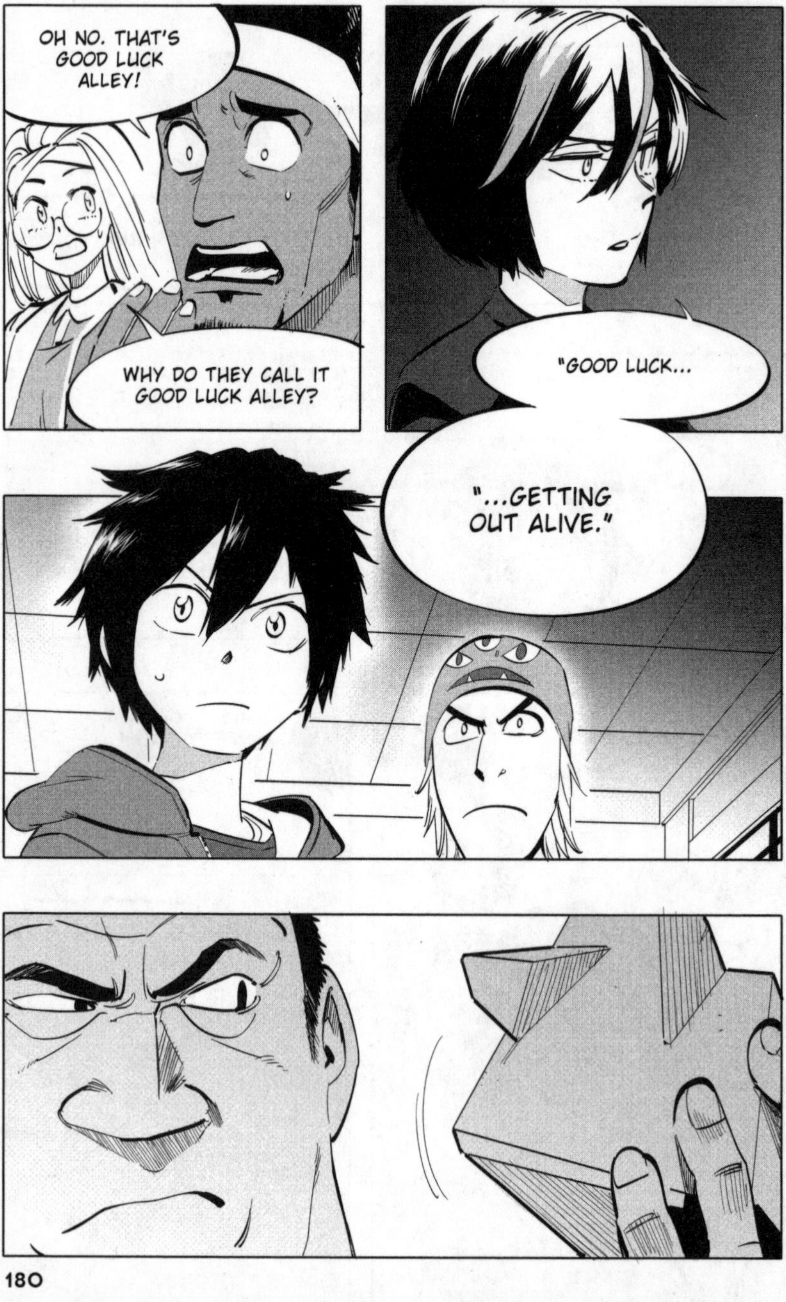
OH NO. THAT'S GOOD LUCK ALLEY!
WHY DO THEY CALL IT GOOD LUCK ALLEY?
"GOOD LUCK...
"...GETTING OUT ALIVE."

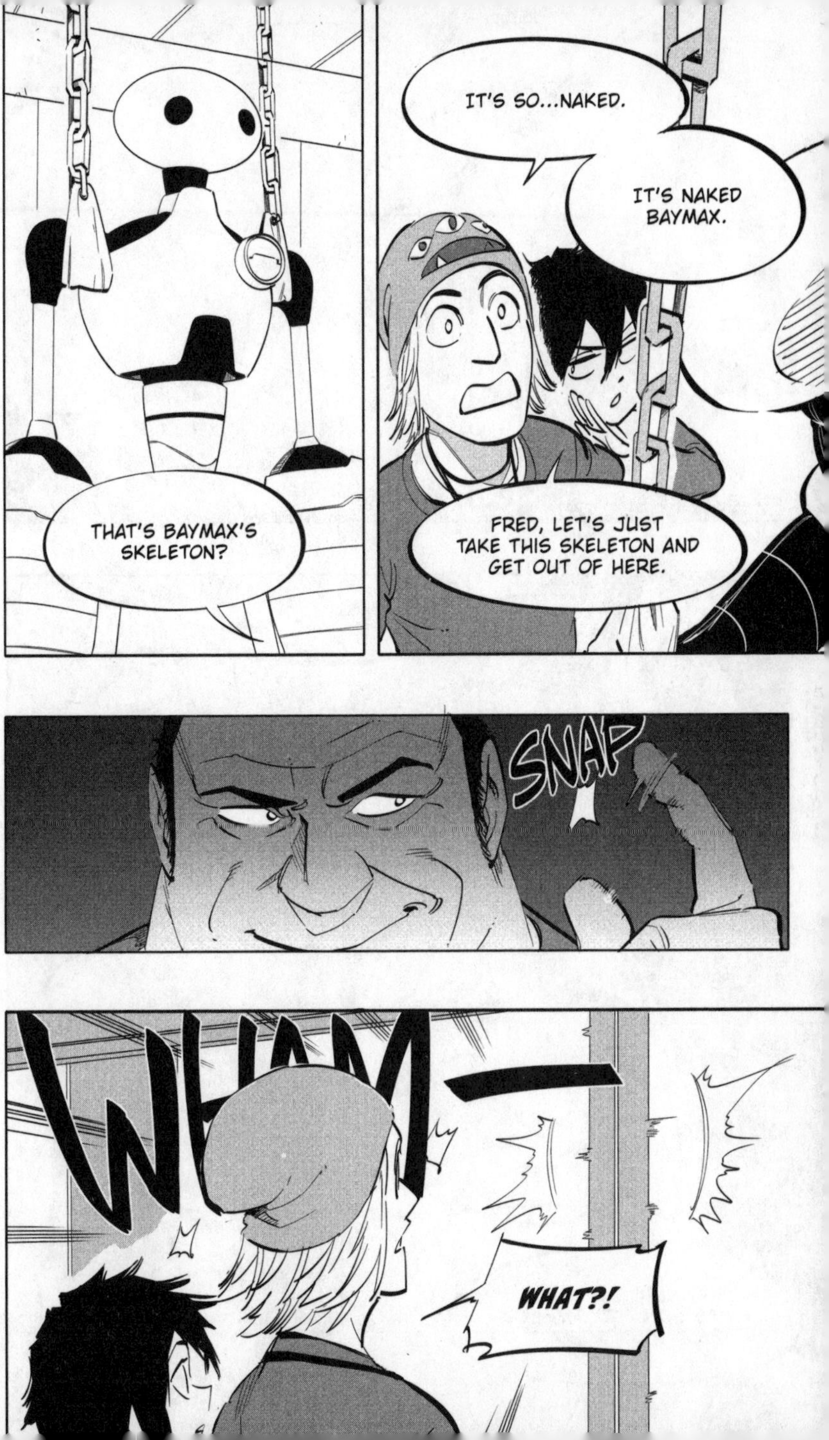
THAT'S BAYMAX'S SKELETON?
IT'S SO...NAKED.
IT'S NAKED BAYMAX.
FRED, LET'S JUST TAKE THIS SKELETON AND GET OUT OF HERE.
SNAP
WHAM—
WHAT?!

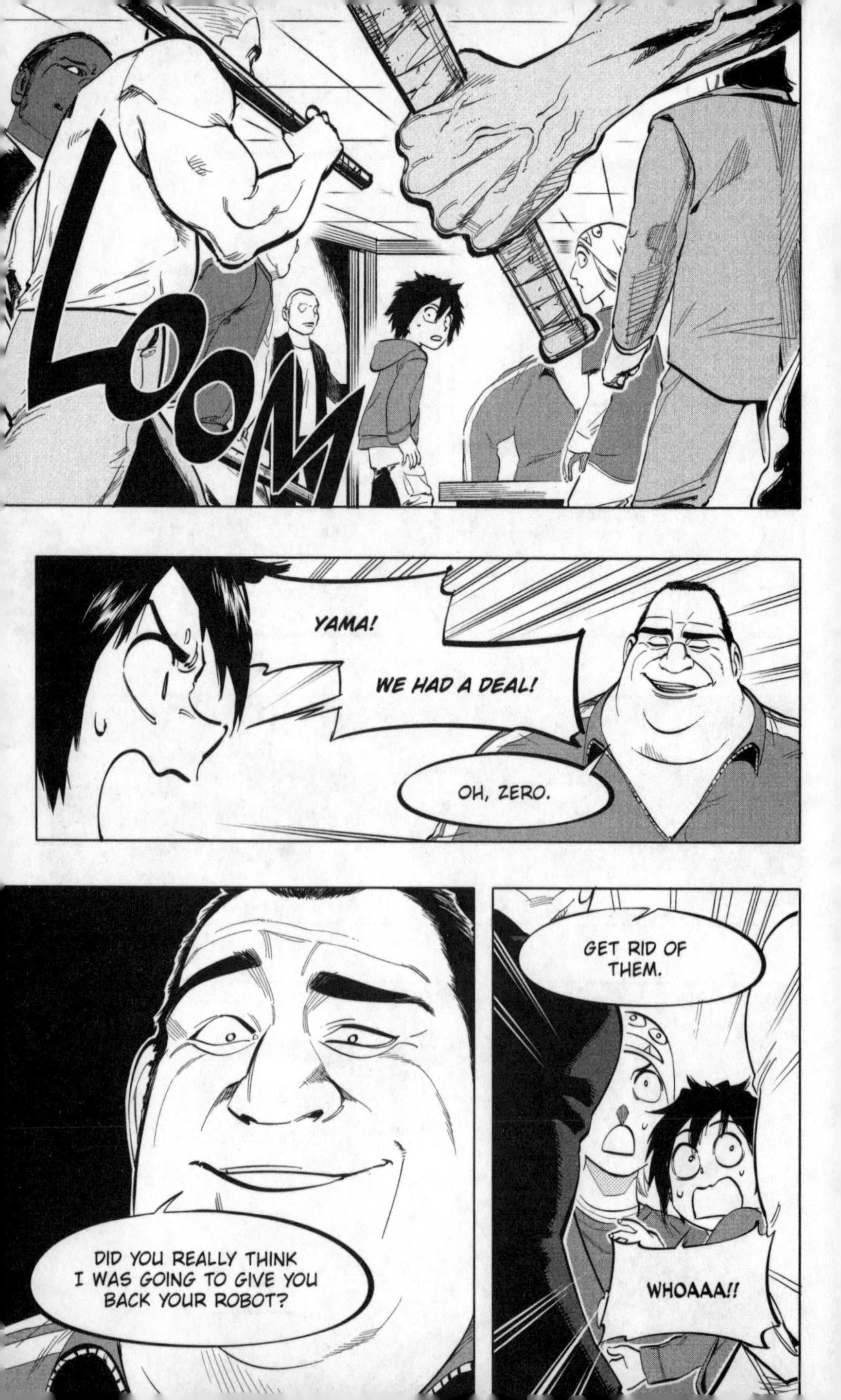
LOOM
YAMA!
WE HAD A DEAL!
OH, ZERO.
DID YOU REALLY THINK I WAS GOING TO GIVE YOU BACK YOUR ROBOT?
GET RID OF THEM.
WHOAAA!!

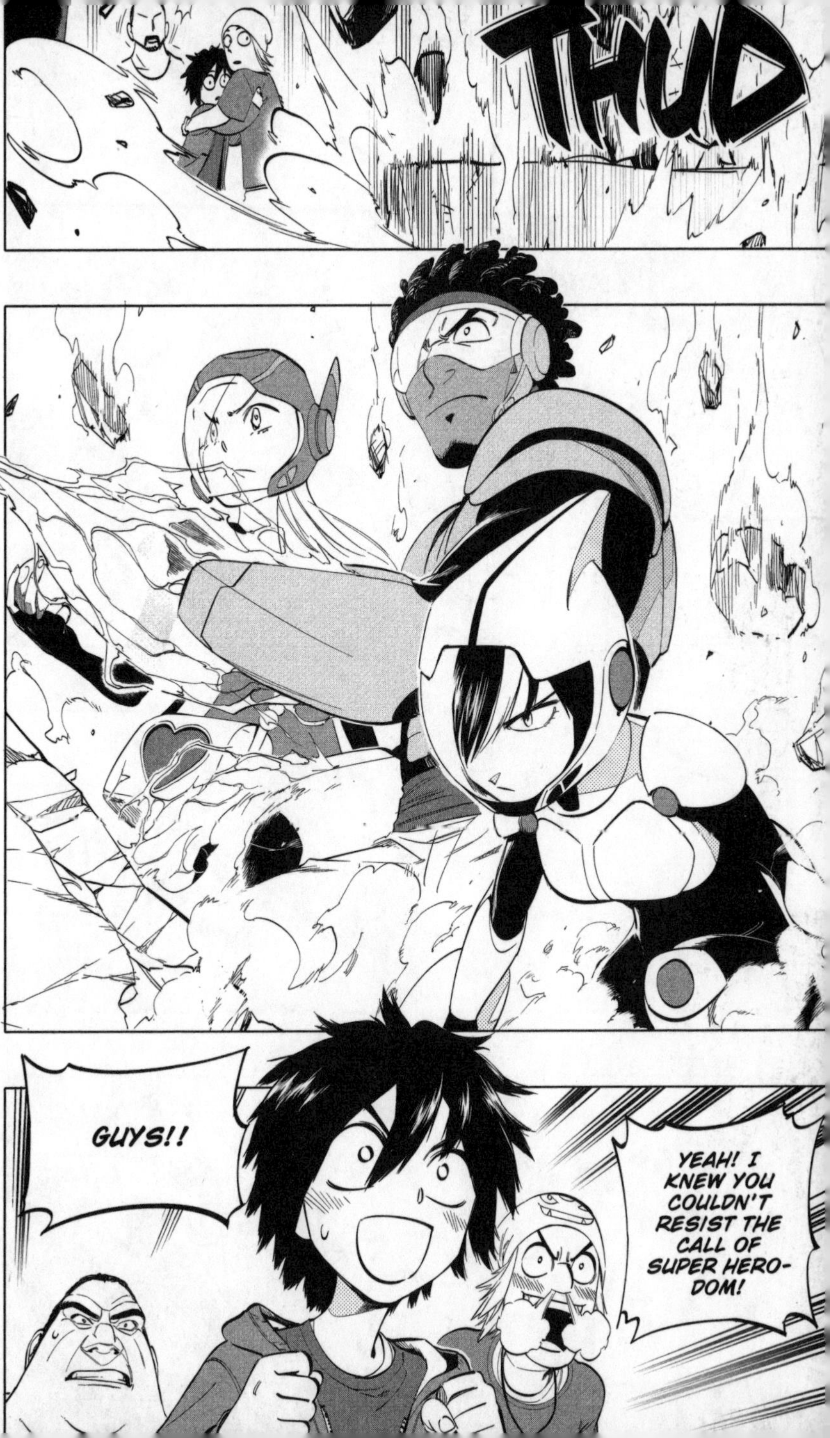
THUD
GUYS!!
YEAH! I KNEW YOU COULDN'T RESIST THE CALL OF SUPER HERO-DOM!

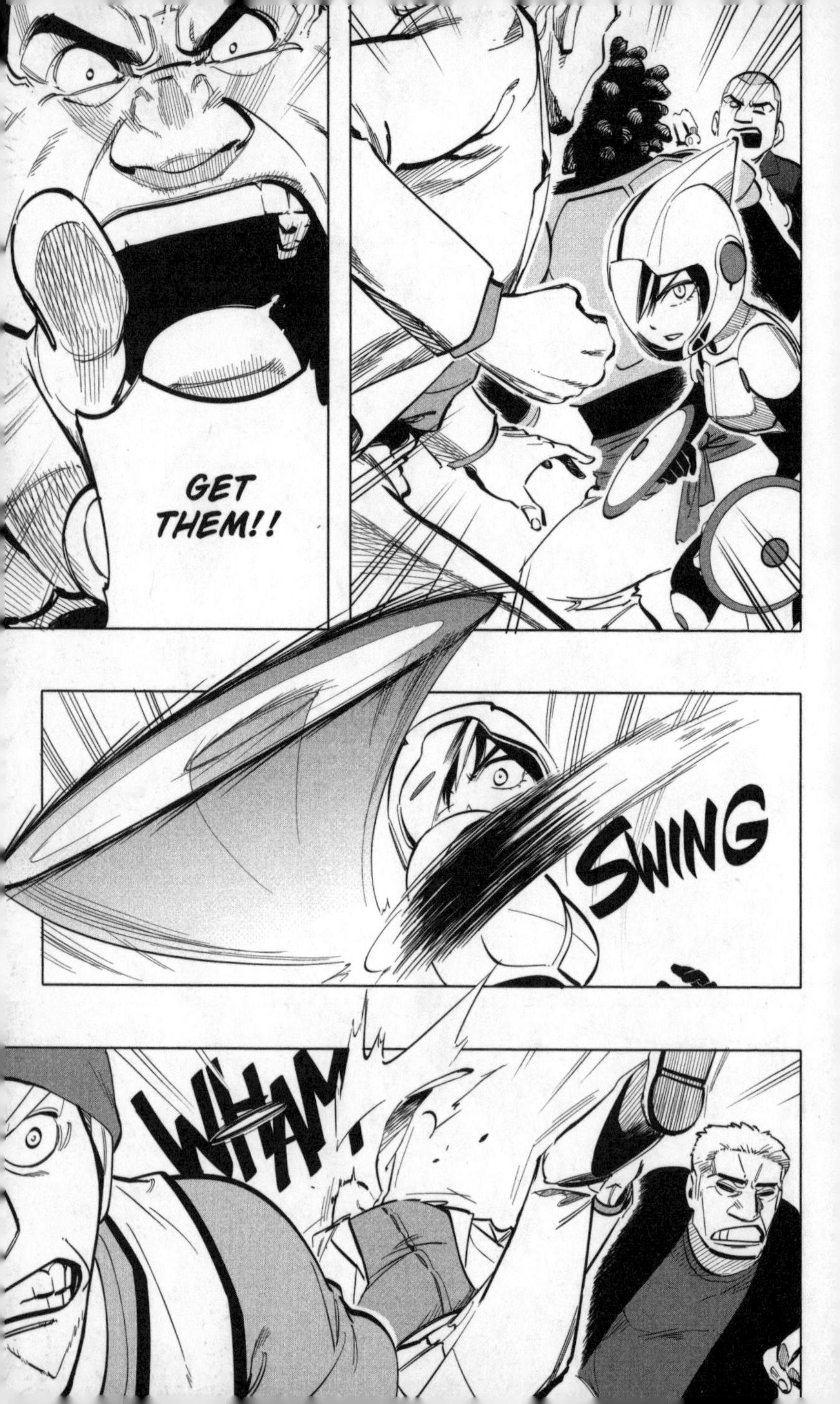
GET THEM!!
SWING
WHAM!

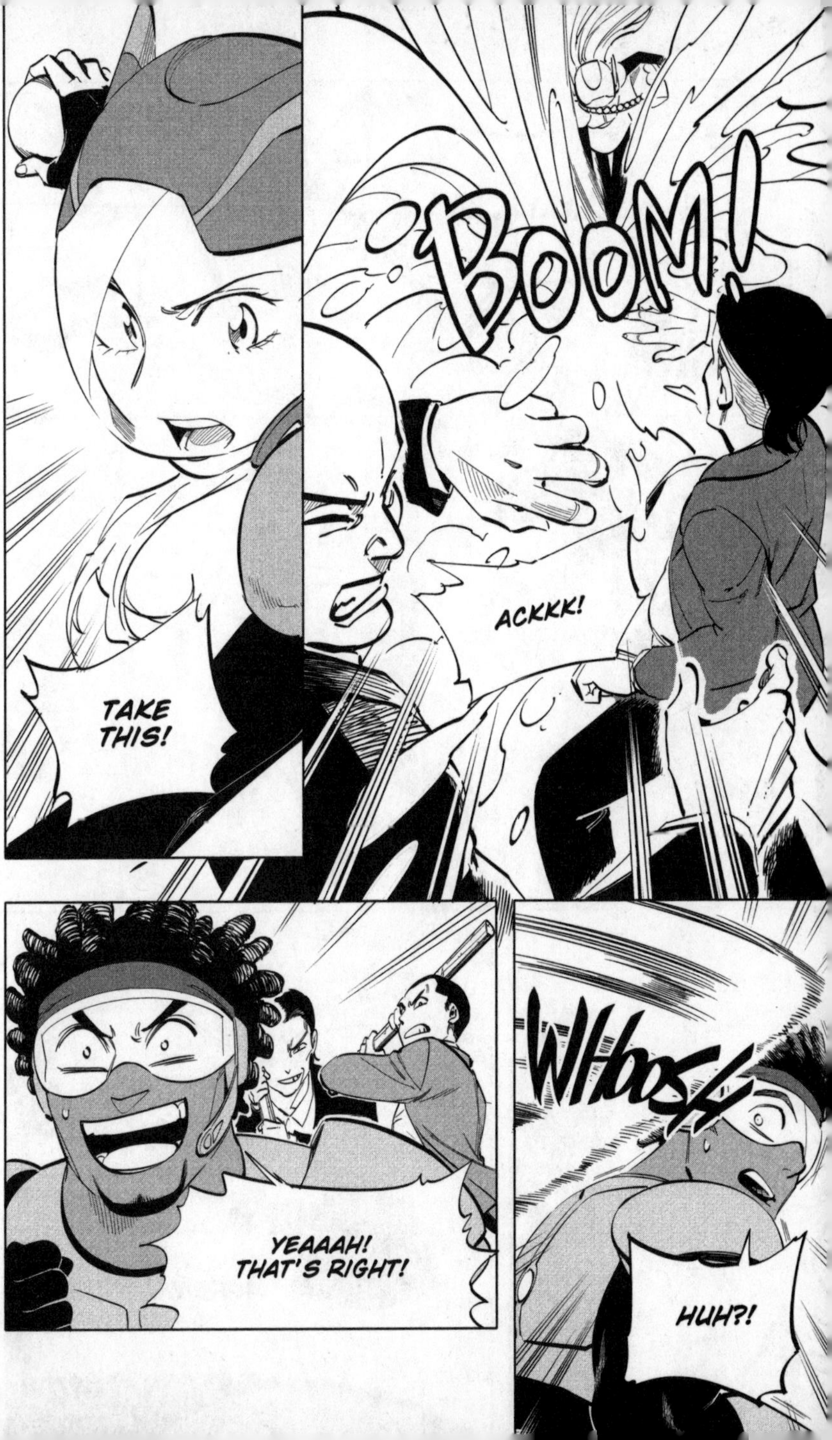
TAKE THIS!
BOOM!
ACKKK!
YEAAAH! THAT'S RIGHT!
WHOOSH
HUH?!

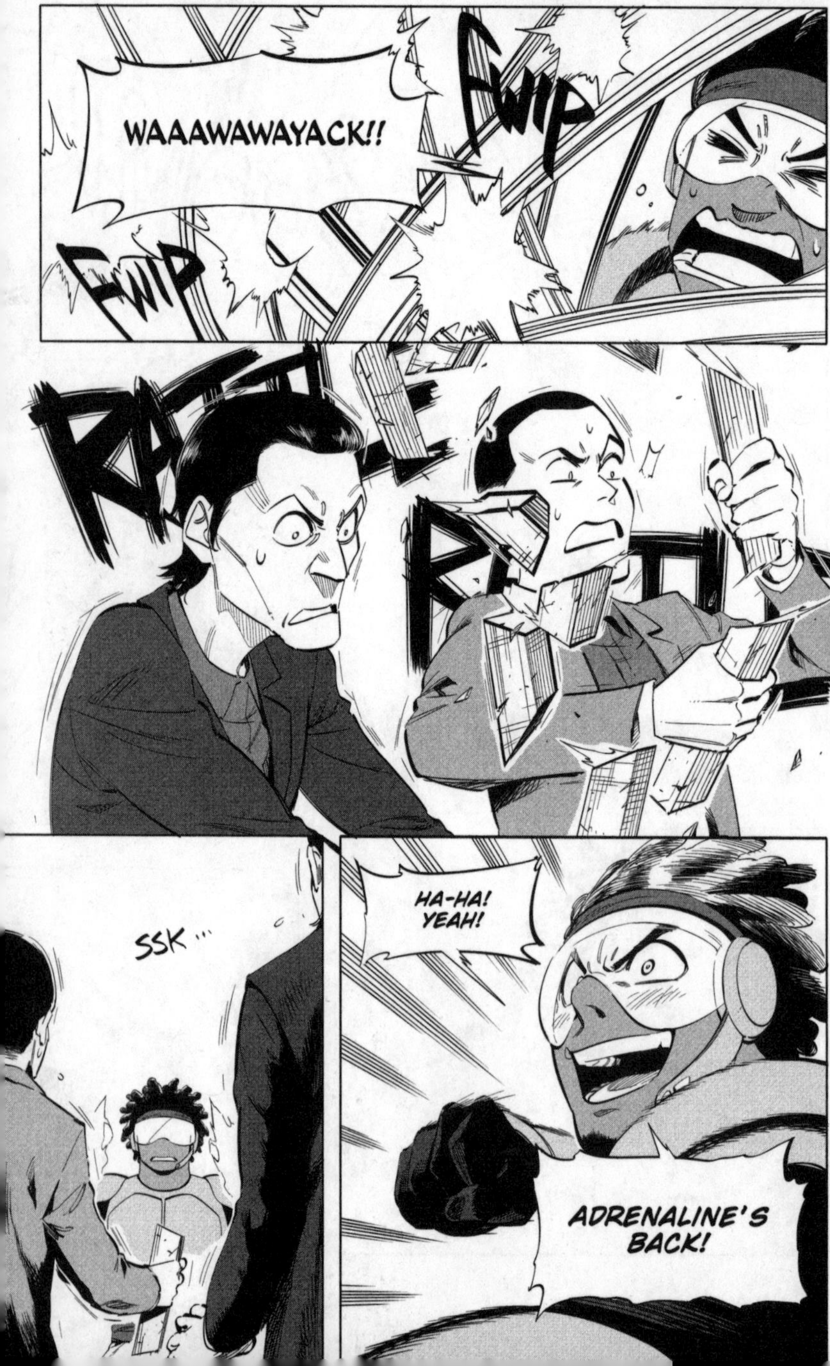
WAAAWAWAYACK!!
FWIP
FWIP
SSK...
HA-HA! YEAH!
ADRENALINE'S BACK!

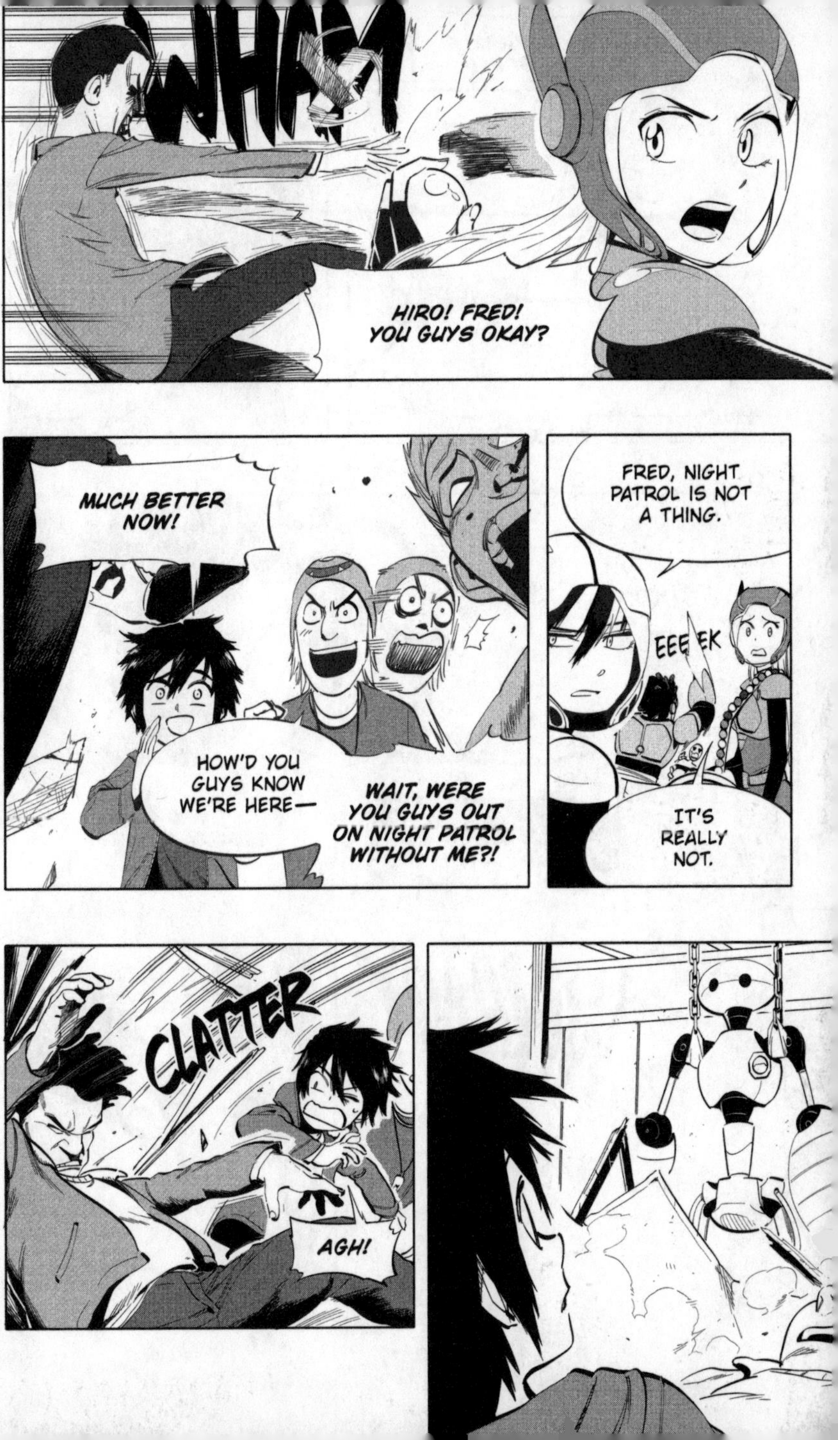
WHAM
HIRO! FRED! YOU GUYS OKAY?
MUCH BETTER NOW!
HOW'D YOU GUYS KNOW WE'RE HERE—
WAIT, WERE YOU GUYS OUT ON NIGHT PATROL WITHOUT ME?!
FRED, NIGHT PATROL IS NOT A THING.
EEEEEK
IT'S REALLY NOT.
CLATTER
AGH!

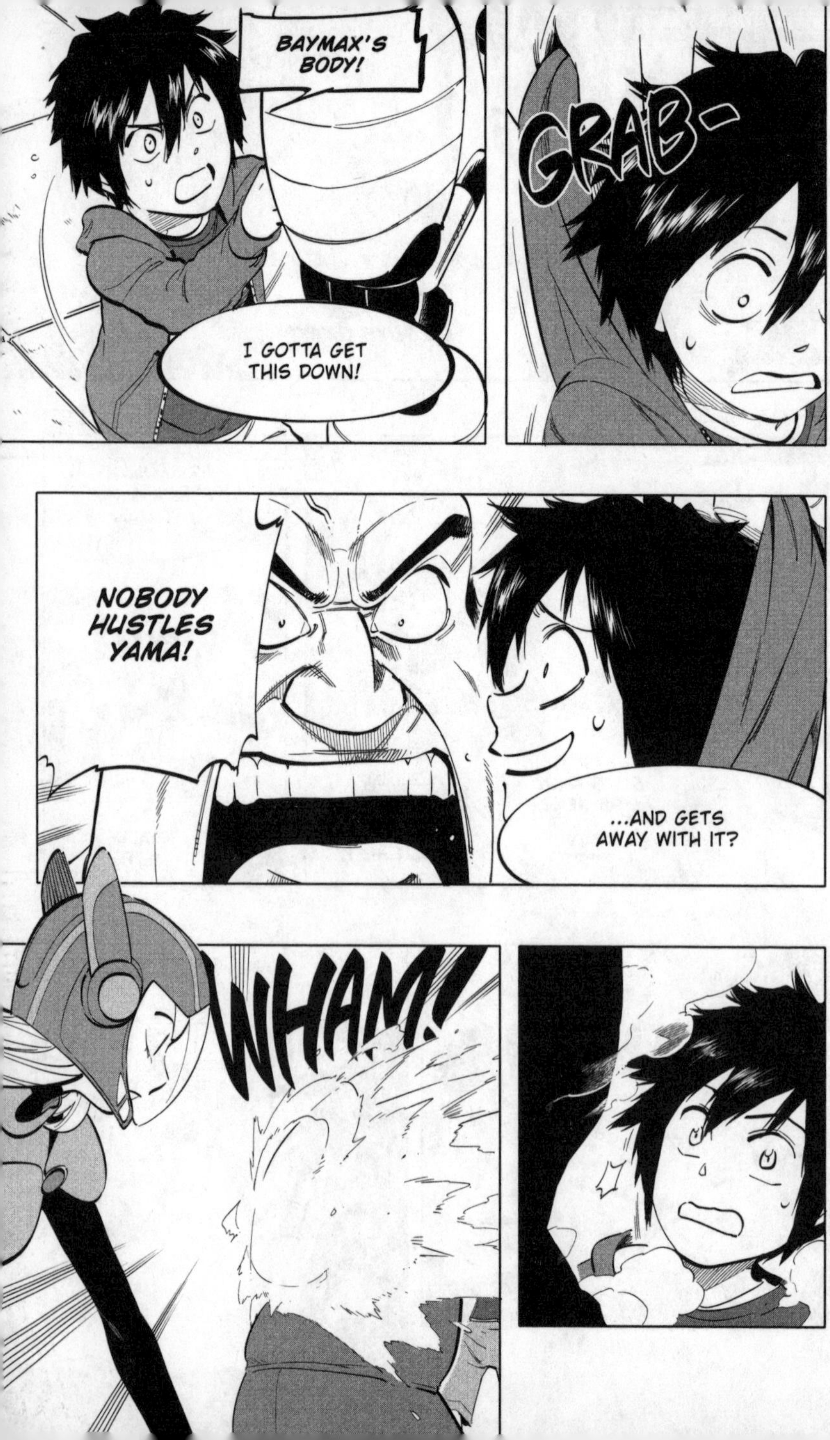
BAYMAX'S BODY!
I GOTTA GET THIS DOWN!
GRAB-
NOBODY HUSTLES YAMA!
...AND GETS AWAY WITH IT?
WHAM!

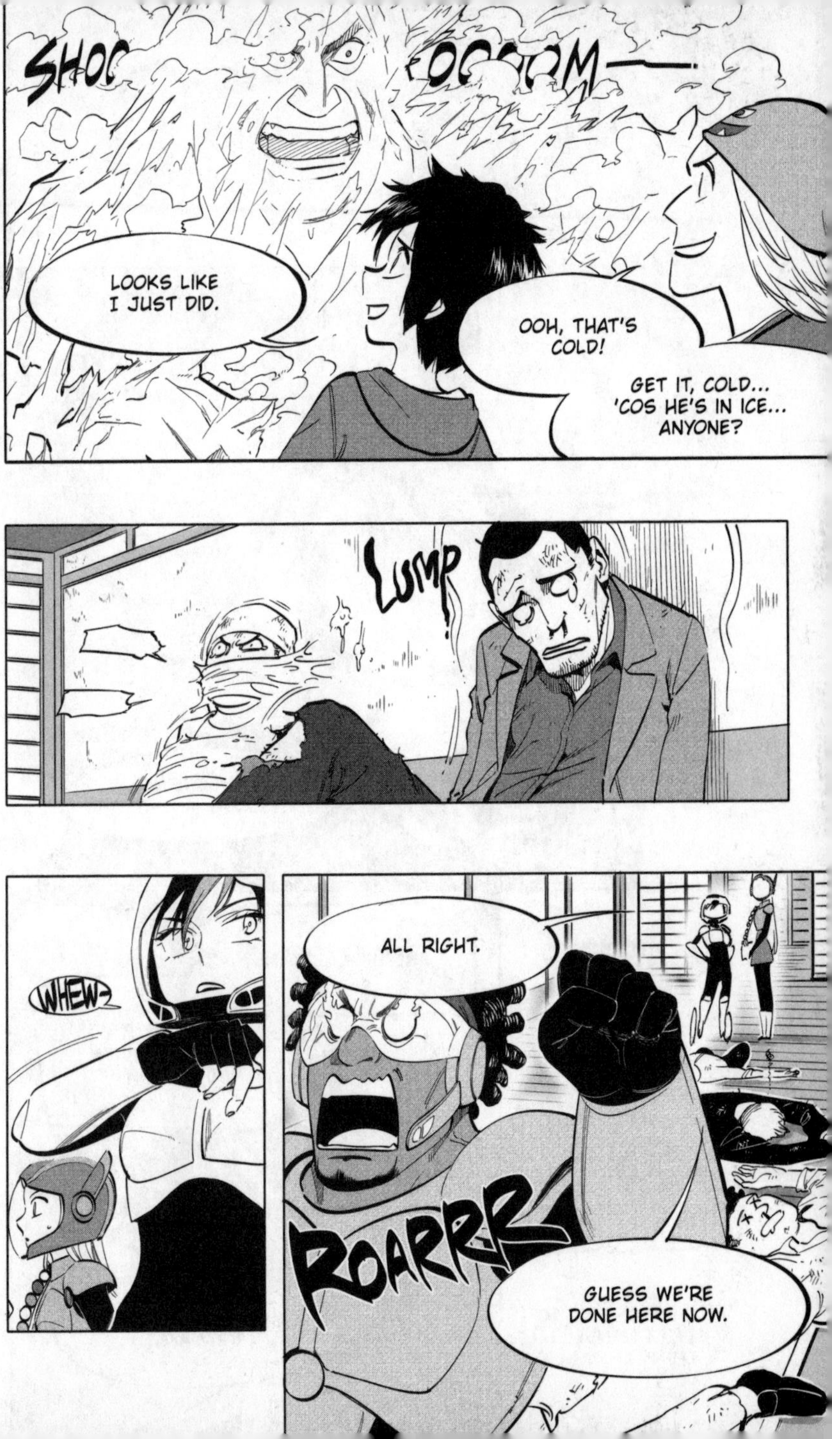

SHOOOOOOOM—
LOOKS LIKE I JUST DID.
OOH, THAT'S COLD!
GET IT, COLD... 'COS HE'S IN ICE... ANYONE?
LUMP
WHEW-
ALL RIGHT.
ROARRR
GUESS WE'RE DONE HERE NOW.

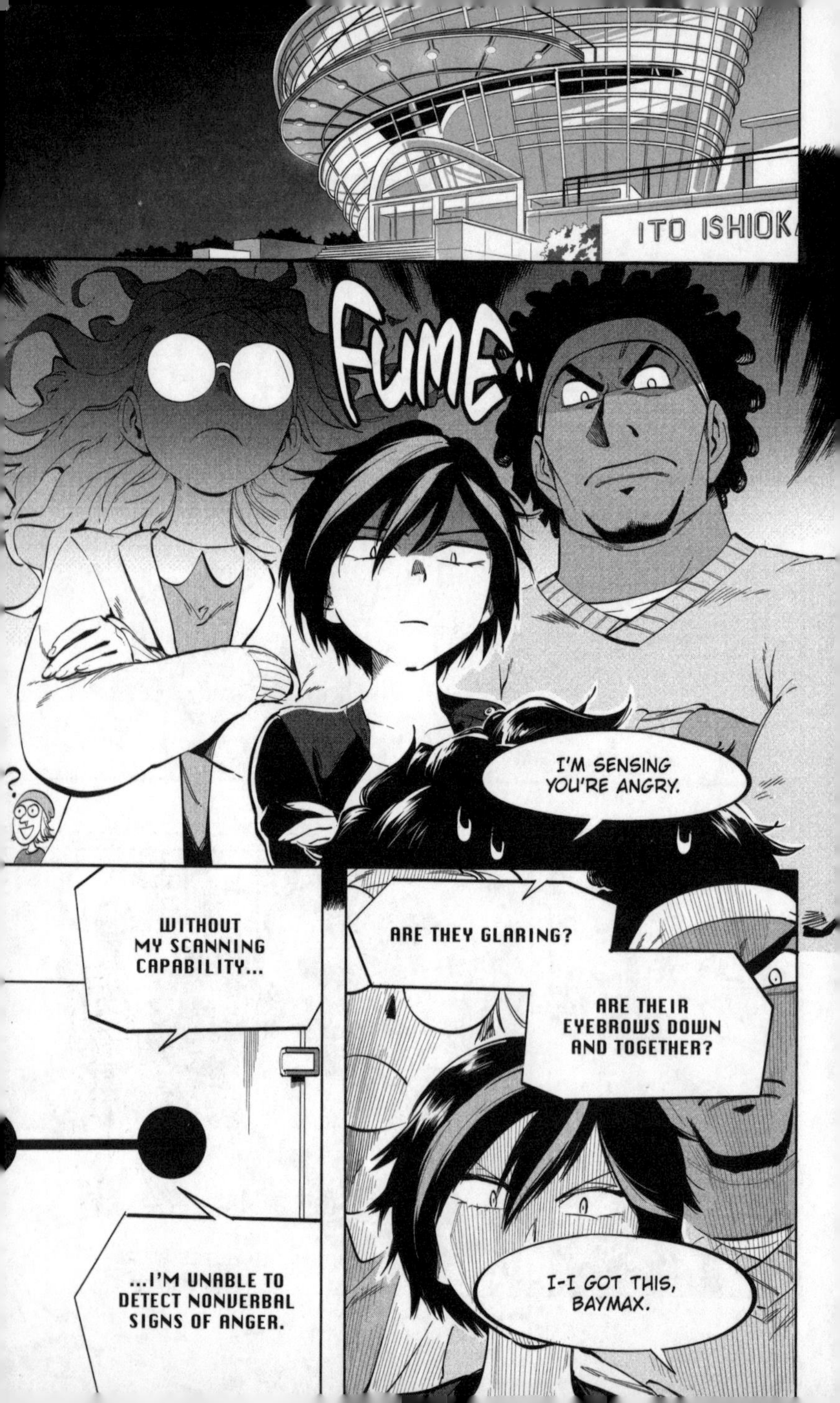
ITO ISHIOK
FUME..
?
I'M SENSING YOU'RE ANGRY.
WITHOUT MY SCANNING CAPABILITY...
...I'M UNABLE TO DETECT NONVERBAL SIGNS OF ANGER.
ARE THEY GLARING?
ARE THEIR EYEBROWS DOWN AND TOGETHER?
I-I GOT THIS, BAYMAX.

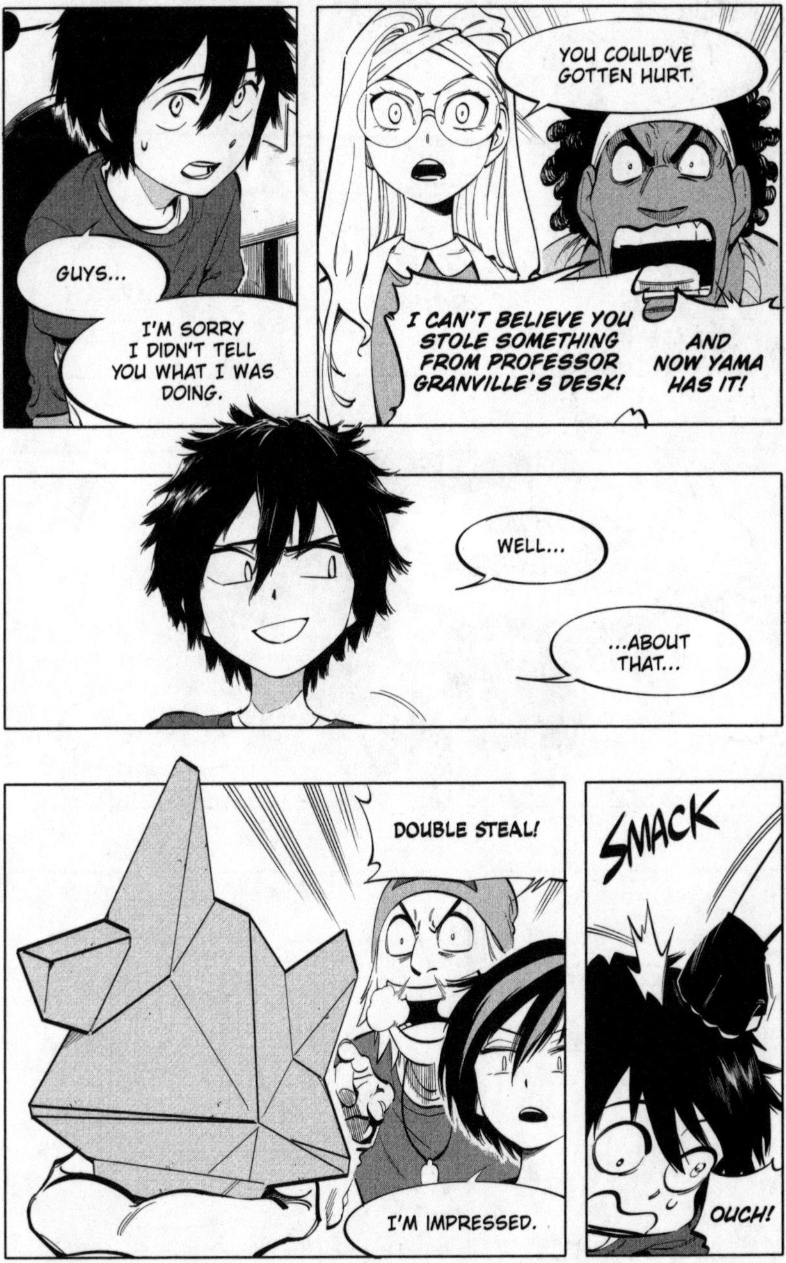
GUYS...
I'M SORRY I DIDN'T TELL YOU WHAT I WAS DOING.
YOU COULD'VE GOTTEN HURT.
I CAN'T BELIEVE YOU STOLE SOMETHING FROM PROFESSOR GRANVILLE'S DESK!
AND NOW YAMA HAS IT!
WELL...
...ABOUT THAT...
DOUBLE STEAL!
I'M IMPRESSED.
SMACK
OUCH!

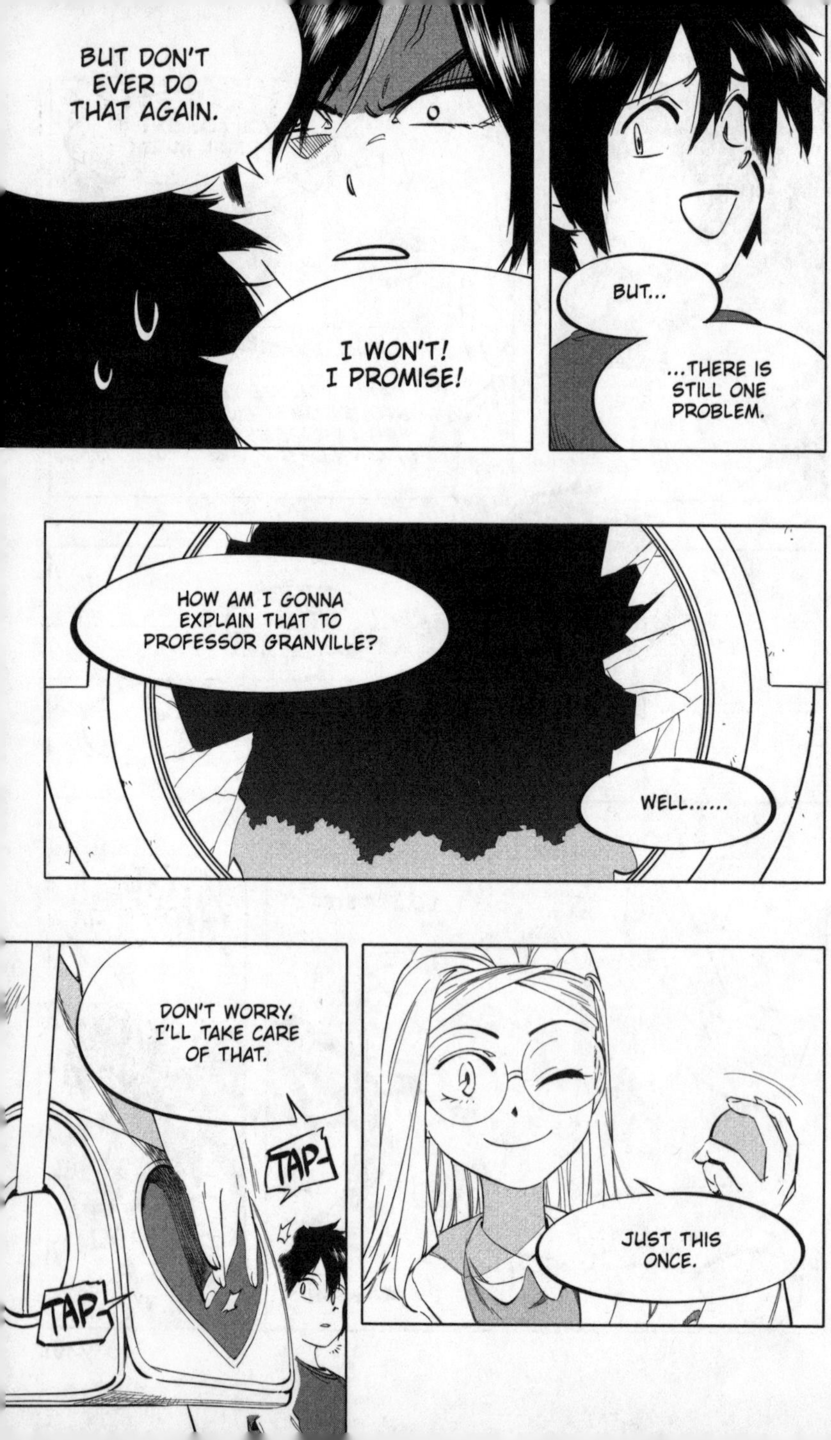
BUT DON'T EVER DO THAT AGAIN.
I WON'T! I PROMISE!
BUT...
...THERE IS STILL ONE PROBLEM.
HOW AM I GONNA EXPLAIN THAT TO PROFESSOR GRANVILLE?
WELL......
DON'T WORRY. I'LL TAKE CARE OF THAT.
TAP-
TAP-
JUST THIS ONCE.

BEEP——

DIAGNOSTICS
IN PROGRESS

BEEP——

BEEP——

...ESS

BEEP——

BEEEEP

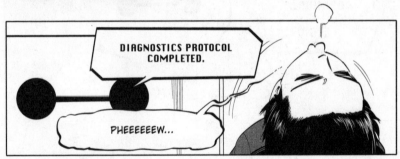

DIAGNOSTICS PROTOCOL COMPLETED.

PHEEEEEEW...

ONE LAST THING, THEN.

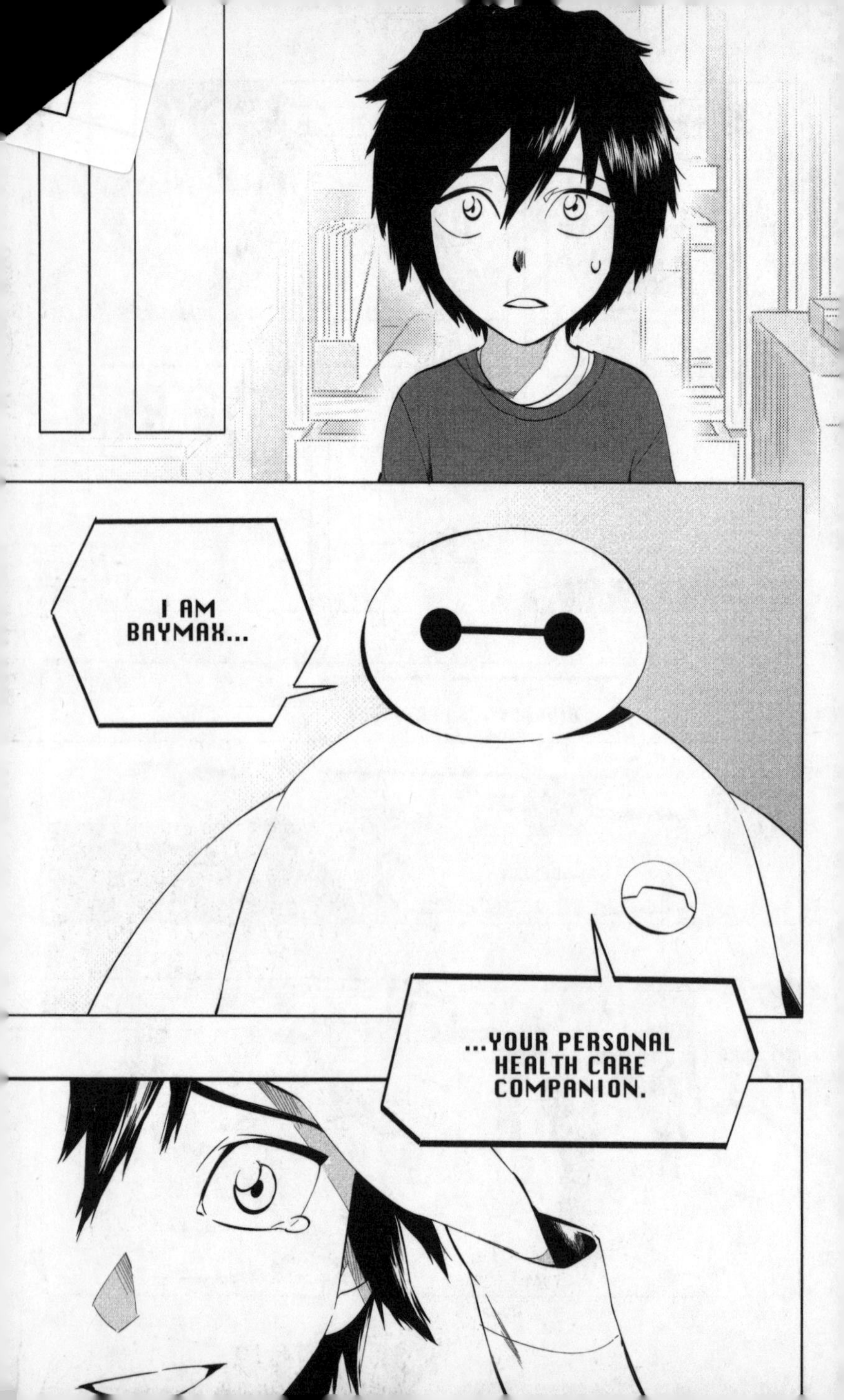
I AM BAYMAX...
...YOUR PERSONAL HEALTH CARE COMPANION.

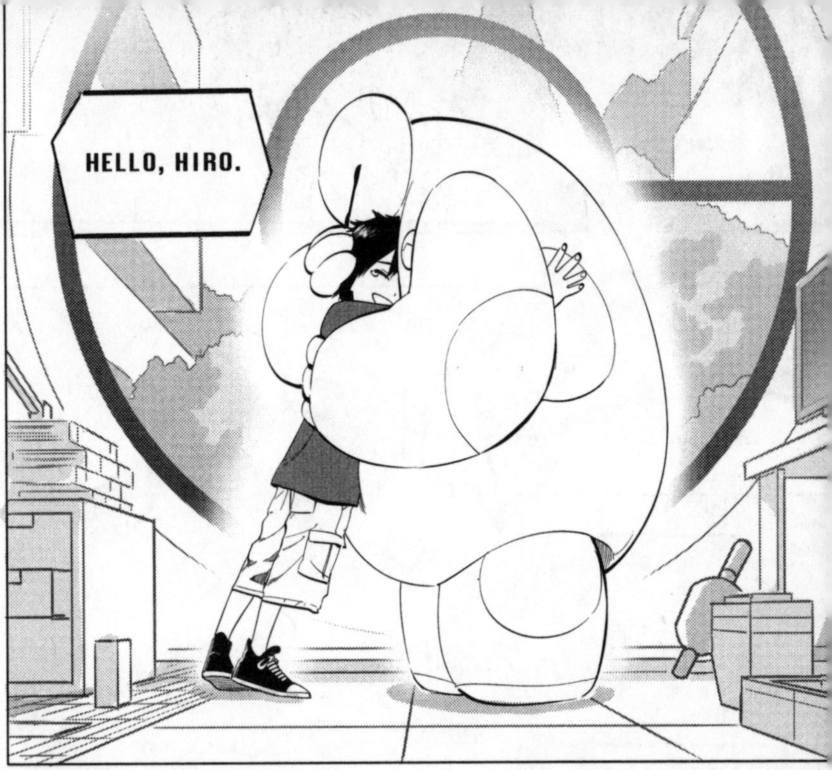
HELLO, HIRO.
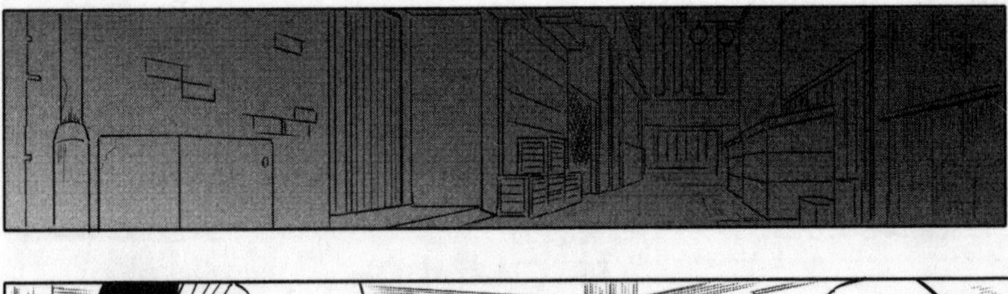
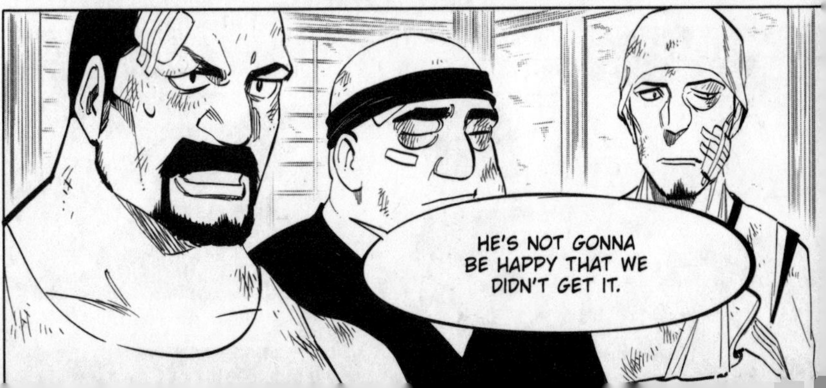
HE'S NOT GONNA BE HAPPY THAT WE DIDN'T GET IT.

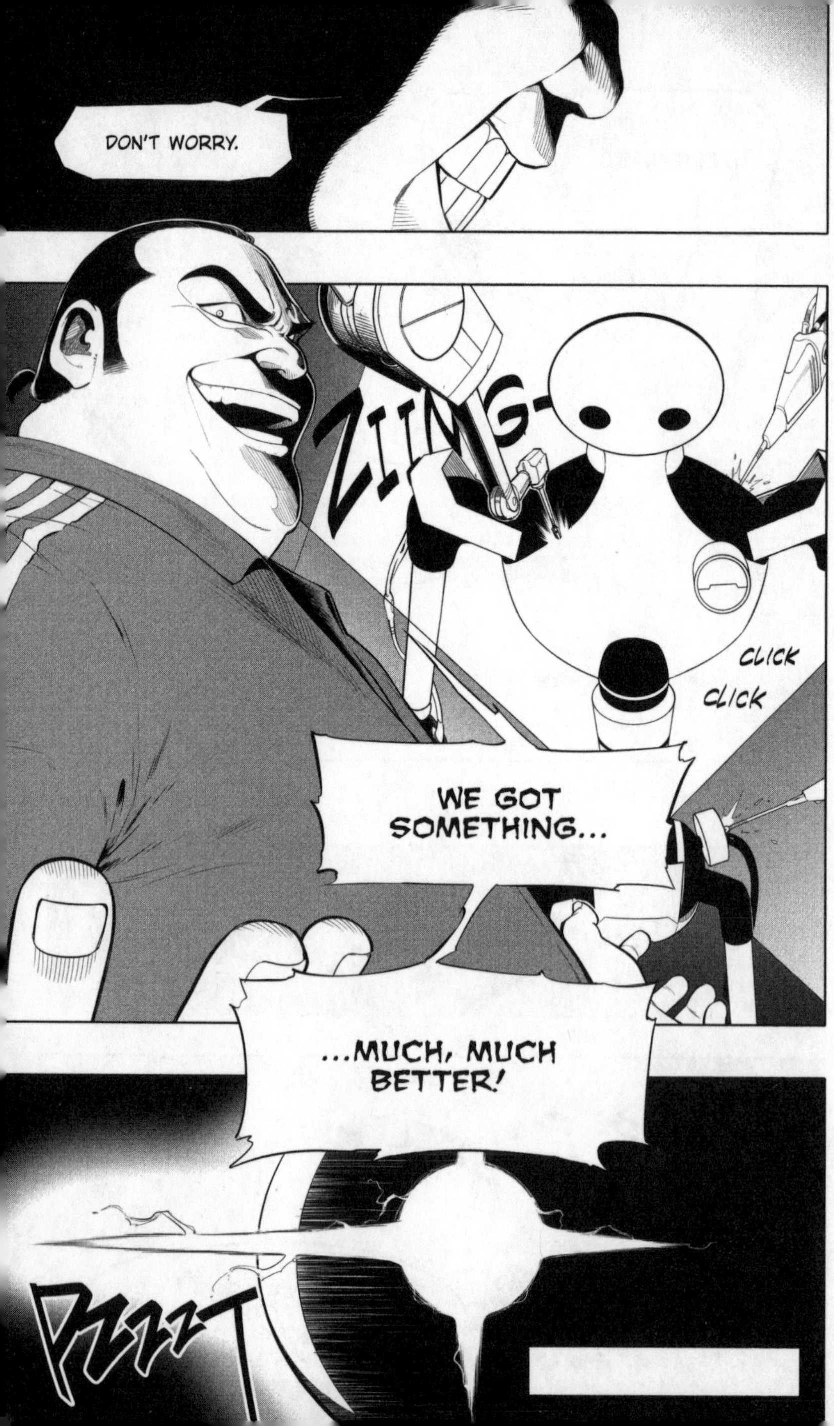
DON'T WORRY.
ZIING-
CLICK
CLICK
WE GOT SOMETHING...
...MUCH, MUCH BETTER!
BZZZT

See You in Volume 2!

EPISODE 1 BONUS ①

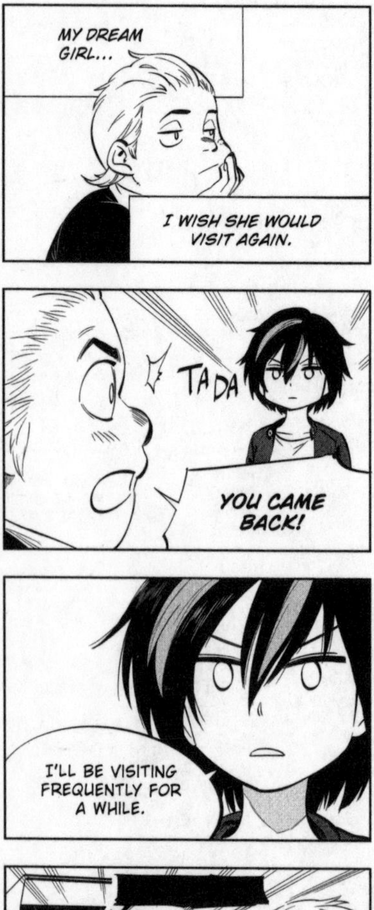
MY DREAM GIRL...
I WISH SHE WOULD VISIT AGAIN.
TA DA
YOU CAME BACK!
I'LL BE VISITING FREQUENTLY FOR A WHILE.
[redacted]
PEW
PEW
SHE SET NEW HIGH SCORES FOR ALL THE GAMES AND LEFT.
I NEED TO DEVELOP MORE GAMES!

EPISODE 1 BONUS ②

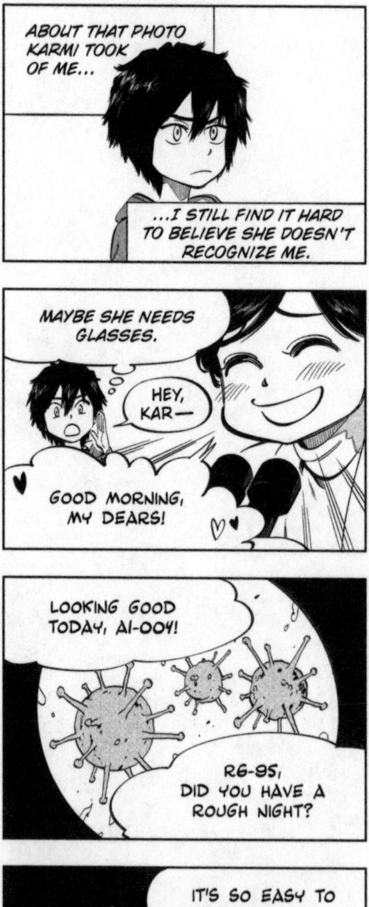
ABOUT THAT PHOTO KARMI TOOK OF ME...
...I STILL FIND IT HARD TO BELIEVE SHE DOESN'T RECOGNIZE ME.
MAYBE SHE NEEDS GLASSES.
HEY, KAR—
GOOD MORNING, MY DEARS!
LOOKING GOOD TODAY, AI-004!
R6-95, DID YOU HAVE A ROUGH NIGHT?
IT'S SO EASY TO TELL HOW YOU GUYS FEEL!
NOPE. IT'S JUST THAT SHE ONLY HAS EYES FOR THE VIRUSES.

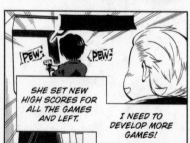

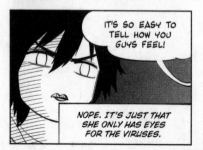

EPISODE 2 BONUS ①

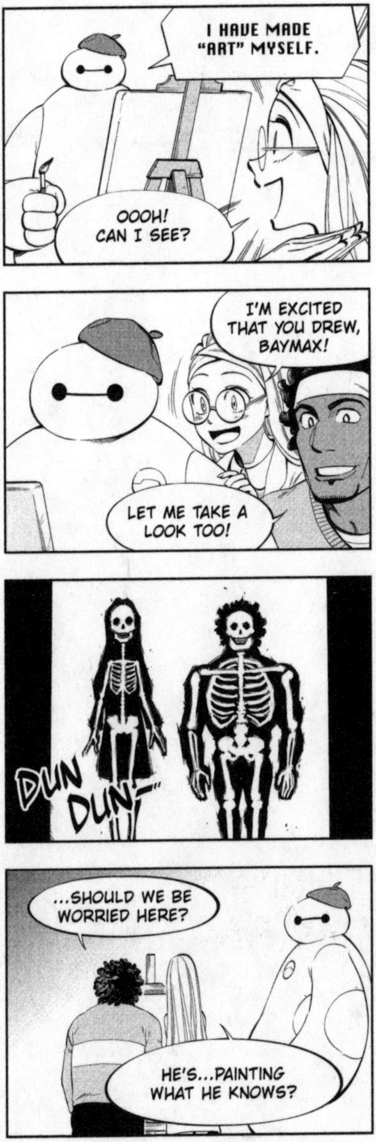
I HAVE MADE "ART" MYSELF.
OOOH! CAN I SEE?
I'M EXCITED THAT YOU DREW, BAYMAX!
LET ME TAKE A LOOK TOO!
DUN DUN
...SHOULD WE BE WORRIED HERE?
HE'S...PAINTING WHAT HE KNOWS?

EPISODE 2 BONUS ②

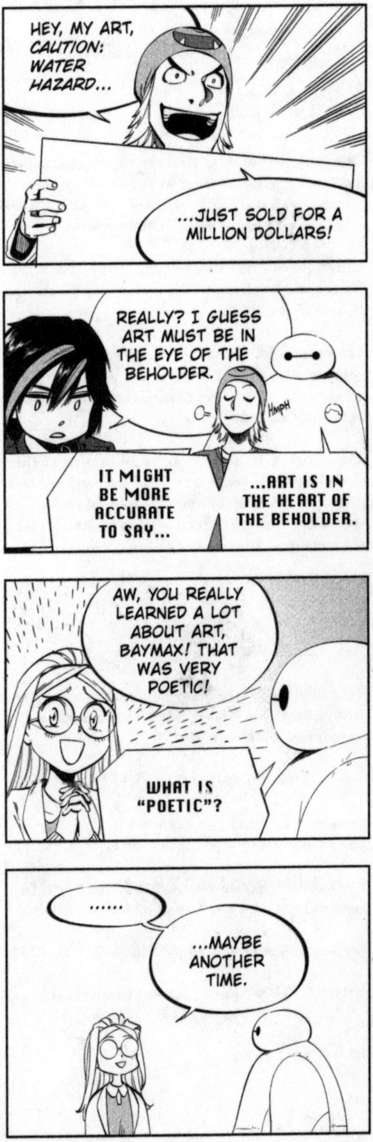
HEY, MY ART, CAUTION: WATER HAZARD...
...JUST SOLD FOR A MILLION DOLLARS!
REALLY? I GUESS ART MUST BE IN THE EYE OF THE BEHOLDER.
HMPH
IT MIGHT BE MORE ACCURATE TO SAY...
...ART IS IN THE HEART OF THE BEHOLDER.
AW, YOU REALLY LEARNED A LOT ABOUT ART, BAYMAX! THAT WAS VERY POETIC!
WHAT IS "POETIC"?
......
...MAYBE ANOTHER TIME.

Art and Adaptation:
Hong Gyun An
Lettering: JY Editorial

Copyright © 2021 Disney Enterprises, Inc. All Rights Reserved. "Big Hero 6" Team and Characters created by: MAN OF ACTION.

Yen Press, LLC supports the right to free expression and the value of copyright. The purpose of copyright is to encourage writers and artists to produce the creative works that enrich our culture.

The scanning, uploading, and distribution of this book without permission is a theft of the author's intellectual property. If you would like permission to use material from the book (other than for review purposes), please contact the publisher. Thank you for your support of the author's rights.

JY
150 West 30th Street, 19th Floor
New York, NY 10001

Visit us at jyforkids.com · facebook.com/jyforkids · twitter.com/jyforkids · jyforkids.tumblr.com · instagram.com/jyforkids

First Edition: August 2021

JY is an imprint of Yen Press, LLC.
The JY name and logo are trademarks of Yen Press, LLC.

The publisher is not responsible for websites (or their content) that are not owned by the publisher.

Library of Congress Control Number: 2021939554

ISBNs: 978-0-316-47464-1 (paperback)
       978-0-316-47466-5 (ebook)

10 9 8 7 6 5 4 3 2 1

WOR

Printed in the United States of America